SEMANTICS IN ACTION – APPLICATIONS AND SCENARIOS

Edited by **Muhammad Tanvir Afzal**

Semantics in Action – Applications and Scenarios
Edited by Muhammad Tanvir Afzal

Published by InTech

Janeza Trdine 9, 51000 Rijeka, Croatia

Copyright © 2012 InTech

All chapters are distributed under the Creative Commons Attribution 3.0 license, which allows users to download, copy and build upon published articles even for commercial purposes, as long as the author and publisher are properly credited, which ensures maximum dissemination and a wider impact of our publications. After this work has been published by InTech, authors have the right to republish it, in whole or part, in any publication of which they are the author, and to make other personal use of the work. Any republication, referencing or personal use of the work must explicitly identify the original source.

As for readers, this license allows users to download, copy and build upon published chapters even for commercial purposes, as long as the author and publisher are properly credited, which ensures maximum dissemination and a wider impact of our publications.

Notice

Statements and opinions expressed in the chapters are these of the individual contributors and not necessarily those of the editors or publisher. No responsibility is accepted for the accuracy of information contained in the published chapters. The publisher assumes no responsibility for any damage or injury to persons or property arising out of the use of any materials, instructions, methods or ideas contained in the book.

Publishing Process Manager Vedran Greblo

Technical Editor Teodora Smiljanic

Cover Designer InTech Design Team

Additional hard copies can be obtained from orders@intechopen.com

Semantics in Action – Applications and Scenarios, Edited by Muhammad Tanvir Afzal
p. cm.
ISBN 978-953-51-0536-7

We are IntechOpen, the world's leading publisher of Open Access books

Built by scientists, for scientists

4,100+
Open access books available

116,000+
International authors and editors

120M+
Downloads

151
Countries delivered to

Our authors are among the
Top 1%
most cited scientists

12.2%
Contributors from top 500 universities

CLARIVATE ANALYTICS
BOOK CITATION INDEX
INDEXED

WEB OF SCIENCE™

Selection of our books indexed in the Book Citation Index
in Web of Science™ Core Collection (BKCI)

Interested in publishing with us?
Contact book.department@intechopen.com

Numbers displayed above are based on latest data collected.
For more information visit www.intechopen.com

For EU product safety concerns:
IN TECH d.o.o., Prolaz Marije Krucifikse Kozulić 3, 51000 Rijeka, Croatia,
info@intechopen.com or visit our website at intechopen.com.

Meet the editor

Muhammad Tanvir Afzal, PhD., is an Assistant Professor in the department of Computer Science at Mohammad Ali Jinnah University, Islamabad, Pakistan, adjunct professor at Graz University of Technology, Graz, Austria, editor-in-chief of a reputed journal such as: Journal of Universal Computer Science, and group leader of an active research group: Centre for Distributed and Semantic Computing. He earned his PhD with distinction from Graz University of Technology, Austria and secured Gold Medal in his Masters from Quaid-i-Azam University, Islamabad, Pakistan. He has published over 50 research articles in reputed journals and conferences. His research activities encompass the area of Semantic Web, Social Web, Sentiment Analysis, Digital Libraries, eLearning, and Information Integration. He is editor/reviewer/session chair of many journals and conferences. He is supervising/co-supervising number of PhD students in Austria, Pakistan, and Malaysia, and is involved in number of international research projects.

Contents

Preface

Semantics is the research area touching the diversified domains such as: Philosophy, Information Science, Linguistics, Formal Semantics, Philosophy of Language and its constructs, Query Processing, Semantic Web, Pragmatics, Computational Semantics, Programming Languages, and Semantic Memory etc. The current book is a pleasant combination of number of great ideas, applications, case studies, and practical systems in diversified domains. The book has been divided into two volumes. The current one is the second volume which highlights the state-of-the-art areas in the domain of Semantics. This volume has been divided into four sections and ten chapters. The sections include: 1) Software Engineering, 2) Applications: Semantic Cache, E-Health, Sport Video Browsing, and Power Grids, 3) Visualization, and 4) Natural Language Disambiguation.

Section 1 presents work in the domain of Software Engineering. This section includes three chapters. First chapter employs model transformation language semantics for aspect composition. The presented work highlights state-of-the-art in the domain, proposes model composition semantics, and provides formal notions and algorithms. The implementation details using ATL semantics and evaluations have been provided. Second chapter presents a static slice monad transformer for program slicing based on monadic semantics. The work is an extended version of the previously published papers by the authors in the same area. Third Chapter presents a framework for modeling and generation of web service oriented context aware system to improve human-machine interaction.

Section 2 highlights applications of semantics in four areas such as: semantic cache, e-health, video browsing, and power grid. The section has been divided into four chapters. First chapter presents a semantic cache system. The state-of-the-art provides insights into contemporary systems. Subsequently, a new semantic cache system such as: sCacheQP, has been proposed. The algorithms have been discussed in details with a case study highlighting the major contributions and challenges in the area. Second chapter highlights the use of Semantics in the area of eHealth for providing semantic interoperability. The prototype has been successfully implemented and tested for a local laboratory in Pakistan. Third chapter presents a semantic approach for sport video browsing. Soccer video high-level semantics detection approaches have been described and evaluated. Subsequently, from the detected highlights, a semantic based soccer video browsing approach is proposed which carries out video content browsing using a book-like structure. Fourth chapter describes a futuristic intelligent self-describing power grid based on ontologies. The prototype applications demonstrate that the rule based techniques when applied on domain ontologies, are capable to facilitate the coding of industrial applications and their customization for user needs.

Section 3 presents innovative visualization techniques to infer semantics. This section comprises of two chapters. First chapter is a study to propose a methodology to visualize conflict structures of public debate by analyzing debate minutes based on corpus-based discourse analysis. An innovative visualization has been proposed and demonstrated for a data which is able to extract insights from public debate domain, for example, do citizens agree with each other?, do experts and administration have interest conflict? etc. Second chapter elaborates an idea of visualizing program semantics. With enough details, examples, theories, and visualization, the chapter argues that the Petri nets can be extended to formally visualize the semantics of a program.

Section 4, the last section of this book, discusses about natural language disambiguation for resolving topic-focus ambiguities using natural language semantics. The procedural semantics of TIL were shown to provide rigorous analyses such that sentences differing only in their topic-focus articulation were assigned different constructions producing different propositions (truth-conditions) and having different consequences. However, the proposed approach is not able to dictate *which* disambiguation is the intended one, thus leaving room for pragmatics.

I would like to thank authors who participated to conclude such a nice worth-reading book. I am also thankful to In-Tech Open access Initiative for making accessible all of the chapters online free of cost to the scientific community.

Dr. Muhammad Tanvir Afzal
Department of Computer Science
Mohammad Ali Jinnah University, Islamabad,
Pakistan

Section 1

Software Engineering

1

Using Model Transformation Language Semantics for Aspects Composition

Samuel A. Ajila, Dorina Petriu and Pantanowitz Motshegwa
Department of Systems and Computer Engineering,
Carleton University, Ottawa, ON,
Canada

1. Introduction

Modern software systems are huge, complex, and greatly distributed. In order to design and model such systems, software architects are faced with the problem of cross-cutting concerns much earlier in the development process. At this level, cross-cutting concerns result in model elements that cross-cut the structural and behavioral views of the system. Research has shown that Aspect Oriented (AO) techniques can be applied to software design models. This can greatly help software architects and developers to isolate, reason, express, conceptualize, and work with cross-cutting concerns separately from the core functionality (Ajila et al., 2010; Petriu et al, 2007). This application of AO techniques much earlier in the development process has spawned a new field of study called Aspect-Oriented Modeling (AOM). In AOM, the aspect that encapsulates the cross-cutting behavior or structure is a model, just like the base system model it cross-cuts. A system been modeled has several views including structural and behavioral views. Therefore, a definition of an aspect depends on the view of interest. Unified Modeling Language (UML) provides different diagrams to describe the different views. Class, Object, Composite Structure, Component, Package, and Deployment diagrams can be used to represent the structural view of a system or aspect. On the other hand, Activity, State Machine, and Interaction diagrams are used to model the behavioral view. Interaction diagrams include Sequence, Interaction Overview, Communication, and Timing diagrams.

After reasoning and working with aspects in isolation, the aspect models eventually have to be combined with the base system model to produce an integrated system model. This merging of the aspect model with the base model is called Aspect Composition or Weaving. Several approaches have been proposed for aspect composition using different technologies/methodologies such as graph transformations (Wittle & Jayaraman, 2007), matching and merging of model elements (Fleury et al., 2007), weaving models (Didonet et al., 2006) and others. The goal of this research is to compose aspect models represented as UML sequence diagrams using transformation models written in Atlas Transformation Language (ATL).

Composing behavioral models (views) represented as UML Sequence diagrams is more complex than composing structural views. Not only is the relationships between the model elements important but the order is equally paramount. Several approaches have been proposed for composing behavioral aspects with core system behavior, and these include graphs transformations [Whittle et al., 2007] and generic weavers [Morin et al., 2008]. In this research work we view composition as a form of model transformation. Aspect composition can be considered a model transformation since it transforms aspect and primary models to an integrated system model. Toward this end, we propose and focus on an approach that uses model transformations to compose both primary and aspect models represented as UML Sequence diagrams (SDs). SDs modeling the primary model and generic aspect models is created using Graphical UML modeling tools like Rational Software Architect (RSA). Model transformations are then used to instantiate the generic aspect models in the context of the application to produce context specific aspect models. Binding rules used for instantiating the generic aspect are represented as mark models that conform to a metamodel. Using other model transformations, the context specific aspect models are then composed with the primary model to produce an integrated system model. Verification and validation is performed, not only to verify that composition was successful, but also to ensure that the composed model is a valid UML model that can be processed further and shared with other researchers.

The rest of this chapter is structured as follows. Section two presents Model Driven approach, Aspect-Oriented techniques and technologies, and Atlas Transformation Language (ATL). We present our approach to model composition in section three starting with an example. We introduce our model composition semantics and definitions in section four - giving formal notions and three major algorithms (pointcut detection, advice composition, and complete composition) that define the basis of our work. Section five presents the design and implementation of our model composition using ATL semantics. We introduce and analyze a case study based on phone call features in section six. Section seven gives our conclusion, limitations, and future work.

2. Model Driven Engineering/Development/Architecture (MDE/MDD/MDA)

In Model Driven Engineering (MDE) everything is a model. A model refers to a simplified view of a real world system of interest; that is, an abstraction of a system. MDE considers models as the building blocks or first class entities (Didonet et al, 2006). A model conforms to a metamodel while a metamodel conforms to a metametamodel. MDE is mainly concerned with the evolution of models as a way of developing software by focusing on models. With this new paradigm of software development, the code will be generated automatically by model to code transformations. Model Driven Development (MDD) is copyrighted term by Object Management Group (OMG). One of the most important operations in MDE/MDD is model transformation. There are different kinds of model transformations including model to code, model to text, and model to model. Our interest in this paper is in model to model transformations. Figure 2.1 shows the process of model transformation. Since every artifact in MDE is a model, the model transformation is also a model that conforms to a metamodel. The transformation model defines how to generate models that conform to a particular metamodel from models that conform to another metamodel or the same metamodel. In Figure 2.1, the transformation model M_t transforms M_a to M_b. M_t conforms to MM_t while M_a and M_b conform to MM_a and MM_b respectively. The three metamodels conform to a common metametamodel MMM.

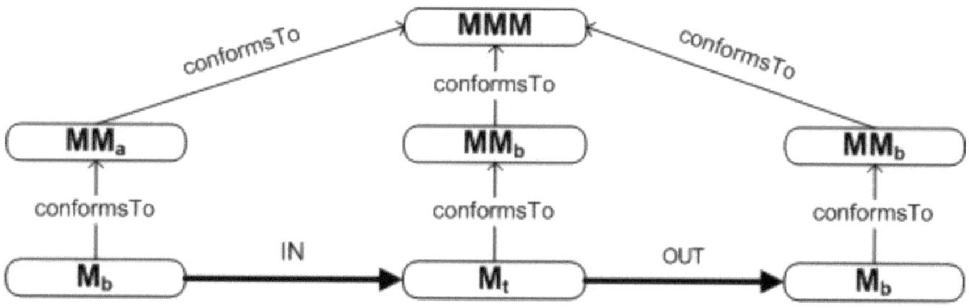

Fig. 2.1. Overview of Model Transformation Adopted from (ATL-User-Manual, 2009).

OMG's Model-Driven Architecture (MDA) is a term copyrighted by OMG that describes an MDE approach supported by OMG standards; namely, UML, Meta-Object Facility (MOF), MOF-Query/View/Transformation (QVT), XML Metadata Interchange (XMI) and Common Warehouse Metamodel (CWM). MDA decouples the business and application logic from the underlying platform technology through the use of the Platform Independent Model (PIM), Platform Specific Model (PSM) and model transformations. The PIM describes a software system independently of the platform that supports it while PSM expresses how the core application functionality is realized on a specific platform. Given a specific platform, the PIM is transformed to PSM. Platform in this case refers to technological and engineering details that are independent of the core functionality of the application. For example, middleware (e.g., CORBA), operating system (e.g., Linux), hardware, etc.

2.1 Aspect-Oriented (AO) techniques/technologies

The size of modern software systems has increased tremendously. Software architects and developers have to design and develop systems that are not only enormous, but are more complex, and greatly distributed. These systems naturally have many cross-cutting concerns (requirements) whose solutions tend to cross-cut the base architecture and system behavior. Such concerns include security, persistence, system logging, new features in software product lines, and many others. Aspect-Oriented techniques allow software developers and architects to conceptualize and work with multiple concerns separately (Groher & Voelter, 2007; Kienzle et al., 2009; Petriu et al., 2007). These techniques allow us to modularize concerns that we cannot easily modularize with current Object-Oriented (OO) techniques (Whittle & Jayaraman, 2007). The final system is then produced by weaving or composing solutions from separate concerns (Petriu et al., 2007). Klein et al. point out that dividing and conquering these cross-cutting concerns also allows us to better maintain and evolve software systems (Klein et al., 2007).

Aspect Oriented Programming (AOP) applies AO techniques at code level (France et al., 2004; Petriu et al., 2007). AOP was introduced to enhance Object-Oriented Programming to better handle cross-cutting concerns that cause code scattering and tangling, which leads to code that is very difficult to maintain and impossible to reuse or modify. AOP addresses these issues by introducing a class like programming construct called an *aspect* which is used to encapsulate cross-cutting concerns. Just like a class, an aspect has attributes (state) and methods (behavior). An aspect also introduces concepts well known to AO community; namely, *join points, advice,* and *pointcut.* Join points are points in the code where the cross-cutting behavior is to be inserted. AspectJ (a popular AOP Java tool) supports join points for method invocations, initializing of attributes, exception handling, etc (Colyer et al., 2004). A *pointcut* is used to describe a condition that matches join points, that is it is a way of defining join points of interest where we want to insert the cross-cutting functionality. This cross-cutting behavior to be inserted at a join point is defined in the *advice*. AspectJ supports *before*, *after*, and *around* advices (Colyer et al., 2004).

Recent work in AO has focused on applying AO techniques much earlier in the development process (Kienzle et al., 2009; Klein et al., 2007; Morin et al., 2008; Petriu et al., 2007). In Aspect Oriented Modeling (AOM), Aspect-Oriented techniques are applied to models (unlike AOP). Whittle et al. define an AO model as "a model that cross-cuts other models *at the same level of abstraction*" (Whittle et al., 2006). Aspects are considered models as well; hence, it makes sense to define (or abstract) other concepts such as pointcuts and advices as models. However, the precise definition of a joint point, pointcut or advice depends on our modeling view. For example, in a structural view, such as a class diagram, an aspect is defined in terms of classes and operations/methods whereas in a behavioral view, such as a sequence diagram, an aspect is defined in terms of messages and lifelines. This has resulted in several approaches to AOM most of which have focused on separation and weaving (composition) of structural (class diagrams) and behavioral views (sequence, activity, and state diagrams) (Klein et al., 2007; Morin et al., 2008; Petriu et al., 2007). Several approaches have been proposed for composing aspects in AOM. These include using graph transformations (Gong, 2008; Whittle & Jayaraman, 2007), semantics (Klein et al., 2006), executable class diagrams (ECDs), weaving models (Didonet et al., 2006), generic approaches and frameworks (Fleury et al., 2008; Morin et al., 2008), etc. Composition primarily involves deciding what has to be composed, where to compose, and how to compose (Didonet et al., 2006). Aspect composition can either be symmetric or asymmetric. In symmetric composition, there is a clear distinction between the models to be composed; that is, one model plays the role of a base model while the other is declared an aspect model (Jeanneret et al, 2008). This distinction is absent in asymmetric composition.

2.2 Atlas transformation language

The Atlas Transformation Language (ATL) is a model transformation language from the ATLAS INRIA & LINA research group (ATL-User-Guide, 2009). The language is both declarative and imperative, and allows developers to transform a set of input models to a number of output target models. In ATL, source or input models can only be navigated but cannot be modified (Jouault & Kurtev, 2005) whereas target models are write-only and cannot be navigated. Figure 2.2 below shows an overview of an example of an ATL transformation (Family2Person) from [ATL_Examples] that transforms a Family model to a Person model. The Family model conforms to an *MMFamily* metamodel whereas the Person model conforms to an *MMPerson* metamodel. The ATL, *MMFamily*, and *MMPerson* metamodels all conform to the Ecore metametamodel which is a metamodel for the Eclipse Modeling Framework. Families2Persons.atl is an ATL model or program that transforms a Family model to a Person model.

ATL has three types of units that are defined on separate files (ATL-User-Guide, 2009); namely, ATL modules, queries and libraries. ATL has types and expressions that are based on the Object Constraint Language (OCL) from OMG. ATL has primitive types (Numeric, String, Boolean), collection type (sets, sequences and bags) and other types, all of which are

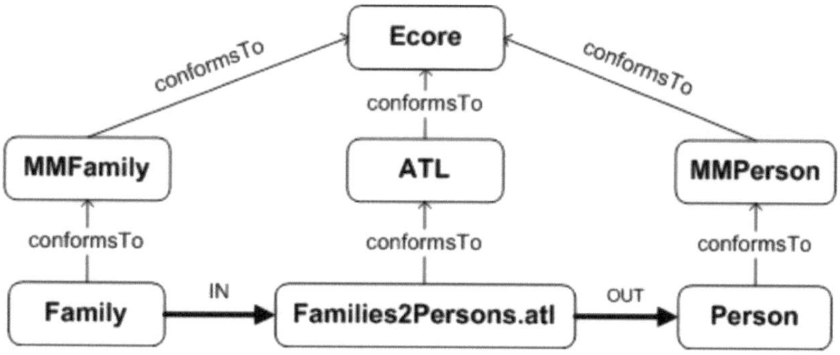

Fig. 2.2. Overview of the Family to Person ATL Transformation.

sub-types of the *OCLAny* abstract super-type. An ATL module or program, like Families2Persons.atl in the previous example, defines a model to model transformation (Jouault & Kurtev, 2005). It consists of a header, helpers (attribute and operation helpers) and transformation rules (matched, called and lazy rules) (Jouault & Kurtev, 2005). The header defines the module's name, and the input and target models. ATL operation helpers are more like functions or Java methods, and can be invoked from rules and other helpers. Attribute helpers unlike operation helpers do not take any arguments. All helpers are, however, recursive and must have a return value. Rules define how input models are transformed to target models. They are the core construct in ATL (Jouault & Kurtev, 2005). ATL supports both declarative and imperative rules. Declarative rules include matched rules and lazy rules. Lazy rules are similar to matched rules but can only be invoked from other rules. A matched rule consists of source pattern and target pattern (Jouault & Kurtev, 2005). A source pattern is defined as an OCL expression and defines what type of input elements will be matched (ATL-User-Guide, 2009). An ATL model is compiled, and then executed on the ATL engine that has two model handlers; namely, EMF (Eclipse Modeling framework) and MDR (Meta Data repository) (ATL-User-Guide, 2009). Model handlers provide a programming interface for developers to manipulate models (Jouault & Kurtev, 2005). The EMF handler allows for manipulation of Ecore models while MDR allows the ATL engine to handle models that conform to the MOF 1.4 (Meta Object Facility) metametamodel (ATL-User-Guide, 2009). For example, the ATL transformation in Figure 4.1 would require an EMF model handler since the metamodels conform to Ecore.

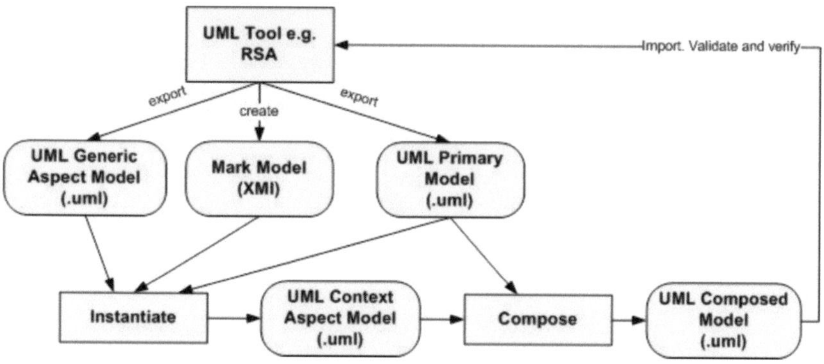

Fig. 3.1. Our AOM Composition Approach.

3. Our approach to model composition

Our approach shown in the Figure 3.1 is an adaptation of the approach proposed by Petriu et al. in (Petriu et al., 2007). Using a UML modeling tool, like RSA (Rational Software Architect) from IBM, the primary and generic aspect models are modeled in UML and then exported to a UML 2.1 (.uml) format file. The mark model is created in an XMI file. The *Instantiate* and *Compose* operations in Figure 3.1 are defined as ATL model transformations. We first instantiate a generic aspect model to the context of the application by using a model transformation that takes the primary, generic aspect and mark models as input, and transforms them to a context specific aspect model. We then invoke a second transformation that will take as input the newly created context specific aspect model and the primary model, and then output a composed target model.

3.1 Example

Let us introduce a simple example to provide a better view of our approach and the definitions of the various concepts used in the approach. This example is adapted from Klein et al. (Klein et al., 2007). It illustrates the weaving of a simple security aspect into a primary model. The primary model consists of a single scenario. In fact, our composition approach assumes that the primary model has only one sequence diagram (SD) and models a particular instance of a use case. This example consists of a login scenario shown in Figure 3.2 below. The model shows a simple iteration between instances of Server and Customer. The Customer attempts to log into the Server by sending a *login* message. The Customer's login details are incorrect; hence, the Server sends a *try_again* message to the Customer to attempt another login. The Customer then sends a *login* message with the correct details this time and the Server responds with an *ok* message.

The primary model does not have any security features. So, we want to add some security mechanism to the scenario so that when a customer attempts login and fails, the system should do something about that exception. We can model this security mechanism as a Security Aspect model that will detect a presence of a message from the Customer to the Server, and a reply from the Server back to the Customer. The presence of this sequence of messages is defined in the aspect's pointcut. The new behavior we want to add to the primary model in order to enhance security is defined in the aspect's advice. However, to make the aspect reusable and more useful, it has to be generic but not specific to our example or situation. This way we can reuse the aspect and in different situations and scenarios.

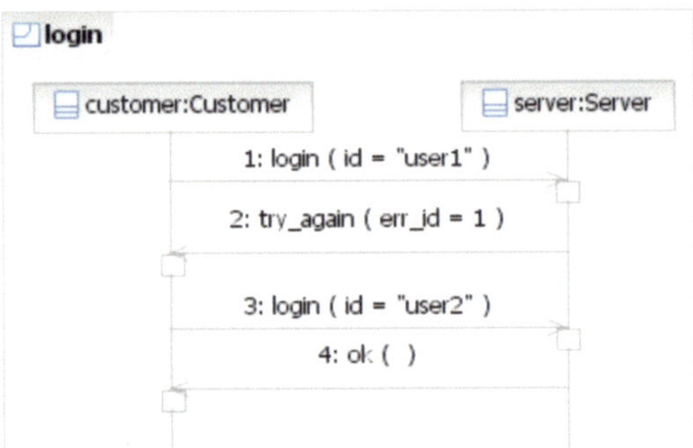

Fig. 3.2. The Primary Model - A Login Scenario for a Security Aspect Example.

To create a generic aspect we adopt the use of template parameters used by France et al. (France et al., 2004) and others (Kienzle et al., 2009; Petriu et al., 2007) to define generic roles played by the participants and messages in the generic aspect model. These generic roles are then bound to specific roles (names) when the generic aspect is instantiated. Figure 3.3 shows the pointcut and advice that make up our generic security aspect model. It should be noted that in case of multiple aspects, each aspect will be modeled separately. The lifelines (participants) and messages in the model are made generic. The pointcut in Figure 3.3a defines that the aspect detects any sequence of messages between a lifeline that plays the role of |client and lifeline that plays the role of |server such that |client sends a message tied to the role |operation and |server responds with |retry. During instantiation these template parameters (roles) will be set (bound) to concrete names of appropriate lifelines and messages.

As already mentioned, the advice represents the new or additional behavior we want executed if the pointcut matches, that is, if we find the sequence of messages defined in the pointcut in our primary model. The advice in Figure 3.3b declares that we want |server to invoke a self call after receiving |operation and before sending |retry to |client. So our advice in this case adds new behavior (the |handle_error self call). The idea is that during composition, as we shall see later, we replace whatever was matched by pointcut with what is defined in the advice.

Before an aspect can be composed with the primary model, the generic aspect model must first be instantiated to the context of the application to produce a Context Specific Aspect Model. This is achieved by "binding" the template parameters to application specific values. For example, we want to bind "customer" to |client because in our primary model, customer plays the role of |client.

Instantiating our generic aspect model using the bindings in Table 1, we obtain the context specific aspect model shown in Figure 3.4. The pointcut from the context specific aspect will then match the sending of a *login* message from *customer* to *server* and a try*_again* message from *server* back to *customer*, which is what we want. Its advice declares that the *save_bad_attempt* self call will be added to the server hopefully for the server to do something useful and security related.

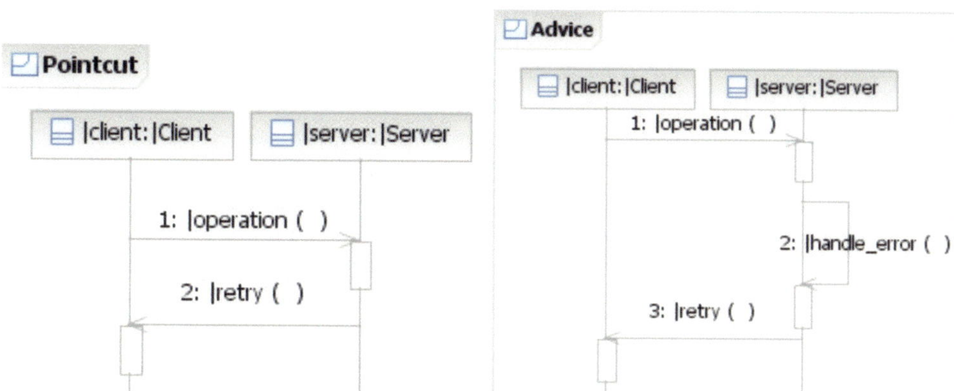

(a) pointcut (b) Advice

Fig. 3.3. Generic Aspect Model.

Parameter	Binding value	Comment
|client	customer	Lifeline object name.
|server	server	Lifeline object name.
|Client	Customer	The name of the type for the lifeline object.
|Server	Server	The name of the type for the lifeline object.
|operation	login	
|reply	try_again	
|handle_error	save_bad_attempt	

Table 1. Example of Security Aspect Binding Rules.

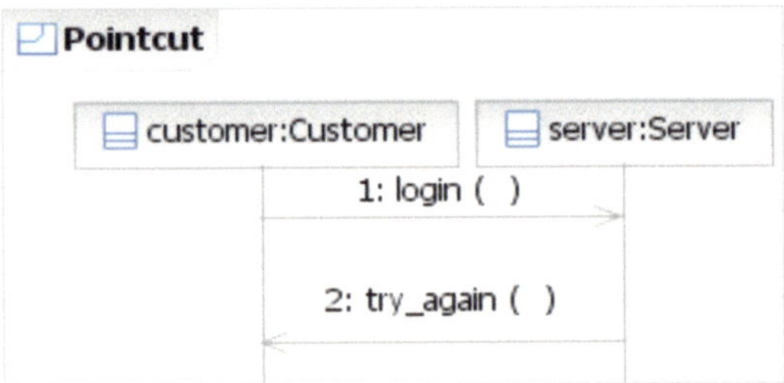

(a) Pointcut

(b) Advice

Fig. 3.4. Context Specific Aspect Model.

3.2 Model composition

After instantiating a context specific aspect model, a complete integrated system is obtained by composing the primary model with the context specific aspect model. We view composition as a form of model transformation as shown in Figure 3.5. Therefore, our aim is to transform the input models (Primary and Context Specific Aspect) to a target composed model. As shown in Figure 3.5, both the input and output models conform to an EMF implementation of the UML metamodel specification while our ATL program or model conforms to the ATL metamodel. All the metamodels conform to the EMF's Ecore metametamodel. As in other aspect composition approaches composition has to be performed on different views, that is, structural or behavioral views. Our main focus is on the behavioral view. Composition inevitably results in some model elements been replaced, removed, added or merged (Morin et al., 2008; Gong, 2008). Similarly in our approach, all model elements from the context specific aspect model that are not already in the primary model, will be added to the composed model but elements common to both models will be merged. All join point model elements (from primary model) are replaced by advice elements. The rest of the elements from the primary model will be added to the composed model. A formal definition of our models and the proposed algorithm (for matching and composing) are based on UML metamodel classes. The specification for the UML metamodel (OMG, 2009) is enormous and also includes metaclasses for other UML diagrams that we are not interested in. Therefore, it makes sense to look only at some of the important classes whose objects are used in creating sequence diagrams (SDs).

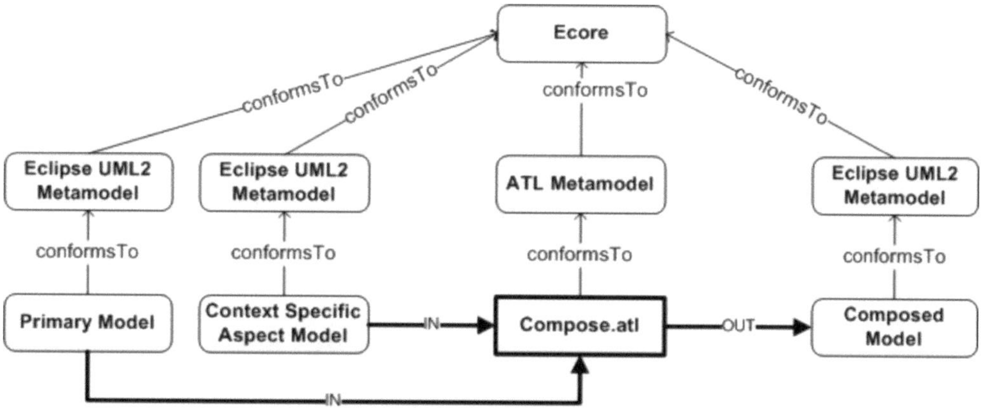

Fig. 3.5. Aspect Composition as an ATL model transformation.

4. Model composition semantics and definitions

A sequence diagram shows the order in which messages are exchanged among participants; hence, order is crucial [Hamilton & Miles, 2006; Pilone & Pitman, 2005). The messages or interactions, to be precise, on a specific lifeline are totally ordered but interactions between two lifelines are partially ordered. The most important model elements in a SD are probably lifelines (participants), messages, message ends, and the enclosing interaction. Figure 4.1 is a simplified class diagram of the Interactions Metamodel showing the relationships among the metaclasses for these model elements.

A complete description of each metaclass can be obtained from the UML specification (OMG, 2009). The *InteractionFragment* abstract class represents a general concept of an interaction (OMG, 2009). An *Interaction* is a sub class of *InteractionFragment* that represents the modeled behavior or interactions (exchange of messages) between participants (lifelines)[OMG09]. An *Interaction* essentially encloses *Messages*, *Lifelines* and other *InteractionFragments*. The enclosed *InteractionFragments* are stored in an ordered list referenced by the *fragment* role. This ordering is exploited in our algorithms for matching and composing SDs. A *Message* models the kind of communication between participants [OMG09]. There are five main types of messages; namely, synchronous, asynchronous, delete, create, and reply messages [Hamilton+06]. Each message is accompanied by a pair of MessageOccurrenceSpecifications (MOSs). The *sendEvent* MOS represents the sending of the message while *receiveEvent* MOS models the reception of the message. Each MOS also has a reference to the lifeline for which the message is received or sent from through the *covered* association. In return, each *Lifeline* has a reference to a list of *InteractionFragments* or specializations of *InteractionFragment* (including MOSs), which cover the lifeline, through the *coveredBy* association.

The events that we are interested in are specializations of the *MessageEvent* abstract class mainly the *SendOperationEvent* (SOE) and *ReceiveOperationEvent* (ROE) classes. These types of events occur during the sending or receiving of a request for an operation invocation (OMG, 2009).

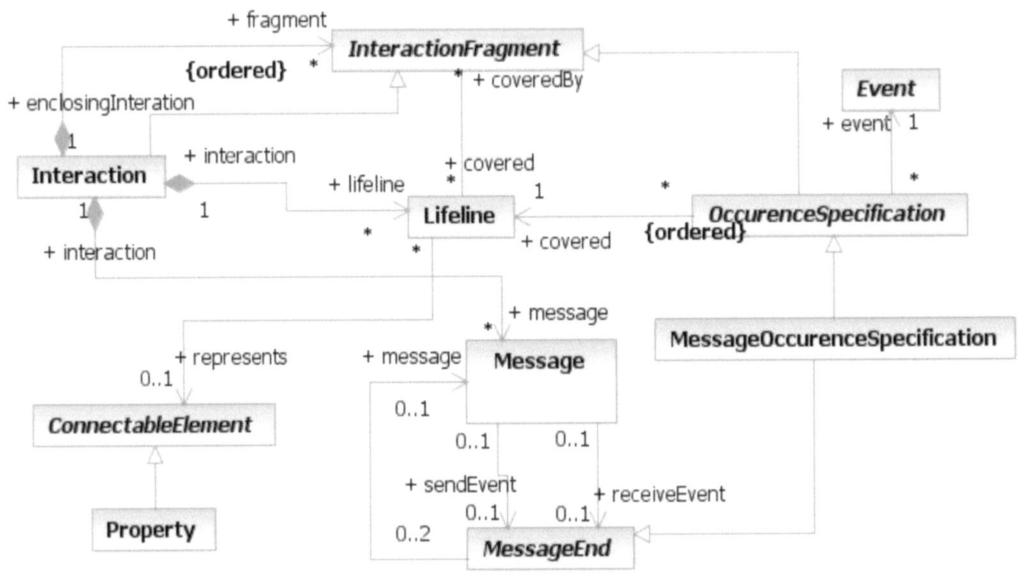

Fig. 4.1. Simplify Metamodel for Sequence Diagrams.

4.1 Sequence Diagram (SD) Composition

As previously described, our AOM approach has a primary model, one or more generic aspect models and a mark model. The primary model describes the core system functionality (behavior) without cross-cutting concerns. The generic aspect models describes (encapsulate) cross-cutting concerns which could otherwise be scattered across core functionality; for example, new features (in software product lines), security, persistence, etc. Before composing the primary model with an aspect model we first instantiate the generic aspect model in the context of the application with the help of a mark model. We employ an ATL transformation model that takes the primary, generic aspect, and mark models as input, and produces a context specific aspect model as output. We would like to point out that the mark model does not necessarily have to specify all the bindings for the template parameters in cases where some of the bindings can be matched or implied from the primary model. A second ATL transformation model then takes as input the primary and context specific models to produce the composed model. Defining a generic aspect improves re-usability since the same aspect can be instantiated and then composed with the primary model multiple times until a complete integrated system model is obtained. Since we are mainly interested in the behavioral view (of our primary and aspect models), our work is mainly focused on the composition of interactions diagrams in the form of SDs. As described earlier, the aspect model consists of a pointcut and an advice defined as SDs where the pointcut is the behavior to detect and the advice is the new behavior to compose or weave at the join points [Klein et al., 2007]. Before composing, we first have to identify all our join points by matching the pointcut SD with the primary model. The pointcut SD consists of message or a sequence of messages between lifelines; therefore, we want to find the occurrence of these sequences of messages in the primary model and then insert the defined cross-cutting behavior (defined in the advice SD) at every join point. Composition is essentially inserting this new behavior; that is, composition is achieved by replacing the join points with the advice SDs. Before instantiating a generic aspect, we first have to ensure that the aspect can be applied to the primary model; that is, whether its pointcut matches. A formal definition of matching will be given later. Also during composition we have to find where to weave. This makes pointcut detection or finding join points a core operation. The algorithm designed for pointcut detection manipulates the SD metaclasses by exploiting the relationship between *InteractionFragments* and their ordered list of fragments in an interaction. It also makes use of the fact that a sequence of messages (and indeed a SD) is essentially a list of ordered fragments.

4.1.1 Formal notations for defining aspects and primary models

Let,

- **P** be a sequence of fragments, that is, *InteractionFragments* (CombinedFragments and MOSs), from the aspect's pointcut SD.
- **A** be a sequence of fragments from the aspect's Advice SD.
- **C** be a sequence of fragments from the primary model SD.

Note that a sequence is an ordered collection/list.

Then, **P** = Sequence{f_1, ..., f_ψ} where ψ = number of fragments in **P** and f_i is either a *CombinedFragment* (CF) or a MessageOccurrenceSpecification (MOS), such that,

f_i =	If instance of	where
CF(O, Λ)	CF	**O** is a sequence of operands in the **CF** and each operand is also a sequence of fragments just like **P**. This is the case with nested CFs. **Λ** is a list of lifelines covered by the **CF**.
MOS(L_i,E_i,M_i)	MOS	L_i is a lifeline covered by f_i. E_i is an event associated with f_i. M_i is a message associated with f_i.

and,

C = Sequence{c_1, ..., c_μ} where μ = number of fragments in **C** and c_i is also either a CF or a MOS, such that,

c_i =	If instance of	where
CF(O, Λ)	CF	**O** is a sequence of operands in the **CF** and each operand is also a sequence of fragments just like **C**. This is the case with nested CFs. **Λ** is a set of lifelines covered by the **CF**.
MOS(L_i,E_i,M_i)	MOS	L_i is a lifeline covered by c_i, E_i is an event associated with c_i. M_i is a message associated with c_i.

4.1.2 Aspect and primary models definition

Using the above notation, we will define an aspect model as a pair of fragment sequences, that is, **Aspect** = **(P, A)** where **P** and **A** are the sequences defined earlier. This definition is adapted from Klein et al. in (Klein et al., 2006; Klein et al., 2007); However, Klein et al. define a simple SD as a tuple that consists of a set of lifelines, a set of events, a set of actions and partial ordering between the messages (Klein et al., 2007). This is different from our definition of a sequence of fragments. Using our definition, the primary model = **C**, a sequence of fragments from the primary model SD. Then our pointcut **P** matches **C** if and only if there exists two sub-sequences M_1 and M_2 in C such that, $C = M_1 \oplus P \oplus M_2$, where $\oplus$ denotes a union of sequences. $A \oplus B$ returns a sequence composed of all elements of A followed by the elements of B. If the **P** matches **C** several times, say *n* times, then we can say, $C = M_1 \oplus P \oplus M_2 \oplus \ldots \oplus M_n \oplus P \oplus M_{n+1}$. This definition is an adaptation of the definition given by Klein et al. in (Kleinet al., 2006).

4.1.3 Join point definition

Part of the sequence **C** that corresponds or matches **P** is the join point. In other words, a join point is a sub sequence of **C** that is equal to the sequence **P**. Equal here means that fragments at the same corresponding location in **P** and join point (same index on either sequences) are equal. For example, if elements at position 1 in **P** and in the join point are both MOSs, they can only be equal if and only if they cover similar lifelines (same name and type), have the same message, and have other features that are similar. More details for checking for equality will be given in the design and implementation section. Since the size (number of fragments) of **P**, hence the size of a join point, is fixed we can afford to keep track of only fragments at the beginning of each join point. With this assumption we can define; **S** = Sequence$\{s_1, \ldots, s_n\}$, a sequence of fragments at the beginning of each join point where $n > 1$ is number of join points matched by **P**. A join point, J_i is then given by a sub sequence of **C** from index of s_i in **S** to the index of s_i plus ψ minus 1. That is, if; x_i = **indexOf**(s_i) and $y_i = x_i + \psi - 1$, where ψ = number of elements in **P**, then, J_i = C->**subSequence**(x_i,y_i) for $1 \leq i \geq n$.

4.2 Composition algorithms - assumptions and requirements

The below algorithm and indeed the other algorithms to be introduced later, make the following assumptions:

- The input models are well formed and valid; hence, the sequences **S**, **P**, and **A** are valid. For example, we do not have empty sequences. We also assume that the aspect models (generic and context specific) consists of two interactions (SDs) named Advice and Pointcut, and that the primary model represents one interaction or scenario; therefore, consists of one instance of *Model*, one instance of *Collaboration*, and one instance of *Interaction*.
- We can correctly compare any two fragments regardless of their specialization, for example, comparing a MOS with a CF.
- Nested CFs have been properly and consistently unrolled.
- A lifeline's name is the same as that of the represented object (property).
- Message have arguments with primitive UML types (strings and integers).
- We can ignore other fragments like *BehaviorExecutionSpecifications* (BESs) and *ExecutionOccurrenceSpecifications* (EOSs) focusing only on MOSs and CFs (and their operands), and still achieve accurate pointcut detection.

4.2.1 Pointcut detection algorithm

The pseudo code for the algorithm that detects or matches pointcuts and returns **S** is given below. The algorithm begins by creating an empty sequence **S** on line 2. It then iterates over all fragments c_i in **C** checking if c_i is equal to f_1, the first element in our pointcut **P** on line 9. If the elements are **not** equal, the algorithm moves to the next c_i. However, if the fragments (c_i and f_1) are equal, it obtains $\mathbf{J_i}$, a sub sequence of **C** starting from c_i and with the same size as **P**, on line 10.

Algorithm-1 Pointcut Detection Algorithm
Input : **P** = Sequence{f_1, ..., f_ψ}, **C** = Sequence{c_1, ..., c_μ}
where ψ = number of fragments in **P**, and μ = number of fragments in **C**
Output : **S** = Sequence{s_1, ... ,s_n}

```
1.   begin
2.        S = Sequence{}
3.        foreach c_i in C do
4.             //compute the location of the end of the potential join point
5.             k = i + ψ -1
6.             if k > μ then //make sure we have a valid location
7.                  break
8.             end if
9.             if c_i = f_1 then
10.                 J_i = C->subSequence(i,k) // Potential join point
11.                 /* check if fragment at the same location in P is equal to the
12.                 corresponding element in the join point */
13.                 if pairWiseMatch(P, J_i) then
14.                      S->enqueue(c_i)
15.                 end if
16.            end if
17.       end loop
18.       return S
20.  end
```

On line 13 the algorithm then compares **P** and $\mathbf{J_i}$, side-by-side by checking if each pair of fragments at index *j* on both sequences is equal for $1 \leq j \geq \psi$. If this is true, then indeed $\mathbf{J_i}$ is a join point. So the algorithm inserts the first element (c_i) of the join point into **S** and loops back to line 3. It continues looping until it has checked all the elements of **C** or the condition on line 6 is true to ensure we do not fall off the edge. More details on the implementation of this algorithm and its functions, like *pairWiseMatch*, will be discussed in the next section.

4.2.1.1 Algorithm-1 complexity

If the algorithm-1 has to visit all fragments in **C** (when $\psi = 1$) then both functions on lines 10 and 13 will take constant time, that is, O(1) which makes the algorithm linear or O(n). If **P** is the same size as C ($\psi = \mu$), then the algorithm has to loop only once but both *subSequence* and *pairWiseMatch* functions are O(n); hence, the algorithm is again linear. However, if $\psi < \mu$ then again both functions (i.e., *Sequence* and *pairWiseMatch*) are, in the worst case, linear and the algorithm will have to loop several times each time invoking the two functions making the algorithm quadratic, that is $O(n^2)$; therefore, in general the algorithm is $O(n^2)$.

4.2.2 Complete composition algorithm

After detecting the pointcut and obtaining our join points, the next step is to weave the advice at the join points. Since the advice has already been bound to the context of the application during aspect instantiation, weaving the advice is simplified to replacing a join point with the advice. This is trivial with only one join point. Challenges arise when we have multiple join points because we have only one advice from the aspect model. We can either duplicate the advice or work with one join point at a time. Both options were explored but duplicating the advice (without duplicating the aspect model) proved to be complex due to the inability to navigate target models in ATL, and the nested relationships between *InteractionFragments*. Focusing one join point at a time is easier and more elegant. The complete composition algorithm presented in this section achieves this. Let us first introduce abbreviations that we will use in the algorithm.

- **GAM** = Generic Aspect Model
- **CSAM** = Context Specific Aspect Model (Instantiated generic aspect model)
- **MM** = Mark Model
- **PM** = Primary Model
- **CM** = Composed Model

The pseudo code of the Complete Composition Algorithm is given below. The three functions defined in this algorithm represent the ATL transformations used to implement this algorithm as we shall see in the next chapter. The algorithm begins by retrieving *n* the number of join points matched in the primary model (PM) using the *JoinPointsCount* function on line 2. This function implements algorithm-1 (Pointcut detection Algorithm) to return a sequence of fragments at the beginning of each join point, and then finds the size of that sequence. The details of the implementation of this function will be given in next chapter. The number of join points determines if the algorithm will execute lines 6 to 10, and not necessarily the number of times the loop will iterate. If n > 0, that is, we have at least one join point, the algorithm instantiates the GAM to create a CSAM on line 6. This corresponds to the instantiate process shown in Figure 5.1. It then composes PM with CSAM by weaving the advice at the first join point using the *Compose* function on line 8 to produce our composed model.

Algorithm-2 Complete Composition Algorithm
Input :GAM, MM, PM
Output :CM

```
1.      begin
2.              n = JoinPointsCount(GAM, MM, PM)
3.              temp = PM
4.              while n > 0
5.                      // instantiate our generic aspect model
6.              CSAM = Instantiate(GAM, MM, temp)
7.                      // compose advice and first join point
8.                      CM = Compose (temp,CSAM)
9.              temp = CM
10.             n = JoinPointsCount(GAM, MM,temp)
11.             end while
12.             return CM
13.     end
```

The algorithm then checks the CM for more join points on line 10. If more are found, it returns to line 6 to instantiate the GAM using CM (new primary model). It then creates another CM and checks for more join points. The algorithm continues looping until no join points are found.

As it is, this algorithm has a potential nasty flaw in the form of positive feedback, which, if left unattended, can cause the algorithm to loop indefinitely in some cases! The problem is rooted on the fact that composing an aspect in most cases results in the addition of new model elements (fragments, messages and lifelines) which in turn can produce more join points. This means that after composition on line 8, the algorithm may find more join points on line 10 causing the algorithm to iterate again and again. For example, if the pointcut is defined as a single message MSG1, and the primary model has two invocations of this message, then we have two join points. If the advice adds three instances of the same message MSG1, then after composition (1st iteration) we will have four join points. After the second iteration well have six, then eight, etc. With the number of join points increasing all the time the algorithm will never terminate. This problem is easily solved by tagging model elements from advice during instantiation on line 6. To be precise we only have to tag MOSs (fragments). Then when pointcut matching during the invocation of *JoinPointsCount* (implementing algorithm-1), we check for that tagging. If a potential join point has at least one tagged fragment, then we know that this join point emerged only after composition; therefore, it is immediately disqualified.

4.2.2.1 Algorithm-2 complexity

The complexity of algorithm-2 is difficult to analyze because on the surface the algorithm appears to be linear on the number of join points. However, the algorithm is not necessarily linear on the number fragments. We have already seen that detecting the number of join points is quadratic. Therefore, if that is nested within a loop, we could say that (in general) the algorithm is cubic, that is, $O(n^3)$

4.2.3 Advice composition algorithm

At the core of the *Compose* function, used by the Complete Composition Algorithm described above, is the Advice Composition algorithm that weaves the advice at the join point. Recall the definition of an **Aspect** = (**P**, **A**). We will use definition again where by "**Aspect**" we are referring to a context specific aspect model. Our main interest is mainly on the advice sequence **A**. Recall that,

- **A** = Sequence{a_1, ..., a_ω}, a sequence of fragments from the aspect model advice SD, where ω = number of fragments in **A**.
- **C** = Sequence{c_1, ..., c_μ}, a sequence of fragments from the primary model, where μ = number of fragments in **C**.
- **S** = Sequence{s_1, ... ,s_n}, a sequence of fragments at the beginning of each join point, where $n > 1$ is number of join points matched by **P**.
- A join point, $\mathbf{J}_i$ is then given by a sub sequence of C from index of s_i in **S** to the index of $s_i + \psi$-1; That is, If, x_i = indexOf(s_i) and $y_i = x_i + \psi - 1$, then, $\mathbf{J}_i$ = C->subSequence(x_i,y_i) for $0 \leq i \geq n$
- **P** is a sequence of fragments from the pointcut SD.

Since our Complete Composition Algorithm is concerned with one join point at a time, our Advice Composition algorithm needs to work with only one join point; that is, the join point that begins with s_1 (the first element in **S**). Then, let $\mathbf{C_{CM}}$ be a sequence of fragments from the composed model. Recall again that;

With the notation defined, we can now describe our Advice Composition algorithm. Its pseudo code is given on the next page. In a nut shell, the algorithm simply replaces the join point with the advice. The algorithm first checks if we have a join point. If so, it obtains the first element of **S**, on line 5. Using that element, the algorithm finds the location (x_1) at the beginning and at the end (y_1) of the join point, as shown on lines 6 and 7. The algorithm then obtains a sub sequence of fragments from **C** (primary model) before the start of the join point, on line 12. Note that indexing for our sequence data structure starts at 1 instead of zero as in Java lists or arrays. On line 16, the algorithm returns a sequence of fragments after the last element of the join point to the end of **C**. The composed model is then given by $\mathbf{C_{CM}}$ = *sub_before* ⊕ **A** ⊕ *sub_after*, that is, the union of *sub_before*, **A** and *sub_after*.

Algorithm-3 Advice Composition
Input : **C**, **A**, **P**, **S** - where ψ = number of fragments in **P**
Output : $\mathbf{C_{CM}}$

```
1.  begin
2.      if S->isEmpty() then
3.          CCM = {}
4.      else
5.          s1 = S->first()        //fetch the tail of the 1st join point
6.          x1 = C->indexOf(s1)    //find its location in C
7.          y1 = x1 + ψ-1          //find the location of the join point's head
8.          sub_before = {}
9.          sub_after = {}
10.         if x1 > 1 then
11.             //get all fragments before the join point
12.             sub_before = C->subSequence(1,x1-1)
13.         end if
14.         if y1 < μ then
15.             //get all fragments after the join point
16.             sub_after = C->subSequence(y1+1, μ)
17.         end if
18.         //Insert the advice in place of the join point
19.         CCM = Sequence {sub_before, A, sub_after}
20.     end if
21.     return CCM
22. end
```

4.2.3.1 Algorithm-3 complexity

Creating *sub_before* and *sub_after* is linear in the worse case. Creating C_{CM} is also O(n) in the worst case; hence, the above algorithm is clearly linear.

5. Design and Implementation

In the previous section, we introduced our definition of primary, aspect and mark models. We also introduced our approach to AOM composition, and discussed our Complete Composition Algorithm that uses two other algorithms to detect join points, and compose the primary and aspect models. In this chapter we describe how the Complete Composition Algorithm was implemented using ATL transformations to realize the functions *JoinPointsCount(...)*, *Instantiate(...)* and *Compose(...)* employed by the algorithm. These functions were implemented as ATL transformation models and used to transform several input models to desired target models to achieve composition of SDs. Before giving the implementation details of these transformation models, we would like to first justify some of our design decisions and also describe how we designed our mark model.

5.1 Design decisions

Several key decisions were taken in this work. These include:

- The use of ATL transformation models for composition instead of, say, graph transformations or general programming languages (e.g., Java). Aspect composition or weaving can be considered a form of model transformation because we take at least two input (primary and aspect) models and produce at least one target model (composed). Therefore, model transformation approaches can be used for aspect composition. ATL was chosen because it is mature and has a rich set of development tools that are built on top of flexible and versatile Eclipse platform. ATL is based on OCL; therefore, it is not difficult for a developer with some OCL experience to learn. ATL was also chosen because no work on behavioral aspect composition, that we are aware of, has been attempted using ATL.
- The use of RSA 7.5 as a modeling tool of choice. RSA 7.5 is not free but we already have a license for it. It is a great UML modeling tool. It has excellent support for SDs. It is easy and intuitive to use. It allows for easy model migration. We can export or import UML models as .uml or XMI files. It allows for model validation (not available in some of the tools) which we found very useful. RSA can also generate a sequence diagram from an imported model. This makes verification of our composed model easy and less error prone.
- The use of a mark model. ATL Transformations only work with models; therefore, our binding rules have to be in the form of a model that has a metamodel. Mark models are a convenient way to work with parameterized transformations. MDA, certainly, allows for use of mark models in model transformations (Happe et al., 2009). Happe et al. use mark models to annotate performance models in their work on performance completions (Happe et al., 2009).
- Ignoring BehaviorExecutionSpecifications (BESs) and Execution Occurrence Specifications (EOSs) model elements during pointcut detection and composition. As stated in the previous section, we are convinced that we can ignore these two and still achieve accurate pointcut detection. This is because BESs and EOSs are used to define the duration of execution of behavior (OMG, 2009) of say, a message invocation. Our work is focused on detecting the occurrence of a sequence of messages (interactions between participants) and doing something when we find the sequence. We are not concerned about how long the participant will execute after a message invocation.

During early stages of system modeling or at high levels of system abstraction, BESs and EOSs are not really applicable or useful; therefore, our decision to ignore them is reasonable.

5.2 Designing mark model metamodel

A mark model helps define binding rules for instantiating generic aspect models. These rules are merely template parameter and value pairs stored in mark model instances. In MDE, a model must have a metamodel that it conforms to, and our mark model is no exception. Since the mark model is to be used in ATL transformations (with an EMF model handler), its metamodel must conform to a metametamodel that is the same as the ATL metamodel, that is, Ecore as shown in Figure 4.1 and Figure 4.2. ATL development tools include KM3 (Kernel MetaMetaModel) which is textual notation for defining metamodels (ATL_Manual, 2009). The code snippet below shows a KM3 definition of the metamodel for our mark model which we named *BindingDirectives*. The metamodel has one class with a *parameter* and *binding* value attributes of type *String*. This essentially means that the instances of the mark model will be a collection of objects with initialized parameter and binding attributes.

```
package BindingDirectives {
        class BindingDirective {
                attribute parameter : String;
                attribute binding : String;
        }
        package PrimitiveTypes {
                datatype String;
        }
}
```

The metamodel is defined in a *.km3* file which is then converted (injected) to an Ecore format encoded in XMI 2.0 using injectors in the ATL IDE (ATL_Manual, 2009). Once the metamodel has been defined, we can begin creating mark models in an XMI format.

5.3 Implementation of the complete composition algorithm

As mentioned earlier, the Complete Composition Algorithm uses the *JoinPointsCount*, *Instantiate*, and *Compose* transformations to produce a composed model (SD). These transformations in return implement the other two algorithms (Pointcut detection and Advice Composition algorithm) to achieve their objectives.

5.3.1 Getting the Number of Join Points

The *JoinPointsCount* transformation is implemented by the ATL transformation model shown in Figure 5.1. It returns the number of join points found in the primary model given a pointcut defined in a generic aspect, and binding rules defined in a mark model. The transformation produces a simple UML target model that contains the number of join points found. The number of join points must be returned in a model because an ATL transformation (module) has to produce a model but not a string or integer. The

JoinPointsCount transformation is implemented in an ATL module creatively named **JoinPointsCount** as shown below by its header definition.

module JoinPointsCount;
create NUMJOINPOINT:UML2 **from** PRIMARY:UML2, ASPECT:UML2, BIND:BD;
uses PointcutMatchHelpers;

...

The header declares that the transformation takes as input two UML2 models (bound to variables PRIMARY and ASPECT), a model that conforms to the BD (Binding Directive) metamodel, that is the mark model bound to the variable BIND. The transformation then produces a UML2 target model bound to the variable NUMJOINPOINT. The header also declares that the transformation uses the *PointcutMatchHelpers* ATL library. This is where common or general purpose helpers such as the ones used for pointcut detection (and used also by other transformations) are defined. This helps reduce code duplication and allows for a better code maintenance.

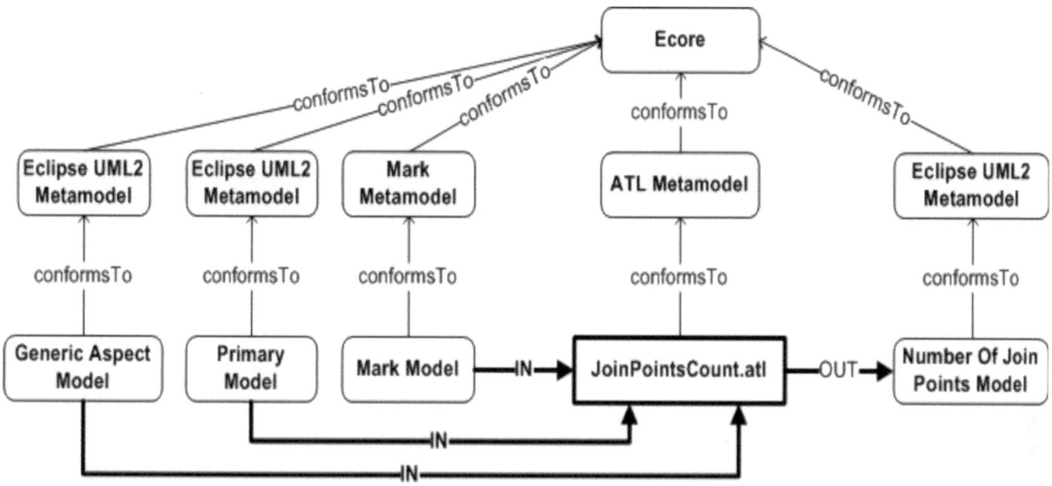

Fig. 5.1. An Overview of the *JoinPointsCount* ATL Transformation.

5.3.2 JoinPointsCount helpers

The transformation employs several helpers listed in Appendix A. It also uses some of the helpers defined in the *PointcutMatchHelpers* library listed in Appendix B. Please note that aspect model here refers to the generic aspect model (not context specific) which is one of the input models to the transformation.

5.3.3 JoinPointsCount rules

Rules are used to generate the target model in ATL. Our *JoinPointsCount* transformation has two simple declarative rules (one matched rule and one lazy rule) that generate a UML model to store the number of join points found. A proper UML model should have a *Model* container element that packages all the other modeling elements. The list of contained objects is then referenced by the *packagedElement* attribute or association. The *Model* matched rule is the main rule that generates a *Model* element. We want the rule to match only one element. Therefore, its source pattern defines that the rule should match an element of type **UML2 Model** from the input aspect model as it can be seen on line 2 in the code snippet for the rule below. The rule's target pattern defines that a **UML2 Model** element will be generated.

```
1. rule Model {
2.    from s : UML2!Model(s.fromAspectModel() )
3.    to t : UML2!Model (
4.      name <- 'NumberOfJoinpoints',
5.           packagedElement <- Sequence {
6.      thisModule.CreateLiteralInteger(thisModule.numJoinPoints,
7.                      'NumberOfJoinpoints'),
8.                                        ...
```

The attributes of the target elements will be initialized as defined from line 4. A *Model* element has a name and a collection of packaged elements. The *name* attribute is set to 'NumberOfJoinpoints'. The *packagedElement* attribute will be set to a sequence containing a **UML2 LiteralInteger** element generated by the invoked *CreateLiteralInteger* lazy rule. This lazy rule is passed the number of join points and a string (name) as parameters. The number of join points is, therefore, returned in a **UML2 LiteralInteger** model element packaged in a **UML2 Model** element. The code snippet for the *CreateLiteralInteger* lazy rule is shown below. The rule creates a *LiteralInteger* model element and initializes its name and value attributes with a string (desired name) and an integer (number of join points found by our transformation) respectively.

```
lazy rule CreateLiteralInteger  {
   from count : Integer,  name :String
   to t: UML2!LiteralInteger  (
         name <- name,
    value <- count
                                          ...
```

5.4 Instantiating A generic aspect model

The *Instantiate* transformation is implemented by the ATL transformation shown in Figure 5.2. This transformation instantiates a generic aspect model and produce a context specific aspect model. It inputs a primary model, generic aspect model and a mark model, and outputs a context specific aspect model.

The *Instantiate* ATL module, whose header is shown below, implements the *Instantiate* transformation. The header declares that the module creates a target **UML2 model** bound to the CONTEXTSPECIFIC variable.

```
module Instantiate;
create CONTEXTSPECIFIC : UML2 from PRIMARY : UML2, ASPECT : UML2, BIND : BD;
uses PointcutMatchHelpers;
                                        ...
```

The module has two UML2 source models (bound to variables PRIMARY and ASPECT) and one source model bound to the variable BIND that conforms to our *Binding Directives*

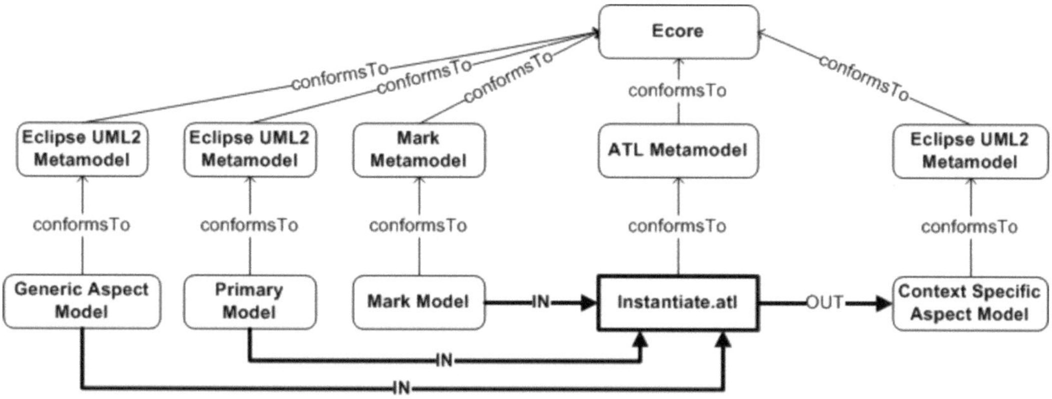

Fig. 5.2. An overview of the *Instantiate* ATL Transformation.

metamodel (BD); that is, a mark model. The header also declares that the module imports the *PointcutMatchHelpers* library.

5.5 Instantiate helpers

Just like the *JoinPointsCount*, this module also uses some of the helpers defined in the *PointcutMatchHelpers* library listed in Appendix B. This transformation also uses helpers defined within its module. Before we can generate the context specific aspect model, we have to ensure that we have a join point where we can weave. The *pointcutMatched* attribute helper returns true if we have at least one join point. It is used as a guard condition for all the rules that generate the target model elements as we shall see later. This ensures that no model element will be generated if there are no join points. The details of this helper are shown below.

```
helper def: pointcutMatched : Boolean =
        thisModule.joinPointsFragments()->notEmpty();
```

The helper returns true if the sequence that contains all the fragments at the beginning of each join point (returned by *joinPointsFragments()*) is not empty. Since *pointcutMatched* is defined as an attribute helper, it is evaluated once and the result cached. This means that successive calls to the helper will be faster which improves performance especially in our case where the helper is called many times by all the rules.

5.5.1 Instantiate rules

Several rules are required to generate a complete context specific aspect model. In fact, we have a rule for every model element type required for a well formed UML sequence diagram. These rules include several matched rules and a handful of lazy rules. Just like in the previous transformation, our target UML model should have a *Model* container element that packages all the other modeling elements. The rule that generates the target *Model* element is shown below.

```
1. rule Model {
2.    from s : UML2!Model (
3.                    s.fromAspectModel() and thisModule.pointcutMatched
4.          )
5.    to t : UML2!Model (
6.          name <- s.createAspectName(),
7.                    packagedElement <- s.packagedElement
8.          )
9. }
```

The source pattern specifies that the rule matches elements of type **UML2 Model**. It also has a condition that the matched element should come from the aspect model (using *fromAspectModel()* helper), and also that *pointcutMatched* must be true, as mentioned earlier. There is only one *Model* element from the aspect model. If at least one join point was found, then only one **UML2 Model** element will be created on the target model since the target pattern declares that the rule creates an instance of **UML2 Model**. Its packaged elements will be initialized to the list from the matched element as defined on line 7 above. The name will be initialized with the string returned by the *createAspectName()* helper on line 6 above. The UML specification describes that an *Interaction* can be contained in a *Collaboration*. Collaborations are used to show the structure of cooperating elements with a particular purpose (OMG, 2009). Indeed, the primary and aspect models created using RSA have interactions contained within collaborations. The *Collaborations* matched rule has the task of generating *Collaboration* objects that enclose the interactions for the advice and pointcut. Recall that the aspect model consists of the advice and pointcut SDs (interactions). The rule is described by the code snippet shown below.

```
1.    rule Collaborations {
2.       from s : UML2!Collaboration (
3.                    thisModule.aCollaborations->includes(s) and
4.                    thisModule.pointcutMatched
5.             )
6.       to t : UML2!Collaboration (
7.             name <- s.name,
8.                    ownedBehavior <- s.ownedBehavior,
9.             ownedAttribute <- s.ownedAttribute,
10.            ownedConnector <- s.ownedConnector
11.            )
12.   }
```

The guard condition for this rule's source pattern ensures that only collaborations from the aspect model (and not from primary model) are matched. It checks if a collaboration is included in the collection of collaborations from the aspect model returned by the *aCollaborations* attribute helper. The attributes of the generated collaboration, including the enclosed interactions (*ownedBehavior*), are initialized from those of the matched collaboration as shown on lines 7 to 10 above. The *aInteractions* and *pInteractions* rules are used to create *Interaction* target elements for the advice and pointcut respectively. The rules are almost identical with slight differences in the source pattern guard. The code below gives details of the *aInteractions* rule. The difference between the rules is in line 3. The guard for *aInteractions* rule ensures that the rule matches the interaction from the aspect's advice which has the name "Advice".

```
1.  rule aInteractions {
2.     from s : UML2!Interaction (
3.                     s.name = 'Advice' and thisModule.pointcutMatched
4.           )
6.     to t : UML2!Interaction  (
7.       name <- s.name,
8.                     lifeline <- s.lifeline,
9.             fragment <- s.fragment,
10.            message <- s.message,
11.                    ownedAttribute <- s.ownedAttribute,
12.                    ownedConnector <- s.ownedConnector,
13.                    generalOrdering <- s.generalOrdering,
14.            ownedBehavior <- s.ownedBehavior,
15.            covered <- s.covered
16.            )
17. }
```

The guard for the *pInteractions* rule matches the interaction from the aspect's pointcut which has the name "Pointcut". Both rules then initialize the attributes of the generated interactions using the values from the attributes of the matched source elements as it can be seen from lines 7 to line 15.

The *Lifelines* rule generates lifelines for both the advice and pointcut SDs. The rule matches all lifelines from the advice model as shown on line 3 of rule's code snippet on the next page. The *aLifelines* helper returns all lifelines from the generic aspect model (advice and pointcut SDs). The generated lifeline's attributes are then initialized as shown from lines 6 to 8. This rule probably best shows how helpers are used to assist rules in creating the target models other than been used as guard conditions in the source pattern. We can see on line 6 that binding is achieved by using the *bind()* helper to initialize the name of the generated lifeline.

```
1.  rule Lifelines {
2.     from s : UML2!Lifeline (
3.            thisModule.aLifelines->includes(s)and thisModule.pointcutMatched
4.            )
5.     to targetLifeline : UML2!Lifeline (
6.       name <- s.bind(),
7.                    coveredBy <- thisModule.getMOSByLifeline(s),
8.                    represents <- s.represents
9.            )
10. }
```

5.6 Composing aspect models

After obtaining a context specific aspect model from the previous transformation (*Instantiate*), the next step is to compose the context specific aspect model with the primary model. This is achieved by the *Compose* ATL transformation whose overview is shown in

Figure 3.5. The transformation inputs the primary and context specific source models, and produces a composed target model. Both the source models and the output model conform to the UML2 metamodel. This transformation is implemented by the *Compose* ATL module. The code snippet below shows a description of the module's header.

```
module Compose;
create COMPOSED : UML2 from PRIMARY : UML2, ASPECT : UML2;
uses PointcutMatchHelpers;
...
```

As expected, the header declares that the module creates a UML2 Model bound to the variable COMPOSED from two UML2 source models bound to the variables PRIMARY and ASPECT for the primary and aspect models respectively. The module also uses some helpers from the *PointcutMatchHelpers* library.

5.6.1 Compose helpers

Our *Compose* transformation has a number of helpers. All the helpers have a necessary role to play but some roles are, certainly, more important than others. For example, the *getTargetFragments* attribute helper has the privilege of returning the composed sequence of fragments, that is, *sequence {sub_before, A, sub_after}* from algorithm-3. The code definition of this helper is shown below. The helper begins by ensuring that there is, at least, one join point by calling the *pointcutMatched* helper on line 2, which we have described earlier. If there exists a join point, *getTargetFragments* then obtains a sequence of fragments before the join point by invoking the *lowerFragSub* helper on line 4, a sequence of fragments from the advice (by invoking *getAspectFragments*) on line 5, and a sequence fragments after the join point on line 6. It returns a flattened sequence consisting of those sequences. The fragments returned by *getTargetFragments* are used to initialize the fragment attribute of the interaction generated by our transformation.

```
1.  helper def : getTargetFragments : Sequence(UML2!InteractionFragment) =
2.          if thisModule.pointcutMatched then
3.            Sequence {
4.                thisModule.lowerFragSub(thisModule.firstJPIndex),
5.                thisModule.getAspectFragments('Advice'),
6.                thisModule.upperFragSub(thisModule.firstJPIndex +
7.                thisModule.numPCTFs-1)
8.              }->flatten()->asSequence()
9.        else
10.             Sequence{}
11.       endif;
```

The *getTargetFragments* helper also serves as the base of our composition process. Almost all the other elements to be used in generating the target model are rooted from this helper. The *targetCFs* helper, which returns all combined fragments to be used for generating combined fragments in the target model, iterates through fragments returned by *getTargetFragments* returning all instances of *CombinedFragment*. The *targetOperands* helper, in return, iterates through the sequence of combined fragments returned by *targetCFs* to obtain all instances of *InteractionOperand*.

5.6.2 Compose rules

Several rules are defined for creating the composed target model. Rules in the *Compose* transformation probably use more helpers compared to the two previous transformations, mainly because in this transformation more elements are removed or added. This requires modifications to many associations between model elements. The code below is that for the *Model* matched rule which is used to create the **UML2 Model** element.

```
1.  rule Model {
2.     from s : UML2!Model (
3.              s.fromPrimaryModel()  and thisModule.pointcutMatched
4.              )
5.     to t : UML2!Model (
6.                    name <- thisModule.getModelName(s.name, thisModule.aModel),
7.                          packagedElement <- Sequence {
8.                          thisModule.targetClasses,
9.                          thisModule.pCollaborations,
10.                                     thisModule.getTargetEvents()
11. ...
```

The rule matches elements of type **UML2 Model** from the primary model, and provided the pointcut matches as defined by the source pattern on lines 2 and 3. The rule creates instances of *Model* as declared on line 5. Since the primary model consists of one instance of the *Model* class, this rule will generate only one instance. It then initializes the created instance with the use of several helpers as defined on lines 6 to 11. The *getModelName* helper generates a string used to initialize the name attribute. The *packageElement* list attribute is initialized to a sequence of classes returned by *targetClasses*, a collaboration from the primary returned by *pCollaborations*, and a sequence of events returned by the *getTargetEvents()* operation helper. These three helpers are defined in the context of the module; hence, the use of the keyword *thisModule*.

```
rule Messages{
   from s : UML2!Message (
            thisModule.targetMessages->includes(s) and
            thisModule.pointcutMatched
            )
   to t : UML2!Message (
            name <- s.name,
            sendEvent <- s.sendEvent,
            receiveEvent <- s.receiveEvent,
            messageSort <- s.messageSort,
            argument <-  s.argument->collect (e  |
                                  if  e.oclIsTypeOf(UML2!LiteralString) then
                                             thisModule.CreateLS(e)
                                  else
                                             if  e.oclIsTypeOf(UML2!LiteralInteger) then
                                                       thisModule.CreateLI(e)
                                             else
                                                       OclUndefined
                                             endif
...
```

The *Messages* rule shown below is used to generate messages for the target model. This rule is more interesting since it calls a few lazy rules to help initialize some of the attributes of the target messages to be created. The rule matches all messages included in *targetMessages* and creates messages for the target model. The generated message is initialized as defined from line 7. On line 12, the *argument* attribute is initialized by calling a suitable lazy rule. We are only interested in primitive type message arguments (integers and strings); therefore, we have two lazy rules for creating an instance of *LiteralInteger* or *LiteralString* depending on the argument type for the matched message.

The rule uses ATL's built-in *oclIsTypeOf(t: oclType)* operation to check the type of the argument for the matched message. If it is a *LiteralString* then the *CreateLS* lazy rule is called but if it is a *LiteralInteger* the *CreateLI* lazy rule is called instead. If the argument is neither an integer nor a string, the message's argument attribute is initialized to *OclUndefined*, ATL's equivalent of null. All the rules that are used by the Compose transformation to generate the composed model are listed in Appendix C.

6. Case studies - phone call features as aspects

This case study of a cell phone application was adapted from Whittle and Jayaraman in (Whittle et al., 2007). The application has three use cases but we are only interested in two; namely, *Receive a Call* and *Notify Call Waiting* (Whittle et al., 2007]. The *Receive a Call* use case is considered to be the base model and the *Notify Call Waiting* is considered the aspect. Figure 6.1 shows a dynamic view of the *Receive a Call* use case modeled as a sequence diagram. This will be our primary model. When the user's phone receives a call (*incomingCall* message), it alerts the user by displaying the appropriate information about the caller on the phone's display (Whittle et al., 2007) by sending a *displayCallInfo* message to the display. The phone also sends a *ring* message to the ringer. The user then has several options captured by an **alt** combined fragment. The user can accept the call by sending a *pickUp* message to the phone and later end the call by sending a *hangUp* message. Alternatively, if the user chooses not to accept the call, the user can send a *disconnect* message to the phone. If the user elects to ignore the call, the phone will ring for a specified amount of time and then time out ending the scenario. As mentioned, the *Notify Call Waiting* scenario or feature is considered an aspect. The approach (graph transformations) taken by Whittle and Jayaraman (Whittle & Jayaraman, 2006) does not have the notion of generic or context specific models like our approach. Therefore, Figure 6.2 shows our representation of the behavioral model of the *Notify Call Waiting* scenario as a generic aspect model.

The pointcut is defined as a sequence of parameterized |accept and |end messages from the receiver lifeline to the phone lifeline. This will match a sequence of two messages that will be bound to |accept and |end from the lifeline bound to |receiver. The advice shown in Figure 5.2b is slightly more complex. It introduces messages that if bound properly, will place the current call on hold (Whittle et al., 2007). The behavior defined by the advice is only applicable when the user is currently on call; therefore, we must ensure that the advice is weaved between the *pickUp* and *hangUp* messages on the primary model (Whittle et al., 2007). To achieve this, we will bind |accept and |end to *pickUp* and *hangUp* respectively, as shown on lines 9 and 10 of the mark model below. The |receiver parameter is bound to *user* so the pointcut matches *pickUp* and *hangUp* from the user to the phone.

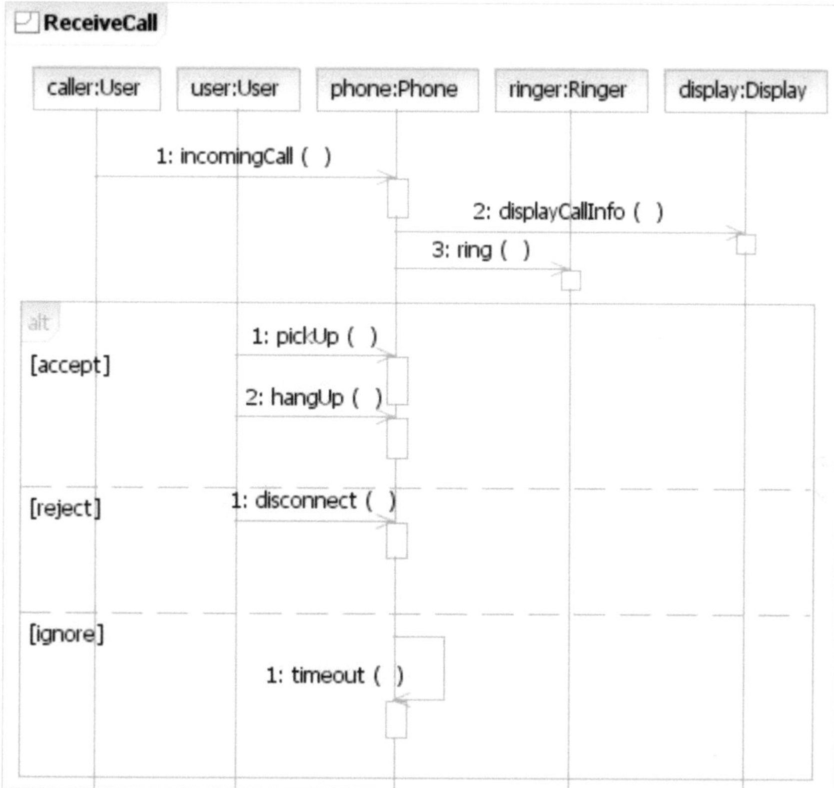

Fig. 6.1. Receive a Call Primary Model Adapted from (Whittle et al., 2007).

```
<?xml version="1.0" encoding="ISO-8859-1"?>
<xmi:XMI xmi:version="2.0" xmlns:xmi="http://www.omg.org/XMI"
xmlns="BindingDirectives">
  <BindingDirective parameter="|receiver" binding="user"/>
  <BindingDirective parameter="|sender"   binding="caller"/>
  <BindingDirective parameter="|anotherRequest" binding="incomingCall"/>
  <BindingDirective parameter="|notify" binding="displayCallInfo"/>
  <BindingDirective parameter="|acknowledge" binding="ok"/>
  <BindingDirective parameter="|accept"   binding="pickUp"/>
  <BindingDirective parameter="|end"                binding="hangUp"/>
  <BindingDirective parameter="|suspend" binding="putOnHold"/>
  <BindingDirective parameter="|Client"   binding="User"/>
  <BindingDirective parameter="|notifier"   binding="display"/>
  <BindingDirective parameter="|Transducer"       binding="Display"/>
</xmi:XMI>
```

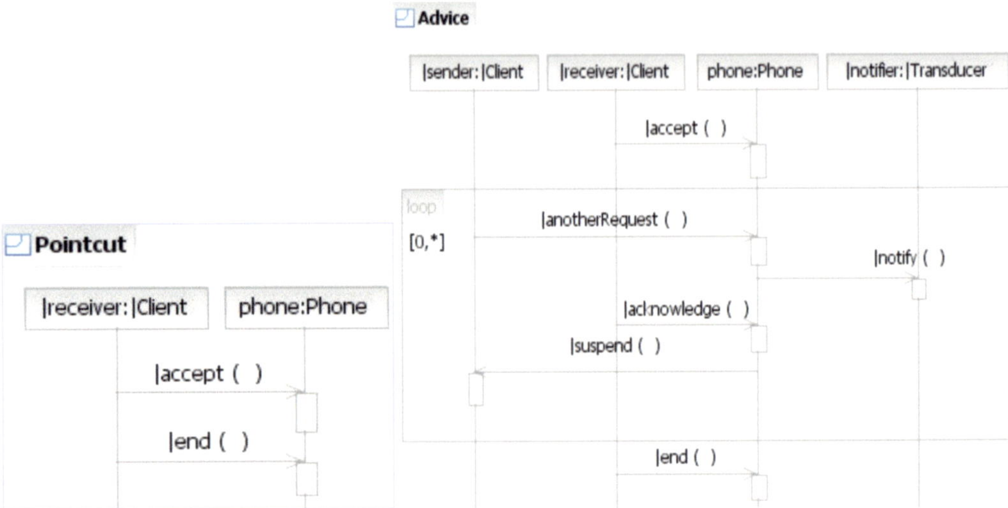

(a) Pointcut (b) Advice

Fig. 6.2. Notify Call Waiting Generic Aspect Model.

The rest of the parameters are bound as defined by the mark model. Recall that by binding these parameters from the generic aspect model, we are actually instantiating it to produce a context specific aspect model. This is done by the *Instantiate* ATL transformation as discussed in earlier sections. However, before going into the trouble of instantiating a context specific aspect (and composing it with the primary model), we must first determine if the pointcut matches, and if so, how much join points were found. Getting the number of join points is performed by the *JoinPointsCount* transformation which takes the generic aspect, the primary and mark models as input, and produces a target model that contains the number of join points. Executing this transformation produces the model shown in Figure 6.3 (when viewed on Eclipse's uml editor). The model contains a *LiteralInteger* object with the name *NumberOfJoinpoints* and which has a value of one, that is, our primary model has one join point.

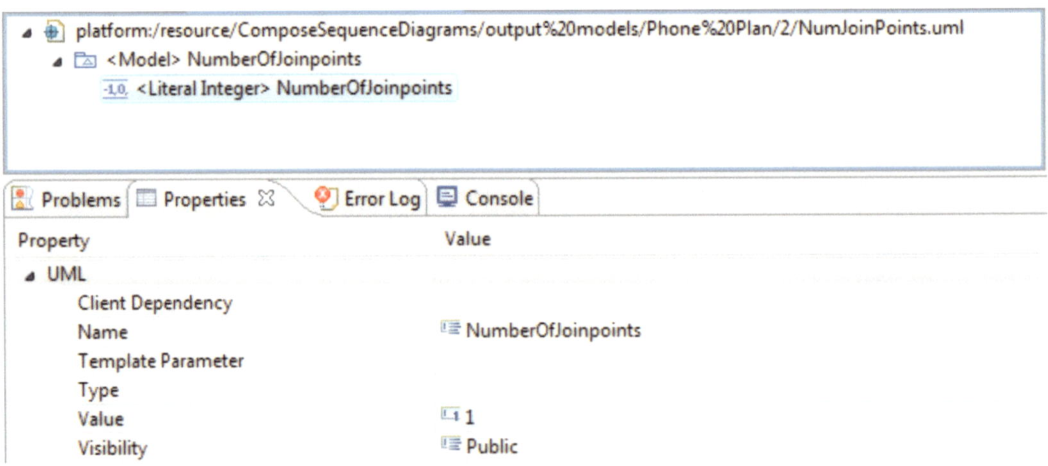

Fig. 6.3. JoinPointsCount Output Model.

With only one join point, our composition algorithm only has to loop once; hence, no loop unrolling is required. The next step is to validate our models using both RSA and our custom *validator* package. Running the *ValidateComposedModel* class from our custom package to validate the composed model (CM) produces the output shown below.

Reading model CM from disk ...Validating CM
Model container is valid
All Classes are valid :)
All Class Operations are valid :)
All Message events are valid :)
Collaboration model element ReceiveCall is valid :)
All Owned attributes in ReceiveCall are valid :)
Interaction model element ReceiveCall is valid :)
All Message Occurrence Specifications in ReceiveCall are valid :)
All Messages in ReceiveCall are valid :)
All lifelines in ReceiveCall are valid :)
Our model and all its model elements meet our validation requirements

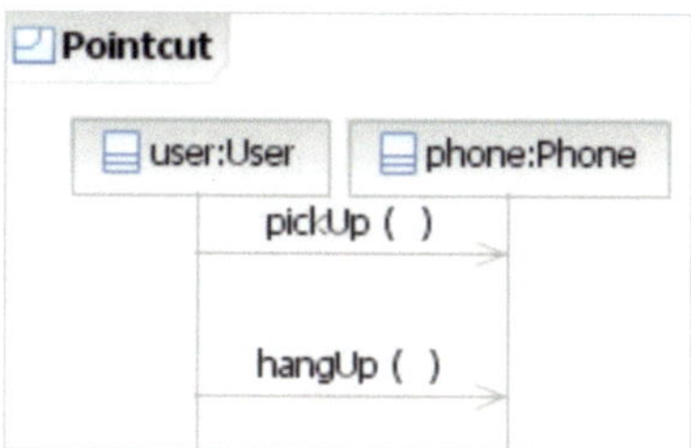

(a) Pointcut

(b) Advice

Fig. 6.4. Context Specific Aspect Model.

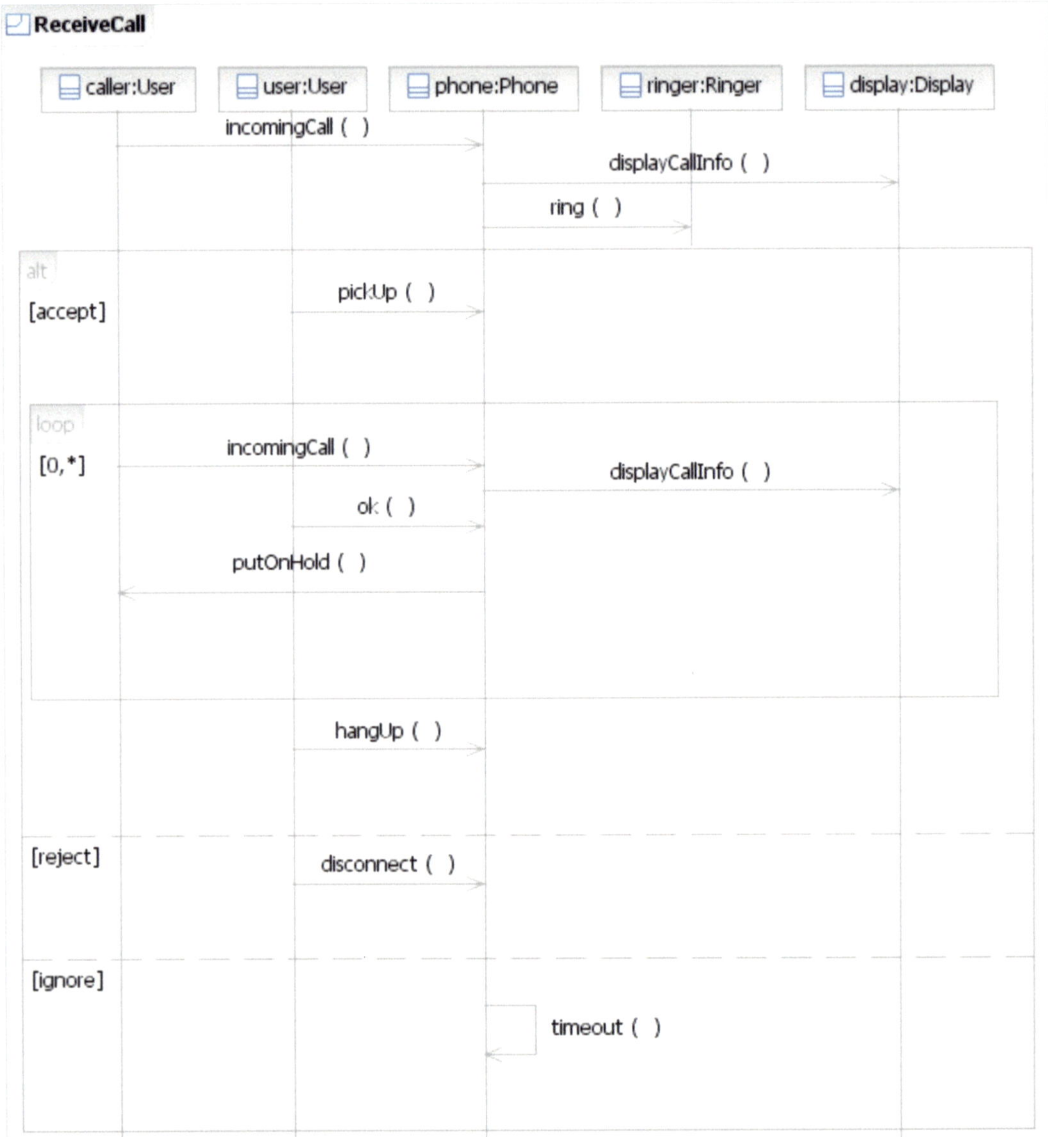

Fig. 6.5. Composed Model.

Running the *ValidateComposedModel* to validate the context specific aspect model (CSAM) also shows that the model is valid. Both models are valid according to the checklist defined in our *validator* package. Both models are then imported into RSA for validation and visual inspection.

Figure 6.4 and 6.5 show the context specific aspect and composed model SDs created on RSA after importing the models. The pointcut was properly bound. We can see in Figure 6.4a that |accept and |end are bound to *pickUp* and *hangUp* while |receiver and |Client have been bound to *user* and *User* respectively. Figure 6.4b shows that the advice has also been bound as specified by the mark model. Figure 6.5 shows a sequence diagram for our composed model. We can see that the advice has been properly weaved into the **alt** combined fragment's first operand. This way, if the user chooses to accept a call and another *incomingCall* message is received by the phone the phone's display will show the new caller's information. The user can then send an *ok* message to phone to put the caller on hold.

7. Conclusion

The main objective of this work is to compose aspect models represented as UML sequence diagrams (SDs) using the Atlas Transformation Language (ATL). Toward this end, we proposed a formal definition of SDs in terms of an ordered list of interaction fragments, and in the process defined three algorithms for pointcut detection, advice composition and complete composition. We designed and implemented the Complete Composition algorithm to achieve composition of the primary model and generic aspect models. We consider aspect composition as a form of model transformation; therefore, the algorithm is implemented using model transformations written in the ATL model transformation language. We also designed a simple metamodel in Ecore for mark models used to define binding rules which are used to instantiate generic aspect models. We finally designed and implemented a custom Java package to help validate the composed model. The Java classes check the composed model elements against a list of defined constraints designed to ensure that essential model elements are present in the composed model and are properly initialized.

The Complete Composition Algorithm proposed and implemented composes behavioral views of both primary and aspect models represented as UML sequence diagrams. The primary model defines the core system behavior without cross-cutting concerns while the aspect models represent behavior that cross-cuts the primary model. The models are described in UML Sequence diagrams created using an eclipse-based modeling tool (RSA) and then exported to a UML2.1 file for composition and validation.

Using ATL, a mature model transformation language, the Complete Composition Algorithm is implemented using three transformation models; namely JoinPointsCount, Instantiate, and Compose. The JoinPointsCount transformation determines the number of join points in the primary model given the pointcut from the aspect model. The aspect models are made generic so that they can be more reusable; therefore, they must first be instantiated before they can be composed with the primary model. The Instantiate transformation is used to instantiate generic aspect models in the context of the application using a set of binding rules defined in mark models to produce context specific aspect models. The Compose transformation then takes the primary model and context specific aspect model as inputs, and produces a composed model. This process is repeated as many times as there are join points and aspect models until a complete integrated system is obtained.

To test our design and implementation, several test cases and case studies were successfully conducted. Validation was achieved by using custom Java classes to check the model against a set of defined constraints. The composed model was also validated using RSA's built-in validation feature. To verify composition, a sequence diagram was generated from the model's UML2.1 file using RSA. The generated sequence diagram was then visually inspected to see if the composition was performed properly.

Using ATL for composing models does have its challenges. The inability to navigate target models or modify input models makes intricate weaving of aspects a hard problem. However, the benefits of using a versatile language that allows for powerful expressions may outweigh the challenges.

7.1 Limitations and future work

This work is part of an ambitious quest for a complete AOM composition framework and a set of tools that can allow software architects and developers to easily apply AO techniques to model driven software development. There are several limitations that must be addressed, and new features to be added before our composition approach can be more useful. These include:

- Improved string pattern definition and matching for template parameters.
- Non primitive message and operation argument types.
- Support for Interaction Occurrences.
- Support for BehaviorExecutionSpecifications (BESs), ExecutionOccurrenceSpecifications (EOSs) and other model elements.
- Structural view composition.
- Invoking ATL from Java.
- An eclipse plug-in to help in the creation of the mark model.

Our approach currently supports the use of the wildcard "*" for defining template parameters. This gives some flexibility when defining generic aspect models. However, to allow for powerful expressions, we need to use regular expressions. Currently ATL (version 2.0.x) does not support the use of regular expressions for comparing or matching strings. ATL only uses regular expressions for replacing and splitting strings. Future research may include development of a custom string ATL library that will provide helpers that implement regular expression matching operations.

Furthermore, we have assumed that messages in the primary and aspect models have simple arguments that are either strings or integers. However, messages can have arguments that are instances of classes defined in the structural view of the system. Therefore, the current use of lazy rules to create message arguments (and class operation parameters) may not be ideal. Future work would look at a more efficient and elegant way of creating message arguments in the target model. Interaction Occurrences provide a way to reuse and manage complex SDs. They are a notation for copying one SD (basic) into another one, which may be larger (Pilone et al., 2005). Our current composition approach has no support processing interaction occurrences; therefore, future research would look into including interaction occurrences in pointcut detection and composition. This will provide challenges because the use of interaction occurrences means that the primary model SD or the aspect model SDs may contain more than one instance of *Interaction* depending on the number of interaction occurrences.

Recall that BESs and EOSs were ignored in our composition approach. Future work could look into how these model elements can be processed with other interaction fragments. We would also add support for other model elements that are not currently supported; like, connectors, signals (and related events), gates, etc.

Future research would also include composition of other behavioral views (Statechart and Activity diagrams) and structural views (class diagrams) of the primary model and aspect models. Our current approach does achieve some composition of structural model elements from the primary and aspect models but does ignores associations between the structural elements.

8. Acknowledgement

This research work was partly sponsored by NSERC (Natural Sciences and Engineering Research Council) of Canada through grant number EGP 401451-10.

9. Appendix A - JointPointsCount helpers

Helper Name	Return type	Purpose
aMessages	Sequence	Returns all messages from the aspect model.
aOperations	Sequence	Returns all class operations from the aspect model.
aLifelines	Sequence	Returns all lifelines from the aspect model.
aSendEvents	Sequence	Returns all SOEs from the aspect model.
aRecvEvents	Sequence	Returns all ROEs from the aspect model.
aProperties	Sequence	Returns all lifeline properties the aspect model.
allBindings	Sequence	Returns all binding rules from the mark model.

10. Appendix B - PointcutMatchHelpers library

Helper name	Return type	Purpose
adviceMOSEncoding()	String	A tagging string for advice MOSs
getAspectFragments(sd)	Sequence	Returns MOSs and CFs from a given SD from the aspect model.
getPrimaryFragments()	Sequence	Returns MOSs and CFs from a given SD from the primary model.
getFragments()	Sequence	Returns MOSs and CFs within the context CF.
getFragments()	Sequence	Returns MOSs and CFs within the context Interaction Operand.
sameEventType(e1, e2)	Boolean	Returns true if the given *MessageEvents* are both ROE or SOE
PairwiseMatchFragments (src, tgt)	Boolean	Checks if the fragments at the same index from *src* and *tgt* sequences are "equal".

getBinding(name)	String	Retrieves the binding value from the mark model for the given template parameter.
bindingDefined(String)	Boolean	Returns true if a binding value exists for the given parameter.
samePropertyType(pct , core)	Boolean	Returns true if the given *Properties* have the same type (class).
equals(mos) Context = MOS	Boolean	Checks if the context and supplied MOSs are equivalent.
invalidMOSName()	Boolean	Returns true if the context MOS has been tagged meaning it was added from a previous composition iteration
getLifelineMOS()	Sequence	Returns MOSs that cover the context lifeline.
getAspectSD (name)	Interaction	Returns an SD (Advice or Pointcut) from the Aspect Model.
getMessageLifelines (m)	Sequence	Returns the sender and receiver lifelines for the given message.
getSDLifelines (sd)	Sequence	Returns all lifelines in a given SD.
getSDMessages (sd)	Sequence	Returns all messages in a given SD.
createMOSName (code, idx)	String	Generates a name for the context MOS given our tagging string and MOS index in the sequence of MOS.
fromAspectModel() Context = Model	Boolean	Returns true if the context model is from the aspect model.
fromAspectModel() Context = Interaction	Boolean	Returns true if the context Interaction is from the aspect model.
fromPrimaryModel() Context = Model	Boolean	Returns true if the context model is from the primary model.
fromPrimaryModel() Context = Message	Boolean	Returns true if the context message is from the primary model.
notInPrimaryModel() Context = Class	Boolean	Returns true if the context class is from the primary model.
notInPrimaryModel() Context = MessageEvent	Boolean	Returns true if the context MessageEvent is from the primary model.
notInPrimaryModel() Context = Operation	Boolean	Returns true if the context operation is from the primary model.
equals(c) Context = Class	Boolean	Returns true the context class is the same as the supplied class; that is, if they have the same name.
classMatch (c1 , c2)		Returns true if the two classes are equal.

equals(o) Context = Operation	Boolean	Returns true if the context operation is the same as the supplied operation.
equals(e) Context = MessageEvent	Boolean	Returns true if self is the same as the supplied event; that is, they are of the same type and have the same operation.
equals(f) Context = CombinedFragment	Boolean	Returns true if the context CF is the same as the given interaction fragment which also has to be CF.
equals(f) Context = InteractionOperand	Boolean	Returns true if the context interaction operand is equal to the given interaction fragment .
getMOSs() Context = InteractionOperand	Sequence	Returns all MOSs enclosed by the context interaction operand.
getMOSs() Context = CombinedFragment	Sequence	Returns all MOSs enclosed by the context CF.
PairwiseMatchOperands (src,tgt)	Boolean	Returns true if the given sequences of operands have matching pair of operands, that is, the operands at the same index are equal.
PairwiseMatchMOSs (src, tgt)	Boolean	Checks if the elements at the same index from the *src* and *tgt* sequence are equal.
joinPointsFragments()	Sequence	Returns fragments at the start of the join points.
getMaxInt()	ValueSpecificationAction	Returns the *maxInt* value of the given Interaction constraint.
getMinInt()	ValueSpecificationAction	Returns the *minInt* value of the given Interaction constraint.

11. Appendix C – Compose rules

Rule	**Purpose**
Model	Generates a *Model* element that contains all the other target model elements.
Collaborations	Creates a *Collaboration* that contains the composed model interaction.
Interactions	Generates the *Interaction* that owns fragments, lifelines, messages, etc.
CombinedFragments	Generates all *CombinedFragments* including nested ones.
InteractionOperands	Generates all *InteractionOperands*.

InteractionConstraints	Creates all the constraints.
OpaqueExpressions	Generates *OpaqueExpressions* for *InteractionConstraints.*
Lifelines	Generates all lifelines.
Messages	Produces messages for the target model.
MOSs	Creates all *MessageOccurrenceSpecifications* (MOSs).
ROEs	Generates *ReceiveOperationEvents* for *receiveEvent* MOSs.
SOEs	Produces *SendOperationEvents* for *sendEvent* MOSs.
Operations	Generates operations for classes.
Classes	Generates classes.
Properties	Generates all *Properties* for lifelines.
lazy rule CreateLUN	Creates *LiteralUnlimitedNaturals* that are used for guard conditions.
lazy rule CreateLS	Creates strings that are used for guard conditions and arguments for messages.
lazy rule CreateLI	Creates integers that are used for guard conditions and arguments for messages.
lazy rule CreateParam	Creates parameters for operations in the target model.

12. References

http://wiki.eclipse.org/ATL/User_Guide, last accessed on September 22, 2009.

Samuel A. Ajila, Dorina Petriu, and Pantanowitz Motshegwa, *Using Model Transformation Semantics for Aspects Composition,* 2010 IEEE 4th International Conference on Semantic Computing (IEEE-ICSC 2010), pp 325-332, Carnegie Mellon University, Pittsburgh, PA, USA, September 22 - 24, 2010

ATLAS group LINA & INRIA Nantes, "ATL User Manual version 0.7," Online resource available at: http://www.eclipse.org/m2m/atl/doc/ATL_User_Manual[v0.7].pdf, last accessed on September 22, 2009.

O. Barais, J. Klein, B. Baudry, A. Jackson, and S. Clarke, "Composing Multi-View Aspect Models," In Proceedings of the Seventh International Conference on Composition-Based Software Systems, pages 43-52, 2008.

A. Colyer, A. Clement, G. Harley, M. Webster, "Eclipse AspectJ. Aspect-Oriented Programming with AspectJ and the Eclipse AspectJ Development Tools,"Addison Wesley Professional, December 14, 2004, ISBN : 0-321-24587-3

M. Didonet Del Fabro, J. Bézivin, and P. Valduriez, "Weaving Models with the Eclipse AMW plug-in," In: Eclipse Modeling Symposium, Eclipse Summit Europe 2006, Esslingen, Germany, 2006.

F. Fleurey, B. Baudry, R. France, and S. Ghosh, "A Generic Approach for Automatic Model Composition," Lecture Notes In Computer Science archive Models in Software Engineering: Workshops and Symposia at MoDELS 2007, Nashville, TN, USA, September 30 - October 5, 2007,pages 7-15, 2008, Springer-Verlag Berlin, Heidelberg.

R. France, I. Ray, G. Georg and S. Ghosh, "Aspect-Oriented Approach to Design Modeling," IEEE Proceedings - Software, Special Issue on Early Aspects: Aspect -Oriented Requirements Engineering and Architecture Design, 151(4):173-185, August 2004.

H. Gong, "Composition of Aspects Represented as UML Activity Diagrams.", Master's thesis, Carleton University, 2008.

I. Groher, and M. Voelter. "XWeave: models and aspects in concert," In Proceedings of the 10th international workshop on Aspect-oriented modeling, March 2007.

K. Hamilton, and R. Miles, "Learning UML 2.0", O'Reilly, April 2006, ISBN-10: 0-596-00982-8 .

J. Happe, S. Becker, C. Rathfelder, H. Friedrich, and R. H. Reussner, "Parametric Performance Completions for Model-Driven Performance Prediction," Journal of Systems and Software, Volume 82 Issue 1, January 2009, Elsevier Science Inc.

I. Jacobson, and P. Ng, "Aspect-oriented software development with use case," Addison-Wesley Professional, December 30, 2004, ISBN-10: 0321268881.

C. Jeanneret, R. France, and B. Baudry, "A reference process for model composition," In Proceedings of the 2008 AOSD workshop on Aspect-oriented modeling, April 2008.

J.M. Jézéquel, "Model Transformation Techniques Model Techniques," Online resource available at: http://modelware.inria.fr/static_pages/slides/ModelTransfo.pdf, last accessed in August 30, 2009

F. Jouault, and I. Kurtev, "Transforming Models with ATL," In proceedings of the Model Transformation in Practice Workshop, October 3rd 2005.

J. Kienzle, W. A. Abed, and J. Klein, "Aspect-oriented multi-view modeling," In Proceedings of the 8th ACM international conference on Aspect-oriented software development, March 2009.

J. Klein, L. Hélouët, and J.M. Jézéquel, "Semantic-based Weaving of Scenarios," AOSD 06, March 20-24, Bonn, Germany, 2006

J. Klein, F. Fleurey, and J.M. Jézéquel, "Weaving Multiple Aspects in Sequence Diagrams," Transactions on AOSD III, LNCS 4620, pp. 167–199, 2007

Kompose website, http://www.kermeta.org/kompose/ last accessed on September 23, 2009.

M. Milanovic, "Complete ATL Bundle for launching ATL transformations programmatically." Online resource available at: http://milan.milanovic.org/download/atl.zip, last accessed on September 10, 2009.

B. Morin, J. Klein, O. Barais, and J.M. Jézéquel, "A generic weaver for supporting product lines," In proceedings of the 13th international workshop on Software architectures and mobility, Leipzig, Germany, May 2008.

Object Management Group, "UML Superstructure Specification, v2.1.1," Online resource available at: http://www.omg.org/docs/formal/07-02-05.pdf, last accessed last accessed on July 20, 2009.

Object Management Group, "UML Superstructure Specification, v2.2," Online resource available at: http://www.omg.org/docs/formal/09-02-02.pdf, last accessed on August 22, 2009.

OpenArchitectureware website, http://www.openarchitectureware.org/ last accessed on September 23, 2009.

D.C. Petriu, H. Shen, and A. Sabetta, "Performance Analysis of Aspect- Oriented UML Models", Software and Systems Modeling (SoSyM), Vol. 6, No. 4., pages. 453-471, 2007, Springer Berlin / Heidelberg

D. Pilone, and N. Pitman, "UML 2.0 in a Nutshell", O'Reilly, (June 2005) ISBN: 0-596-00795-7

G. Straw, G. Georg, E. Song, S. Ghosh, R. France, and J. M. Bieman, "Model Composition Directives," LNCS 3273, pages 84-97, 2004, Springer Berlin / Heidelberg

J. Whittle, J. Araújo, and A. Moreira, "Composing aspect models with graph transformations," In Proceedings of the 2006 international workshop on Early aspects at ICSE, pages 59-65, Shanghai, China, 2006

J. Whittle, and P. Jayaraman, "MATA: A Tool for Aspect-Oriented Modeling Based on Graph Transformation," At MoDELS'07: 11th International Workshop on Aspect-Oriented Modeling, Nashville TN USA, Oct 2007.

M. Woodside, D.C. Petriu, D.B. Petriu, J. Xu, T. Israr, G. Georg, R. France, J.M. Bieman, S.H. Houmb, and J. Jürjens, "Performance analysis of security aspects by weaving scenarios extracted from UML models," Journal of Systems and Software, Volume 82 , Issue 1 (January 2009), pp 56-74, 2009

2

Program Slicing Based on Monadic Semantics

Yingzhou Zhang[1,2,3]
[1]*College of Computer, Nanjing University of Posts and Telecomm., Nanjing*
[2]*Jiangsu High Technology Research Key Lab. for Wireless Sensor Networks,*
[3]*Key Lab of Broadband Wireless Communication and Sensor Network Technology, Ministry of Education Jiangsu Province, Nanjing, China*

1. Introduction

A program slice consists of those statements of a program that may directly or indirectly affect the variables computed at a given program point (Weiser, 1984). The program point p and the variable set V, denoted by <p, V>, is called a slicing criterion. Program slicing has applications in software testing and debugging, measurement, re-engineering, program comprehension and so on (Kamkar, 1995; Tip, 1995; Harman, 2001; Binkley, 1996; Gallagher, 1991).

Program slicing algorithms can be roughly classified as static slicing and dynamic slicing methods, according to whether they only use statically available information or compute those statements that influence the value of a variable occurrence for a specific program input. Most of the existing slicing algorithms rely on relation graphs such as system dependence graphs (SDG) or program dependence graphs (PDG). These slicing methods are incremental, sequential, not combinatorial or not parallelizable easily for multi-core systems. However modern programming languages support modularized programming and programs might consist of a set of modules. So the program analysis should reflect this design technology, and their methods (including program slicing) should be flexible, combinable, and parallelizable for improving the efficiency.

As the behavior of a program is determined by the semantics of the language, it is reasonable to expect an approach for program slicing based on formal semantics of a program. On the basis of this view, this paper proposes an approach for program slicing based on modular monadic semantics, called *modular monadic slicing*. It can compute slices directly on abstract syntax, without explicit construction of intermediate structures such as dependence graphs.

The program slicing methods focused on the semantics of programs can be found in ref. (Hausler, 1989; Ouarbya, 2002; Venkatesh, 1991). These methods are based on the standard denotational semantics of a program language. As mentioned in ref. (Moggi, 1991; Liang & Hudak, 1996; Wansbrough, 1997; Mosses, 1998; Zhang & Xu, 2004), traditional denotational semantics lack modularity and reusability. A better solution was to use *monads* (Moggi, 1991) to structure denotational semantics, with the help of *monad transformers* (Moggi, 1991; Wadler, 1992; Espinosa, 1995) which can transform a given monad into a new one with new operations. S.Liang et al. used monads and monad transformers to specify the semantics of programming language; called it *modular monadic semantics*. In this paper, we will employ it in our program slicing algorithm.

In our previous work (Zhang et al, 2004, 2005, 2006; Zhang & Xu, 2005; Wu et al. 2006), we abstracted the computation of program slicing as a simple slice monad transformer, which took only the label set L as its parameter, without reflecting explicitly the change of the slice table Slices. In ref. (Zhang, 2007), we presented theoretical foundation for our previous work. Based on these theories of the monadic slicing and from the view of the practical implementation, this paper will redesign the static slice monad transformer. The extensibility and reusability of our monadic method will be showed by easily introducing a new program feature (such as pointers) to slicing analysis.

The rest of the paper is organized as follows: In Section 2, we briefly introduce and illustrate the concepts of modular monadic semantics through a simple example language. The computation of program slicing is abstracted as *slice monad transformer* in Section 3. In Section 4, we discuss and illustrate our static slicing algorithm in detail. In Section 5, we show how our slicing algorithm can be readily adapted to an extension for the example language with pointers. In Section 6 and 7, we address the implementation, the time and space complexity analysis. We conclude this paper with directions for future work in Section 8.

Along the paper, the presentation follows the monadic semantics style. We use Haskell[1] notation with some freedom in the use of mathematical symbols and declarations. For brevity and convenience, we will omit the type constructors in some definitions.

2. Modular monadic semantics

In this section, we briefly review the theory of monads (Wadler & Thiemann, 2003; Moggi, 1989), monad transformers and modular monadic semantics (Liang, 1998). Readers familiar with these topics may skip the section, except for the last three paragraphs (about the syntax and monadic semantics of an example language).

2.1 Monads and monad transformers

Monads, originally coming from philosophy, were discovered in category theory in the 1950s and introduced to the semantics community by Moggi in 1990s (Moggi, 1989). After this work, Wadler popularized Moggi's ideas in the functional programming community (esp. in Haskell) (Wadler, 1995). In the monad-based view of computation, a monad is a way to structure computations in terms of values and sequences of computations using those values (Newbern, 2002). The monad determines how combined computations form a new computation and frees the programmer from having to code the combination manually each time it is required. From this view, a monad can be thought as a strategy for combining computations into more complex computations.

In Haskell, monads are implemented as a type constructor class with two member operations/functions.

---

[1] Haskell is an advanced purely functional programming language. Please visit its official website (http://www.haskell.org or http://haskell.org) for more information.

class Monad m **where**
$return :: a \to m\ a$
$(\gg=) :: m\ a \to (a \to m\ b) \to m\ b$

Here, *return* is the Haskell name for the unit and >>= (pronounced "bind") is the extension operation of the monad. The above definition of the monad class means: a parameterized type m (which may think of as a function from types to types) is a monad if it supports the two operations *return* and >>= with the types given. Using the combinator analogy, a monad m is a combinator that can apply to different values. $m\ a$ is a combinator applying to a value of type a. The *return* operation puts a value into a monadic combinator. The >>= operation takes the value from a monadic combinator and passes it to a function to produce a monadic combinator containing a new value, possibly of a different type. The >>= operation is known as "bind" because it binds the value in a monadic combinator to the first argument of an operation.

To be a proper monadic combinators, the *return* and >>= operations must work together according to some simple laws. Monads laws state in essence that >>= operation (sequential composition) is associative, and *return* is its unit/identity. Failure to satisfy these laws will result in monads that do not behave properly and may cause subtle problems when using the do-notation[2].

A monad (call it m) therefore defines a type of computation. The nature of the computation is captured by the choice of the type m. The *return* operation constructs a trivial computation that just renders its argument as its result. The >>= operation combines two computations together to make more complex computations of that type.

To make the use of monads more convenient, we adopt the following syntactic sugar (which is similar to S. Liang's notation and the do-notation in Haskell as well):

$$\{e\} \equiv e$$
$$\{m; e\}_m \equiv m \gg= \backslash\ \_ \to \{e\}$$
$$\{x \leftarrow m; e\}_m \equiv m \gg= \backslash\ x \to \{e\}$$
$$\{\mathbf{let}\ exp; e\} \equiv \mathbf{let}\ exp\ \mathbf{in}\ \{e\}$$

In practice, the computations can't be performed in isolation. In this case, we need a monad that combines the features of the two monads into a single computation. It is impossible in general to combine two monads to form a new monad. Moreover, it is inefficient and poor practice to write a new monad instance with the required characteristics each time a new combination is desired. Instead, there is the technique, called monad transformers (Liang, 1998), which can transform a given monad into a new one that has both the new operations and maintains those of the former monad. The concept of monad transformers was rediscovered by D.Espinosa in Moggi's original work. He developed a system, Semantic Lego, which implemented Moggi's original *monad constructors* to give a modular semantics for languages.

---

[2] Do notation is an expressive shorthand for building up monadic computations. In short, the do notation allows us to write monadic computations using a pseudo-imperative style with named variables. The result of a monadic computation can be "assigned" to a variable using a left arrow ← operator.

In Haskell, a monad transformer can be defined as any type constructor *t* such that if *m* is a monad, so is "*t m*", by using the two parameter constructor class MonadTrans:

$$\textbf{class}\ (\text{Monad}\ m,\ \text{Monad}\ t\ m) \Rightarrow \text{MonadTrans}\ t\ m\ \textbf{where}$$
$$\quad lift :: m\ a \rightarrow t\ m\ a$$

The member function *lift* lifts a monadic computation in the inner monad *m* into the combined monad "*t m*". Furthermore, we expect a monad transformer to add features, without changing the nature of an existing computation. This can be obtained by the properties of *lift* function above (also called *monad transformer laws*). The monad transformer laws guarantee the basic lifting property that any program, which does not use the added features, should behave in the same way after a monad transformer is applied. Intuitively, these laws say that lifting a null computation brings about a null computation, and that lifting a sequence of computations is equivalent to first lifting them individually, and then combining them in the lifted monad.

For example, Figure 1 gives the environment monad transformer, EnvT, which can be used to add environment reading functionality to other monads. In Figure 1, the functions *rdEnv* and *inEnv*, return the current environment and perform a computation in a given environment, respecitively.

```
newtype EnvT r m a = EnvT {runEnvT :: r → m a}
instance (Monad m) ⇒ Monad (EnvT r m) where
  return a = EnvT (\_→ return a)
  m ≫= k  = EnvT (\r→ {a ← runEnvT m r; runEnvT (k a) r} )
instance MonadTrans (EnvT r) where
    lift m = EnvT (\_→ m)
class (Monad m) ⇒ EnvMonad r m where
    inEnv :: r → m a → m a
    rdEnv :: m r
instance (Monad m) ⇒ EnvMonad r (EnvT r m) where
    inEnv r m = EnvT (\_→ runEnvT m r)
    rdEnv = EnvT (\r→ return r)
```

Fig. 1. Environment monad transformer EnvT(Liang,1998).

2.2 Modular monadic semantics

Modular monadic semantics specifies the semantics of a programming language by mapping terms to computations, where the details of the environment, store, etc. are hidden within a monad. This is difference from traditional denotational semantics, which maps a term (an environment or a continuation) to an answer. The modular monadic semantics is composed of two parts: *modular semantic building blocks* and *monad transformers*. Semantic building blocks define the monadic semantics of individual source language features. They are independent of each other.

Monad transformers define the kernel-level operations in a modular way. Multiple monad transformers can be composed to form the underlying monad used by all the semantic building blocks. The crucial property of modular monadic semantics is the division of the monad *m* into a series of monad transformers, each representing a computation. As mentioned in the previous section, monad transformers provide the power to represent the abstract notion of programming language features, but still allow us to access low-level semantic details. The concept of lifting allows us to consider the interactions between various features. In some sense, *monad transformers can be designed once and for all* (Liang, 1998), since they are entirely independent of the language being described. From this view, we can draw the computation of program slicing as an entity that is independent of the language being analyzed. This will be discussed in the next section. Before doing it, we illustrate the modular monadic semantic description of a very simple imperative programming language **W**.

The **W** language considered in this paper is very similar to the language described in ref. (Slonneger & Kurtz, 1995).The abstract syntax and semantic building blocks of the **W** language are provided in Figure 2 and 3 respectively. In Figure 3, the identifier ***Fix*** denotes a fixpoint operator; *xtdEnv* and *lkpEnv* are the updating and lookup operators of environments Env, respectively; *updSto* and *alloc* are the updating and allocation functions of stores Loc, respectively; *rdEnv* and *inEnv* are the basic operators of the enviornment monad EnvMonad (given in Figure 1); *putValue* and *getValue* are the writting and reading functions of I/O actions, respectively. Following Venkatesh's assumption for expressions in ref. (Venkatesh, 1990), we also assume that the labeled expressions have no side-effects. The expressions, whose syntax is left unspecified for the sake of generality, consist of operations over identifiers and are uniquely labeled. The label is for the entire expression.

Domains:

arg: Arg (Arguments); b: Blk (Blocks); c: Cmd (Commands);

d: Dec (Declarations); e: Exp (Expressions); ide: Ide (Identifiers);

l: Label (Labels); p: Prg (Programs); t: Type (Types)

Abstract Syntax:

p :: = **program** ide **is** b

b :: = d **begin** c **end**

d :: = **const** ide = l.e | **var** ide : t | d_1; d_2

c :: = ide := l.e | c_1; c_2 | skip | **read** ide | **write** l.e

| **while** l.e **do** c **endwhile** | **if** l.e **then** c_1 **else** c_2 **endif**

Fig. 2. Abstract syntax of the **W** language.

In modular monadic semantics, the monad definition is simply a composition of the corresponding monad transformers, applied to a base monad. In this paper, we use the input/output monad IO as the base monad. We then select some monad transformers, say StateT and EnvT, and apply them to the base monad IO, forming the combined monad ComptM:

$$\text{ComptM} \equiv (\text{EnvT} \cdot \text{StateT})\ \text{IO}$$

The environment monad transformer adds an environment to the given monad. The *return* function ignores the environment, while ≫= passes the inherited environment to both sub-computations. Equipped with the monad transformers, the resulting monad ComptM can support all of the semantic building blocks in Figure 3, which gives the formal semantic description we expected.

Domains:

r: Env (Environments); *loc*: Loc (Stores); *s*: State (States); *v*: Value (Values)

Semantics Functions:

M :: Prg → ComptM ()

M⟦ **program** ide **is** b ⟧ = ***B***⟦ b ⟧

B :: Blk → ComptM ()

B⟦ d **begin** c **end** ⟧ = {*r'* ← ***D***⟦ d ⟧; *inEnv r'* ***C***⟦ c ⟧ }

D :: Dec → ComptM Env ; ***E*** :: Exp → ComptM Value

D⟦ **const** ide = l.e ⟧ = {*v* ← ***E***⟦ l.e ⟧; *r* ← *rdEnv*; *xtdEnv* (ide, *v*, *r*) }

D⟦ **var** ide : t ⟧ = {*loc* ← *alloc*; *r* ← *rdEnv*; *xtdEnv* (ide, *loc*, *r*)}

D⟦ d_1; d_2 ⟧ = {*r* ←*rdEnv*; *r'*←*inEnv r* ***D***⟦ d_1 ⟧; *inEnv r'* ***D***⟦ d_2 ⟧)}

C :: Cmd → ComptM ()

C⟦ ide := l.e ⟧ = {*v* ← ***E***⟦ l.e ⟧; *r* ← *rdEnv*; *loc* ← *lkpEnv*(ide, *r*); *updSto*(*loc*, *v*)}
C⟦ c_1; c_2 ⟧ = {***C***⟦ c_1 ⟧; ***C***⟦ c_2 ⟧ }
C⟦ skip ⟧ = *return* ()
C⟦ **if** l.e **then** c_1 **else** c_2 **endif** ⟧ = {*v* ← ***E***⟦ l.e ⟧; ***case*** *v* ***of*** **TRUE** → ***C***⟦ c_1 ⟧
FALSE → ***C***⟦ c_2}
C⟦ **while** l.e **do** c **endwhile** ⟧ = ***Fix*** (*f*→ {*v* ← ***E***⟦ l.e ⟧;
case *v* ***of*** **TRUE** →*f* · ***C***⟦ c ⟧
FALSE → *return* () })
C⟦ **read** ide ⟧ = {*loc* ← *lkpEnv*(ide, *rdEnv*); *v* ← *getValue*; *updSto*(*loc*, *return v*)}
C⟦ **write** l.e ⟧ = { *v* ← ***E***⟦ l.e ⟧; *putValue v* }

Fig. 3. Semantic building blocks of the **W** language.

3. Static slice monad transformer

As mentioned above, each monad transformer represents a single notion of computation. Since static program slicing can be viewed as a computation, we can abstract it as a language-independent notion of a computation by using a *static slice-monad transformer*

SliceT. Its definition is given in Figure 4, where *l* denotes a set of labels of expressions that were required to compute the current statement; *st* denotes a slice table Slices whose data structure is defined as follows:

type Var = String
type Labels = [Int]
type Slices = [(Var, Labels)]
lkpSli :: Var → Slices → ComptM Labels
updSli :: (Var, ComptM Labels) →Slices →ComptM ()
mrgSli :: Slices → Slices → ComptM Slices

Here, [] denotes a table data structure. The three operators, *lkpSli*, *updSli* and *mrgSli*, represent to lookup the slice of a variable in a given Slices table, to update a table Slices through a variable with its slice, and to merge two given slice tables into a new one, respectively.

In the similar way as ref. (Zhang, 2005, 2007), the following theorems are straightforward. These theorems guarantee the correctness of the definition of the slice monad transformer in Figure 4.

Theorem 1. *SliceT l st m* is a monad.
Theorem 2. *SliceT l st* is a monad transformer.

A static slice-monad transformer *SliceT l st*, taking an initial set of labels and a slice table, returns a computation of a pair of the resulting value and the new slice table. The operator *return* returns the given value with the unchanged slice table. The operator >>= takes a monad *m* and a function *k*. It passes the initial set of labels *l* and slice table *st* to the monad *m*; this yields a value *a* paired with an intermediate slice table *st'*; function *k* is applied to the value *a*, yielding a monad (*k a*); this yields in *l* and *st'* the final result paired with the final slice table.

The lifting function *lift* says that a computation in the monad *m* behaves identically in the monad *SliceT l st m* and makes no changes to the slice table. The operation *rdLabel*/*inLabel* and *getSli*/*setSli* support reading/setting of the parameter *l* and *st* in the static slice-monad SliceMonad, respectively.

With the use of the transformer *SliceT*, other monads can be easily transformed into the static slice-monad SliceMonad. For instance, we can lift respectively the basic operators of monads StateMonad and EnvMonad through *SliceT* as shown in Figure 4.

4. A monadic static slicing algorithm

The static slice for a variable in a program is the collection of all possible computations of values of that variable. In this section, we only consider end slicing for a single variable, i.e. the slicing criterion is <p, v>, where v the variable of interest, and p the end program point. One can easily generalize this to a set of points and a set of variables at each point by taking the union of the individual slices (Binkley, 1996).

The main idea of monadic static slicing algorithms can be briefly stated as follows: for obtaining a static slice, we firstly apply the slice transformer SliceT to semantic building blocks of the program analyzed. It makes the resulting semantic description include

```
newtype SliceT l st m a = SliceT {runSliceT :: (l, st) → m (a, st)}
instance (Monad m) ⇒ Monad (SliceT l st m) where
  return a = SliceT (\(_, st)→ return (a, st) )
     m ≫= k  = SliceT (\(l, st)→ {(a, st') ← runSliceT m (l, st);
                                              runSliceT (k a) (l, st')} )
instance MonadTrans (SliceT l st) where
     lift m = SliceT (\(_, st)→ {a ← m; return (a, st)} )
class (Monad m) ⇒ SliceMonad l st m where
     rdLabel :: m l
     inLabel :: l → m a → m a
     getSli :: m st
     setSli :: st → m st
instance (Monad m) ⇒ SliceMonad l st (SliceT l st m) where
     rdLabel     = SliceT return
     inLabel l m  = SliceT (\(_, st)→ runSliceT m (l, st) )
     getSli      = SliceT (\(_, st)→ return (st, st) )
     setSli st  = SliceT (\(l, _)→ return (l, st) )
instance (EnvMonad r m, MonadTrans (SliceT l st) m)
   ⇒ EnvMonad r (SliceT l st m) where
     inEnv r (SliceT l st m) = SliceT (\(l,st)→ inEnv r (runSliceT m (l,st)) )
     rdEnv = lift rdEnv
instance (StateMonad s m, MonadTrans (SliceT l st) m)
   ⇒ StateMonad s (SliceT l st m) where
     update = lift . update
```

Fig. 4. Static slice-monad transformer SliceT.

program slice semantic feature. According to the semantic description, we then compute static slices of each statement in sequence. Finally we will obtain the static slices of all single variables in the program. In fact, with the process of analyzing a program, the Slices table, which includes the current individual program slices for all variables of this program, is modified steadily according to the monadic slicing algorithm.

Concretely, with respect to the example program **W** mentioned in Section 2, Figure 5 gives the main part of our monadic static algorithm. Figure 5 gives the rules of when and how to modify the current slice table. It adds the computation of static slicing into program analysis modularly, with the help of the monad transformers SliceT given in Section 3. SliceT can be composed with other transformers such as EnvT and StateT as follows, and apply them to monad IO, forming the underlying monad ComptM:

$$\text{ComptM} \equiv (\text{SliceT} \cdot \text{StateT} \cdot \text{EnvT})\ \text{IO}$$

In Figure 5 (or the monadic slicing algorithm in a sense), for each computation of a labeled expression l.e, there is an intermediate set L' as follows:

$$L' = \{\text{l}\} \cup L \cup \bigcup_{x \in Refs(\text{l.e})} lkpSli(x,T)$$

where T represents the current slice table before analyzing the expression l.e; *Refs*(l.e) denotes the set of variables appeared in l.e. The relation above means that after an expression l.e included in the current expression is computed, the initial set L should be transformered by adding the label of expression l.e, i.e., label l, and all sets of labels of expressions influenced by the variables of the expression l.e.

In addition, the *updSli* operation of the Slices type is applied to record the result of the static slicing in program analysis. In case of the language **W**, only when describe the semantics of assignment statement and initial assignment statement within a variable declaration, the corresponding operator *updSli* should be added in as shown in Figure 5.

A static slice includes the statements that possibly affect the variable in the slicing criterion. Therefore, for capturing these possible statements, in Figure 5 we ought to add the operator *mrgSli* into semantic descriptions of conditional statement and loop statement.

After the last statement of a program is analyzed, we could obtain, from the result Slices table, the static slice of each single variable (say *var*) of the program, which is the set of labels of all expressions influenced on the *var* variable:

$$L = lkpSli\ (var, getSli)$$

For getting the final result of the static slices, i.e., a syntactically valid subprogram, we -- following Venkatesh (Venkatesh, 1990) -- define *Syn*(s, *L*) for language **W** in Figure 6, where s is a W-program analyzed. It guides us how to construct a syntactically valid subprogram of s from the set *L*. It just gives a strategy for returning the final result/subprogram from a given set *L*, so it could be changed to cater to different people's need. For example, if one does not consider variable declaration as part of slices, then one might change the corresponding term in Figure 6 as follows:

"**var** ide : t " : "skip"

The correctness proofs of our monadic static slicing algorithms can refer to their termination theorem and their consistency with PDG-based slicing algorithms, given in ref. (Zhang, 2007). In fact, the term L and $\bigcup_{x \in Refs(l.e)} lkpSli(x,T)$ in the above definition of L' can accurately capture control dependences and data dependences related, respectively.

For more about the algorithm, we now illustrate to use the rules in Figure 5 to compute the static slice w.r.t. <8, sum> of an example **W** program in Figure 7. Its each expression is uniquely labeled through the label (marked in source program) of the place where the expression presences. So the fourth expression is "i := 1".

According to the rule/semantics of assignment statements in Figure 5, after the third expression (i.e. "sum := 0") is analyzed, its intermediate set L (whose initial value is ϕ) is changed to L':

$$L' = \{3\} \cup L \cup lkpSli\ (\text{sum}, T) = \{3\} \cup \phi \cup \phi = \{3\}$$

Where T is the current slice table, including the static slices of the "i" and "sum" variables, written briefly as L(i) and L(sum), respectively. Since this expression is an assignment one, the related data in Slices need to update through *updSli*, i.e. L(sum) = L' = {3}. Similarly, after the 4th expression is analyzed, we have

$$L' = \{4\} \cup L \cup lkpSli\ (\text{i}, T) = \{4\};\ \ \text{L(i)} = \{4\}$$

And keep going for the 5th-7th expressions, we obtain

$$\text{5th: } L' = \{5\} \cup \phi \cup \mathrm{L(i)} = \{4, 5\}$$

$$\text{6th: } L'' = \{6\} \cup L' \cup (\mathrm{L(sum)} \cup \mathrm{L(i)}) = \{3, 4, 5, 6\};\ \mathrm{L(sum)} = \{3, 4, 5, 6\}$$

$$\text{7th: } L'' = \{7\} \cup L' \cup \mathrm{L(i)} = \{4, 5, 7\};\ \mathrm{L(i)} = \{4, 5, 7\}$$

$$\boldsymbol{M} :: \mathrm{Prg} \rightarrow \mathrm{ComptM}\ ()$$

$$\boldsymbol{M}[\![\ \textbf{program}\ \mathrm{ide}\ \textbf{is}\ \mathrm{b}\ ]\!] = \textit{return}\ ()$$

$$\boldsymbol{B} :: \mathrm{Blk} \rightarrow \mathrm{ComptM}\ ()$$

$$\boldsymbol{B}[\![\ \mathrm{d}\ \textbf{begin}\ \mathrm{c}\ \textbf{end}\ ]\!] = \textit{return}\ ()$$

$$\boldsymbol{D} :: \mathrm{Dec} \rightarrow \mathrm{ComptM\ Env} \quad \boldsymbol{E} :: \mathrm{Exp} \rightarrow \mathrm{ComptM\ Value}$$

$$\boldsymbol{D}[\![\ \textbf{const}\ \mathrm{ide} = \mathrm{l.e}\ ]\!] = \{\ L \leftarrow \mathit{rdLabels};\ T \leftarrow \mathit{getSli};$$
$$L' \leftarrow \{\mathrm{l}\} \cup L \cup \bigcup_{x \in \mathit{Refs}(\mathrm{l.e})} \mathit{lkpSli}(x, T)\ ;\ \mathit{updSli}(\mathrm{ide}, L', T)\ \}$$

$$\boldsymbol{D}[\![\ \textbf{var}\ \mathrm{ide} : \mathrm{t}\ ]\!] = \textit{return}\ ()$$

$$\boldsymbol{D}[\![\ \mathrm{d}_1;\ \mathrm{d}_2\ ]\!] = \textit{return}\ ()$$

$$\boldsymbol{C} :: \mathrm{Cmd} \rightarrow \mathrm{ComptM}\ ()$$

$$\boldsymbol{C}[\![\ \mathrm{ide} := \mathrm{l.e}\ ]\!] = \{\ L \leftarrow \mathit{rdLabels};\ T \leftarrow \mathit{getSli};$$
$$L' \leftarrow \{\mathrm{l}\} \cup L \cup \bigcup_{x \in \mathit{Refs}(\mathrm{l.e})} \mathit{lkpSli}(x, T)\ ;\ \mathit{updSli}(\mathrm{ide}, L', T)\ \}$$

$$\boldsymbol{C}[\![\ \mathrm{c}_1;\ \mathrm{c}_2\ ]\!] = \{\boldsymbol{C}[\![\ \mathrm{c}_1\ ]\!];\ \boldsymbol{C}[\![\ \mathrm{c}_2\ ]\!]\ \}$$
$$\boldsymbol{C}[\![\ \mathrm{skip}\ ]\!] = \textit{return}\ ()$$
$$\boldsymbol{C}[\![\ \textbf{if}\ \mathrm{l.e}\ \textbf{then}\ \mathrm{c}_1\ \textbf{else}\ \mathrm{c}_2\ \textbf{endif}\ ]\!] = \{\ L \leftarrow \mathit{rdLabels};\ T \leftarrow \mathit{getSli};$$
$$L' \leftarrow \{\mathrm{l}\} \cup L \cup \bigcup_{x \in \mathit{Refs}(\mathrm{l.e})} \mathit{lkpSli}(x, T)\ ;$$
$$\mathit{inLabels}\ L'\ \boldsymbol{C}[\![\ \mathrm{c}_1\ ]\!];\ T1 \leftarrow \mathit{getSli};\ \mathit{setSli}(T);$$
$$\mathit{inLabels}\ L'\ \boldsymbol{C}[\![\ \mathrm{c}_2\ ]\!];\ T2 \leftarrow \mathit{getSli};\ \mathit{mrgSli}(T1, T2)\ \}$$

$$\boldsymbol{C}[\![\ \textbf{while}\ \mathrm{l.e}\ \textbf{do}\ \mathrm{c}\ \textbf{endwhile}\ ]\!] = \boldsymbol{\mathit{Fix}}\ (\lambda f.\ \{L \leftarrow \mathit{rdLabels};\ T \leftarrow \mathit{getSli};$$
$$L' \leftarrow \{\mathrm{l}\} \cup L \cup \bigcup_{x \in \mathit{Refs}(\mathrm{l.e})} \mathit{lkpSli}(x, T)\ ;$$
$$f \cdot \{\mathit{inLabels}\ L'\ \boldsymbol{C}[\![\ c\ ]\!];\ T' \leftarrow \mathit{getSli};\ \mathit{mrgSli}(T, T')\}\})$$

$$\boldsymbol{C}[\![\ \textbf{read}\ \mathrm{l.ide}\ ]\!] = \{L \leftarrow \mathit{rdLabels};\ T \leftarrow \mathit{getSli};\ L' \leftarrow \{\mathrm{l}\} \cup L;\ \mathit{updSli}(\mathrm{ide}, L', T)\}$$
$$\boldsymbol{C}[\![\ \textbf{write}\ \mathrm{l.e}\ ]\!] = \textit{return}\ ()$$

Fig. 5. Monadic semantics of static slicing for **W** programs.

```
    program Example is
1   var sum
2   var i
    begin
3    sum := 0 ;
4    i := 1;
5    while i < 11 do
6      sum := sum + i;
7      i := i + 1
       endwhile;
8   write sum
    end
```

Fig. 7. An example program.

Because of the loop of While statement, the 5th-7th expressions are analyzed again:

$$\text{5th: } L'' = \{5\} \cup L' \cup \mathrm{L(i)} = \{4, 5, 7\}$$

$$\text{6th: } L''' = \{6\} \cup L'' \cup (\mathrm{L(sum)} \cup \mathrm{L(i)}) = \{3, 4, 5, 6, 7\};$$

$$\mathrm{L(sum)} = \{3, 4, 5, 6, 7\}$$

$$\text{7th: } L''' = \{7\} \cup L'' \cup \mathrm{L(i)} = \{4, 5, 7\};\ \mathrm{L(i)} = \{4, 5, 7\}$$

Now, if the whole loop body is analyzed over again in this way, the slice L(sum) and L(i) will not be changed again, reaching their fixpoint. So after finishing the analysis of the last statement (8h), we obtain the final table Slices as follows:

$$\mathrm{L(i)} = \{4, 5, 7\};\ \mathrm{L(sum)} = \{3, 4, 5, 6, 7\}$$

According the rules of *Syn*(s, *L*) in Figure 6, we can obtain the final result of static slice w.r.t. <8, sum> of the example program.

5. Extending W language with pointers

The modular monadic approach mentioned previously is flexible enough that we can easily introduce a new program feature to analysis. In this section, we will illustrate this power by considering an extension of the language **W** with pointers. We shall show how to adapt the implementation to this extension, with a small change in our existing monadic slice algorithm.

The introduction of a pointer will lead to aliasing problems (Horwitz, 1989; Hind, 1999) (i.e. multiple variables access the same memory location), so we need pointer analysis to obtain the corresponding data dependency information. In order to represent the unbounded data

Syn(s, *L*) = case s of	
"**program** ide **is** b " :	***if*** *Syn*(b, *L*) = "skip" ***then*** "skip" ***else*** "**program** ide **is** b"
"d **begin** c **end** " :	***if*** *Syn*(d, *L*)=*Syn*(c, *L*)="skip" ***then*** "skip" ***else*** "d **begin** c **end**"
"**const** ide = l.e " :	***if*** $l \in L$ ***then*** "**const** ide = l.e" ***else*** "skip"
"**var** ide : t " :	***if*** ide $\in \{var\} \cup \bigcup_{l \in L} Refs(\text{l.e})$ ***then*** "**var** ide : t " ***else*** "skip"
"d_1; d_2 " :	*Syn*(d_1, *L*); *Syn*(d_2, *L*)
"ide := l.e " :	***if*** $l \in L$ ***then*** "ide := l.e" ***else*** "skip"
"c_1; c_2 " :	*Syn*(c_1, *L*); *Syn*(c_2, *L*)
"skip " :	"skip"
"**read** ide " :	***if*** ide $\in \{var\} \cup \bigcup_{l \in L} Refs(\text{l.e})$ ***then*** "**read** ide" ***else*** "skip"
"**write** l.e " :	"skip"
"**if** l.e **then** c_1 **else** c_2 **endif** ":	***if*** (*Syn*(c_1, *L*) = *Syn*(c_2, *L*) = "skip") $\wedge$ ($l \notin L$) ***then*** "skip"
	else "**if** l.e **then** *Syn*(c_1, *L*) **else** *Syn*(c_2, *L*) **endif** "
"**while** l.e **do** c **endwhile** " :	***if*** (*Syn*(c, *L*) = "skip") $\wedge$ ($l \notin L$) ***then*** "skip"
	else "**while** l.e **do** *Syn*(c, *L*) **endwhile**"

Fig. 6. The definition of *Syn*(s, L), where L = *lkpSli*(*var*, *getDSli*).

structures in a finite way for the presence of pointers, we consider that all point in the same procedure applied to form an array of heap space, and will deal with this array as a whole. The extended algorithm combines the point-to analysis by data-flow iteration with forward monad slicing. With the illumination of this idea, the key issue to be addressed is the solution to assignments. The other statements (such as conditional statements, loop statements, etc.) could be resolved by adding point-to computation to the existing slicing methods. Before going on, we introduce a data structure for point-to analysis.

Similar to the Slices datatype in Section 3, we design an abstract datatype PT for point-to analysis:

type Var = String
type PtSet = [Var]
type PT = [(Var, PtSet)]
getPT :: ComptM PT
setPT :: PT → ComptM PT
lkpPT :: Var → PT → ComptM PtSet

$$updPT :: \text{Var} \rightarrow \text{PtSet} \rightarrow \text{PT} \rightarrow \text{ComptM ()}$$

$$mrgPT :: \text{PT} \rightarrow \text{PT} \rightarrow \text{ComptM PT}$$

The point-to table, PT, is a table of pairs of a single variable and its associated point-to set (a set of variables). It has five operators *getPT, setPT, lkpPT, updPT* and *mrgPT,* which return and set the current table of point-to sets, lookup a point-to set corresponding to a variable in a given table of point-to sets, update some point-to sets corresponding to a list of variables in a given table of point-to sets, and merge two table of point-to sets into one table, respectively.

With the pointers, we sometimes need to update the slices or the point-to sets of some variables at the same time, so we extend the operator *xtdSli* for Slices datatype, and the operator *xtdPT* for PT datatype as follows:

$$xtdSli :: [\text{Var}] \rightarrow \text{Labels} \rightarrow \text{Slices} \rightarrow \text{ComptM ()}$$

$$xtdPT :: [\text{Var}] \rightarrow \text{PtSet} \rightarrow \text{PT} \rightarrow \text{ComptM ()}$$

Now we can study in depth the assignment statements with pointers. For simplicity, we only consider single dereference of a pointer (e.g. *x), since multi-dereference (e.g. **x) can be divided into multiple single dereferences. We decompose an assignment into a left-value expression (such as x or *x), and a right-value expression (also notated as l.e, but may contain *y or &y). So we need to expand the definition of *Refs*(l.e) in Section 4. The variables appeared in a right-value expression can be divided into three categories: reference variables, dereference variables and address variables. So we have

$$Refs(\text{l.e}) = \{\text{x} \mid \text{x is a reference variable}\} \cup \{\text{y} \mid \text{y is a dereference variable}\}$$

$$\cup \{\text{z} \mid \text{z} \in \boldsymbol{lkpPT}(\text{y}, \boldsymbol{getPT}), \text{ where y is a dereference variable}\}$$

The detail algorithm of *Refs*(l.e) is shown in Figure 8, where the *PtInfo*(l.e) function can obtain the point-to information generated by l.e.

The algorithm in Figure 8 addresses the issues of the reference and point-to information of a right-value expression, and hence facilitates the expansion of the existing slicing algorithm in Figure 5. The final expansion for the static slices of a **W** program with pointers is shown in Figure 9, which is generated by adding the bold and blue terms in Figure 5.

By introducing point-to analysis to our previous monadic slicing, we presented (in Figure 9) an approach of monadic slicing for a program with pointers. This approach obtained the point-to information through the data-flow iteration. Being different from the traditional methods where the point-to information and slicing are analyzed in two different phases, they are computed in the same phase in our method, by combining the forward monad slicing with data-flow iteration. Instead of recording point-to information for every statement, we only need to record the information for current analysis statements. So our method saves space without losing the precision. In addition, our approach also reserves the excellent properties of compositionality and language-flexibility from the original monadic slicing method.

Input: an expression (e.g. e)

Output: the reference set, *Refs*, and the point-to set, *PtInfo*, of the expression

Algorithm:

case e **of**

e is the expression of the form &y →

$Refs(e) = \phi$; $PtInfo(e) = \{y\}$

e is the expression of the form *y →

Let ys = ***lkpPT***(y, ***getPT***) where ys is the current point-to set of y;

$Refs(e) = \{y\} \cup ys$; $PtInfo(e) = \bigcup_{v \in ys} \boldsymbol{lkpPT}(v, \boldsymbol{getPT})$

e is a pure variable such as y →

Let ys = ***lkpPT***(y, ***getPT***);

$Refs(e) = \{y\}$; $PtInfo(e) = ys$

e is the compound expression with two sub-expressions e_1 and e_2 →

$Refs(e) = Refs(e_1) \cup Refs(e_2)$; $PtInfo(e) = PtInfo(e_1) \cup PtInfo(e_2)$

e is a constant of a value type →

$Refs(e) = \phi$; $PtInfo(e) = \phi$

end case;

Fig. 8. The algorithm for the reference set and the point-to set of an expression.

6. Implementation and complexity analysis

In this section, we will implement the monadic slicing algorithms, and analyze its complexity as well.

Because of the use of monad transformers, modular denotational semantics achieves a high level of modularity and extensibility. Despite this, it is still executable: there is a clear operational interpretation of the semantics (Wadler, 1995). In ref. (Liang, 1995, 1998; Wadler, 1995), some modular compilers/interpreters using monad transformers were constructed. On the basis of these works, our monadic approach for static program slicing is feasible. Based on Labra's language prototyping system LPS (Labra et al, 2001), we developed a simple monadic slice prototype MSlicer (for more, see ref. (Zhang, 2007) or its website: https://sourceforge.net/projects/ lps). Its implementation language is Haskell, which is a purely functional language with lazy evaluation. The beauty of laziness allows Haskell to deal with infinite data, because Haskell will only load the data as it is needed, and because the garbage collector will throw out the data after it has been processed. Using higher-order

$$\boldsymbol{M} :: \text{Prg} \rightarrow \text{ComptM ()}$$

$\boldsymbol{M}[\![$ **program** ide **is** b $]\!] = \textit{return}\ ()$

$$\boldsymbol{B} :: \text{Blk} \rightarrow \text{ComptM ()}$$

$\boldsymbol{B}[\![$ d **begin** c **end** $]\!] = \textit{return}\ ()$

$$\boldsymbol{D} :: \text{Dec} \rightarrow \text{ComptM Env} \quad \boldsymbol{E} :: \text{Exp} \rightarrow \text{ComptM Value}$$

$\boldsymbol{D}[\![$ **const** ide = l.e $]\!] =$

$\{ L \leftarrow \textit{rdLabels};\ T \leftarrow \textit{getSli};\ P \leftarrow \textit{getPT};\ \text{ps} = \textit{PtInfo}(\text{l.e});\ \text{xs} = \textit{lkpPT}(\text{ide}, P);$

if (ide is of the form *x) then

$L' \leftarrow \{l\} \cup L \cup \bigcup_{r \in Refs(\text{l.e}) \cup \{x\}} lkpSli\ (r, T)\ ;\ \textit{xtdSli}(\text{xs}, L', T);\ \textit{xtdPT}(\text{xs}, \text{ps}, P);$

else

$L' \leftarrow \{l\} \cup L \cup \bigcup_{x \in Refs(\text{l.e})} lkpSli(x,T)\ ;\ \textit{updSli}(\text{ide}, L', T);\ \textit{updPT}(\text{ide}, \text{ps}, P)\}$

$\boldsymbol{D}[\![$ **var** ide : t $]\!] = \textit{return}\ ()$

$\boldsymbol{D}[\![\ d_1;\ d_2\ ]\!] = \textit{return}\ ()$

$$\boldsymbol{C} :: \text{Cmd} \rightarrow \text{ComptM ()}$$

$\boldsymbol{C}[\![$ ide := l.e $]\!] =$

$\{ L \leftarrow \textit{rdLabels};\ T \leftarrow \textit{getSli};\ P \leftarrow \textit{getPT};\ \text{ps} = \textit{PtInfo}(\text{l.e});\ \text{xs} = \textit{lkpPT}(\text{ide}, P);$

if (ide is of the form *x) then

$L' \leftarrow \{l\} \cup L \cup \bigcup_{r \in Refs(\text{l.e}) \cup \{x\}} lkpSli\ (r, T)\ ;\ \textit{xtdSli}(\text{xs}, L', T);\ \textit{xtdPT}(\text{xs}, \text{ps}, P);$

else

$L' \leftarrow \{l\} \cup L \cup \bigcup_{x \in Refs(\text{l.e})} lkpSli(x,T)\ ;\ \textit{updSli}(\text{ide}, L', T);\ \textit{updPT}(\text{ide}, \text{ps}, P)\}$

$\boldsymbol{C}[\![\ c_1;\ c_2\ ]\!] = \{\boldsymbol{C}[\![\ c_1\ ]\!];\ \boldsymbol{C}[\![\ c_2\ ]\!]\}$

$\boldsymbol{C}[\![$ skip $]\!] = \textit{return}\ ()$

$\boldsymbol{C}[\![$ **if** l.e **then** c_1 **else** c_2 **endif** $]\!] =$

$\{ L \leftarrow \textit{rdLabels};\ T \leftarrow \textit{getSli};\ P \leftarrow \textit{getPT};\ L' \leftarrow \{l\} \cup L \cup \bigcup_{x \in Refs(\text{l.e})} lkpSli(x,T)\ ;$

$\textit{inLabels}\ L'\ \boldsymbol{C}[\![\ c_1\ ]\!];\ T1 \leftarrow \textit{getSli};\ P1 \leftarrow \textit{getPT};\ \textit{setSli}(T);\ \textit{setPT}(P);$

$\textit{inLabels}\ L'\ \boldsymbol{C}[\![\ c_2\ ]\!];\ T2 \leftarrow \textit{getSli};\ P2 \leftarrow \textit{getPT};\ \textit{mrgSli}(T1, T2);\ \textit{mrgPT}(P1, P2)\}$

$\boldsymbol{C}[\![$ **while** l.e **do** c **endwhile** $]\!] =$

$\textbf{Fix}(\lambda f.\ \{L \leftarrow \textit{rdLabels};\ T \leftarrow \textit{getSli};\ L' \leftarrow \{l\} \cup L \cup \bigcup_{x \in Refs(\text{l.e})} lkpSli(x,T)\ ;\ P \leftarrow \textit{getPT};$

$f \cdot \{\textit{inLabels}\ L'\ \boldsymbol{C}[\![\ c\ ]\!];\ T' \leftarrow \textit{getSli};\ P' \leftarrow \textit{getPT};\ \textit{mrgSli}(T, T');\ \textit{mrgPT}(P, P')\ \}\})$

$\boldsymbol{C}[\![$ **read** l.ide $]\!] = \{ L \leftarrow \textit{rdLabels};\ T \leftarrow \textit{getSli};\ L' \leftarrow \{l\} \cup L;\ P \leftarrow \textit{getPT};$

if (ide is of the form *x) then $\textit{xtdSli}(\textit{lkpPT}(x, P), L', T)$

else $\textit{updSli}(\text{ide}, L', T)\ \}$

$\boldsymbol{C}[\![$ **write** l.e $]\!] = \textit{return}\ ()$

Fig. 9. Monadic slicing semantics for the **W** language with pointers.

functions from the libraries, Haskell modules can be written to concisely describe each language feature (Peterson et al, 1997; Thompson, 1996). Features such as arbitrary precision integer arithmetic, list comprehensions, infinite lists, all come in handy for the effective monadic slicing of a large program.

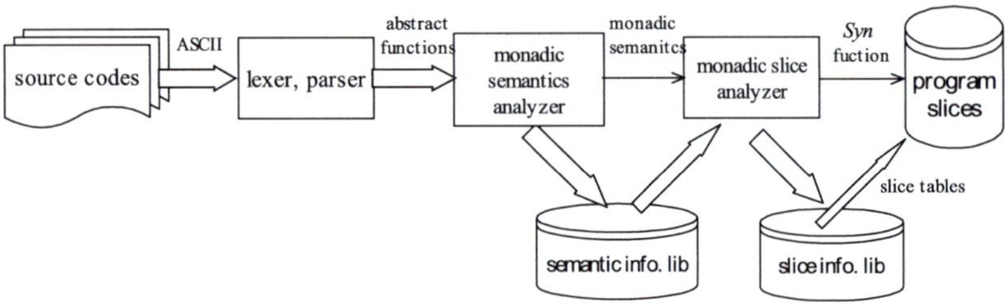

Fig. 10. The framework of the prototype MSlicer.

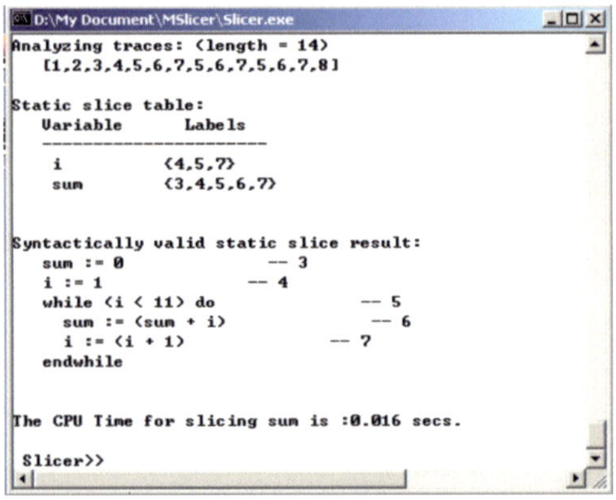

Fig. 11. The slice results of the sample program in Figure 7 from our MSlicer.

m	**statements**
1	var v1 = 1;
	⋮
5	var v5 = 5;
6	while (1 < 2) do
	⋱
5+*l*	while (1 < 2) do
6+*l*	v1 := v2;
	⋮
10+*l*	v5 := v1
	endwhile;

Fig. 12. A loop sample with *l* while statements.

Figure 10 gives the framework of the monadic slicer MSlicer. Figure 11 gives the static slice results for the example program in Figure 7 from our current monadic slicer. The final results also include the output value, analysis trace, static slice table and CPU time.

In practice, in order to obtain good performance, we choice the Haskell type IntSet instead of the original set type of Labels (i.e. [Int]) in Section 3. The implementation of IntSet is based on big-Endian Patricia trees (Okasaki & Gill, 1998; Morrison, 1968). This data structure performs especially well on binary operations like union and intersection. Many operations have a worst-case complexity of **O(min(*n*,*W*))**, where n is the number of elements; W is the number of bits in an Int (32 or 64). This means that the operation can become linear in the number of elements with a maximum of W.

The measures of system size used below are those associated with the data structure of program slice Slices (which is a Hash table).

In a modular compiler/interpreter, our slice monad transformer could be modularly and safely combined into the semantic buildings, so the complexity analysis is restricted to L' and *Syn*(s, L) of a concrete programming language. In the case of our example language **W**, the intermediate label set L' can be determined in worst-case time $O(v \times m)$, where v refers to the number of single variables in the program analyzed; and m is the number of labeled expressions in the program. To determine the *Syn*(s, L) shown in Figure 6 may cost $O(\min(m,W))$. Therefore the time cost of the predominant part of program slicing in the monadic slicing algorithm is bounded by $O(v \times m \times n)$, where n is the number of all labeled expressions appeared (perhaps repeatly) in the sequence of analyzing the program. In addition, an extra time cost $O(v \times \min(m,W))$ needs to get the executable slices of all single variables. Now we can see that the worst-case time of the whole static slice is $O(v \times m \times n)$. Since we finally obtain the static slices of all variables after the last statement is analyzed, the program slice of each variable, on the average, costs $O(m \times n)$. In fact, $n = O(m^2)$ at worst, for more see the following loop statement shown in Figure 12. So all of its static slices will cost the worst-case time $O(m^3)$.

To analyze the space complexity of the algorithms, we pay our attention to the constructions *Refs*(l.e), Slices, L' and L. We need space $O(v \times v)$ and $O(v \times m)$ to save *Refs*(l.e) and Slices, respectively. According to the definition of slice monad transformer SliceT in Figure 4, we need more intermediate labels when SliceT is applied to loop statements (e.g. while statements). So it takes the space $O(k \times m)$ to save intermediate labels, where k refers to the maximal times of analyzing the loop statements in the program (until the slice stabilizes) . The label set L will cost the space $O(m)$. Therefore, the total space cost is $O(v \times v + v \times m + k \times m)$.

By analyzing the complexity of algorithms in Figure 8 and 9, we find that the cost of point-to analysis is less than the cost of slicing. So our expansion algorithm to pointers has no additional complexity.

We have tested the complexity analysis of our monadic static algorithms by using the program with l while loop statements shown in Figure 12, which is similar to the while program in ref. (Binkley & Gallagher, 1996). From the results given in Figure 13, we can see that $n = O(m^2)$ at worst. This shows that the prototype monadic slicer MSlicer without optimization (such as BDD or SEQUITUR (Zhang et al, 2003) for the slice and trace tables) can compute slices for large analysis histories in reasonable time and space. (The experiments run on a Pentium Willamette (0.18) Windows PC system with 1GB RAM).

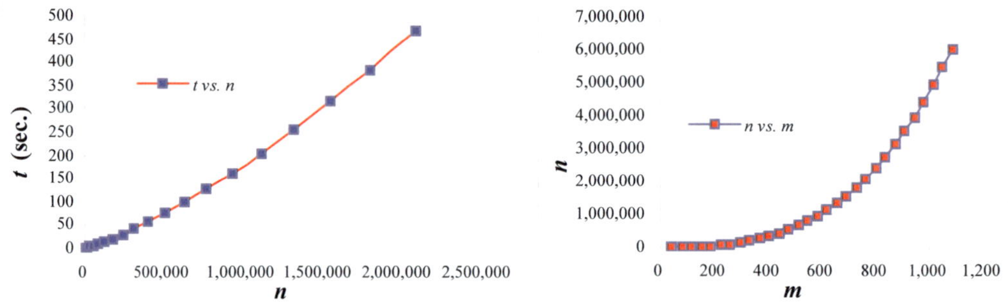

(a) t vs. n (b) n vs. m

Fig. 13. The relations between CPU time, *t*, and the number of all labeled expressions analyzed in practice, *n*, or the number of labeled expressions in the program, *m*.

7. Related work and comparisons

The original program slicing method was expressed as a sequence of data flow analysis problems (Weiser, 1984). An alternative approach was relied on program dependence graphs (PDG) (Ottenstein & Ottenstein, 1984). Most of the existing slicing methods were evolved from the two approaches. A few program slicing methods focused on the semantics of programs.

G.Canfora et al.'s *conditioned slicing* (Canfora et al, 1998) adds a condition in a slicing criterion. Statements that do not satisfy the condition are deleted from the slice. M.Harman et al.'s *amorphous slicing* (Harman & Danicic, 1997) allows for any simplifying transformations which preserve this semantic projection. These two methods are not really based on formal semantics of a program. P.A.Hauser et.al 's *denotational slicing* (Hausler, 1989; Ouarbya et al, 2002) employs the functional semantics of a program language in the denotational (and static) program slicer. G.A.Venkatesh (Venkatesh, 1991) also took account of denotational slicing with formal slicing algorithms including dynamic and static. This approach is indeed based on the standard denotational semantics of a program language. The language Venkatesh considered is a very simply one without pointers. We have extended it in this paper to a more realistic programming language containing pointers, but take an entirely different approach called *modular monadic slicing*.

Compared with the existing static slicing algorithms, the monadic static-slice algorithm has excellent flexibility, combinability and parallelizability properties, because it has abstracted the computation of static slicing as an independent entity, *static slice-monad transformer*. Our algorithm has allowed that static slices could be computed directly on abstract syntax, with no needs to explicitly construct intermediate structures such as dependence graphs.

In respect of accuracy, in Section 4 or in ref. (Zhang, 2007) we have stated that the slice results of monadic static slicing algorithm are not less precise than PDG-based ones. This is because the term L and $\bigcup_{r \in Refs(\mathrm{l.e})} lkpSli\ (r, getSli\ )$ in the definition of L' can accurately capture control dependences and data dependences respectively, which are the base of PDG-based algorithms.

According to the complexity analysis (in Sections 6) for monadic slicing algorithms, their time complexity of each variable is averagely $O(m^3)$ time. While the intra-procedural slicing algorithms based on dataflow equations can compute a slice in $O(v \times n' \times e)$ time, or averagely in $O(n' \times e)$ time for each variable, where n' is the number of vertices in the control flow graph (CFG) and e the number of edges in CFG (Weiser, 1984). Although the PDG-based algorithms extract slices in linear time (i.e. $O(V + E)$, where V and E are the number of vertices and edges in the slice, respectively) after the PDG has been computed, a PDG can be constructed in $O(n' \times e + n' \times d)$ time, where d is the number of definitions in the program (Tip, 1995). Here V, n', e and d are the same complexity level of m, so the whole time of PDG-based algorithms (including the PDG-construct time) is also $O(m^3)$ nearly.

8. Conclusions and future work

In this paper, we have proposed a new approach for program slicing. We have called it *modular monadic program slicing* as it is based on modular monadic semantics. We have abstracted the computation of program slicing as a language-independence object, *slice monad transformer*. Therefore, the modular monadic slicing has excellent flexibility and reusability properties comparing with the existing program slicing algorithms. The modular monadic slicing algorithm has allowed that program slices could be computed directly on abstract syntax, with no needs to explicitly construct intermediate structures such as data flow graphs or dependence graphs.

As the behavior of a program is determined by the semantics of the language, it is reasonable to present the modular monadic program slicing. Furthermore, it is feasible, because modular monadic semantics is executable and some modular compilers/interpreters have already been existed.

For our future work, we will analyze slicing for programs with special features such as concurrent, object-oriented, exceptions and side-effects, by combining slice monad transformer with existing ones such as concurrent (Papaspyrou, 2001), object-oriented (Labra, 2002), non-determination, exceptions and side-effects (Moggi, 1991; Wadler, 1992, 2003). At the same time, we will improve our prototype of monadic slicers and give more comparisons with other slicing methods in experiments.

9. Acknowledgments

We thank Dr. J.Labra for his cooperating with us in the implementation of the slicer. This work was supported in part by the National Natural Science Foundation of China (60703086, 60903026, 60873049, 60973046), the Priority Academic Program Development of Jiangsu Higher Education Institutions(PAPD), Qing Lan Project of Jiangsu Province, NSF of Jiangsu Higher Education Institutions of China (10KJB520015),"Climbing"Program of Nanjing University of Posts and Telecommunications of China (NY210009), Open Foundation of Guangxi Key Laboratory of Trusted Software(Guilin University of Electronic Technology).

10. References

Weiser M (1984). Program Slicing. *IEEE Transaction on Software Engineering*, vol. 16, no. 5, pp. 498-509.

Kamkar M (1995). An Overview and Comparative Classification of Program Slicing Techniques. *Journal of Systems and Software*, vol. 31, no. 3, pp. 197-214.

Tip F (1995). A Survey of Program Slicing Techniques. *Journal of Programming Languages*, vol.3, no.3, pp.121-189.

Harman M & Hierons R (2001). An Overview of Program Slicing. *Software Focus*, vol. 2, no. 3, pp. 85-92.

Binkley D & Gallagher K (1996). Program Slicing. *Advances in Computers*, vol. 43, pp. 1-50.

Gallagher K & Lyle J (1991). Using Program Slicing in Software Maintenance. *IEEE Transactions on Software Engineering*, vol. 17, no. 8, pp. 751-761.

Hausler P (1989). Denotational Program Slicing. *Proceeding of 22th Annual Hawaii International Conference on System Sciences*, vol. 2, pp. 486-495.

Ouarbya L; Danicic S & Daoudi M, et al (2002). A Denotational Interprocedural Program Slicer. *Proceeding of 9th IEEE Working Conference on Reverse Engineering*, IEEE Press, Virginia, pp. 181-189.

Venkatesh G (1991). The Semantic Approach to Program Slicing. *ACM SIGPLAN Conference on Programming Language Design and Implementation*, Toronto, Canada, pp. 26-28.

Moggi E (1991). Notions of Computation and Monads. *Information and Computation*, vol. 93, pp. 55-92.

Liang S & Hudak P (1996). Modular Denotational Semantics for Compiler Construction. *Proceeding of 6th European Synposium on Programming Languages and Systems, ESOP'96. LNCS 1058*, Springer-Verlag, Berlin, pp. 219-234.

Wansbrough K (1997). A Modular Monadic Action Semantics. Master thesis, University of Auckland, Auckland.

Mosses P (1998). Semantics, Modularity, and Rewriting Logic. *Proceeding of 2nd International Workshop on Rewriting Logic and its Applications, ENTCS 15*, Elesvier Press, Netherlands.

Zhang Y Z & Xu B W (2004). A Survey of Semantic Description Frameworks for Programming Languages. *ACM SIGPLAN Notices*, vol. 39, no. 3, pp.14-30.

Wadler P (1992). Comprehending monads. *Mathematical Structures in Computer Science*, vol. 2, pp. 461-493.

Espinosa D (1995), "Semantic Lego", PhD dissertation, Columbia University, Columbia.

Liang S; Hudak P & M. Jones (1995). Monad Transformers and Modular Interpreters, *22nd ACM SIGPLAN-SIGACT Symposium on Principles of Programming Languages, POPL'95*, ACM Press, New York, pp. 333-343.

Zhang Y Z; Xu B W & Shi L, et al (2004). Modular Monadic Program Slicing, *The 28th Annual International Computer Software and Applications Conference, COMPSAC 2004*, Hong Kong, China, pp. 66-71.

Zhang Y Z; Xu B W & Labra G (2005). A Formal Method for Program Slicing, *Australian Software Engineering Conference, ASWEC'05*, Australian, pp. 140-148.

Zhang Y Z & Xu B W (2005). A Slice Monad Transformer and Its Applications in Program Slicing, *The 10th IEEE International Conference on Engineering of Complex Computer Systems,* ICECCS'05, Shanghai, China, pp. 147-154.

Wu Z Q; Zhang Y Z & Xu B W (2006). Modular Monadic Slicing in the Presence of Pointers, *In: Alexandrov V N, Albada G D, Sloot P M, et al, eds. 6th International Conference on Computational Science. LNCS 3994.* Reading: Springer-verlag, pp.748-756.

Zhang Y Z; Labra G & del R (2006). A Monadic Program Slicer, *ACM SIGPLAN Notices*, vol. 41, no. 5, pp. 30-38.

Zhang Y Z (2007). A Novel Formal Approach to Program Slicing, *Science in China F: Information Sciences*, vol. 50, no. 5, pp. 657-670.

Wadler P & Thiemann P (2003). The Marriage of Effects and Monads, *ACM Transactions on Computational Logic*, vol. 4, no. 1, pp. 1-32.

Moggi E (1989). An Abstract View of Programming Languages, *LFCS Report, ECS-LFCS-90-113*, University of Edinburgh, http://www.lfcs.informatics.ed.ac.uk/reports/90/ECS-LFCS- 90-113/

Liang S (1998). Modular Monadic Semantics and Compilation, PhD dissertation, University of Yale, Yale.

Wadler P (1995). Monads for Functional Programming, *Lecture Notes on Advanced Functional Programming Techniques, LNCS 925*, Springer-Verlag, Berlin, pp. 24-52.

Newbern J (2002). All About Monads, http://www.haskell.org/all about_monads/html /index.html

Slonneger K & Kurtz B (1995). *Formal Syntax And Semantics of Programming Language: A Lab Based Approach.* Addison & Wesley.

Venkatesh G (1990). Semantics of Program Slicing, *Bellcore TM-ARH-018561.*

Horwitz S; Pfeiffer P & Reps T (1989). Dependence Analysis For Pointer Variables, In: *Proceedings of the SIGPLAN Conference on Programming Language Design and Implementation*, pp. 28-40.

Hind M; Burke M & Carini P, et al (1999). Interprocedural Pointer Alias Analysis, ACM Transactions on Programming Languages and Systems, 21(4): 848~894.

Kahl W (2003). A Modular Interpreter Built with Monad Transformers, *Course Lectures on Functional Programming*, CAS 781.

Labra G; Luengo D & Cueva L (2001). A Language Prototyping System Using Modular Monadic Semantics, *Workshop on Language Definitions, Tools and Applications, LDTA'01*, Netherlands.

Peterson J; Hammond K & Augustsson L, et al (1997). Report on the Programming Language Haskell 1.4, A Non-strict Purely Functional Language, *Yale University Technical Report, YALEU/DCS /RR-1106.*

Thompson S (1996). *Haskell: The Craft of Functional Programming*, Addison-Wesley, Harlow, England.

Okasaki C & Gill A (1998). Fast Mergeable Integer Maps, *Workshop on ML*, September, pp.77-86.

Morrison D (1968). PATRICIA-- Practical Algorithm To Retrieve Information Coded In Alphanumeric, *Journal of the ACM*, vol. 15, no. 4, pp. 514-534.

Zhang X; Gupta R; Zhang Y (2003). Precise Dynamic Slicing Algorithms, *Proceedings of the 25th International Conference on Software Engineering*, IEEE CS Press, Washington DC, pp. 319-329.

Ottenstein K & Ottenstein M (1984). The program dependence graph in a software development environment, *ACM SIGPLAN Notices*, vol.19, no. 5, pp. 177-184.

Canfora G; Cimitile & De L (1998). Conditioned Program Slicing, *Information and Software Technology*, vol. 40, no. 11/12, pp. 595-607.

Harman M & Danicic S (1997). Amorphous Program Slicing, *IEEE International Workshop on Program Comprehesion, IWPC'97*, IEEE CS Press, Los Alamitos, pp. 70-79.

Papaspyrou N (2001). A Resumption Monad Transformer and its Applications in the Semantics of Concurrency, *Technical Report CSD-SW-TR-2-01*, National Technical University of Athens, Software Engineering Laboratory.

Labra G; Luengo D & Cueva L, et al (2002). Reusable Monadic Semantics of Object Oriented Programming Languages, *Proceeding of 6th Brazilian Symposium on Programming Languages, SBLP'02*, PUC-Rio University, Brazil.

CCMF, Computational Context Modeling Framework – An Ontological Approach to Develop Context-Aware Web Applications

Luis Paulo Carvalho[1] and Paulo Caetano da Silva[2]
[1]*UNIFACS-University of Salvador/IRT-Instituto Recôncavo de Tecnologia*
[2]*UNIFACS-University of Salvador*
Brazil

1. Introduction

The purpose of software is to help people to perform their activities and fulfill their objectives. In this regard, the human-software relationship could be enhanced if software could adapt to changes automatically during its utilization (Brézillon, 1999). Context is defined by (Dey, 2001) as any type of information which characterizes an entity. An entity is any person, place or object that is relevant to the interaction between users and software. According to (Dey & Abowd, 1999) context-awareness is the capability of software to use context to offer services to users. For instance, a context-aware system may trigger an alarm in a device near to a user to remind him of the departure time of a planned trip (Yamato et al. 2011). In this example, context is used to provide a service to the user: the reminding of a personal activity. It is not, however, a trivial task to associate context with software in the same level of abstraction as humans do when they communicate with each other. (Dey & Abowd, 1999) considers that such ability is naturally inherited from the richness of the human languages and the common understanding of how the world works and from an implicit understanding of daily situations. Thus, with the intention of enhancing the offering of services from software to humans, it is important to transmit these capacities to computational environments.

As maintained by (Sheng & Benatallah, 2005), web services have become a promising technology for the development of internet-oriented software. Services are autonomous platform-independent software that executes tasks ranging from providing simple answers to users requests to the execution of complex processes. Web services are services that utilize the internet and its open technologies, e.g. WSDL, Web Service Description Language, SOAP, Simple Object Access Protocol, UDDI, Universal Description, Discovery and Integration, and XML, eXtensible Markup Language, to supply functionalities to other applications (Berbner et al. 2005). (Kapitsaki et al. 2009) assure that the handling of context is of vital importance to web services, since it promotes dynamic behavior, content adaptation and simplicity of use to end users. However, the association between web services and context is not easy to achieve because adequate mechanisms are not offered to developers in order to support the description and representation of context-related information and its later utilization by web services.

Considering the lack of appropriate technologies to extend software to integration of context and web services, this work proposes:

1. A framework, CCMF (Carvalho & Silva, 2011), Computational Context Modeling Framework, which relies on the reuse of artifacts and tools to automate analysis and development activities related to the making of context-aware web applications;
2. The instantiation of CCMF considering 2 different case studies: (a) Integration of CCMF and CCMD (Carvalho & Silva, 2011), Computational Context Modeling Diagram (to be presented in Section 3.1); (b) The embedding of ontologies in CCMF. Both cases intending to enable the development of context-aware web applications;
3. The analysis of the coupling between the framework and the 2 targeted technologies (CCMD and Ontologies) in order to evaluate the advantages and disadvantages of each approach.

This work is organized as follows: Section 2 presents related works. The framework is described in Section 3. In Section 4, CCMF is coupled with CCMD and ontologies to develop a context-aware web application (both approaches are compared). Section 5 enfolds conclusions and future works.

2. Related works

(Carvalho & Silva, 2011) gathered requirements from related literature - e.g. (Topcu 2011), (Hoyos et al. 2010), (Dey et al. 2001), (Vieira, 2008), (Bulcão, 2006), (Schmidt, 2006) - with the intention of enumerating important characteristics for the modeling of the information which influences the utilization of software and to provide guidelines to base the creation of the framework. Table 1 lists the requirements.

<table>
<tr><th></th><th>Requirement</th><th>Purpose</th></tr>
<tr><td>I</td><td>It must support the development of context-aware software as a two-phase task: specification of context information (structure) and adaptation</td><td>The separation into two phases promotes the decoupling of aims, allowing designers to focus on specific activities related to each development phase</td></tr>
<tr><td>II</td><td>It must categorize the information into context dimensions</td><td rowspan="2">By modeling the context focus and dimensions, designers are able to orderly identify and structure context information, promoting the readability of the model</td></tr>
<tr><td>III</td><td>It has to identify the context focus of a task</td></tr>
<tr><td>IV</td><td>It must support the transfer of context information and artifacts between development phases</td><td>The effort required to perform next development steps (e.g. modeling of adaptation) is lessened by the input of artifacts from previous phases (e.g. modeling of structures)</td></tr>
<tr><td>V</td><td>It must promote the diversity of context information in a domain-independent manner</td><td>So that designers can model context-aware systems to automate tasks of a variety of scenarios</td></tr>
<tr><td>VI</td><td>It has to support the reuse of distributed computing systems such as services</td><td>To base context adaptation on web services API, e.g. Google Agenda API (GAgenda, 2011)</td></tr>
</table>

Table 1. Requirements for developing context-aware software (Carvalho & Silva, 2011)

The following works were evaluated against the requirements (listed in Table 1):

1. CMS-ANS (Bonino et al. 2007), Context Management Service/Awareness and Notification Service, a framework that allows context sources to publish information and client software to be notified when specific contexts are acquired;
2. CONON (Wang et al. 2004), CONtext Ontology, a two-layered ontology intended to promote the sharing of context structures among agents and services;
3. CMP (Simons, 2007), Context Modeling Profile, uses stereotypes to extend the class diagram of UML to model context. In the same way, ContextUML (Sheng & Benatallah, 2005) adds stereotypes to the UML (in specific, to the class diagram) to model context-aware web services;
4. CEMantTIKA Case (Patrício, 2010), composed of a set of customized diagrams - based on the Eclipse platform and JBoss Drools (JBDrools, 2009) - that model context structures and adaptations of context-aware software;
5. (Bastida et al. 2008) proposes WSBPEL (WSBPEL, 2007), Web Service Business Process Execution Language, to model adaptation based on context information extracted from software requirements;
6. (George & Ward, 2008) modify the WSBPEL engine to support the addition of context variables and sources (i.e. the sources are used to fill information in the variables);
7. CAMEL (Grassi & Sindico 2009), Context-Awareness ModEling Language, composed of UML-oriented diagrams made specifically to model context structures and adaptation;
8. (Yamato et al. 2010) proposes dynamic adaptations of composite web services utilizing semantic context metadata to select equivalent functionalities from clusters of web services.

Table 2 shows the result of the evaluation of the works against the proposed requirements (filled cells indicate that the requirement was fulfilled).

	I	II	III	IV	V	VI
CMS-ANS		■				■
CONON		■			■	
CMP	■				■	
ContextUML	■			■	■	■
CEManTIKA Case	■		■	■	■	
(Bastida et al. 2008)	■			■	■	■
(George and Ward 2008)	■			■	■	■
CAMEL	■			■	■	
(Yamato et al. 2010)				■	■	■

Table 2. Evaluation of related works against the requirements (Carvalho & Silva, 2011).

Since the aforementioned related works do not fulfill all of the requirements (described in Table 1), CCMF is proposed as set of activities intended to automate the analysis and development of context-aware web applications. In Section 3, the framework is described and it is discussed its association with reusable development languages, tools and artifacts. A case study in which CCMF is applied is presented in Section 4.

3. CCMF, Computational Context Modeling Framework

CCMF is composed of a set of analysis and development activities which are intended to lessen the effort demanded by the development of context-aware web applications. This is achieved from: (a) the reuse of artifacts and third-part tools, modeling languages and technologies and (b) the automation of the execution of targeted activities, which are described in next paragraphs.

As shown in Figure 1, the framework is composed of two layers containing specific activities to be carried by developers. Its upper layer comprises the activities related to the definition of structures of context information and its externalization to the adaptation modeling mechanism, a WSBPEL diagram. Such externalization is made possible by the transformation of the context structures into a context medium. Provided that XML-based languages enable the interoperation of computational agents, e.g web services (Alboaie et al. 2003), XSD (XSD, 2001), XML Schema Definition, documents are used by the framework to enable the utilization of context by web services integrated to the WSBPEL diagram. Respectively, the definition of context structures and the transformation of these structures into context mediums are performed by the activities identified by numbers 1 and 2.

Once the context medium is created, it can be transformed into language-specific context classes. Considering, for instance, JAVA as the development language, XMLBeans API (XMLBeans, 2009) can be used to transform the XSD schema into JAVA serializable classes. The resulting classes can be instantiated as objects that are capable of encapsulating their attributes into XML documents. Later on, web services can rely on such documents to exchange complex context data between each other, i.e. the serialization via XML documents is necessary to interoperate web services in a manner that the information about context is used to parameterized the adaptation. The generation of the serializable classes is performed by the activity number 3.

After having modeled the context structures, the developer must define how the context information must be used to automate adaptations. This activity (identified by number 4), the first one of the framework´s lower layer, depends on WSBPEL to base the context adaptation on web services. In this case, web services must be gathered and integrated to a WSBPEL diagram in order to utilize context information to parameterize responses to situations of use. Along with the deployment of the composite context-aware web service (by activity number 5), a WSDL document is created. This document describes the web service with the purpose of allowing the remote calling of its functionalities by other computational agents (e.g. handheld-embedded applications, other web services). To ease the effort required by the creation of these agents, the WSDL document can be transformed into language-specific source code (by executing the activity identified by the number 6). The source code is intended to provide ways to client software to access the composite web service in order to be served by adaptation functionalities.

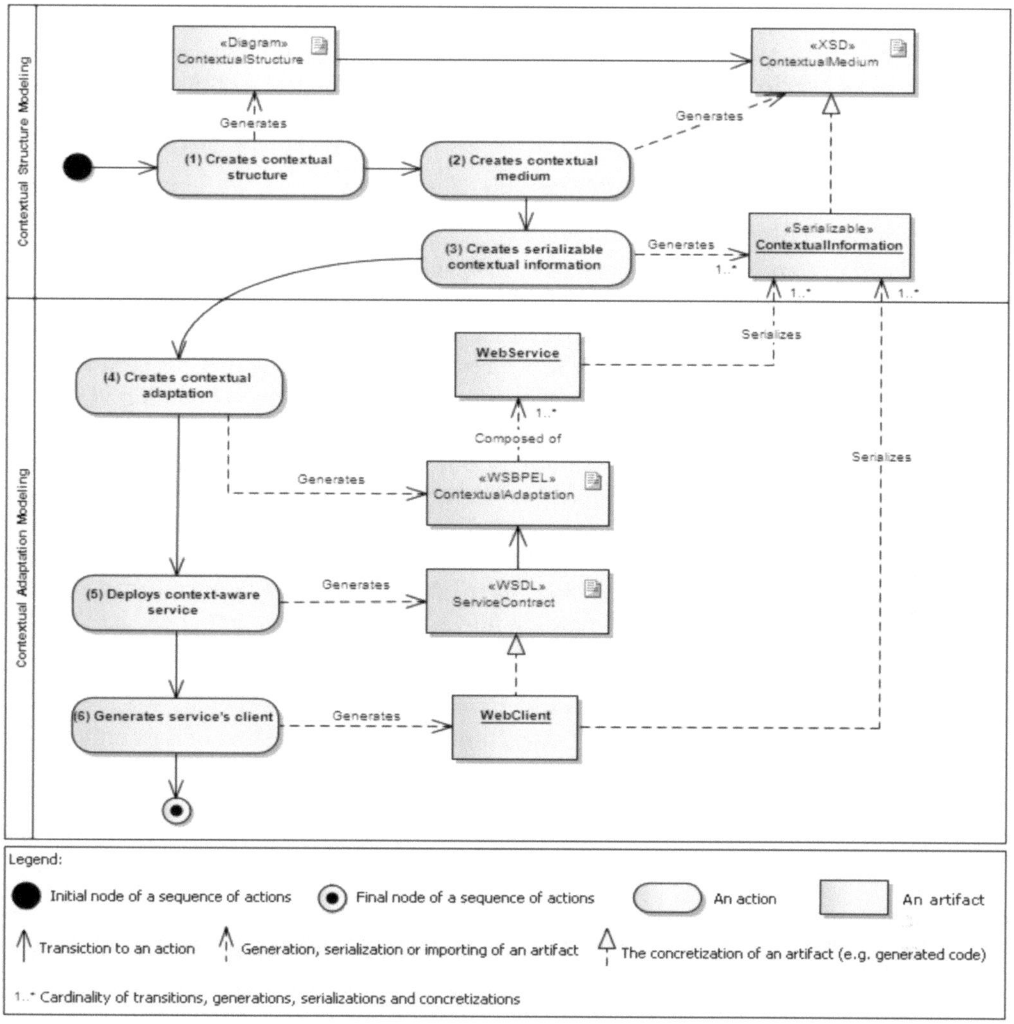

Fig. 1. CCMF - Computational Context Modeling Framework (Carvalho & Silva, 2011)

Provided the activities depicted in Figure 1, CCMF is capable of:

1. Modeling structures of context information (upper layer of the framework) and the adaptation (lower layer of the framework);
2. Enabling the reuse of development artifacts, e.g. by transforming a context medium (a XSD document) into XML-based classes in order to serialize complex context data between web services;
3. Supporting the reuse of distributed computing systems such as web services. In this case, the adaptation mechanism is placed "in the cloud" and it can be reused by other computational agents over the internet.

In Section 3.1, it is described a diagram, CCMD, Computational Context Modeling Diagram, which automates the execution of activity number 1 of CCMF, the modeling of context structures, i.e. CCMD can be coupled with the upper layer of CCMF to define the sets of information which may interfere in situations of use of software. In Section 3.2 ontologies are introduced as a replacement for CCMD, being analyzed what are the necessary adaptations to be applied to the framework in order to enable the use of ontologies to model context-aware web applications.

3.1 CCMD – Computational Context Modeling Diagram

CCMD is composed of a set of stereotypes which allows the creation of diagrams to model concepts related to computational context, e.g. the context focus and dimensions. According to (Brézillon & Pomerol, 1999) the context focus corresponds to a step in the solution of a problem or in a decision making process. (Vieira, 2008) states that the focus can represent a relationship between an agent and a task, in which the agent is responsible for performing the task. For instance, referring to the modeling of software that bases the scheduling of meetings on computational context, the focus might indicate that a secretary (the agent) must perform the task "prepare meeting". The focus is important to context modeling because it enables developers to identify specific sets of context information in relation to the task executed by an agent. Once the focus is identified, the related information can be grouped as context dimensions. As indicated by (Brézillon & Bazire, 2005) the context dimensions enables the categorization of context information and have the main purpose of helping software designers to specify, model and fill information into adequate structures (Bulcão, 2006). CCMD models the following context dimensions identified by (Abowd & Mynatt, 2000):

1. "Location" represents spatial characteristics of the context information;
2. "Temporal" ("Time") comprises any date/time-related information of the context;
3. "Participant" represents entities (other than the agent) which participates in the execution of the task;
4. "Motivation" ("Preferences") is related to the objectives of the agent and participants;
5. "Activity" corresponds to activities performed during the execution of the task.

The task, the context focus and dimensions are illustrated in Figure 2. Number 1 points to the task. The context focus is represented by the stereotype linked to number 2. Number 3 is associated with the stereotypes that represent the context dimensions.

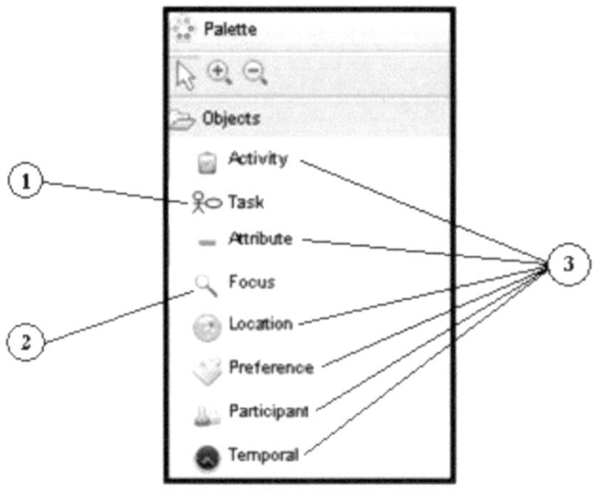

Fig. 2. Stereotypes of CCMD (Carvalho & Silva, 2011).

A concrete implementation of the stereotypes of CCMD can be generated via EuGENia (EuGENia, 2011) plugin to embed the modeling of context in the Eclipse IDE. EuGENia defines a declarative language which abstracts away the details of the coding of diagrams. The declarative metadata of CCMD is transformed by EuGENia into artifacts which input graphic-related data into Eclipse's GMF (GMF, 2010), Graphical Modeling Framework, and EMF (EMF, 2009), Eclipse Modeling Framework. As a result, it is generated a diagram (CCMD) to be used via Eclipse IDE to model context information structures. The graphical elements of CCMD are shown in Figure 3. Next to number 1, it is represented the "Task" from which the context focus is extracted. The "Focus" is placed next to number 2. The "Preference" is modeled by the element next to the number 3. Each "Participant" is symbolized by the element pointed by number 4. The "Location" is positioned near to number 5. The "Activity" is represented by the element next to number 6. The "Temporal" ("Time") dimension is situated nearby the number 7.

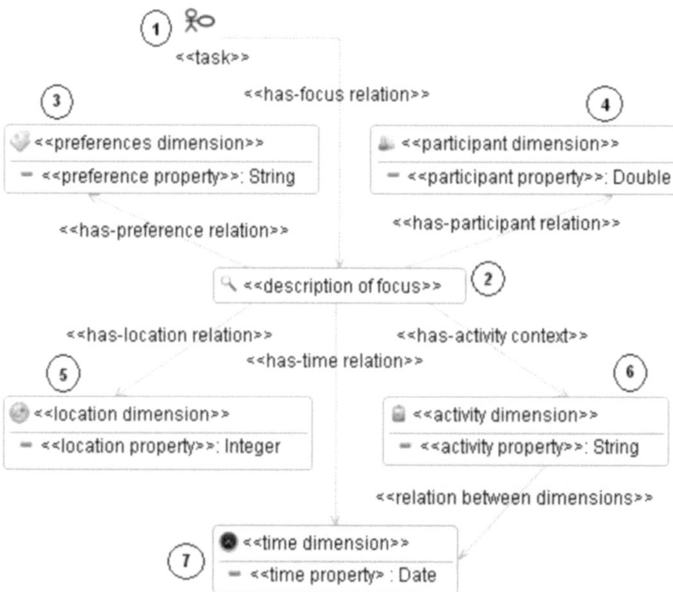

Fig. 3. Concrete implementation of CCMD stereotypes (Carvalho & Silva, 2011)

The instantiation of CCMF and its coupling with CCMD is described in Section 4.1. The framework is used to implement a context-aware web application. The modeling activities enumerated in Figure 1 are exemplified as well as the reuse of tools and artifacts.

3.2 Ontologies

As stated by (Noy, 2004; Chen et al. 2004), ontologies are believed to be a key feature in the making of context-aware distributed systems due to the following reasons:

1. Ontologies enable the sharing of knowledge by open dynamic agents (e.g. web services);
2. Ontologies supply semantics for intelligent agents to reason about context information;
3. Ontologies promote the interoperability among devices and computational agents.

Considering that the abovementioned advantages ensure that ontologies side with the purpose of CCMF, which is to promote the reuse and interoperability of distributed computational agents (e.g. web services) with the intention of automating the creation of context-aware web applications, it is proposed the coupling of CCMF with an ontological approach. In this case, it must be surveyed how ontologies are capable of supporting the representation of context structures and the generation of context-aware adaptations mechanisms.

(Bontas et al. 2005) defines ontology reuse as the process in which available (ontological) knowledge is used to generate new ontologies. By reusing existent ontologies the cost of implementation is reduced, since it avoids the manual codification of a new one. Moreover, two different ontologies can be bound together as one to represent concepts of broader domains, i.e. a given ontology can be associated with others with the intention of modeling concepts of a domain in order to represent the sum of the information represented by each of the combined ontologies. Therefore, the framework must be evolved as to allow the collecting and binding of ontologies with the intention of supplying structures of information to model computational context.

Another aspect of ontologies that motivates modifications on the development activities of CCMF is related to their capability of having a dual purpose (Reinisch et al. 2008): ontologies are able to represent knowledge and also to store and generate instances of such knowledge to interoperate agents. In comparison with the set of activities of the former framework (Figure 1), the handling of CCMD and the XSD/XML-based artifacts can be replaced by ontologies, because they can be accessed directly by the web services of the context-aware composition in order to enable the saving and retrieval of the context information. As a consequence, the effort required to model a context-aware composite web service is lessened, because it is not necessary to deal with the instantiation and manipulation of serializable objects and XML documents, i.e. the utilization of ontologies causes the removal and substitution of activities from the original framework (the one illustrated in Figure 1 of Section 3).

The modified framework is shown in Figure 4. The activity identified by number 1 represents the collecting and binding of existent ontologies in the making of a new one, which must be suitable to model information of the context-aware application's domain. The second activity is that of customizing the ontology to better represent context information. This activity can be exemplified by the definition of associations between natively dissociated classes and/or the addition of new classes and attributes to candidate ontologies. The third activity creates the context adaptation and bases it on the utilization of composite web services. The web services of the composition are able to add and select instantiated individuals from the ontology in substitution to serializations via XML documents. The deployment of the composite web service is performed by activity number 4. The generated WSDL contract is reused in the making of client software by activity number 5.

Thus, the adapted framework, hereafter O-CCMF, Ontology-driven Computational Context Modeling Framework, is able to (re)use ontologies through a smaller set of activities dedicated to the development of context-aware web-applications.

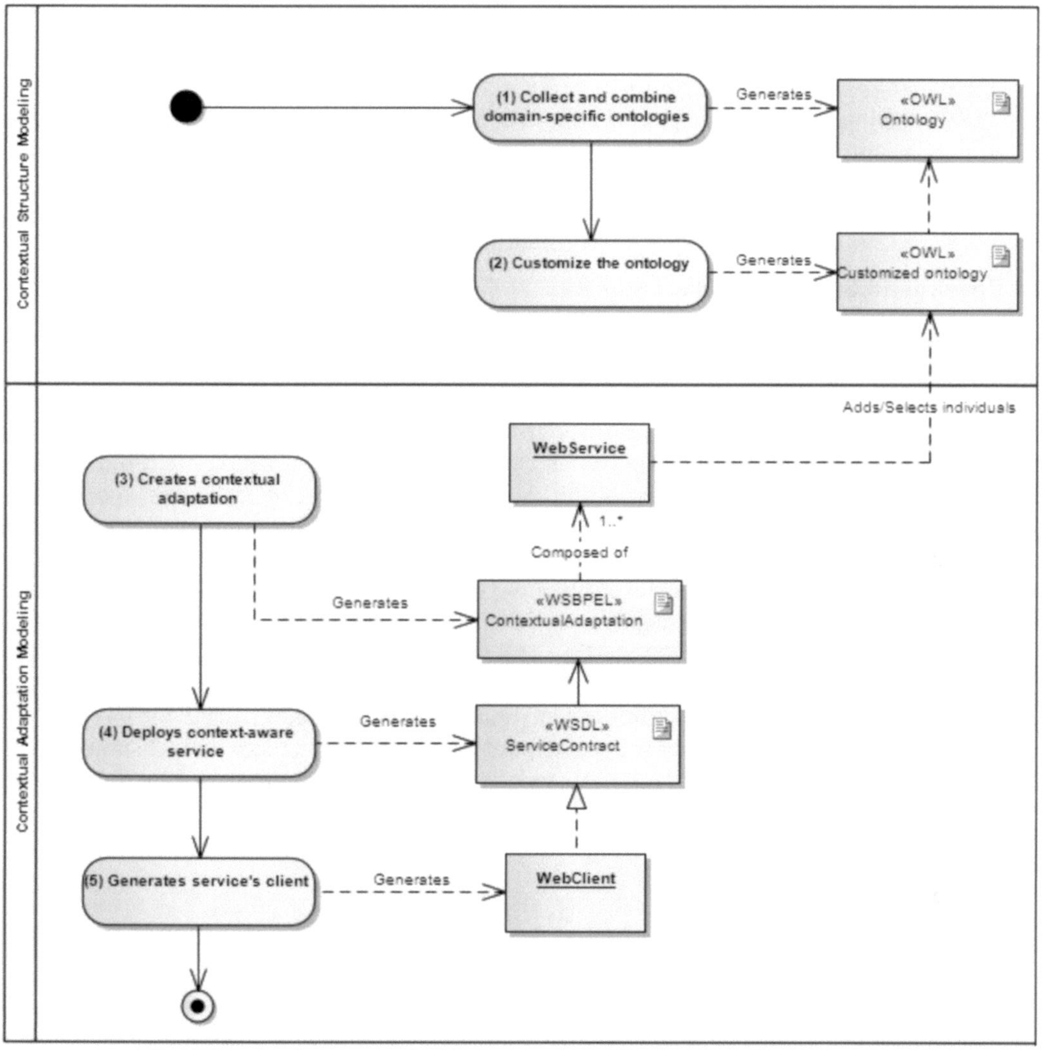

Fig. 4. O-CCMF - Ontology-Driven Computational Context Modeling Framework

The two versions of CCMF, the one coupled with CCMD and O-CCMF are exemplified as study cases in Section 4. They are used to develop the same context-aware web application. Later on, both approaches are evaluated against the requirements identified in Section 2 (Table 1).

4. Case studies

As a proof of concept of the application of CCMF and O-CCMF, it is proposed the creation of a context-aware meeting alert application. The frameworks are used to model and develop an application that must send alerts to participants of meetings according to the requirements defined by (Antoniou et al. 2007):

1. If the participant is located near to the place where the meeting is going to happen, he must receive an alerting message 5 minutes before the meeting;
2. If the participant is located in a place far from where the meeting is going to happen, the message must be sent within 40 minutes;
3. If the meeting is going to happen in the rush hour, 10 minutes are added to the interval;
4. If it is raining, another 10 minutes are added;
5. If the meeting's subject is about giving a class, 30 minutes are added in order to allow the participant to prepare himself for the class.

4.1 Developing the meeting alert application with CCMF

The first activity of the framework is that of modeling the context information structures. Figure 5 shows a graphical instantiation of CCMD which is used to represent the context data that parameterizes the context adaptation of the meeting alert application. The element next to number 1 represents the task under which a context focus is identified (next to number 2). The focus aids designers in determining the specific set of context information that is necessary to enable the adaptation, i.e. the combination of tasks and focus helps designers to restrain the scope of analysis of context structures. Once the focus is identified, the datasets of context information can be added to CCMD. The meeting is symbolized by the element next to number 3. The location of the meeting is represented by the element next to number 5. The temporal dimension is represented by the element identified by number 6 and contains information about the starting and ending datetime of the meeting. The list of participants is represented by the element next to number 4. Each participant has its own geographic location (latitude/longitude coordinates) which is represented by the element next to number 7. The locations of the participants are used to calculate their distances from the location of the meeting. The preferable weather condition is represented by the element next to number 8.

Fig. 5. Meeting alert context information modeled by CCMD (Carvalho & Silva, 2011)

After using CCMD to define context structures, a context medium must be generated (activity 2 of the framework). The purpose of the context medium is to integrate the framework with different sources of context information (e.g. CCMD). Figure 6 shows an excerpt from a XSD document generated by the CCMD that represents the meeting and its location, its participants and the date/time-related information.

```
<complexType name="meeting">
 <sequence>
  <element name="location" type="gagenda:location" minOccurs="1" maxOccurs="1"/>
  <element name="temporal" type="gagenda:temporal" minOccurs="1" maxOccurs="1"/>
  <element name="participant" type="gagenda:participant" minOccurs="0"
maxOccurs="unbounded"/>
 </sequence>
 <attribute name="title" type="string"></attribute>
 <attribute name="description" type="string"></attribute>
</complexType>
```

Fig. 6. Context medium exported by CCMD as a XSD document (Carvalho & Silva, 2011).

The context medium (XSD document) enables the framework to transform the context structure into other formats of reusable artifacts. For instance, in order to interoperate the web services, with the purpose of implementing the context adaptation of the meeting alert software, the XSD document can be converted into serializable JAVA classes (by the XMLBeans API). This transformation corresponds to the third activity of the framework and it generates a library that makes possible the exchanging of context data between web services, e.g. a certain web service fills context information into a serializable object, which automates the creation of a XML document that is serialized toward other web services. By receiving the XML document as an input, the targeted web service deserializes the context information back into a high level JAVA object. Figure 7 illustrates an example of a XML document which serializes context information related to a meeting.

```
<data:meetings title="Meeting professor Paulo Caetano"
 description="Meeting professor Paulo Caetano to talk about the dissertation"
xmlns:data="http://www.data.agenda.adapters.google.unifacs.edu.br">
 <data:location address="Rua Ponciano de Oliveira, 126, Rio Vermelho, CEP 41950-275, Salvador,
Ba, Brasil">
 </data:location>
 <data:temporal start="2011-08-23T17:30:00.000-03:00" end="2011-08-23T18:30:00.000-03:00">
 </data:temporal>
 <data:participant name="luis paulo" email="luispsc@yahoo.com.br"></data:participant>
 <data:participant name="paulo caetano" email="paulocaetano.dasilva@gmail.com">
</data:participant>
</data:meetings>
```

Fig. 7. XML-based serializable information (Carvalho & Silva, 2011).

Once the modeling of the context structures is made available, it must be defined how the software is adapted to situations of use. Prior to designing the adaptation, using the BPEL Visual Designer for Eclipse IDE (BPELEclipse, 2010), web services has to be found so to make possible the collecting and processing of the context data. Table 3 lists services API's used to automate the adaptation of the meeting alert application.

API/Service	Usage
Google Agenda	It supplies information about meetings
Yahoo Weather Forecast	It offers information about weather conditions
Google Geocoding (GGCoding, 2011)	It converts address-based locations of meetings to geographic coordinates
Google Geodirections API (GDirections, 2011)	It calculates the distance from each participant to to meeting's location

Table 3. Services API's used to automate the adaptation of the meeting alert application

The XML document in Figure 7 contains data retrieved from a web service based on the Google Agenda API. Figure 8 shows an example of an event added to the user's agenda. Next to number 1, it is shown the title of the event. Its description is placed near to number 2. Next to 3, the event's starting and ending date and time are shown. Event's location is identified by the number 4. The list of participants is placed near to number 5.

Fig. 8. Google Agenda as a source of context information (Carvalho & Silva, 2011)

The WSBPEL diagram illustrated in Figure 9 models a workflow in which the web services of Table 3 are used to automate the context adaptation. The action identified by the number 1 request events from Google Agenda. The location of the event is processed to determine the weather condition in the area where the meeting is going to happen. This is performed by the action identified by number 2. Since the location of the event is not expressed as a latitude-longitude pair, Google Geocoding is executed to translate the address of the event into geographic coordinates (next to number 3). The distance from each participant to the event's location is calculated by Google Directions (near to the number 4). Once all of the context information is retrieved and processed by the web services, the WSBPEL diagram evaluates the amount of time within which the alert messages must be sent to participants. If the participant is located near to event's location[1], the message is sent within 5 minutes. If not, the message is sent within 40 minutes (conditional test next to number 5). If it is going

[1] Participants within a radius of 3.000 meters are considered near to event's location.

to rain (test placed near to number 6), another 10 minutes are added. If the event happens during the rush hour, the interval is increased in 10 minutes (condition evaluated next to number 7). If the event is about giving a class[2], another 30 minutes are added to the interval so that the participant will be able to ready himself in order to give the class.

Fig. 9. Context adaptation based on WSBPEL (Carvalho & Silva, 2011).

After the modeling of the context adaptation, the BPEL designer is able to generate a WSDL document that externalizes the new generated composite web service to client applications. Figure 10 shows an example of the result of the adaptation supplied by the meeting alert web service.

[2] The description of the event is searched for the word "class" and similars.

> To participant identified by 'luispsc@yahoo.com.br' the alert message must be sent within 50 minutes!
> To participant identified by 'paulocaetano.dasilva@gmail.com' the alert message must be sent within 15 minutes!

Fig. 10. Adaptation supplied by the meeting alert web service (Carvalho & Silva, 2011)

4.2 Coupling CCMF and Ontologies

The O-CCMF can, as well, be used to develop the meeting alert application. In this section, its activities are performed to re-implement the software.

The first activity of O-CCMF is that of finding the appropriate ontologies to enable the modeling of context information. For instance, in relation to the meeting alert application, SOUPA, Standard Ontology for Ubiquitous and Pervasive Applications, (Chen et al. 2004) can be used for this purpose. SOUPA comprises two sub-ontologies, SOUPA Core and SOUPA Extension, which contain, among others, classes suitable for the representation of meetings. In Figure 11, such classes are highlighted (in yellow).

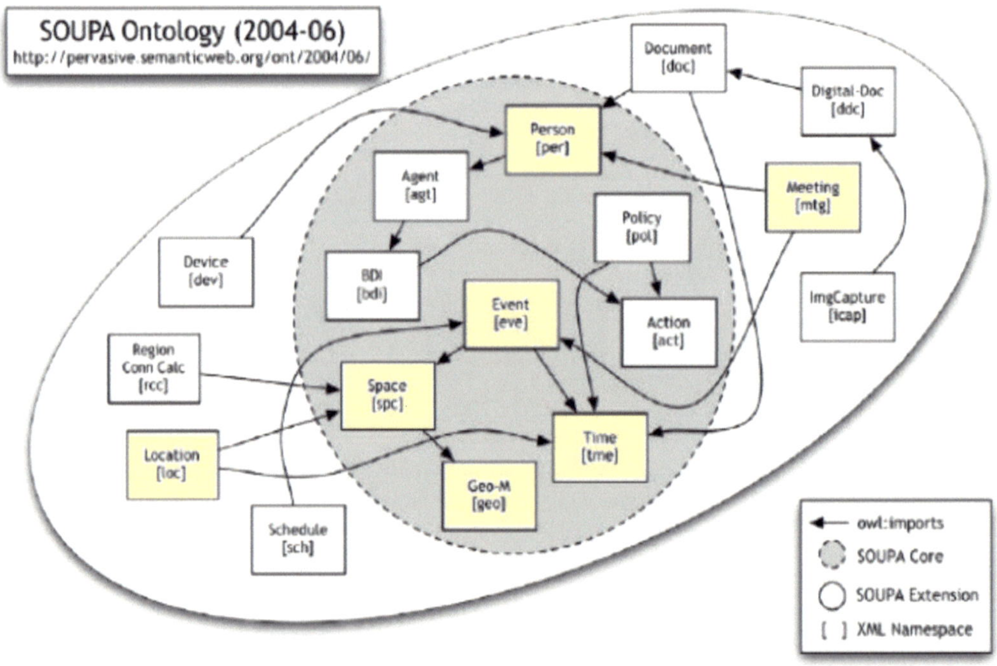

Fig. 11. Classes of SOUPA (Chen et al. 2004).

Considering the set of context information contained in Figure 5, SOUPA must be coupled with other ontology in order to represent weather conditions, since the adaptation requires the evaluation of such information prior to furnishing context adaptation. With that purpose, the *OWEATHER*, Weather Ontology, (Gajderowicz, 2008) is bound to SOUPA to provide classes which enable the modeling of weather-related information. Figure 12 shows the three layers of abstraction of the *OWEATHER* ontology. The upper layer, Class Level 1, contains a top generic Weather class under which grouping classes (e.g. Wind, Precipitation at Class Level 2) are defined. Class Level 3 contains classes that represent specific natural phenomena (e.g Gusting, Rain).

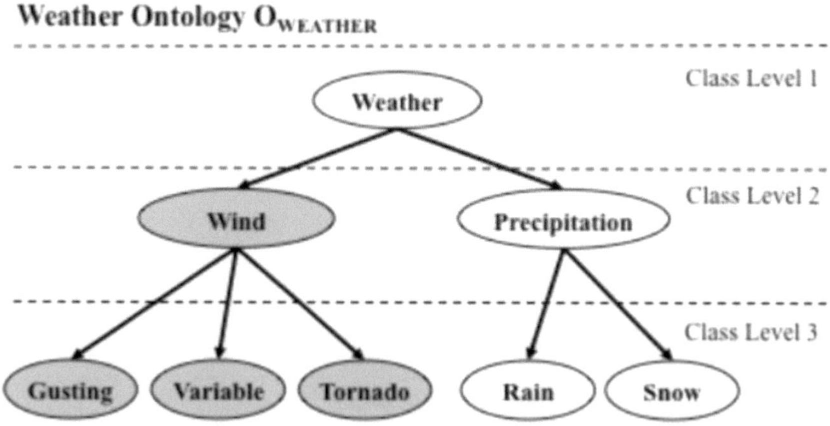

Fig. 12. Classes of *OWEATHER* (Gajderowicz, 2008).

The union of SOUPA and *OWEATHER* produces a new ontology, MAO (Meeting Alert Ontology), which enables the modeling of the context structures for the meeting alert application. Table 4 relates the classes contained in MAO to the context information defined using CCMD (in Figure 5).

Source ontology	Ontology classes	CCMD classes
SOUPA	Meeting + Event (MeetingEvent)	Meeting
	Location	Location
	Time	Temporal
	Geo-M	Geolocation
	Person	Participant
OWEATHER	Weather	Weather

Table 4. Ontology classes to represent context information.

The resulting ontology can be populated by information related to meetings. In Figure 13, number 1 points to a "MeetingEvent" individual (instance of the "MeetingEvent" class of MAO) being exhibited by Protégé (Protégé, 2011). Protégé is a free, open-source platform that provides a suite of tools to construct domain models and knowledge-based applications with ontologies. Number 2 identified the class-to-class properties of the event, i.e. its relation with other complex classes of the ontology. The "hasParticipant" element represents an association between an event and its participants, i.e. the individuals "LuisPaulo" and "PauloCaetano" that are instances of the class "Person". The "hasStart" and "hasEnd" elements are related, respectively, to the starting and ending date and time of the event (they are instances of the "Time" class). The "locatedAt" element is intended to represent the spatial location of the event, i.e. the place where the meeting is intended to happen. The ontology also supplies information about the meeting's title and description (elements pointed by number 3).

Fig. 13. The "Event" individual of the meeting alert ontology.

Although, it is possible to combine different ontologies in the production of a new one, e.g. the combination of SOUPA and *OWEATHER* produces MAO, it is necessary to adapt the ontology to better express the context information. For instance, Event and Meeting were two dissociated concepts of SOUPA, but, considering the meeting alert application, they had to be combined in a single class, MeetingEvent, so that it would supply a unique way to represent meeting-related events. This adaptation exemplifies the execution of activity 2 of the O-CCMF (as illustrated in Figure 4).

The meeting event information of Figure 13 was retrieved from a web service based on the Google Agenda API and stored in MAO using the OWL API (OWLAPI, 2011). The composite web service (the one illustrated in Figure 9 of Section 4.1) was altered with the intention of using the OWL API and ontologies (SOUPA and *OWEATHER* grouped in MAO) as a replacement for the XML serializable classes (i.e. the JAVA XML Beans classes originated from XSD documents). In this case, the ontologies promote the sharing of a common vocabulary that replaces the serialization of context information via XML documents. As a concrete example of this form of interoperability, Figure 14 illustrates how individuals retrieved from Google Agenda are added to MAO with the intention to parameterize the execution of other web services, e.g. the one originated from the Google Geocoding API. This is done by the "getEventEntries" method that selects event entries found in user's agenda and inserts them in the meeting alert ontology. Once the Geocoding converts the address of the meeting to geographic coordinates, they are compared to the current location of the participants to determine how far/near they are from meeting's location. The location is also used by Yahoo Weather Forecast to evaluate the rain likelihood, i.e. the service analyzes the weather-related information to determine if it is going to rain in the area where the meeting is intended to happen.

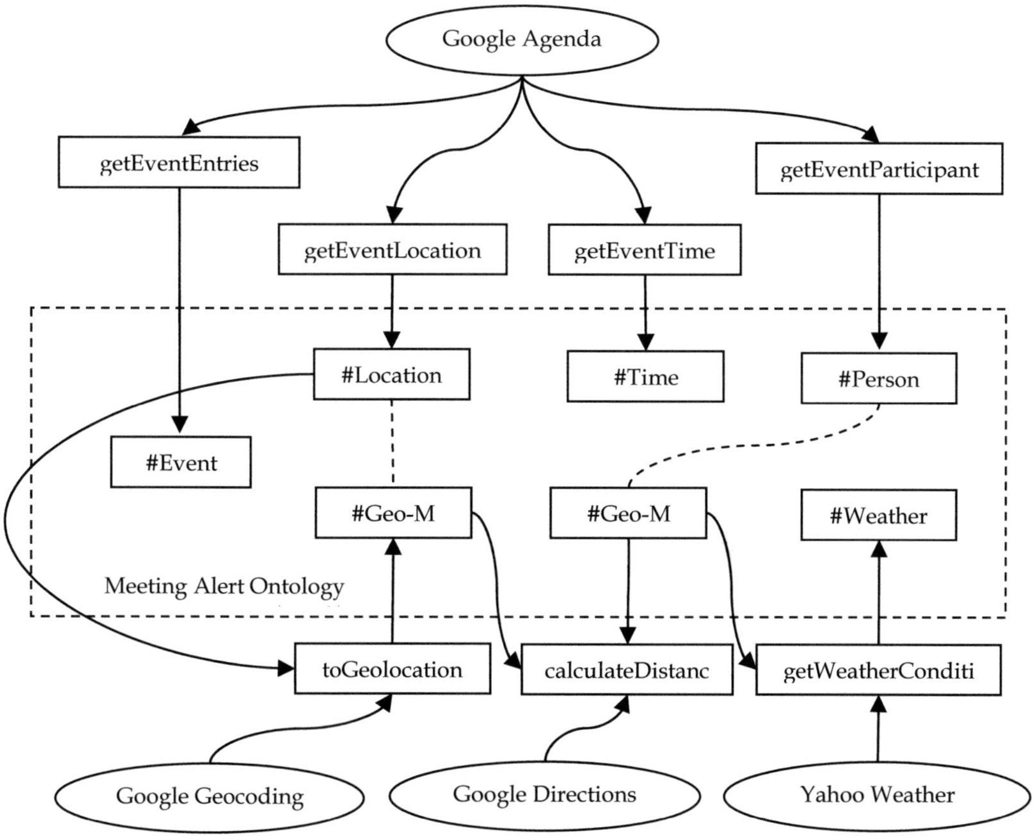

Fig. 14. Using the MAO ontology to interoperate web services.

Considering the scenario depicted in Figure 14, the context adaptation is less influenced by the overhead of modeling serializations via XML. In the making of the meeting alert web application, for instance, it was possible to produce web services which took no parameters as input and, likewise, returned no output, because the context information was selected and saved directly to the ontology (no serialization of context information needed). As a consequence, the modeling of the context adaptation can rather rely on choreographed web services in substitution to orchestrations. Figure 15 illustrates the difference between orchestration and choreography (Gǎbor et al. 2004). The orchestration (left side of Figure 15) requires that the execution of web services is controlled by one agent which describes how services interact with each other. The WSBPEL, for instance, is an orchestrator of web services. In a choreography (right side of Figure 15), each web service involved in the process describes the part they play in the interaction which is performed in a collaborative manner.

The choreography can be exemplified by the interaction between the Geocoding and Directions web services. The Directions web service is able to extract the geographic coordinates inserted into the ontology by the Geocoding web service. This is performed in a i.e. choreographed manner, since the direct manipulation of the meeting alert ontology by

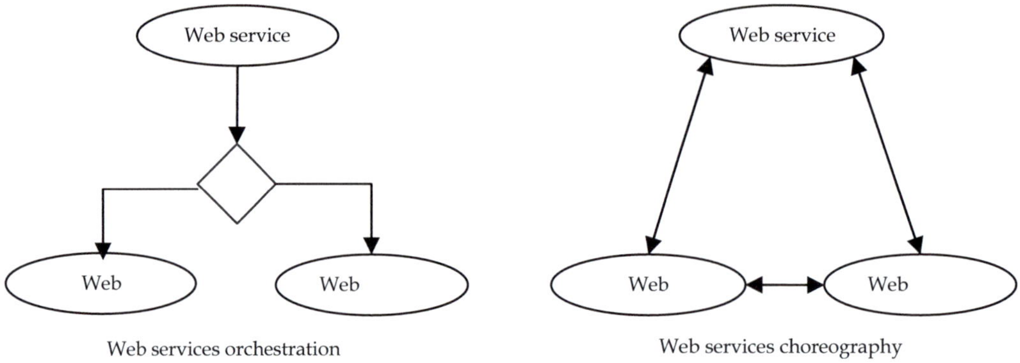

Fig. 15. Choreography and orchestration of web services (Peltz, 2003).

the web services promotes an internalized sharing of context information, without the intervention of controlling agents, such as an orchestration mechanism. As an opposite example, the WSBPEL diagram (e.g. the one illustrated in Figure 9, Section 4.1) is responsible for transferring the context information from one service to other, i.e. using WSBPEL, software designers must model an appropriate sequence of actions so that the context information is interchanged among services. In this case, the WSBPEL workflow acts like a controlling agent.

4.3 Comparing CCMF and O-CCMF

Provided the two scenarios of development of context-aware web applications, the ontological approach, O-CCMF, leads on a reduced framework in comparison with the former version, CCMF, because ontologies have the characteristic of being artifacts suited for both the storage and sharing of information among computational agents. The meeting alert ontology, for instance, represents structures of context information and, too, it encloses the instances of its own ontological classes (individuals). On the contrary, considering that CCMF utilizes CCMD to only model the context information with no regard as to afford the mechanisms to allow the direct storage and instantiation of its classes as concrete objects, it is required from CCMF the transformation of CCMD into XSD/XML documents to support the sharing of context information. Consequently, as computational agents are able to add and select individuals directly from ontologies, the context adaptation can be automated by a workflow that groups and interoperates web services in a collaborative manner, i.e. the adaptation is served to client software by choreographed web services as a replacement to orchestrated ones, in a way that the orchestration eases the modeling of the adaptation by not requiring the provision of serializations.

Table 5 relates the requirements identified in Section 2 (Table 1) to CCMF and O-CCMF, indicating how they were fulfilled by each framework.

Requirement	CCMF	O-CCMF
It must support the development of context-aware software as a two-phase task: specification of context information (structure) and adaptation	CCMD is coupled to the framework to represent context structures. WSBPEL diagram models the adaptation	CCMD is replaced by combined ontologies to represent context information. WSBPEL is maintained to create the adaptation
It must categorize the information into context dimensions	CCMD contains stereotypes that represent the context focus and dimensions	No specific data structures represent the focus and dimensions. It could be, though, added to ontologies (e.g. MAO) during the execution of the customization activity (activity 2 of the framework)
It has to identify the context focus of a task		
It must support the transfer of context information and artifacts between development phases	The transference is performed by XML documents and XML serialization API's	The usage of ontology is twofold: it represents the context and it enables the interoperability of web services by instantiated individuals
It must promote the diversity of context information in a domain-independent manner	CCMD does not constrain the domain	Although ontologies are known for representing specific knowledge domains, they can be combined to support broader concepts
It has to support the reuse of distributed computing systems such as services	Achieved by the usage of orchestrated web services	Achieved by the usage of choreographed web services

Table 5. Evaluating the frameworks against the requirements.

CCMF and O-CCMF are capable of assisting developers in the creation of context-aware web applications. Adopting one or the other as development framework is a matter of deciding what it is the intended context information source: diagrams such as CCMD or ontologies. Another criterion would be the intended method of creating composite web services to serve context adaptation to client software: orchestrated (CCMF) or choreographed (O-CCMF) web services.

5. Conclusion and future work

Related works, as those described in Section 2, are likely to subject the modeling and development of context-aware applications to the utilization of ontologies or diagrams-oriented solutions (e.g. stereotyped UML class diagram). By introducing CCMF, a model-driven framework, and its ontology-oriented variation, O-CCMF, this work points to a heterogeneous scenario where context information is collected from different sources and adaptations are served by varied web services. Such diversification demands adaptive approaches from development solutions, as, for instance, the ability to deal with different modeling technologies (e.g. ontologies, diagrams) in a decoupled manner. Instead of favoring one specific form of development of context-aware web applications, CCMF and O-CCMF promote the reuse of a mixed set of artifacts, tools, API's, information and functionalities sources.

In regard to CCMF, its coupling with CCMD intends to grant to developers an immersive environment in which concepts of computational context (context focus and dimensions) orients the design of context information and adaptation. An advantage that is not provided by O-CCMF. However, contrary to ontologies, CCMD (and CCMF, consequently) does not rely on a single artifact to represent classes and instances of context information. Thus, CCMF has to be coupled with extra mechanisms (e.g serializable JAVA classes) to workaround such limitation which is naturally overcame by O-CCMF.

Both frameworks rely on web services to automate context adaptation and to serve it to remote clients across the internet. One advantage that arises from this approach is that of making possible the addition of further context information and adaptation steps to enhance context-awareness mechanisms. For instance, improvements in the Google Agenda API can be automatically propagated to client software without needing to distribute modification patches. Conversely, faulty web services might lessen the quality of served adaptations. For example, in case a specific functionality of the Google Agenda API either becomes deprecated or fails to retrieve some important context information, client software may not succeed in supplying context-awareness to end users.

Currently, the following tasks must be carried out in order to supplement this work:

1. The ontology-driven framework must be evaluated against further study cases to analyze weather the WSBPEL diagram can be decoupled from the framework in order to favor other composition mechanisms, e.g. the WSCI, Web Service Composition Interface (Gábor et al. 2004), which is representative of the choreography approach;
2. Reasoning mechanisms based on the semantics supplied by ontologies must be surveyed in order to enhance the adaptation. For instance, the conditional test that evaluate if the participant is the same location of the event could be inferred from the ontology by the web service that schedules the alerts;
3. The ontological approach promotes the binding of existent ontologies in the definition of domain-specific context information. Therefore, the searching for fitting available ontologies must be adequately supported by the framework. It must be surveyed how this activity can be better assisted by the coupling O-CCMF with available third-part tools and processes.

6. References

Abowd, G. D. & Mynatt. E. D. (2000). Charting past, present, and future research in ubiquitous computing. *ACM Trans. Comput.-Hum. Interact. 7*, pp. 29-58

Alboaie, L.; Buraga, S. C. & Alboaie, S. (2003). tuBiG: a layered infrastructure to provide support for Grid functionalities, *Proceedings of the second international conference on Parallel and distributed computing*, Washington, DC, USA, pp. 9-14

Antoniou, G.; Bikakis, A.; Karamolegou, A. & Papachristodoulou, N. (2007). A context-aware meeting alert using semantic web and rule technology. *International Journal of Metadata, Semantics and Ontologies 2007*, Vol. 2, No.3, pp. 147 - 156

Bastida, L.; Nieto, F. J. & Tola, R. (2008). Context-aware service composition: a methodology and a case study, *Proceedings of the 2nd international workshop on Systems development in SOA environments*, New York, USA, pp. 19-24

Bonino, L. O.; Wijnen, R. P. & Vink, P. (2007). A service-oriented middleware for context-aware applications. In *Proceedings of the fifth international workshop on middleware for pervasive and ad-hoc computing*. New York, NY, USA

Bontas, E. P.; Mochol, M. & Tolksdorf, R. (2005). Cases on Ontology reuse. *Proceedings of the 5th International Conference on Knowledge Management*

BPELEclipse (2010). BPEL Eclipse Designer. Available from http://www.eclipse.org/bpel

Brézillon, P. (1999). Context in problem solving: a survey. *Knowl. Eng. Rev. 14*, 1, pp. 47-80.

Brézillon, P. & Bazire, M. (2005). Understanding Context Before Using It. *5th International and Interdisciplinary Conference, CONTEXT-05*, v. LNAI 3554, Springer Verlag, Paris, France, pp. 29-40

Brickley, D. & Miller, L (2003). FOAF vocabulary specification. RDFWeb Namespace Document, RDFWeb, xmlns.com.

Bulcão, R. (2006). Um processo de software e um modelo ontológico para apoio ao desenvolvimento de aplicações sensíveis a contexto. Serviço de pós-graduação do ICMC-USP, São Carlos, São Paulo, Brasil

Carvalho, L. P. & Silva, P. C. (2011). CCMD - Computational Context Modeling Diagram - And WSBPEL Integration. *IADIS Applied Computing International Conference*. Rio de Janeiro, Brasil, November

Chen, H.; Perich, F.; Finin, T. & Joshi, A. (2004). SOUPA: Standard Ontology for Ubiquitous and Pervasive Applications. *1st Annual Int'l Conf. on Mobile and Ubiquitous Systems: Networking and Services*, August

Dey, A. K. (2001). Understanding and Using Context. *Personal and Ubiquitous Computing, Special issue on Situated Interaction and Ubiquitous Computing* 5, 1, pp. 4-7

Dey, A. K. & Abowd, G. D. (1999). Towards a better understanding of context and context-awareness, *Proceedings of the first international symposium on handheld and ubiquitous computing*, H. Gellersen, Ed. Lecture Notes in computer science. Springer-Verlag, London, England, pp. 304-307

Dey, A. K.; Abowd, G. D. & Salber, D. (2001). A conceptual framework and a toolkit for supporting the rapid prototyping of context-aware applications, *Human-computer interaction*, vol. 16

EMF (2009). Available from http://www.eclipse.org/modeling/emf

EuGENia (2011). Available from http://www.eclipse.org/gmt/epsilon/doc/eugenia/

Gábor, V.; Andersson, B. & Wohed, P. (2004). An Ontology based Analysis of BPEL4WS and WSCI. *Proceedings of the 3rd Nordic Conference on Web Services (NCWS 2004)*, ISBN 91-7636-431-3. Växjö, Sweden

GAgenda (2011). Google Agenda API. Available from http://code.google.com/intl/pt-BR/apis/calendar/

Gajderowicz, B. (2011). Using decision trees for inductively driven semantic integration and ontology matching. Thesis, Ryerson University, Program of Computer Science. Available from http://www.scs.ryerson.ca/~bgajdero/msc_thesis/document/b-gajderowicz-msc-thesis.pdf

GDirections (2011). Google Directions API. Available from http://code.google.com/intl/pt-BR/apis/maps/documentation/directions/

GGCoding (2011). Google GeoCoding API. Available from http://code.google.com/intl/pt-BR/apis/maps/documentation/geocoding/

GMF (2010). Graphical Modeling Framework (Graphical Modeling Project - GMP). Available from http://www.eclipse.org/modeling/gmp

George, A. A. & Ward, P. A. (2008). An architecture for providing context in WS-BPEL processes, *Proceedings of the 2008 conference of the center for advanced studies on collaborative research: meeting of minds*, New York, NY, USA, Article 22

Grassi, V. & Sindico, A. (2009). Model driven development of context aware software systems, *Proceedings of International Workshop on Context-Oriented Programming*, New York, USA, pp. 1-5

Hoyos, J. R.; Molina, J. G. & Botia, J. A. (2010). MLContext: A Context-Modeling Language for Context-Aware Systems, *Proceedings of Electronic Communications of the European Association of Software Science and Technology*

JBDrools (2009). JBoss Drools. Available from http://www.jboss.org/drools/drools-flow

Noy, N. F. (2004). Semantic integration: A survey of ontology-based approaches. *SIGMOD Record*, 33(4), Dec. 2004

OWLAPI (2011). The OWL API. Available from http://owlapi.sourceforge.net/index.html

Patrício, R. F. (2010). CEManTIKA CASE: uma ferramenta de apoio ao desenvolvimento de Sistemas Sensíveis ao Contexto, UFPE, Recife, Pernambuco, Brasil

Peltz, C. (2003). Web Service Orchestration and Choreography. Available from http://wpage.unina.it/rcanonic/didattica/at/documenti/wsOrchestration.pdf

Protégé (2011). Protégé Ontology Editor. Available from http://protege.stanford.edu/

Reinisch, C.; Granzer, W.; Fraus, F. & Kastner, W. (2008). Integration of Heterogeneous Building Automation Systems using Ontologies. *Proc. of the 34th Annual Conference of the IEEE Industrial Electronics Society (IECON '08)*, Nov. 2008, pp. 2736–2741

Schmidt, D. C. (2006). Guest Editor's Introduction: Model-Driven Engineering. IEE Computer 39(2), pp. 25-31

Sheng, Q. Z. & Benatallah, B. (2005). ContextUML: A UML-based modeling language for model-driven development of context-aware web services, *Proceedings of the International Conference on Mobile Business*, Washington, DC, USA, pp. 206-212

Simons, C. 2007. CMP: A UML context modeling profile for mobile distributed systems, *Proceedings of the 40th Annual Hawaii International Conference on System Sciences*, Hawaii, USA

Topcu, F. (2011). Context modeling and reasoning. Available from http://www.snet.tu-berlin.de/fileadmin/fg220/courses/SS11/snet-project/context-modeling-and-reasoning_topcu.pdf

Vieira, V. 2008. CEManTIKA: A domain-independent framework for designing context-sensitive systems, Centro de Informática - UFPE, Recife, Pernambuco, Brasil

XMLBeans (2009). Apache XML Beans 2.5. Available from http://xmlbeans.apache.org/

XSD (2001). W3C XML Schema 1.1. Available from http://www.w3.org/XML/Schema

Yamato, Y.; Nakano, Y. & Sunaga, H. (2010). *Context-aware service composition and change-over using BPEL engine and semantic web*. Intech Open Access Publisher. Rijeka, Croatia

YWForecast (2011). Yahoo Weather. Available from http://developer.yahoo.com/weather/

Wang, X. H.; Gu, T.; Zhang, D. Q. & Pung, H. K. (2004). Ontology based context modeling and reasoning using OWL, *Proceedings of the 2004 communication networks and distributed systems modeling and simulation conference*, San Diego, CA, USA

WSBPEL (2007). OASIS Web Service Business Process Execution Language (WSBPEL) 2.0. Available from http://www.oasis-open.org/committees/wsbpel/

Section 2

Applications: Semantic Cache, E-Health, Sport Video Browsing, and Power Grids

4

Semantic Cache System

Munir Ahmad, Muhammad Abdul Qadir, Tariq Ali,
Muhammad Azeem Abbas and Muhammad Tanvir Afzal
Centre for Distributed and Semantic Computing,
Faculty of Computing,
Mohammad Ali Jinnah University Islamabad,
Pakistan

1. Introduction

One of the economical ways to develop a very large scale database is to distribute it among multiple server nodes. Main problem in these types of systems is retrieval of data within significant time; especially when network or server load is high. This task becomes more critical when data is to be retrieved from the database against frequent queries. Cache is used to increase the retrieval performance of mobile computing and distributed database systems. Whenever data is found locally from the cache it is termed as cache hit. Percentage of user posed queries that can be processed (partially or fully) locally from cache is called hit ratio. So, the cache system should be designed in a way that will increase the hit ratio. Improvement in hit ratio ensures efficient reuse of stored data. Due to efficient reuse of stored data, lesser amount of data is required to be retrieved from remote location.

Typically, cache is organized in three ways, as page, tuple, and semantic. Unit of transfer in page cache is *page* (multiple tuples) and in tuple cache is a *tuple*. In page cache irrelevant tuples may be retrieved for a user query. Retrieval of irrelevant data causes to wastage of valuable resources. Tuple cache overcomes this problem by stopping the retrieval of irrelevant tuples. Major problem (retrieving portion of tuple instead of complete tuple) still exists which cannot be handled using both (page & tuple) of these caching models. These caching schemes (page & tuple) are not able to identify whether the answer is contained in the cache in case of query not fully matched (partial matched). In page and tuple cache schemes all of the data is retrieved from remote site even in the presence of partial data on cache. In simple words portion of page or portion of tuple cannot be reused in the presences of page or tuple caching. As a result hit ratio is not up to that extent to which it should be.

To answer the queries partially from local site concept of semantic cache is introduced. Semantic cache has an ability to increase the hit ratio up to possible extent. Semantic cache provides better performance than page and tuple cache and this system is referred as semantic caching. Semantic caching provides the significance workload reduction in distributed systems, especially in mobile computing as well as improves the performance.

In semantic caching the semantic descriptions of processed query with actual contents are stored. Next posed query is processed for stored semantic descriptions of data in the cache and posed query is divided into probe (portion available at cache) and remainder (portion that is not available at cache and have to retrieved from cache) queries. In this context we can say that there are two major activities query processing and cache management are involved in semantic caching. So, efficiency of the semantic caching will depends on these two major activities (query processing and cache management). Query processing is the process which returns the result against user posed query. In semantic cache query processing is done by dividing the user query into probe and remainder queries on the base of query matching. In fact, efficiency of query processing will depend on the efficiency of division process (query trimming) of user query into sub queries (probe and remainder) as well as on retrieval time against both probe and remainder queries. However, efficiency of query trimming will depends on the semantic indexing. In fact, semantic indexing at cache is a major activity of cache management. In this context we can say that efficient semantic caching system demands efficient query processing and indexing scheme. In this chapter we have discussed the state of art query processing techniques and semantic indexing scheme. We also have presented a query processing scheme sCacheQP and its complete working. Working of sCacheQP is explained with the help of case study.

2. Definitions

This section presents some definitions that are used in rest of the chapter.

Definition 1: Given a user query $Qu = \pi_A\sigma_{P(R)}$; where '*A*' is set of attributes required by user, '*P*' is a condition (WHERE clause) of the user query, and '*R*' is a relation. **User Query's Semantics** will be 3-tupple $<Q_S, Q_F, Q_W>$ where Q_S is a set of required attributes, Q_F is a relation, and Q_W is a condition.

Definition 2: Given a database $D = \{Ri\}$ and its attributes set $A = UA_{Ri}$, $1 \le i \le n$, **Semantic Enabled Schema** will be 6-tupple $<D, R, A, S_A, P, C>$ where '*D*' is the name of database, '*R*' is name of relation, '*A*' is a set of attributes, is a status of attributes, '*P*' is predicate (condition) on which data has been retrieved and cached, and '*C*' is the refrence of contents.

Definition 3: Given a user query $Qu = \pi_A\sigma_{P(R)}$ and Q_C having semantics $<D, R, A, S_A, P, C>$; **Data Set Du** and **Dc** will be retrieved rows in the result of execution of *Qu and* Q_C respectively.

Definition 4: Given a user query Q_U and cached query Q_C with semantics $< Q_S, Q_F, Q_W>$ and $<D, R, A, S_A, P, C>$ respectively; **Probe Query (pq)** will be **Du ∩ Dc**.

Definition 5: Given a user query Q_U and cached query Q_C with semantics $< Q_S, Q_F, Q_W>$ and $<D, R, A, S_A, P, C>$ respectively; **Remainder Query (rq)** will be (**Du** - **Dc**).

Definition 6: Given a user query Q_U and cached query Q_C with semantics $< Q_S, Q_F, Q_W>$ and $<D, R, A, S_A, P, C>$ respectively; **Query Matching** is a process in which user query's semantics $<Q_S, Q_F, Q_W>$ are matched with semantic enabled schema $<D, R, A, S_A, P, C>$. It is further divided into two processes; attribute and predicate matching.

Definition 7: Given a user query Q_U and cached query Q_C with semantics $< Q_S, Q_F, Q_W>$ and $<D, R, A, S_A, P, C>$ respectively; **Attribute Matching** is a process in which user query's attributes $<Q_S>$ are matched with attributes indexed by semantic enabled schema $<A>$. Common attributes (C_A) $Q_S \cap A$ and difference attributes (D_A) $Q_S - A$ are calculated for probe and remainder queries respectively.

Definition 8: Given a user query Q_U and cached query Q_C with semantics < Q_S, Q_F, Q_W> and <*D*, *R*, *A*, S_A, *P*, *C*> respectively; **Predicate Matching** is a process in which user query's condition <Q_W> is matched with condition indexed by semantic enabled schema <*P*>.

Definition 9: Given a user query Q_U and cached query Q_C with semantics < Q_S, Q_F, Q_W, P_A> and <*D*, *R*, *A*, S_A, *P*, *C*>; **Query Trimming** is a process in which user query (Q_U) is divided into probe and remainder query.

Definition 10: Given a user predicate Q_W and cached predicate *P*; **Predicate Implication** ($Q_W \rightarrow P$) holds if and only if Q_W completely overlapped with *P*.

Definition 11: Given a user predicate Q_W and cached predicate *P*; **Predicate Satisfiablity** holds if and only if Q_W partially overlapped with *P*.

Definition 12: Given a user predicate Q_W and cached predicate *P*; **Predicate Unsatisfiablity** holds if and only if Q_W is not overlapped with *P*.

Definition 13: Given a user query Q_U and cached query Q_C with semantics < Q_S, Q_F, Q_W, P_A> and <*D*, *R*, *A*, S_A, *P*, *C*>; **Query Implications** holds if and only if $Q_S \subseteq A$ as well as predicate implication holds.

Definition 14: Given a user query Q_U and cached query Q_C with semantics < Q_S, Q_F, Q_W, P_A> and <*D*, *R*, *A*, S_A, *P*, *C*>; **Query Satisfiability** holds if and only if $Q_S \cap A \mathrel{!=} \Phi$ as well as predicate implication/satisfiability holds.

Definition 15: Given a user query Q_U and cached query Q_C with semantics < Q_S, Q_F, Q_W, P_A> and <*D*, *R*, *A*, S_A, *P*, *C*>; **Query Unsatisfiaility** holds either $Q_S \cap A = \Phi$ or predicate implication/satisfiability does not holds.

3. State of the art

This section presents the brief related work to semantic caching in the context of semantic indexing and query (*SELECT and PROJECT*) processing for relational databases. For detail work survey done by Ahmad et al. (Ahmad et al, 2008) can be considered and for aggregate queries is discussed by Cai et al (Cai et al, 2005). Semantic caching is extensively studied by researchers in both relational and XML databases. In fact, query processing and cache management are two main areas of semantic cache system. In this section we have described the state of the art query processing as well as semantic indexing schemes.

Results of already executed queries are cached to generate more efficient query plans for centralized systems (Roussopoulosl, 1991). Some strategies are defined for cache to prefecth the data by using semantics (Kang et al, 2006). Query refinement technique is introduced to enhance the response time in multimedia databases (Chakrabarti et al, 2000). A predicate based scheme for cache is presented by Keller et al. for client server applications (Keller and Basu, 1996). A scheme with the name of Intelligent Cache Management (Chen et al, 1994) and its extensions are introduced (Ahmed et al, 2005, Altinel et al, 2003, Bashir and Qadir, 2007) to reduce the overhead of page and tuple cache. To answer the queries partially from local site; concept of semantic cache on the base of implication (Sun et al, 1989) and the base of description logic (Ali et al, 2010, Ali and Qadir, 2010) is introduced to increase the hit ratio up to possible extent (Bashir and Qadir 2007, Ahmad et al, 2008a). Idea of amending query is introduced to increase the hit ratio (Ren et al, 2003), graph based query trimming to enhance efficiency (Abbas et al, 2010) and 112 rules (Bashir and Qadir, 2007b) are defined to reduce query processing time by efficient query matching. Rules (112) are only applicable for simple queries (excluding the disjunct or conjunct operator). Jonsson and colleagues presents query matching scheme by using predicate of query (Jonsson et al, 2006). This scheme is not able to handle the SELECT CLAUSE of SQL queries. Query matching algorithm that reduces query processing time in the domain of relational database is also studied in our previous work (Ahmad et al, 2008a, Ahmad et al, 2008, Ahmad et al, 2009]. Work in semantic cache in other domains like web [Lee et al, 1995, Luo et al, 2003] and XML (Chen et al, 2002, Sanaullah et al, 2008) also studied in literature. Importance of semantic cache and disadvantages of page and tuple cache is presented [Ren et al, 2003, Dar et al, 1996] by providing comparisons of semantic cache with page and tuple cache.

There are different structures used to index the semantic description like; flat structure (Dar et al, 1996), 3-level hierarchal (Sumalatha et al, 2007a, 2007b, 2007c) segments (Ren et al, 2003), and 4-HiSIS (Bashir and Qadir, 2007). When semantics of queries are store in a flat structure (Dar et al, 1996) the query matching process is very expensive (time consuming) (Godfrey et al, 1997, Ahmad et al, 2008, Ahmad et al, 2009). Cache is divided into segments (Ren et al, 2003) and chunks (Deshpande et al, 1998) to reduce the cost. Runtime complexity and caching efficiency is improved by division of cache into segments and chunks. List of chunks is build on the base of previous queries and then this list of chunks is used to split the user posed (new) queries into two portions; one answered locally from cache and the second computed remotely (Deshpande et al, 1998). 4-level hierarchal semantic indexing scheme (*4-HiSIS*) is introduced to accelerate the semantic matching (Bashir and Qadir, 2006). In 4-HiSIS; semantic matching accomplished in four steps. At first; database name is matched. After successful matching of the database name; the relation name is matched in the second step. At third, attributes are matched at successful matching of relation match. In the final step predicate matching is performed on the based of successful matching of first three steps. There is a limitation of 4-HiSIS in the context of incompleteness; because there is no refrence of actual contents of cache is stored in 4-HiSIS. This limitation is overcomed by the graph based semantic indexing scheme (Ahmad et al, 2010) by storing the refrence of actual contents. In graph based semantic indexing scheme the matching procedure is performed in five steps. At the state of art graph based indexing is most efficient semantic indexing scheme. It also have a limitation; it has no ability to process the " *Select ** " type and incorrect queries in cache system.

State of the art semantic cache system has limitation in both areas (query processing and cache management i.e semantic indexing schemes). In this chapter we have presented the new scheme for semantic cache query processing. We named this system as sCacheQP. sCacheQP has an ability to overcome the limitaion in the context of query processing which is the main area of the semantic cahce system.

4. Semantic Cache Query Processing (sCacheQP)

This section presents the sCacheQP which is a complete procedure of query processing that overcomes the limitaions of the previous systems. Working and main driver algorithm of the sCacheQP is given in Figure 1 and Figure 2 respectively.

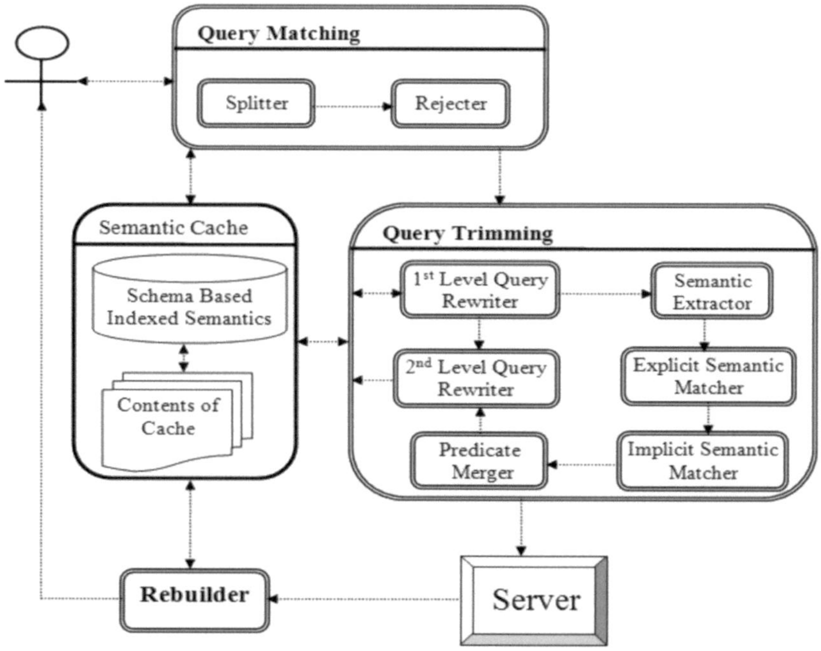

Fig. 1. Working of sCacheQP.

Algrithm1: sCacheQP
INPUT: Q_U (User query)
OUTPUT: F_R (Result against Q_U)
PROCEDURE:

1. Initialization:
   pq:=NULL
   rq1:=NULL
   rq2:=NULL
2. *PORTIONS* := *SPLIT_QUERY* (Q_U)
3. *Reject* := *CHECK_REJECTION* (*PORTIONS*)
4. if (Reject =false) goto step 5 otherwise Reject query and goto step 15
5. C_A, D_A :=1st_Level_Query_Rewriter (Q_S)
6. If(D_A != empty) goto step 7 otherwise goto step 8
7. rq1 := $\pi_{DA}\sigma_{QP}(Q_R)$
8. If (C_A !=empty) goto step 9 otherwise goto step 14.
9. M_C, N_{MCC}, N_{MCU}, *Dvc*, *Dvu* ,*Opc*, *Opu*, *Coc*, *Cou*:=Semantic_Extraction(Q_W, S_W)
10. C_1, N_{C1}:= ExplicitySemanticMatching(M_C, *Dvc*, *Dvu* ,*Opc*, *Opu*)
11. C_2, N_{C2}:= ImplicitSemanticMatching(*Mc*, N_{MCC}, N_{MCU}, C_1, N_{C1})
12. pq, rq2:=PredicateMerging (C_2, N_{C2}, *Coc*, *Cou*)
13. aq :=*GEN_AMEND_QUERY*()
14. F_R:= Rebuilder(pq,rq1,rq2)
15. Exit.

Fig. 2. Main Algorithm of sCacheQP.

4.1 Query matching

In semantic cache, user posed query is matched with the stored semantics on cache. In this process the decision is taken place either data is available at cache or not. Query matching process is accomplished in two sub process splitter and rejecter. Splitter will accept the user query Q_U from the user interface and splits the query on the base of three clauses (*SELECT, FROM, WHERE*) of the query. These three portions are called Q_S (*SELECT: projected attributes in the user query*), Q_F (*FROM*: Relation) and Q_W (*WHERE*: selected rows/tupples on specific condition); and send to the rejecter for initial level checking. Q_W will be empty if there is no condition on user posed query (Ahmad et al, 2009). Algorithm for splitting the user query is presented by Ahmad et al. (Ahmad et al, 2009) and given in figure 3.

Algorithm 2: *SPLIT_QUERY( )*
INPUT: Q_U (User query)
OUTPUT: Q_S, Q_W, Q_F
PROCEDURE:
    Q_S := *SELECT CLAUSE*
    Q_W := *WHERE CLAUSE*
    Q_F := *FROM CLAUSE*
    Return Q_S, Q_W, Q_F.

Fig. 3. Algorithm to Split Query.

Responsibility of rejecter is to checks the validity of user posed query by sending the list of selected attributes (Q_S), relation (Q_F) and predicate attributes (P_A) on the schema based indexing semantics. Predicate attribute is extracted by rejecter from Q_W and included in the list. If attributes list of QS, Q_F and P_A matched with stored schema then processing will be continued otherwise query will be rejected and processing will be stopped. Rejecter also builds Q_S in the case of '*' by retrieving all attributes from schema as a list if predicate attribute exist in schema (Ahmad et al, 2009). Algorithm to validate the user query is presented by Ahmad et al. (Ahmad et al, 2009) and given in figure 4.

Algorithm 4: *CHECK_REJECTION* (Q_S, Q_F, P_A)
INPUT: Q_S, Q_F, P_A
OUTPUT: True/False(
PROCEDURE:
1. If all attributes of Q_S *present in schema*
    If relation of Q_F *present in schema*
        If P_A *is present in schema*
            If(Qs='')*
                return false and build Qs from schema
            Else return true
        Else return true
    Else return true
Else return true

Fig. 4. Algorithm to Reject Incorrect Queries.

4.2 Query trimming

When it has been decided that data is available at cache then second step of sCacheQP is performed. In this step query is divided into two sub queries called probe and remainder queries called query trimming. This process accomplished in two stages. At first stage vertical partition takes place and the attributes that are not available (D_A) at cache directly sent to the server as rq1 (remainder query) with original predicate. We called it 1st level query rewriter (Ahmad et al, 2009) and its algorithm is given in figure 5. The query rq1 will be computed as follow:

$$rq1 = \pi_{DA}\sigma_{QP}(Q_R)$$

Algorithm 5: *1st_Level_Query_Rewritter* (Q_S)
INPUT: Q_S (*SELECT* Clause)
OUTPUT: rq1, C_A
PROCEDURE:
C_A:= Attributes exist in both Qs and Schema
D_A:= Attributes exist in Qs but not in Schema
Return C_A, D_A

Fig. 5. Algorithm for 1st Level Query Rewriter.

Rest of attributes; that are common in both user and cached query forwarded to the predicate processor which worked at second stage. Predicate processor consists of four sub modules; semantic extractor, Explicit Semantic Matcher, Implicit Semantic Matcher, and Predicate Merger. At this stage predicate is simplified by just separating the portions of it on the base of conjunct and disjunct operators. Then semantics of user's query predicate with respect to the cached predicate is extracted in the form of matching columns (*Mc*- similar in both user query predicate and cached predicate), non-matching columns of cache (*NMc*- columns in cached query that are not matched with user query) and non-matching columns of user query (*NMu*- columns in user query that are not matched with cached query). Some other information like; data value of cache predicate (D_{Vc}), data value of user predicate, (D_{Vu}), comparison operator in cache predicate (*Opc*), comparison operator in user predicate (*Opu*). Algorithm to extract the semantics of predicate is given below in figure 6.

Algorithm 6: Semantics Extractor
Input: Q_W ,S_W
Output:
{*Coc[n], Cou[n], Mc[n],, N_{MCC}[n],, N_{MCU}[n], Opc[n], Opu[n], Dvc[n], Dvu[n]*}
Procedure:
1. *M_C [n]*:= List of Columns Present in both Q_W , S_W
2. *N_{MCC}[n]* := List of Columns Present in S_W but not in Q_W
3. *N_{MCU} [n]*:= List of columns present in Q_W but not in S_W
4. *Opc[n]* := operator set of S_W
5. *Opu[n]* := Operator present set of Q_W
6. *Dvc[n]* := Data values in S_W
7. *Dvu[n]* := Data values in Q_W
8. *Coc[n]*:= Connective Operators in *Sw*
9. *Cou[n]*:= Connective Operators in *Qw*
10. return *Coc[n], Cou[n], Mc[n],, N_{MCC}[n],, N_{MCU}[n], Opc[n], Opu[n], Dvc[n], Dvu[n]*

Fig. 6. Algorithm to Extract Semantics from User Query.

```
Algorithm 7: ExplicitSemanticMatching
Input:{Mc[n], OPc[n], OPu[n], DVc[n], DVu[n], Cc[n i], Cu[n]}
Output: {C1[n], NC1[n]}
Method:
Initilaize: C1[n]:=Null, NC1[n]:=Null, i:=0
Repeat from i to n
If(DVc[i] < DVu[i])
    If((OPc[i] ϵ{!=, >,>=}Λ OPu[i] ϵ{>, >=,=}))
        C1[i]←Cc[i] OPc[i] DVc[i]
        NC1[i]←Null
    else if(OPu[i] ϵ{<, <=, !=})
        C1[i] ←Cc [i]OPc[i] DVc[i]
        NC1[i]←(Cu[i] OPu[i]DVu[i])∧(Cc[i]Rev(OPc[i]) DVc[i])
    else
        C1[i] ←Null
        NC1[i]←(Cu[i] OPu[i] DVu[i])
else if(DVc[i] >DVu[i])
    if((OPc[i]ϵ{!=,<,<=}ΛOPu[i]ϵ{<,<=,=}))
        C1[i] ←Cc[i] OPc [i]DVc[i]
        NC1[i]←Null
    else if(((OPc[i] ϵ{!=, >, =, <=, <}ΛOPu[i]ϵ{>, >=, !=}))
        C1[i] ←Cc[i] OPc[i] DVc[i]
        NC1[i]←(Cu[i] OPu[i] DVu[i])∧(Cc[i]Rev(OPc[i]) DVc[i])
    else
        C1[i] ←Null
        NC1[i]←(Cu[i] OPu[i]DVu[i])
else if((DVc[i] = DVu[i])
    if(((OPc[i]ϵ{>=}Λ( OPu[i] ϵ{ >, =}))
      V (OPc[i] = OPu[i])V((OPc[i] ϵ{<=})Λ (OPu[i] ϵ{<,=}))
      V (OPc[i] ϵ{!=}Λ OPu[i]ϵ{<,>}))
        C1 ←Cc OPc DVc
        NC1←Null
    else if(((OPc[i] ϵ{>, <=}Λ OPu[i] ϵ{ >=, !=})
      V (OPc[i]ϵ{<, >=}ΛOPu[i]ϵ{<=, !=})
      V (OPc[i]ϵ{!=,=}ΛOPu[i]ϵ{<=, >=}))
        C1[i] ←Cc[i] OPc [i]DVc[i]
        NC1[i]←(Cu[i] OPu[i] DVu[i])∧(Cc[i] Rev(OPc[i]) DVc[i])
    else
        C1[i] ←Null
        NC1[i]←(Cu[i] OPu[i] DVu[i])
else if((DVc[i]!= DVu[i]) Λ ((OPc[i] ϵ{=, !=}Λ OPu[i] ϵ{!=}))
        C1[i] ←Cc[i] OPc[i] DVc[i]
        NC1[i]←(Cu[i] OPu[i] DVu[i])∧(Cc[i] Rev(OPc[i]) DVc[i])
else
        C1[i] ←Null
        NC1←(Cu[i] OPu[i] DVu[i])
```

Fig. 7. Algorithm to Evaluate Predicate.

After extraction of semantics *Mc*, D_{Vc}, D_{Vu}, *Opc*, and *Opu* sent to the Explicit Semantic Matcher. Explicit Semantic Matcher trims the predicate into two portions; one for remainder (*C1*) and other for probe query (*NC1*). Explicit Semantic Matching algorithm is based on the boundary values as well as on the nature of comparison operators. There are 112 rules defined on the base of boundary values and basic comparison operators (<, <=, >, >=, = =, !=). Algorithm 7 given in figure 7 is used to match and trims the predicate. The output of predicate matching algorithm is predicate that is available at cache (C1) and predicate that is not available at cache (NC1). Working of the algorithm is explained above.

As we have discussed that Explicit Semantic Matching algorithm is based on the boundary value and basic comparison operator. On the base of boundary value and comparison operators; algorithm 7 will trim the predicate into probe and remainder queries.

Remember that predicate matching algorithm having better time complexity is an alternative of satisfiability/implication (Guo et al, 1996) used to help process query in the literature (Ren et al, 2003, Jonsson et al, 2006). Computed values C1, NC1 and NMu sent to the Implicit Semantic Matching algorithm to remove the additional information. Algorithm 8 is used to perform this job that is given below in figure 8.

Algorithm 8: *ImplicitSemanticMatching*
Input:
    $Mc[n]$, $N_{MCC}[n]$, $N_{MCU}[n]$, $C_1[n]$, $N_{C1}[n]$
Output:
    C_2, N_{C2}
Procedure:
Initiliaze $C_2 := Null$, $N_{C2} := Null, i := Null$
Repeat from i to n
1. If ($N_{MCC}[i]$ = null) and ($N_{MCU}[i]$ = null) then
    a. $C_2 := C_1[i]$
    b. $NC2 := N_{C1}[i]$
2. Else If ($N_{MCC}[i]$!=null) and ($N_{MCU}[i]$ = null) then
    a. $C_2 := (C_1[i]) + (N_{MCC}[i])$
    b. $N_{C2} := ((C_1[i] + R\ (N_{MCC}[i]))V(N_{C1}[i])$
3. Else If ($N_{MCC}[i]$ = null) and ($N_{MCU}[i]$!= null) then
    a. $C_2 := (C_1[i]) + (N_{MCU}[i])$
    b. $N_{C2} := N_{C1}[i] + N_{MCU}[i]$
4. Else If ($N_{MCC}[i]$!= null) and ($N_{MCU}[i]$!= null) then
    a. $C_2 := (C_1[i]) + (N_{MCU}[i]) + (NMc[i])$
    b.$N_{C2} := ((C_1[i]) + R(N_{MCC}[i]) + N_{MCU}[i])V((N_{C1}[i]) + (N_{MCU}[i]))$
5. Else If ($Mc[i]$ = = null) then
    a. $C_2 := (N_{MCC}[i]) + (N_{MCU}[i])$
    b. $N_{C2} := N_{MCU}[i] + R(N_{MCC}[i])$

Fig. 8. Algorithm for Implicit Matching.

Algorithm 9: *PredicateMerging*
Input:
    C_2, N_{C2}, *Coc*, *Cou*
Output:
    Cached, N-Cached
Procedure:
If (*Coc &Cou*)ϵ **Λ**
    Cached = ΛC_i
    N-Cached= $V(C_i\ \Lambda NC_j)$ where 1<i,j<n and i!=j
If(*Coc &Cou*)ϵ**V**
    Cached = VC_i where 1<i<n
    N-Cached= VNC_i where 1<i<n
If(*Coc* ϵ**V** *&Cou*ϵΛ)
    Cached = ΛC_i
    N-Cached= $V(C_i\ \Lambda NC_j)$ where 1<i,j<n and i!=j
If(*Cou* ϵ**V** *&Coc*ϵΛ)
    Cached = ΛC_i
    N-Cached= $V((C_i\ \Lambda NC_j)\ V(U_i \Lambda R(U_j))$
        wher1<i,j<n and i!=j

Fig. 9. Algorithm to Merge the Predicate.

Generated cached (C2) and non-cached (NC2) predicates by the Implicit Semantic Matcher are combined by predicate merger. Algorithm to merge the predicate is given in figure 9.

The computed predicates are then sent to the 2nd level query rewriter. Finally, probe and remainder queries will be computed by the 2nd level query rewriter as follow:

pq = *SELECT* C_A From Q_F *WHERE* Ccache
rq2 = *SELECT* C_A FROM Q_F *WHERE* N-Cached

pq will be executed locally ad rq will sent to the server. Then result of both will be sent to the rebuilder to combine the result.

4.3 Query rebuilding

Rebuilder receives the result form server (S_R) which is retrieved across remainder queries (rq1 and rq2) and results from cache (C_R) across probe query (pq) combines both as a final result F_R. Final result is viewed to the user and also updated in the cache contents if required.

5. Case study

To validate our proposed semantic indexing and query processing, we consider the case study of university.

Figure 10 presents the schema of university with two relations employee and students having 4 and 3 fields respectively.

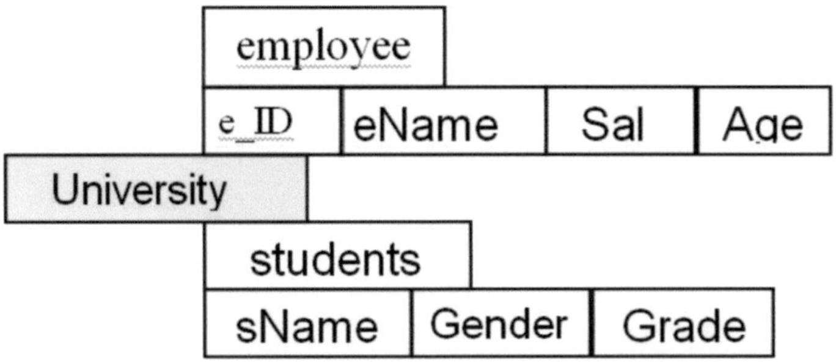

Fig. 10. Schema for University.

For the above given schema of university; there are 15 and 7 segments possible across employee and students relations respectively according to previous work (Ren et al., 2003). In simple words, we can say that there are 15 queries are possible against employee and similarly 7 for students as given in table 1.

In the above example there are 22 possible queries that make separate segments. So the formula to calculate possible segments across a single relation over 'n' attributes is "2n-1". Then add segments across each relation. As in example 15+7 =22: (24-1=15 &23-1=7). Hence, 22 segments are to be visited to check availability of data on cache in the worst case which increases the response time drastically.

S_R	S	S_A	S_P	S_C
employee	S1	e_ID	P1	1
	S2	eName	P1	2
	S3	Sal	P1	3
	S4	Age	P1	4
	S5	e_ID, eName	P3	5
	S6	e_ID, Sal	P4	6
	S7	e_ID, Age	P5	7
	S8	e_ID, eName Sal Age	P6	8
	S9	e_ID Sal Age	P7	9
	S10	e_ID, eName Age	P8	10
	S11	eName Sal	P9	11
	S12	eName Age	P10	12
	S13	Sal Age,eName	P11	13
	S14	e_ID, eName, Sal	P12	14
	S15	Sal, Age	P3	15
students	S16	sName	P21	16
	S17	Grade	P21	17
	S18	Gender	P21	18
	S19	Gender, Grade	P22	19
	S20	Gender, sName	P23	20
	S21	sName, Grade	P24	21
	S22	sName, Grade, Gender	P25	22

Table 1. Possible segments for Given Database.

Schema based hierarchal scheme reduces the number of comparisons to find out whether data is available at cache or not. Only 'n' comparisons are required to check availability of data on cache. Table 1 can be rearranged according to our proposed schema based semantic indexing scheme as in Table 2.

DB Name	**Table Names**	**Fields**	**Status**	**Condition**	**Content**
University	Employee	eName	True	P1	1
		Age	false	Null	Null
		Sal	True	P2	2
		e_ID	True	P3	1
	Students	Gender	false	Null	Null
		Grade	false	Null	Null
		sName	false	Null	Null

Table 2. Schema Based Indexing.

Table 2 represents structure of schema based semantic indexing instead of actual contents. There is only need to compare/match 4 and 3 fields instead of 15 and 7 segments respectively according to previous work. Also it has the ability to reject invalid queries at initial level instead of further processing.

For detailed discussion and simplicity, we consider only employee table of university database. Let us consider there is employee table on server with 4 fields defined in university schema in Figure 10. Employee table on server is given in table 3 below.

e_ID	eName	Age	Sal
110	Asad	20	25000
111	Ali	22	22000
112	Kashif	25	25000
113	Abid	30	15000
114	Adeel	31	42000
115	Komal	37	17000
116	Mahreen	39	30450
117	Tabinda	39	28850
118	Yaseen	40	24450
119	Anees	45	30000
120	Komal	50	30000

Table 3. Employee Table on Database.

Now we divide our case study into five cases in such a way that one can easily understand our contribution and novelty of our approach. For simplicity, each of five cases is discussed standalone and not linked with other. Each case should be considered separately. We have considered that cache is managed from initial for each case.

Case-I: In this case we will take an example that covers the query rejection at initial level.

Let us consider that user has already posed the following query and result has been stored in cache.

*SELECT * FROM* employee *WHERE* age>30

Data on cache will be as given in table 4.

e_ID	eName	Age	Sal
114	Adeel	31	42000
115	Komal	37	17000
116	Mahreen	39	30450
117	Tabinda	39	28850
118	Yaseen	40	24450
119	Anees	45	30000
120	Komal	50	30000

Table 4. Contents on cache in case-I.

Now let us consider user is going to pose following three queries.

1.*SELECT* eName, Age *FROM* emMloyee *WHERE* age>30
(relation is incorrect)
2.*SELECT* eName, Age *FROM* employee *WHERE* gpa>3.0
(predicate attribute is incorrect)
3.*SELECT* ename, rollno *FROM* employee *WHERE* age>30
(Projected attribute is incorrect)

All of three queries should be rejected at initial level; but according to all of previous work query will be posted on server due to unavailability of data on cache.

It is a beauty of our proposed schema based indexing scheme that all of three queries will be rejected and query processing time will be saved. According to our proposed semantic caching architecture list of projected attributes (eName, Age in first query), relation (emMloyee in first query) and predicate attribute is checked from schema based indexing scheme; and query will be rejected due to unavailability of "emMloyee" relation in schema. Similarly, query 2 and 3 will be rejected due to unavailability of "gpa" and "rollno" in employee table respectively and there will be no probe and remainder.

By rejecting query at initial stage; query processing can be saved. In this context our proposed semantic caching scheme has better performance than previous.

Case-II: In this case we will take an example that covers the handling of queries having * in SELECT CLAUSE.

Let us consider that user has already posed the following query and result has been stored in cache.

SELECT eName, Age *FROM* employee *WHERE* age>30

Data for above query will be retrieved and stored on cache will be as given in table 5.

e_ID	eName	Age
114	Adeel	31
115	Komal	37
116	Mahreen	39
117	Tabinda	39
118	Yaseen	40
119	Anees	45
120	Komal	50

Table 5. Contents on cache in case-II.

Note that e_ID is not required but retrieved. It is due to the requirement of key-contained (Ren et al., 2003) contents. Now let us assume that user has posed the following query.

SELECT * *FROM* employee *WHERE* age>30

Now all of the fields of employee required; but according to previous work common set will be calculated (intersection of cached attributes and user's query attributes). There is no way defined to calculate the common set of '*' and some attributes. Here we can say that all of the cached attributes for employee are required, but how can it be decided which of the attributes are not in cache and should retrieved from server.

Here again we need schema at cache (first we need schema for zero level query rejection). If schema is available at cache then SELECT CLAUSE with '*' can be handled easily. By this hit ratio is improved. Splitter splits the query and sent it to the rejecter. Rejecter checks the list of fields with relation and predicate attribute from schema based indexing semantics. Query will not be rejected due to availability of all member of list at schema. Common and difference set of attributes will be computed and sent to the 1st level query matcher. i.e. C_A and D_A will be computed. Remainder query (rq1) with difference attributes (here is only one difference attribute that is 'Sal') will be generated by 1st level query matcher like below.

rq1 = *SELECT* Sal *FROM* employee *WHERE* Age>30

Common attributes (e_ID, Age, eName) will be sent to the Query Generator (QG). Query Generator will generate probe and remainder query on the base of predicate matching. Conditioned attribute (Age) is already retrieved; so there is no need of amending query in this case.

First of semantics of predicate will be computed by semantic extractor as follow.

M_C = Age
NM_C = NULL
NM_U = NULL

After computation of predicate semantics, predicate for probe and remainder query will be computed by using predicate matching algorithm (actually 112 rules are used here). At first, main class of algorithm is selected, here data value of user (DVu=30) is equal to the data value of cache (DVc = 30). So, class 3 of predicate matching will be selected then priority of relational operator will be computed. Relational operator in both queries is '>'; it is low priority (defined in previous work; (Bashir and Qadir, 2007a)) operator. So, following porton of the algorithm will be executed. given below.

$If((O_{Pc} \in \{!=, >, >=\} \wedge O_{Pu} \in \{>, >=, =\}))$
$C_1 \leftarrow C_C\, O_{Pc}\, D_{Vc}$
$N_{C1} \leftarrow$ Null

Here, Cc is Age, operator is '>' and DVc is 30.

So predicate for probe and remainder will be computed we say it C1 (for cached) and NC1 (for non-cached).

C_1 =Age>30
N_{C1} = Null

Due to simple predicate rules defined for complex queries will not be applied. Finally subtraction algorithm will be applied to generate final predicate for probe and remainder queries. As it is computed that NMc and NMu both are Null. So, first case of subtraction algorithm will be applied.

1. **If** (*NMc* = null) and (*NMu* = null)
then
a. $\mathbf{C_2}$:= *C1*
b. $\mathbf{N_{C2}}$:= *NC1*

So, there will be no change in predicate of probe and remainder query. Then, probe query (pq) and second remainder query (rq2) will be generated as below.

pq = SELECT eName, Age FROM employee WHERE Age>30
rq2 = Null

In the last step result of rq1, pq and rq2 is combined by rebuilder.

Case-III: In this case generation of amending query is elaborated.

Let us consider that user has already posed the following query and result has been stored in cache.

SELECT eName, Sal *FROM* employee *WHERE* age>30

Data for above query will be retrieved and stored on cache will be as given in table 6.

E_ID	eName	Sal
114	Adeel	42000
115	Komal	17000
116	Mahreen	30450
117	Tabinda	28850
118	Yaseen	24450
119	Anees	30000
120	Komal	30000

Table 6. Contents on cache in case-III.

Note that e_ID is not required but retrieved. It is due to the requirement of key-contained (Ren et al., 2003) contents. Now let us assume that user has posed the following query.

SELECT eName, Sal *FROM* employee *WHERE* age>35

Here, generation of amending query is discussed. Remaining procedure will be same as discussed in case-II.

Note that data across eName and Sal is present on cache, but predicate attribute (Age) is not on cache. Now some one cannot select the data from cache due to absence of predicate attribute; because some one cannot decide which of the data satisfy the selection criteria (Age>35). To solve this problem, another query called amending query (Ren et al., 2003) to retrieve primary attribute from server on user select criteria as below.

aq = *SELECT* e_ID *FROM* employee *WHERE* Age>35

Then retrieved primary keys will be mapped with keys on cache and data will be presented to user. By this hit ratio is increased.

Case-IV: In this case efficient predicate matching to improve hit ratio by using subtraction algorithm is elaborated with example.

Let us consider that user has already posed the following query and result has been stored in cache.

SELECT eName, Age *FROM* employee *WHERE* Age>30

Data for above query will be retrieved and stored on cache will be as given in table 7.

e_ID	eName	Age
114	Adeel	31
115	Komal	37
116	Mahreen	39
117	Tabinda	39
118	Yaseen	40
119	Anees	45
120	Komal	50

Table 7. Contents on cache in case-IV.

Note that e_ID is not required but retrieved. It is due to the requirement of key-contained (Ren et al., 2003) contents. Now let us assume that user has posed the following query.

SELECT eName, Age *FROM* employee *WHERE* eName = 'Komal'

Now all of the required fields are matched with cached query. Splitter splits the query and sent it to the rejecter. Rejecter checks the list of fields with relation and predicate attribute from schema based indexing semantics. Query will not be rejected due to availability of all member of list at schema. Common and difference set of attributes will be computed and sent to the 1st level query matcher. i.e. C_A and D_A will be computed. Remainder query (rq1) will be null due to empty set of difference attributes (All required attributes are exist on cache). So, remainder query by 1st level query matcher will be like below.

rq1 = *Null*

Common attributes (Age, eName) will be sent to the Query Generator (QG). Query Generator will generate probe and remainder query on the base of predicate matching. Conditioned attribute (Age) is already retrieved; so there is no need of amending query in this case.

First of semantics of predicate will be computed by semantic extractor as follow.

M_C = Null
NM_C = Age
NM_U = eName

After computation of predicate semantics, predicate for probe and remainder query will be computed by using predicate matching algorithm (actually 112 rules are used here). Probe and remainder query will be on the base of these rules like:

CC-QM *← Null*
CNC-QM *← Null*

i.e.

C1 =Null
NC1 = Null

Due to simple predicate rules defined for complex queries will not be applied. Finally subtraction algorithm will be applied to generate final predicate for probe and remainder queries. As it is computed, that NMc and NMu both are not null. So, fourth case of subtraction algorithm will be applied.

4. **Else If** (*NMc* != null) and (*NMu* != null) **then**
a. $\mathbf{C_2}$:= (C_1) + (*NMu*) + (*NMc*)
b. $\mathbf{N_{C2}}$:= ((C_1) + R (*NMc*)+*NMu*)V((NC1)+(NMu))

So, predicate for probe and remainder query will be like below.

C_2 := (Age>30) and (eName = 'Komal')
N_{C2} := (Age<=30) and (eName = 'Komal')

Then, probe query (pq) and second remainder query (rq2) will be generated as below.

```
pq = SELECT eName, Age FROM employee
   WHERE (Age>30) and (eName = 'Komal')
rq2 = SELECT eName, Age FROM employee
   WHERE (Age<=30) and (eName = 'Komal')
```

In the last step result of rq1, pq and rq2 is combined by rebuilder.

6. Conclusion

Caching proved very helpful to reduce the data access latency for distributed and large scale database systems by storing the data against already executed queries. Main problem in caching is to identify the overlapping of required data with stored data. Page and tuple cache are not able to identify the partial overlapping. Semantic cache is capable to answer the overlapped (partially & fully) queries locally. The major challenges of semantic caching are efficient query processing and cache management. For efficient query processing we have proposed and demonstrated the working of sCacheQP system. We have provided complete working and algorithms of sCacheQP. Case study is given to elaborate the sCacheQP. In future, we have a plan to implement the system for data mining and data warehousing.

7. References

Abbas, M.A., Qadir, M.A., Ahmad, M., Ali, T., Sajid, N.A, (2011) "Graph Based Query Trimming of Conjunctive Queries in Semantic Caching", *IEEE International Conference on Emerging Technologies (ICET 2011),* Islamabad, Pakistan, September 5-6, 2011.

Ali, T., Qadir, M.A., Ahmad, M. (2010) "Translation of relational queries into Description Logic for semantic cache query processing" *Information and Emerging Technologies (ICIET) 2010, Karachi Pakistan, 14-16 June 2010*

Ali, T., Qadir, M.A., (2010) "DL based Subsumption Analysis for Relational Semantic Cache Query Processing and Management"10th International Conference on Knowledge Management and Knowledge Technologies, Messe Congress Graz, Austria. 1-3 September 2010

Ahmad, M., Asghar, A., Qadir, M.A., Ali, T. (2010) "Graph Based Query Trimming Algorithm for Relational Data Semantic Cache", *The International Conference on Management of Emergent Digital EcoSystem,* MEDES10, Bangkok, Thailand, October 2010.

Ahmad, M., Qadir, M.A., Razzaque, A., and Sanaullah, M. (2008a), "Efficient Query Processing over Semantic Cache". *Intelligent Systems and Agents, ISA 2008,* indexed by IADIS digital library (www.iadis.net/dl). Held within IADIS Multi Conference on Computer Science and Information Systems (MCCSIS 2008), Amsterdam, Netherland. 22-27 July 2008

Ahmad, M., Qadir, M.A., and Sanaullah, M. (2008b) , "Query Processing over Relational Databases with Semantic Cache: A Survey". *12th IEEE International Multitopic Conference, INMIC 2008, IEEE, Karachi, Pakistan, December 2008.*

Ahmad, M., Qadir, M.A., and Sanaullah, M. (2009) "An Efficient Query Matching Algorithm for Relational Data Semantic Cache". *2nd IEEE conference on computer, control and communication, IC409, 2009.*

Ahmed, M.U, Zaheer, R.A, and Qadir, M.A., (2005). "Intelligent cache management for data grid"; *In Proceedings of the Australasian Workshop on Grid Computing and E-Research,* New South Wales, Australia, 2005.

Altnel, M., Bornhövd, C., Krishnamurthy, C., Mohan, C., Pirahesh, H., and Reinwald, B., (2003)., "Cache Tables: Paving the Way for an Adaptive Database Cache", *Proceedings of the 29th VLDB Conference,* VLDB Endowment, Berlin, Germany, pp. 718-729.

Bashir, M.F and Qadir, M.A., (2006). "HiSIS: 4-Level Hierarchical Semantic Indexing for Efficient Content Matching over Semantic Cache". *INMIC, IEEE,* Islamabad, Pakistan, pp. 211-214.

Bashir, M.F and Qadir, M.A., (2007). "ProQ - Query Processing Over Semantic Cache For Data Grid", *Center for Distributed and Semantic Computing,* Mohammad Ali Jinnah University, Islamabad, Pakistan 2007.

Bashir, M.F., Zaheer, R.A., Shams, Z.M. and Qadir, M.A., (2007). "SCAM: Semantic Caching Architecture for Efficient Content Matching over Data Grid". *AWIC,*Springer Heidelberg, Berlin, 2007. pp. 41-46.

Chakrabarti, K., Porkaew. K., and Mehrotra, S., (2000). "Efficient Query Refinement in Multimedia Databases", *16th International conference on Data Engineering,* IEEE, 2000.

Cai, J., Jia, Y., Yang, S., and Zou, P., (2005) "A Method of Aggregate Query Matching in Semantic Cache for Massive Database Applications". *Springer-Verlag,* Berlin Heidelberg 2005, pp. 435-442.

Chen, C.M. and Roussopoulos, N., (1994). "The Implementation and Performance Evaluation of the ADMS Query Optimizer: Integrating Query Result Caching and Matching," Proc. Int'l Conf. Extending Database Technology, pp. 323-336.

Chen, L., Rundesteiner, E.A., Wang, S., (2002). "XCache -A Semantic Caching System for XML Queries". *In Proceedings of the 2002 ACM SIGMOD international Conference on Management of Data,* ACM Press, New York, pp. 618-618.

Dar, S., Franklin, M.J., Jonnson, B.T., (1996). "Semantic Data Caching and Replacement," *Proceeding of VLDB Conference,* VLDB, pp. 330-341.

Deshpande, P.M. Ramasamy, K., and Shukla, A., (1998). "Caching Multidimensional Queries Using Chunks", *ICMD,* ACM, New York, USA, 1998, pp. 259-270.

Godfrey, P. and Gryz, J., (1997). "Semantic Query Caching for Heterogeneous Databases," *In Proc. 4th KRDB Workshop "Intelligent Access to Heterogeneous Information"*, Athens, Greece, pp.61-66.

Guo, S., Sun, W., and Weiss, M.A., (1996). "Solving Satisfiability and Implication Problems in Database Systems," *Database Systems,* ACM, pp. 270-293.

Jonsson, B. T., Arinbjarnar, M., Thorsson, B., Franklin, M., and Srivastava, D., (2006). "Performance and overhead of semantic cache management", *Internet Technology,* ACM, New York, USA pp. 302–331.

Kang, S.W., Kim, J., Im, S., Jung, H., and Hwang, C.S., (2006). "Cache Strategies for Semantic Prefetching Data", *Proceedings of the Seventh International Conference on Web-Age Information Management Workshops,* IEEE, 2006.

Keller, A.M. and Basu, J., (1996). "A Predicate-Based Caching Scheme for Client-Server Database Architectures", *International Journal* on *Very Large Database,* Springer, Heidelberg, Berlin, , pp. 35-47.

Lee, D. and Chu, W.W., (1999). "Semantic Caching via Query Matching for Web Sources," Proc. CIKM, ACM, Kansas City, USA, pp. 77-85.

Luo, Q., Naughton, J. F., Krishnamurthy, R., Cao, P., and Li, Y., (2000). "Active Query Caching for Database Web Servers", Third International Workshop WebDB on The World Wide Web and Databases Springer, London, UK, pp. 92-104.

Ren, Q., Dunham, M.H., and Kumar, V., (2003). "Semantic Caching and Query Processing". Knowledge and Data Engineering, IEEE Computer Society, 2003, pp. 192-210.

Roussopoulos, N. An incremental Access Method for View Cache: Concept, Algorithms, and Cost Analysis," ACM Trans.Database Systems, vol. 16, no. 3, 1991, 535-563.

Sanaullah, M., Qadir, M.A., and Ahmad, M., (2008) "SCAD-XML: Semantic Cache Architecture for XML Data Files using XPath with Cases and Rules ". 12th IEEE International Multitopic Conference, INMIC 2008, IEEE, Karachi, Pakistan, December 2008.

Sumalatha, M.R., Vaidehi, V., Kannen, A., Rajasekar, M., Karthigaiselven, M., (2007). "Hash Mapping Strategy for Improving Retrieval Effectiveness in Semantic Cache System", ICSCN, IEEE, Chennai, India, pp. 233-237.

Sumalatha, M.R., Vaidehi, V., Kannen, A., Rajasekar, M., Karthigaiselven, M., (2007). "Dynamic Rule Set Mapping Strategy for the Design of Effective Semantic Cache", ICACT, IEEE, Gangwon-Do, Korea, pp. 1952-1957.

Sumalatha, M.R., Vaidehi, V., Kannen, A., Rajasekar, M., Karthigaiselven, M., (2007). "Xml Query Processing - Semantic Cache System". IJCSNS, pp. 164-169.

Sun, X., Kamel, N.N., and Ni, L.M., (1989). "Processing Implication on Queries", Software Engineering, IEEE, Piscataway, USA, pp. 1168-1175.

5

Semantic Interoperability in E-Health for Improved Healthcare

Saman Iftikhar[1], Wajahat Ali Khan[1], Farooq Ahmad[1] and Kiran Fatima[2]
[1]School of Electrical Engineering and Computer Sciences
National University of Sciences and Technology, Islamabad,
[2]Department of Computer Sciences
National University of Computer and Emerging Sciences, Islamabad,
Pakistan

1. Introduction

One of the challenges faced nowadays by the healthcare industry is semantic interoperability. It is the ability of a healthcare system to share information and have that information properly interpreted by the receiving system in the same sense as intended by the transmitting system. Semantic Web (aka Web 3.0) provides the enabling technologies to achieve semantic interoperability. Web Services, as a catalyst in this process, provide seamless communication of information between healthcare systems thus providing better access to patient information and improved healthcare.

Semantic technologies are emerging and several applications ranging from business process management to information security have demonstrated encouraging prospects of its benefits. Role of semantics is also very vital for achieving interoperability in sharing of health records. The aim of this chapter is to establish research and development in the domain of Health Level 7 (HL7) as an application to provide e-health services for the diverse communities. Through this research process, we intend to develop HL7 interface software for healthcare information systems that will provide semantic interoperability between the communicating medical systems. The objective is to facilitate e-health services that are interoperable among a number of domains in this field such as laboratory, patient administration and pharmacy. After its development and testing in the end-user environment, this software solution will be made publicly available under an open-source license. Due to its cutting-edge nature, this software solution has the potential of establishing an international repute for Pakistan in the highly profitable and potent healthcare industry. Since healthcare is a sensitive and critical area as it involves life of human beings, this project will be conducted in a manner to ensure that the resulting software is secure, reliable and maintainable.

This mostly involves research and implementation challenges. Some initiatives are already underway such as Health Services Specification Project (HSSP). It is a joint-venture of HL7 and Object Management Group (OMG), providing standardized service interface specifications. Following the traces of HSSP, our proposal is aimed to design and implement concrete SOA model. The ultimate goal is to define the HL7 Web services as Semantic Web services. Web Services Modeling Framework will provide the platform for automatic web service discovery, composition, and invocation that makes the technology scalable. This purpose of this chapter is to bring improvement in electronic health records by integrating it with semantic web services and semantic registries that will eventually lead to healthcare interoperable systems. One important part is the integration of Service Oriented Architecture (SOA) with HL7. HL7 Pakistan NUST, more specifically, has designed a prototype for the laboratory domain and it has been successfully implemented at the CITI Lab (a local testing laboratory). This successful initial prototype has provided us the baseline to enhance it by embedding semantics in the system in order to enable semantic interoperability.

1.1 Background and rationale

Healthcare systems are critical and demand high accuracy, prompt availability and interoperability. The right use of information and communication system can play vital role in achieving the said requirements; but unfortunately healthcare systems are used mostly as a replacement to manual patient logging. The critical need is to encourage healthcare systems to be more efficient and provide more workable solutions like other industries that have benefited from it e.g. banking, traffic systems and so on. When a patient moves from hospital to hospital, he needs to take all the records and reports with him which is difficult to manage especially in emergency situations. Manual healthcare data system is not only prone to error and loss but also it is not feasible to manage massive data and access any particular record from it. Using healthcare data electronically results in cost-effective, easily accessible, accurate and manageable data processing solutions. In Pakistan, very few healthcare organizations so far have become capable of storing healthcare data electronically but it comes without the ability to share the information. This is mostly due to lack of awareness and implementation of information exchange standards.

Standardization provides us an effective way of communication to achieve the goal of interoperability. HL7 is one of the healthcare standards that allow communication and integration of healthcare systems and allow sharing of data around the globe. The important requirement is to capture relevant information and then make it widely available for others. Therefore, the need is to have a standard that can provide best services in terms of efficiency and reliability. HL7, as it evolves, provides us with a technical business model to fulfill this vision of a diverse, integrated health information system.

The two most important issues that the healthcare industry is facing are integration and interoperability of systems. Countries are not willing to invest in healthcare industry until and unless the healthcare systems to be adopted by them provide interoperability. HL7 is a messaging standard that is used for the exchange of medical information between different communicating parties or devices. The most commonly used versions of HL7 are HL7 V2.x and HL7 V3. HL7 V 2.x is mainly focused on the transfer of message from sender to the receiver rather on interoperability. HL7 V3 focused on the shortcomings of HL7 V2.x and overcome those by targeting semantic interoperability (Neotool). HL7 V3 is based on the standard model called Reference Information Model (RIM). Another potential capability is to make HL7 V3 based systems SOA complaint.

The innovation and the standardization of web services have set the concept of web services as the basic building blocks of information technology systems for Service Oriented

Architectures (SOA) applications. SOA is a solution to handle complex business processes and to achieve interoperability.

Healthcare is a many-to-many business so to cater complexities and bring interoperability among heterogeneous systems; a business process model is required. SOA for our project requires certain standardized specifications to follow in order to claim the compliance with standards. These specifications are formulated mainly by coordination of HL7 and OMG group, under the name of Healthcare Services Specification Project (HSSP). HSSP gives Service Functional Models (SFM) which specifies interface specifications and not the implementation specifications. The document "Service Oriented Architecture and HL7 V3 Methodology" by Special Interest Group (SOA SIG), gives approach for implementing healthcare services in Healthcare domain. Another important document in this series is "The Practical Guide for SOA in Health Care" by HSSP gives concrete guidelines along with mega SOA architecture for Healthcare. These documents are providing main guidelines in our work for getting SOA workflows.

Although SOA framework can be used for designing interoperable systems yet it is not a proper solution for providing true interoperability, i.e. the semantic interoperability. Semantic interoperability is the way to intelligently interpret the transferred knowledge among communicating machines and provide accurate desired results. HL7 V3 provides specifications for different domains like patient administration, specimen, laboratory, observation etc. Every domain supports data and processes particular to that domain in addition to some common elements that are shared among multiple domains. The main focus of this thesis is to bring semantics in the interactions included in laboratory domain. This work refined the meaning of semantic interoperability by representing the interactions and other artifacts with ontologies rather only limited to the vocabulary representation supported by HL7 V3 (Beeler et al., 1999).

In HL7 the semantic interoperability can be seen from two perspectives; data and process. The potentials of semantic data interoperability remain incomplete without semantic process interoperability. Achieving interoperable data would be less effective if there is no semantics in the communication components which can only be achieved when the process is interoperable. Semantic data interoperability means understanding of the data communicated between sender and receiver in such a way that the receiver easily interprets the sender intension of sending the data and properly responds. On the other hand semantic process interoperability is the type of semantic interoperability, which helps in the decision process of the participating parties in communication of HL7 messages on the basis of data contents intended to be exchanged for automation. For bringing semantic interoperability in the HL7 processes, semantic web services are followed for the communication.

HL7 V3 claims to provide semantic interoperability but it only focuses on the semantic data interoperability and semantic process interoperability is still a grey area. HL7 V3 provides data interoperability in the form of terminologies by using vocabularies like SNOMED CT (SNOMED Clinical Terms, 2009), LOINC (LOINC) and HL7's own vocabulary. But semantic interoperability cannot be catered by only taking in to account specified terminologies. To achieve semantic interoperability there is a need of a framework that can support the required constructs for semantic interoperability. Web Service Modeling Framework (WSMF) provides Web Service Modeling Ontology (WSMO) which contains the entities like ontologies, mediators, web services and goals.

One technique for achieving semantic process interoperability is to use simple web services. Web services provide a standard means of interoperable communication between heterogeneous software applications. The complexity is increased for web services when semantic and syntactic heterogeneities are brought in to consideration for the transfer of messages between systems. Therefore, there is a need of using semantic web services for achieving semantic process interoperability. Semantic web services can be used for enhancing the web services capabilities in understanding semantics such that it can be more easily machine process able. This will result in better machine understanding of the web services and the communication would be more effective. Semantic web services should have proper precondition, post-condition, effects and assumptions. There are different approaches used for realizing semantic web services but WSMO is the most preferable as it is the most effective and complete approach amongst all.

There is a need to explore such sophisticated SOA technologies that make the discovery of services for requested users appropriate. In service oriented computing services are used to develop fast, economical, interoperable, evolvable, and extremely distributed applications. Services are self-governing, platform-independent entities that can be described, published, discovered, and loosely coupled. Semantic registries are required for the handling and accessing meaningful information over the semantic web. In present, the services are described, registered and accessed without semantics which is not efficient if the services are to be discovered precisely. In semantic registries the discovery of services is all about the finding of desirable services semantically which have knowledgeable significant properties and relationships. Therefore, the services have to be expressed semantically in semantic registries, so that the semantically described services can be machine comprehensible and precisely used by applications for interoperability of processes through semantic registries and results in semantic SOA.

The issue in using such standards like HL7 V3 is to provide tools and encourage its usage through making them integrated with the existing healthcare systems. Also these standards can be more utilized by following frameworks such as SOA and WSMF. These frameworks can help HL7 standard to achieve true interoperability. In this project our emphasis is to make such open source tools that will help the healthcare industry in achieving such targets.

1.2 Scope and objectives

- To develop standardized services that should be reusable, cost effective and self-maintainable; setting the stage for interoperability in healthcare services.
- To create a hybrid platform by incorporating HL7 V3 standard and Service-Oriented Architecture.
- To model complex healthcare processes in well-defined business language and to capture real life business scenarios, rather than technology-specific terminologies and grammar.
- To contribute the developed platform to the open-source community so other healthcare organizations and hospitals, within and outside the, country can reuse and customize this solution to their specific requirements with minimum efforts.
- To train a reasonable number of professionals and researchers as HL7 based IT researchers, developers as well as users of the HL7 application in the medical related discipline.

1.3 Methodology

The HLH studio architecture as shown in Figure 1 will be used initially to create and parse HL7 V3 message using Java SIG API. The Java SIG API supports generation and parsing of any type of V 3 messages while making corresponding Hierarchical Message Description's (HMD) available. During creation of HL7 message, the HL7 builder tool consumes in-memory Refined Message Information Model (RMIM) objects and taking meta-data from HMDs to create valid serialized XML based message specified by HMD, while in message parsing, the parser tool consumes XML message, validates it against HMD and creates in memory RMIM object graph.

The message generation and parsing is only limited to the Laboratory and Patient Administration domains, their specifications are provided in the HL7 Normative, 2009. The message generation and parsing is the first step towards interoperability. This standard message can then be communicated between communicating parties.

HL7 is a standard used for information exchange among healthcare systems. SOA, on the other hand, is an architecture that enables business agility through the use of common services. HL7 stakeholders realized that by bringing these two realms at one place will generate revolutionary benefits for healthcare. SOA architecture mainly causes interoperable and easy accessible communication which HL7 V3 conventional Messaging Infrastructure (MI) cannot provide.

SOA framework, unlike MI, encompasses service creation, hosting and communication capabilities at one place. Our project needs the basic three elements of SOA; i.e. Producer, Consumer and registry to be realized for rejuvenating our healthcare environment. The producers will be the healthcare organizations, and the consumers are the patients, doctors and other healthcare community. As SOA provides communication according to business case, it supports the academic and business community to get enormous potentials for research and development in healthcare sector. The underlying infrastructure is based on web services, for which HSSP is providing specifications.

Based upon the lessons learned from HSSP specifications, for SOA framework there are some steps that are to be followed. As we are analyzing laboratory and patient administration domain for our case study to be implemented, the laboratory domain artifacts would be analyzed initially. We have to identify services in the laboratory domain by investigating application roles and their interactions. This will lead to decision on operations by studying storyboards, constraints, HL7 information model (DMIM) and trigger events. The description of interface specifications by studying HSSP services' specifications is carried out. The services are then implemented by Web service basic profile and implement orchestration and choreography using business process model workflows. The last step will be registering the services in a proper registry.

Once the HL7 services have been exposed as Web Services, it will be available for everyone to use over the web. The advancement in the Semantic Web has now shifted the simple Web services to the Semantic Web Services. The Semantic Web (SW) approach is to develop languages and mechanisms for expressing information in machine understandable form. The web services that are identified in the SOA framework are to be upgraded to semantic web services. In order to achieve this goal Semantic Web Service (SWS) Architecture review including WSMO, WSML and WSMX should be performed. The identification of process

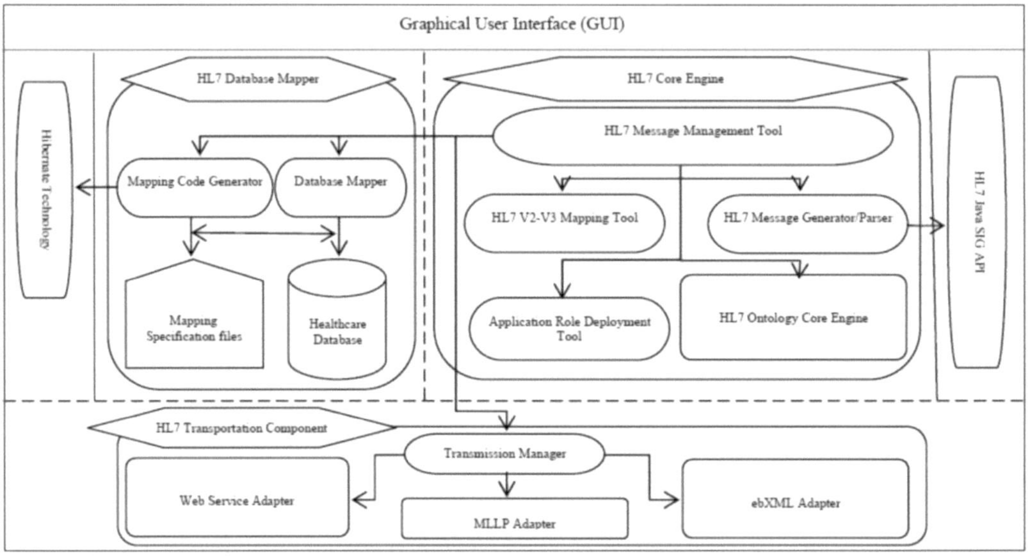

Fig. 1. Architecture for HL7 Studio [14].

flows in HL7 is important for achieving the goal of semantic process interoperability. WSMO entities (ontologies, services, goals and mediators) modeling are the next step to be performed. For HL7 processes we would require to model Interaction ontology and Message Ontology. The interaction ontology would contain all the process artifacts (application roles, trigger events, message types and interactions) while the Message Ontology would contain information related to HL7 V3 message like transmission wrapper, control act wrapper and message payload. The WSMO entities should be modeled using WSMT tool for the semantics to completely take effect. The Adapter component implementation is also an important step as conversion from XML to WSML and WSML to XML is required for overcoming heterogeneity problem and bringing interoperability. To completely utilize the WSMO entities an execution environment WSMX should be implemented. Semantic web services will bring automatic service discovery which will make the timely information transfer of patient resulting in quick access to patient care.

The semantic services are required to be stored, published and retrieved in a repository. The semantic registry would be required for registration/publication of patient and lab domain services semantically, so that the services can be accessed for medical research, decision support systems. Analysis of HL7 standardized referenced information models will be done for semantic information management. Identification of semantic discovery and semantic matchmaking algorithms based on inference and reasoning will be done for best retrieval of requested information services. Analysis of different data exchange mechanisms will be done to exchange medical information across the interlinked semantic registries. Analysis of semantic SOA techniques to make our semantic registries service orientated to ensure semantic interoperability, flexibility and extensibility across heterogeneous environments. Analysis of different electronic health records for its feasibility and integration with semantic SOA semantic registries using HL7 V3. The semantic services related to patient and lab domain will be stored, published and retrieved from the semantic registry that would be helpful for medical research, medical education and diagnosing and curing several diseases.

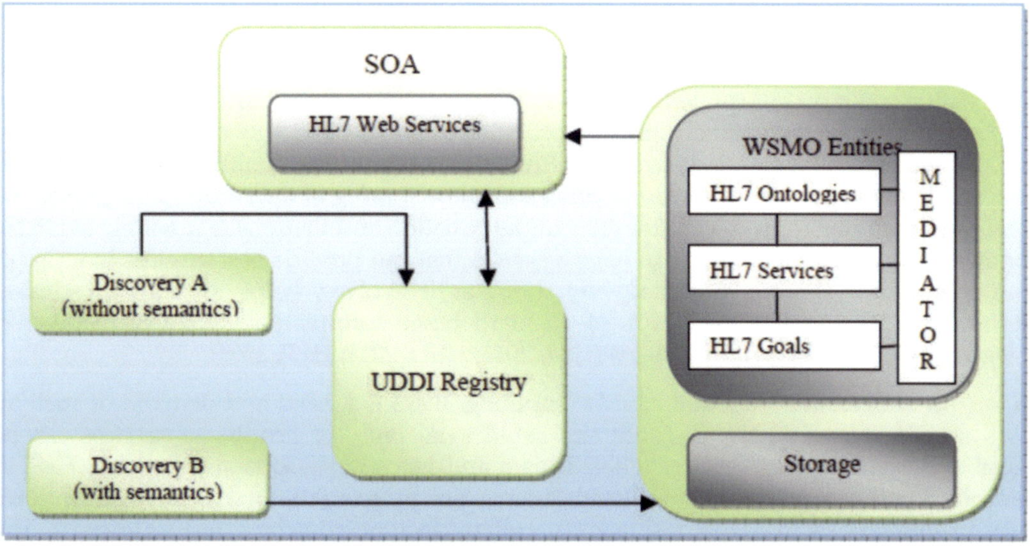

Fig. 2. Generic Architecture of SOA and semantic web services.

Figure 2 shows the generic architecture of how the SOA, semantic web services using WSMF and semantic registries would work together. The discovery would be of the services that are without semantics and semantics based discovery. The discovery without semantics would be through UDDI registry of the web services that are created in SOA framework. The semantic web service discovery would take place by Web Service Execution Environment (WSMX) and the bridge between semantic web services and simple web services is provided by a mechanism called grounding in WSMO.

2. Semantic Electronic Medical Record (SEMR) system as SaaS service model

The advancement in Information and Communication Technology (ICT) is playing increasing role in healthcare and has managed to improve the efficiency of health services to common people. Health informatics plays a vital role in the integration of ICT in healthcare domain. The critical need is to encourage healthcare systems to be more efficient and provide more workable solutions that have benefited from ICT (HIMSS, 2011).

Current syntax based healthcare data systems are not only prone to error and loss but also it is not feasible to manage massive data and access any particular record from it. Therefore healthcare organizations are facing difficulties in managing the large amount of information as well as technological infrastructure. Information retrieval and analysis has turned into a very important challenge for healthcare domain. These challenges can effectively be handled with the help of semantics and cloud computing. Managing healthcare data with semantics results in cost-effective, easily accessible, accurate and manageable data processing solutions. At present EMR systems are designed for hospital operations within the premises, but now have to be modified to support primary care settings of patients, mostly outside of the walls of the hospital. The traditional primary care teams also have to redesign the work-flow as they add new care coordination staff and EMR technology to achieve the desired goal of improving the clinical outcome at reduced costs (Ginsburg, 2006).

Interoperability is the ability of a healthcare system to share information and have that information properly interpreted by the receiving system in the same sense as intended by the transmitting system. Standardization provides us an effective way of communication to achieve the goal of semantic interoperability. HL7 is one of the healthcare standards that allow communication of healthcare systems and allow sharing of data around the globe. The important requirement is to capture relevant information and then make it widely available for others. Therefore, the need is to have a system that can provide best services in terms of meaningful data sharing and discovery. HL7, as it evolves, helps us with a technical business model to fulfill the vision of standard based information exchange in diverse, integrated health information systems (HL7, 2011; HLH, 2011; HL7, 2009).

In the era of Semantic Web and cloud computing, there is a need and demand of such an EMR system where timely, accurate and rapid availability of healthcare services can be possible that can manage patient's health data and helps physicians and patients. EMR is basically a part of local standalone Health Information System (HIS) that is an organization's legal proprietary, it includes hospitals as well as doctors, clinicians and physicians. The basic functionality of an EMR is to allow storage, retrieval and manipulation of records. In order to communicate the information of an EMR system between different branches of a healthcare organization, there is a need to follow a standard that provides interoperability. Since healthcare is a most demanding area as more people are concerned about their health, this system should be scalable, fault tolerant, reliable, secure, timely respondent, sustainable and maintainable.

It is a rarity to deploy an Electronic Medical Record (EMR) system on cloud. Also another challenging task is to incorporate semantic web technologies in EMR's and presenting the complex medical data in a meaningful and intelligent manner in healthcare. This will require the integration of Semantics Web and SaaS model (Software as a Service, 2011) with best featured existing EMR for developing an efficient healthcare semantic web services for the cloud. Some initiatives are underway worldwide such as Health Services Specification Project (HSSP), a joint-venture of HL7 and Object Management Group (OMG, 2011), providing standardized service interface specifications.

Therefore, there is a need to design and implement semantic based healthcare service on cloud for storage, retrieval and manipulation of patient data and medical records. Thus SEMR (Semantic Electronic Medical Record) system will provide the solution for highly intensive patient and medical data sharing, semantic interoperability and management with its availability for larger community access through cloud infrastructure.

2.1 Related work

Some of the current open source EMR systems are listed below with their functionalities and drawbacks.

OpenEMR is an open source clinical practice management system (OpenEMR, 2011). The system can track patient demographics, patient medical records, scheduling, billing, multilingual support and prescription. In short the system provides all basic functionalities that any hospital EMR system can provide but it is restricted to a hospital.

OpenEMR Virtual Appliance (OpenEMR Virtual Appliance, 2011) is a comprehensive open source Medical Practice Management Software Appliance, which provides office scheduling, electronic medical records, prescriptions, insurance billing, accounting and access controls. This appliance has many possible applications, such as a fully functional demo, a testing/developing platform, and as the starting point in real world clinic applications. It can be run on any operating system that supports the VMware Player.

OpenMRS (OpenMRS, 2011) is a full open source healthcare system and has the ability to configure the system to new requirements without programming and to interoperate with other systems whether open or closed. Both of these open source systems are refined under Health Insurance Portability and Accountability Act (HIPAA, 2011) and CCHIT (CCHIT, 2011; CCHIT EMR, 2011) certified.

SequelMed EMR (SequelMed EMR, 2011) is a secure, patient centric, medical record, integrated with Sequel Systems' medical billing software (SequelMed EPM). The system can automate clinical documentation and have Decision Support Tools and Alerts, Integrated Patient Education Protocols, wireless and internet access to medical records.

ClearHealth (Clear-health, 2011) is open source software and include five major areas of healthcare practice operations including scheduling, billing, EMR, HIPAA Security and accounts receivables."

XChart (XChart, 2011) is a paper based project by the Open Healthcare Group that promotes EMR, based in XML.

SmartCare (SmartCare,2011) is software that develops EMR programs and particularly used in Zambia.

Zimbra (Zimbra, 2011) gives e-mail solution for government offices, education institutes and other business environments. Medical professionals can also benefit from its fast backup and recovery of mailboxes, anti-spam and anti-virus protection, this software has also support for BlackBerry and other mobile devices, and their flexible applications. All of these systems are open source and primary care systems.

These systems provide basic clinical practice that is helpful for patients' medical record but do not support interoperability among different workflow components such as laboratory, medical reports, patient administration, pharmacy, insurance, billing, and prescription among medical repositories, hospitals, pharmacies and clinics.

2.2 Methodology

In order to avoid the burden of management of technological infrastructure, SaaS based solution should be used to develop the system on top of cloud infrastructure. To achieve full potential of machine process able SaaS service model based EMR, semantics need to be added. Semantics bring the benefits of unambiguous definition of service functionality and the external interfaces of services reduce human effort in integrating services to SOA, improve dynamism and stability to Web services. Our proposed system will ensure timely delivery of health care information and will ensure its confidentiality. The proposed healthcare system will be developed as semantic web services based on SaaS model and will be deployed on cloud infrastructure. This work will bring significant improvements in current EMR systems through interoperable, automated and seamless meaningful communication.

The ultimate goal is to exploit the EMR system's functionalities as semantic web services. Web Services Modeling Framework (WSMF) will provide the platform for automatic web service discovery, composition, and invocation that makes the product efficient. As EMR system, software will be developed as a service, semantic web technologies will be used to incorporate semantics in the services and the communication will take place through web services and would ensure timely delivery of medical information.

SEMR (Semantic Electronic Medical Record) system will be used to capture and manage patient's data and information by using these two approaches: Semantic Web and Software as a Service (SaaS) service model on cloud. These are emerging approaches that can bring novel way to properly manage patient's data and medical records. SOA and SaaS establish a SaaS service model by leveraging the benefits of SaaS solution and SOA infrastructure. SOA enhances reliability, reduces hardware acquisition costs, leverages existing development skills, and accelerates movement to standards based server and application consolidation. In this way SOA provides a data bridge between incompatible technologies.

Furthermore SaaS solution will provide data and system availability, secure and reliable performance, and maximum system throughput. Communication in the system will be handled by HL7 for semantic interoperability. This system is based on HL7 standard based data exchange format.

The important part of this project is the integration of Semantic Web and SaaS model with best featured existing EMR for developing an efficient healthcare semantic web services for the cloud. This mostly involves research and implementation challenges exist within best featured existing EMR for developing an efficient healthcare semantic web services for the cloud.

2.3 Proposed architecture

The proposed system will be semantic based SaaS service model developed on top of cloud for healthcare domain. SOA and SaaS establish a SaaS service model by leveraging the benefits of SaaS solution and SOA infrastructure. SOA enhances reliability, reduces hardware acquisition costs, leverages existing development skills, accelerates movement to standards-based server and application consolidation, provides a data bridge between incompatible technologies (SOA, 2010).

In the requirement gathering phase literature review and analysis of basic functionalities of EMR systems and SaaS service model would be carried out. Therefore SaaS service model based EMR system would be designed in the first phase. In order to avoid the burden of management of technological infrastructure, we will use SaaS based solution by developing our proposed system on top of cloud infrastructure. To make SaaS service model based EMR and machine process able and achieve its full potential, semantics needs to be added.

Semantics brings the benefits of unambiguous definition of service functionality and external interfaces reduce human effort in integrating services to SOA, improve dynamism and stability to Web services (Semantic SOA, 2011). Therefore the next phase is to upgrade SaaS service model based EMR to Semantic EMR system as SaaS service model for healthcare. In this phase the literature review, analysis and design of semantic web services identification and development for the purpose of fulfilling patient administration requirements would be carried out.

HL7 provides semantic interoperability; therefore the communication in our proposed system is based on HL7 standard based data exchange format. This step will embed HL7 standard in our proposed system for medical data communication.

In the final step an interface of this system can also be provided for smart-phones for physicians and patients to access our system also from outside the patient care premises.

In the architecture four types of services are categorized for SEMR system SaaS service model. The EMR services are part of these categories that are semantic based.

2.3.1 Architectural layout of SaaS based SEMR system

The layered architecture is categorized as presentation layer, business logic layer, data management layer and database layer. The layered architecture is shown in Figure 3.

- **Business process services:**

These services perform the logic of business processes with the help of other services. Business logic is fulfilled by the management of processes and data through data management services. For example request for patient referrals would be fulfilled through underlying data management service provided through message generation service.

- **Data management services:**

These services manage the data for business process services.

- **Metadata services:**

These services provide metadata specifications and standards for message generation, database mapping, and data integration, interoperability, through data modeling, data transformation and data workflows. These services help data management services.

- **Security services**:

These services are responsible for the authorization and authentication of data transmitted and stored for the working of data management services.

The elaborated services architecture is given in Figure 4. We demonstrated the sequence of functionality of Patient Administration service in the following paragraph. In order to use Patient Administration service from our SEMR SaaS service based system we presented patient registration scenario where a doctor registers a patient through our SEMR system Interface. The doctor will give patient demographic information in the form by using our system. As our system is semantic based, the Semantic Gateway service will perform semantic composition. The query of the doctor will be standardized with the help of Message Generation Data Management service that will generate an HL7 message.

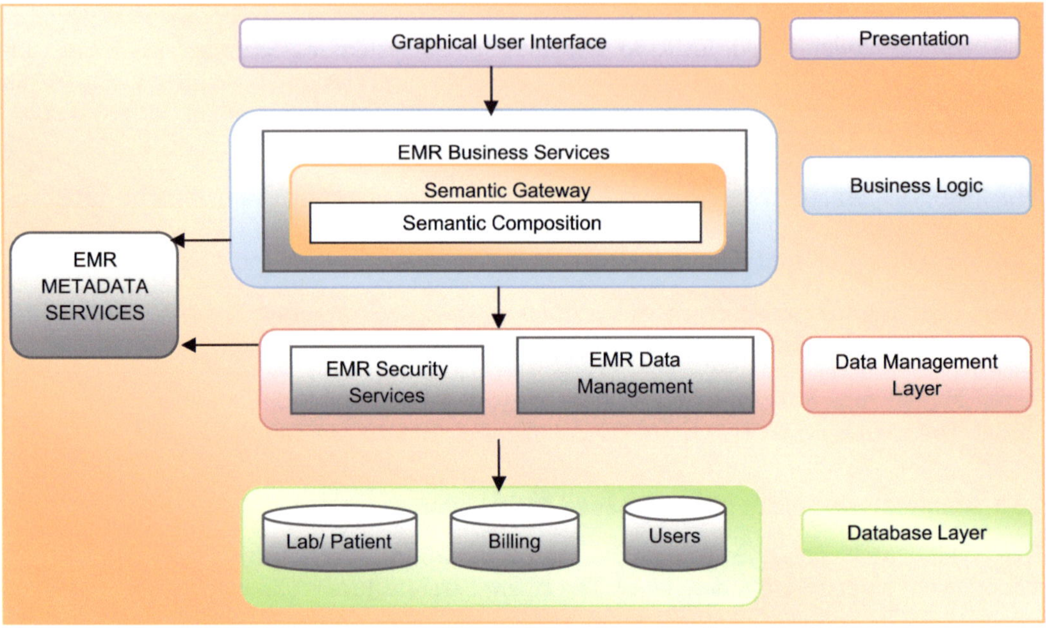

Fig. 3. Architecture for SaaS based SEMR system.

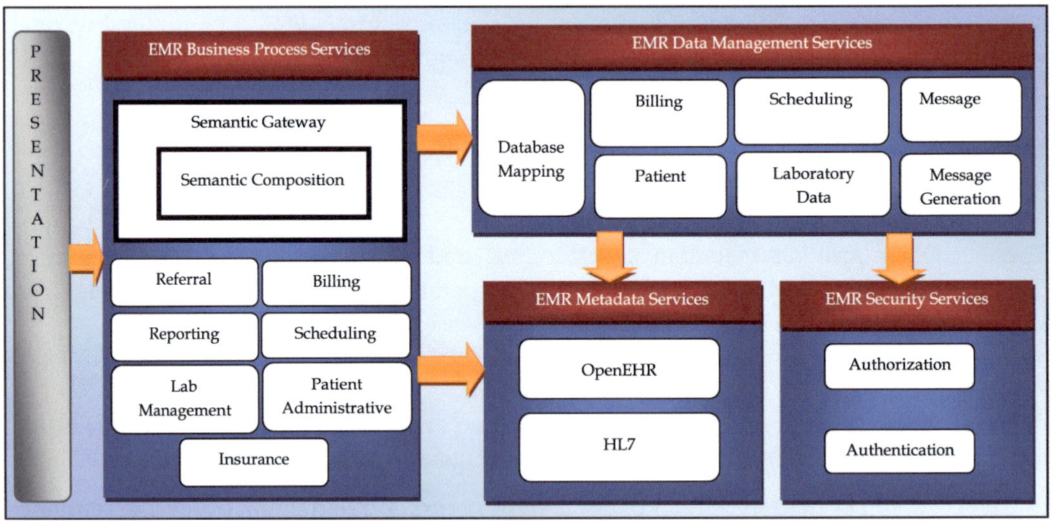

Fig. 4. Elaborated Services Architecture.

The Semantic Gateway service will then discover, select and invoke Patient Administration Business Process service through HL7 message parsing. The Patient Administration service will call the Patient data service for data management. The Patient data service will call the Authorization service to authorize the patient for viewing his medical data. This service will assign user name and password to the patient. Then the Patient data service will store the registered patient in the patient database.

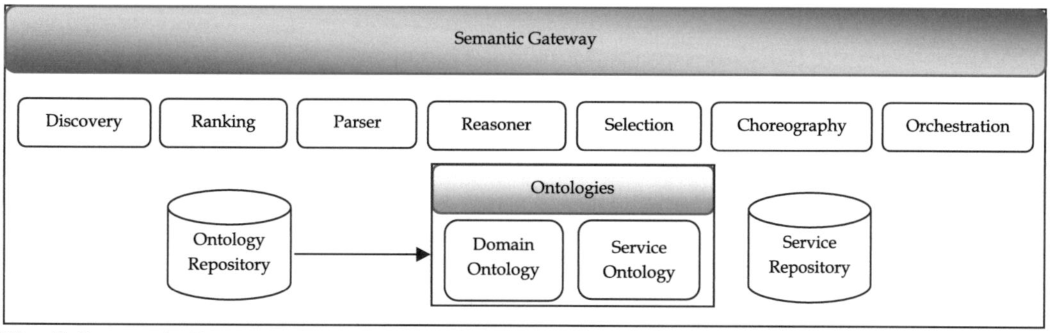

Fig. 5. Semantic Gateway.

Semantic Gateway uses Semantic Gateway service as a part of business process services that is used for taking information from the user and resolving it by using the combination of other services. This provides the semantic annotations to services. Service ontology and Domain ontology are defined for semantic execution. Services and Ontology repositories will be the knowledge bases for the Semantic Gateway service. Reasoner is used in Semantic Gateway for inference about services semantics at runtime. Services of EMR system will be discovered semantically through Semantic Composition business process service. The business logic of this service will perform parsing, choreography, ranking and selection with the help of Semantic Gateway. Semantic gateway is shown in Figure 5. Semantic Gateway is discussed in following sections.

2.3.2 Semantic gateway

The advancement in Information Technology is playing increasing role in healthcare and has managed to improve the efficiency of health services to common people. Health informatics plays a vital role in the integration of Information Technology in healthcare domain. However healthcare organizations are facing problems related to communication of right information to appropriate. Due to data deluge, information retrieval and analysis has become an important problem in various fields including healthcare. Semantic web technologies provide extensible, flexible and efficient information.

The innovation and the standardization of web services provide basic building blocks for information exchange. To exploit web services to their full potential, semantics must be specified. Semantic web technologies play a pivotal role in bringing automation in the process flows. OWL-S provides ontologies for describing web services with the help of semantic constructs in an unambiguous and machine interpretable form. OWL-S follows layered structure of markup languages as HTML, XML, RDF and has built on OWL recommendation of W3C. Its ontologies describe domain concepts of services (e.g., travel, e-business, healthcare information) and business logic. The data flow and controls of the services are related to the domain ontologies through inputs, outputs, preconditions and effects. OWL-S ontologies divide service descriptions in four main parts: process model, service profile, service grounding and the service.

Currently WSMX framework provides automatic service discovery, composition and execution of web services. It provides information exchange between users and service providers and fulfill user specified goal by invoking end point web services. The main strength of WSMO over other semantic web technologies is its discovery mechanism. WSMO is based on the Web Service Modeling Framework (WSMF). WSML is used to describe services' description into Ontologies, Web services, Goals and Mediators (WSMO).

The innovation and the standardization of web services have set the concept of web services as the basic building blocks of information technology systems for Service Oriented Architectures (SOA) applications. The idea is to explore such sophisticated SOA technologies that make the discovery of services for requested users appropriate (Erl, 2005). SOA ensures interoperability, flexibility and extensibility across heterogeneous environments. In service oriented computing services are used to develop fast, economical, interoperable, evolvable, and extremely distributed applications. Services are self-governing, platform-independent entities that can be described, published, discovered, and loosely coupled (Papazoglou, 2007).

Traditional approaches to services publication and discovery have generally relied on the existence of pre-defined registry services like Universal Description, Discovery and Integration (UDDI) (Clement, 2004). Often the description of a service is limited in existing registry, with little or no support for problem specific descriptions. Semantic registries with the use of OWL-S attempt to overcome this limitation and provide a rich semantic description based on ontologies. Semantic matchmaking generally focuses on the problem of identifying services on the basis of the capabilities that they provide. We proposed an OWL-S based Semantic Registry for healthcare information provision. This chapter also presents healthcare service ontology (Iftikhar et al., 2010) developed through the specifications of HL7 Service Functional Model, which is used in our Semantic Registry for publishing and discovering HL7 compliant healthcare semantic web services. HL7 is a well-known healthcare standard that provides specification for standardization of information exchanged among healthcare applications.

In paper (Srinivasan, 2004), Authors have proposed OWL-S/UDDI Matchmaker as an extension of UDDI. Before registering OWL-S based Web Services on UDDI, OWL-S/UDDI Matchmaker converts service profile of these services to UDDI data structure and then stores them on UDDI. During web service discovery, OWL-S/UDDI Matchmaker translates the services back into OWL-S format. Matching takes place between the service request and the published services advertisements present in the registry. The proposed solution enhances the UDDI registry for semantic based searching and capability based matching. UDDI registry has some inherent limitations including lack of semantic representations of contents. The matching process proposed in this paper is restricted to Inputs and Outputs matching of the service profile.

The DAML-S Matchmaker (Paolucci, 2002) was developed by the Intelligent Software Agents Group at Carnegie- Mellon University. The matchmaking system is a database where service providers can register their Web services via DAML-S descriptions through a Web interface. The system then allows service requesters to upload their service requests. The matchmaking algorithm matches the types associated with each input or output parameter. For each parameter (either input or output) there are several degrees of matching, depending on the semantic relationship between the parameters of the advertisement and the request. Based on these results a global matching result is determined.

ebXML Registry (Dogac et al., 2008) give industry groups and enterprises the ability to share business semantic information and business process interfaces in form of XML. This registry has some extensions for medical data registration, annotation, discovery and retrieval in form or archetypes data definitions where registry semantic constructs are used. They provide archetype metadata ontology and describe the techniques to access archetype semantics through ebXML query facilities. They also provide mechanism, how archetype data can be retrieved from underlying clinical information systems by using ebXML Web services.

The FUSION Semantic Registry (Kourtesis and Paraskakis, 2006) is a semantically-enhanced Web service registry based on UDDI, SAWSDL and OWL. This registry augments and enhances the discovery facilities of typical UDDI registry and based on UDDI without changing its implementation. This registry performs matchmaking at data-level and developed by SEERC in the context of research project FUSION and released as open source software. Fusion registry has no matchmaking based on inputs, outputs, preconditions and effects capabilities of services.

Artemis project (Dogac et al., 2006), exploits ontologies based on the domain knowledge exposed by the healthcare information standards like HL7, CEN TC251, ISO TC215 and GEHR. Artemis Web service architecture has no any globally agreed ontologies; rather healthcare institutes resolve their semantic differences through a mediator component. The mediator component works in a P2P manner and uses ontologies in order to facilitate semantic negotiation among involved institutes.

CASCOM is an agent-based approach used for semantic service discovery and coordination in mobile eHealth environment (Fröhlich et al., 2007).

Cesar Caceres is another approach that focuses on Agent-Based Semantic Service Discovery for medical-emergency management (Cáceresc et al., 2006).

COCOON Glue is a prototype of WSMO Discovery engine for the healthcare field to find out the most appropriate advice services (Emanuele and Cerizza, 2005).

Registries are important in a large scale, distributed environment, such as the semantic web. They provide the necessary functionality that allows service providers to expose information of their services to potential users. Various types of approaches that are being followed for storing and accessing information over the web are registry-based discovery mechanisms (Willmott, 2005), indexing methods (UDDI) (Clement, 2004) and publish/subscribe approach (Nawaz et al., 2007). In healthcare domain there is no such mechanism of binding healthcare service providers and requesters in order to discover healthcare data for use in emergency situation. There is lack of registries that provide publish and retrieval of healthcare data through web services. There is no any healthcare services publish in a semantic way for the interoperability of health information exchanged in an efficient manner. Healthcare information is more complex and has diverse dimensions. UDDI (Paolucci, 2002; Srinivasan, 2004) and ebXML (Dogac et al., 2008) do not provide such semantic interoperability in healthcare domain.

2.3.3 Methodology

We proposed a framework based on OWL-S semantic layer which would provide automatic service discovery, composition, invocation and execution of web services for healthcare service providers and end users. Our proposed Semantic Registry would be the key foundation block upon which electronic information is exchanged in an interoperable manner among disparate communities through web services semantics. It would be an Ontology based semantic description model explicitly represents information semantics in abstract and concrete level and resolve heterogeneity.

The system will consist of entry points for the communication to take place. The OWL-S/WSDL grounding mechanism would be used for end point service invocation. In our framework, we proposed to perform goal-oriented discovery with semantic matchmaking of OWL-S ontologies. The proposed use of semantic web services specification language such as OWL-S for describing web services semantically would result in better information exchange. We will incorporate three views of services into user demand to satisfy the requirements of end users in healthcare domain. These views are: customization (who is demanding information), situation (when and where the demand is occurred) and quality (how important the demand is). Service provider, who is going to provide their services for use by appropriate users, will take advantage of the complementary strengths of OWL-S, and these three views of services.

OWL-S has classes of WSDLGrounding for realizing specific elements within WSDL for OWL-S/WSDL Grounding mechanism. This mechanism is more mature as compared to WSMX. WSMX required lowering and lifting mechanism and XSLT transformations for WSMO/WSDL groundings. WSMX also uses RDF and XML as a carrier between WSML and WSDL for grounding mechanism, where loss of semantics can be observed. WSMO provides goal oriented discovery and mediation between ontologies, web services and goals that are not provided by OWL-S. In OWL-S, there is no clear distinction between choreography and orchestration. OWL-S Process Model defines choreography and orchestration. There is no need of separate management for these two processes. In WSMO, the choreography and orchestration are specified clearly. WSMX has interfaces for choreography element (provides the necessary information for communicating with the service), and the orchestration class element, (describes how the service makes use of other services in order to achieve the goal). OWL-S has no Semantic Registry for web service discovery, selection and invocation mechanism, it depends on UDDI for web services discovery. Whereas WSMX framework has three steps of discovery, Goal Discovery, Semantic Web service Discovery and End point service Discovery using any one of the approach: keyword based, light weight and heavy weight discovery.

Our framework would work with both central and distributed computing infrastructures as shown in Figure 1. It will provide services for healthcare information provision and for collaboration of Personal Health Record (PHR) systems, Electronic Health Record (EHR) systems, Health Information Management (HIMS) systems, and other hospital and clinical systems.

Our OWLS Semantic Registry is used for HL7 compliant healthcare semantic web services and metadata publication, discovery, composition and invocation in healthcare domain. One of our major concerns is to describe the HL7 compliant healthcare services publication and discovery. Our vision is to have a Semantic Registry as the key foundation block upon which electronic health information would be exchanged among disparate communities. We already have a proactive approach for efficient discovery based on service category that utilizes semantic-based publish-subscribe model in conjunction with UDDI. In the Service discovery process we analyzed that there are less updates and frequent searches hence push model is the right approach to use. Through our web based Semantic Registry in Figure 6 users can publish and request service descriptions from Service Publish Interface and Service Discovery Interface. The service descriptions stored in OWL-S Profile Repository as OWL-S service profile. The matching algorithm semantically enhances ontology mappings for providing services descriptions to requesters. It assigns scores to individual concepts of the advertised service by concept matching with that of the requested one and then assigns overall ranking to advertisement on the basis of individual scores. The results have shown a significant increase in precision and recall of service discovery as compared to UDDI approach. The users of the UDDI registry can also switch between traditional syntax-based and proposed semantic-based searching. Normal users can access OWL-S profiles and WSDL advertisements through inquiry API provided by UDDI registry. Semantic Matchmaker used in this work (Capability Matching Module) performs Inputs, Outputs, Preconditions and Effects and Service Category Matching. Capabilities of OWL-S web services; Preconditions and Effects represent a "state" before and after the execution of a service respectively. In this paper we enhance the OWL-S semantic web services capability matching to Inputs, Outputs, Preconditions and Effects. In this way this work will cover data as well as functional semantics modeling aspects.

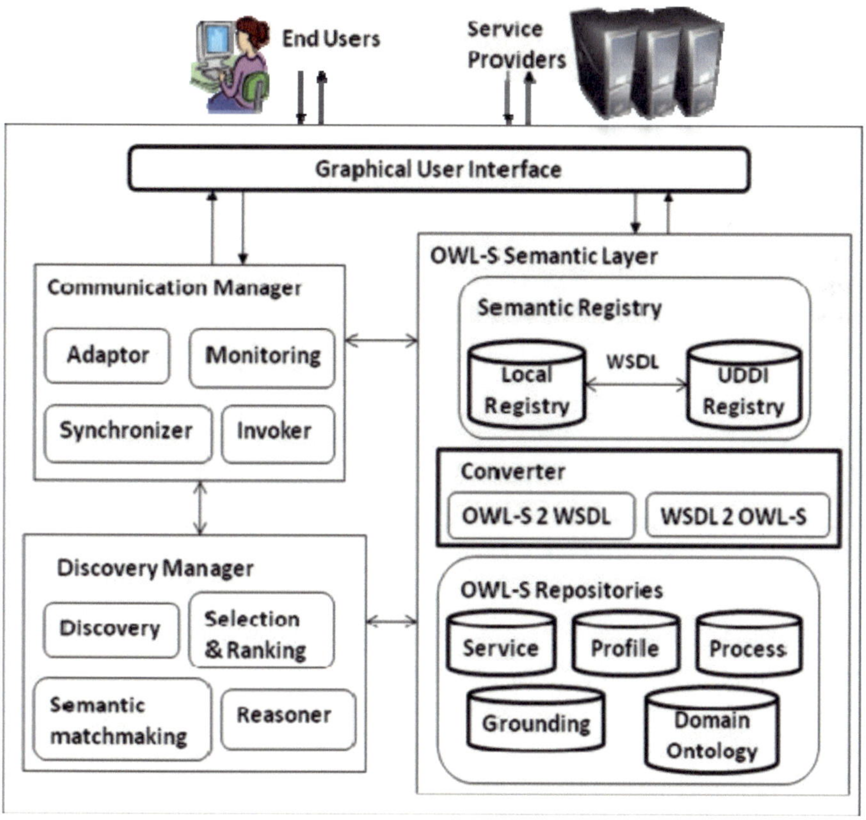

Fig. 6. Semantic Framework.

Our proposed framework Figure 6 consists of following components:

- **Communication Manager**
  - **Adaptor:** End user request will be converted into OWL-S to make it adaptable to internal environment. OWL-S annotations of end user request will be provided to discovery component, which will perform the user oriented discovery with the help of SR, semantic matchmaking, selection & ranking components
  - **Monitoring:** This component will send the request to best selected end point web service candidate.
  - **Invoker:** The response from the end point web service will be given to the user through this component. This component will synchronize all responses from more than one end point web services.
- **OWL-S semantic layer**
  - **OWL-S ontologies:** Semantic descriptions of web services provided by service provider.
  - **Semantic Registry (SR):** SR manages semantic annotations of services provided by service providers in repository and handles discovery process. It also provides OWL-S to WSDL and WSDL to OWL-S translations with the help of OWL-S ontologies.
  - **Repository:** OWL-S ontologies' semantic annotations would be stored in repository to be accessed latter for discovery purpose.
  - **Services domain ontology**
- **Discovery Manager:**
  - **Discovery:** This component will perform keyword based, light weight and heavy weight discovery.
  - **Semantic matchmaking:** During discovery process similar ontologies and web services will be mediated semantically.
  - **Selection & Ranking:** Best candidate end point web service will be selected from the ranked list of web service.
  - **Reasoner:** This component will help selection & ranking component for choosing best candidate.

We developed a healthcare domain services hierarchy through HL7 Service Functional Model (Healthcare Services Specification Project (HSSP)). That services classification is used as healthcare service ontology in our registry for discovery purpose Figure 7.

In order to define HL7 service model specification as in Table 1 for healthcare services publication and discovery through Semantic Registry we consider these two types of services:

1. Business Services provide specific business functionality, such as "Patient Appointment", "Lab Order Management" and so on. These are often further subdivided into "Process Services" and "Core Business Services".
2. Infrastructure (Technical) Services are provided to support the business services and are not specific to healthcare, but are often subject to specific requirements derived from regulation of healthcare information, for example by professional bodies or national legislatures. Examples include: Authorization, Logging, and Transformation.

Fig. 7. Healthcare Service Ontology.

Service specifications	HL7 v3 Artifacts Used [5]
Service	Domain, Topic, Application Role, Trigger Events e.g Lab domain
Interface	Domain, Topic, Application Role, Trigger Events
Capabilities	DIM/D-MIM, Application Role, Storyboards, Activity Diagrams, Use Cases, Trigger Events, (Interaction, CIM/R-MIM, LIM/ HMD, Message Type – if using message oriented level constructs) e.g ApplicationLevelAck, ControlActProcess etc.
Message	RIM, DIM, CIM/R-MIM, CMETs, Vocabulary and Data Types (LIM, HMD, Message Type and Schema – if using actual message level constructs)

Table 1. HL7 Service Specifications.

OWL-S Service profile generated through Jena and OWL-API is as follows:

```
<?xml version="1.0"?>
<rdf:RDF
xmlns:rdf="http://www.w3.org/1999/02/22-rdf-syntax-ns#"
xmlns:xsd="http://www.w3.org/2001/XMLSchema#"
xmlns:rdfs="http://www.w3.org/2000/01/rdf-schema#"
xmlns:owl="http://www.w3.org/2002/07/owl#"
<owl:versionInfo rdf:datatype="http://www.w3.org/2001/XMLSchema#string">
-----OWL ontology for all parameters (input, output, are subclasses of parameters) ----
</owl:Ontology>
 <rdfs:Class rdf:ID="Parameter"/>
<owl:Class rdf:about="#Parameter"> </owl:Class>
 <rdfs:Class rdf:ID="Output"/><rdfs:subClassOf rdf:resource="#Parameter"/>
 <rdfs:Class rdf:ID="Input"/>
 <owl:Class rdf:ID="ServiceCategory">
<owl:Class rdf:ID="Result">
 <rdfs:label>Result</rdfs:label>
-----Preconditions-----
<owl:ObjectProperty rdf:ID="hasPrecondition">
 <rdfs:domain rdf:resource="#Process"/>
 <rdfs:range rdf:resource="&expr;#Condition"/>
</owl:ObjectProperty>
-----Conditional Effects and Effects and Outputs bundled in Results-----
<owl:ObjectProperty rdf:ID="inCondition">
 <rdfs:label>inCondition</rdfs:label>
 <rdfs:domain rdf:resource="#Result"/>
 <rdfs:range rdf:resource="&expr;#Condition"/>
</owl:ObjectProperty>
<owl:ObjectProperty rdf:ID="hasEffect">
 <rdfs:label>hasEffect</rdfs:label>
 <rdfs:domain rdf:resource="#Result"/>
 <rdfs:range rdf:resource="&expr;#Expression"/>
</owl:ObjectProperty>
```

Profile is a subclass of OWLs Service Profile defined below. It is used to acknowledge that there may be different ways to profile services that are different from the way we expressed it so far (HSSP). OWL Profile ontology has no classes for modeling IOPE's. Profile instances will be able to define IOPE's using the schema offered by the Process.owl ontology defined by OWL. Additional Classes, needed to specify details of the OWL-S service profile, are also specified for publication and discovery purpose. These are Service Category, Service Parameters and Quality Rating. We have also specified the definition of Profile that provides a definition of the Profile class. Non-Functional Properties are also defined those provide a definition of properties such as name of the service, contact information, quality of the service, and additional information that may help to evaluate the service. We have also specified Functional Properties like IOPE (Input/Output/Precondition/Effects) that help with the specification of what the service provides. The hasParameter property relates

Profile instances to process:Parameter instances. In addition, the following properties relate Profile to expr:Condition and process:Result: hasPrecondition and hasResult as follows:

- hasResultVar (a Variable) - A variable scoped to the Result block, bound by the result condition.
- inCondition (a Condition)
- withOutput (an OutputBinding of an Output Parameter of the process to a value form)
- hasEffect (an Effect)

The working of the system consists of following phases:

- Information/Web services publication from service providers
- Demand oriented user discovery for healthcare information

OWL-S based semantic web service is consists of three modules: Service Profile, Process Model, and Service Grounding. Service profile is used for advertisement purpose and provides data semantics. In paper (Iftikhar et al., 2010) HL7 compliant health service capabilities were provided for publication to Semantic Registry. In order to provide functional semantics in the service description, process model is also defined for functional description of services. Figure 8 explains information publication.

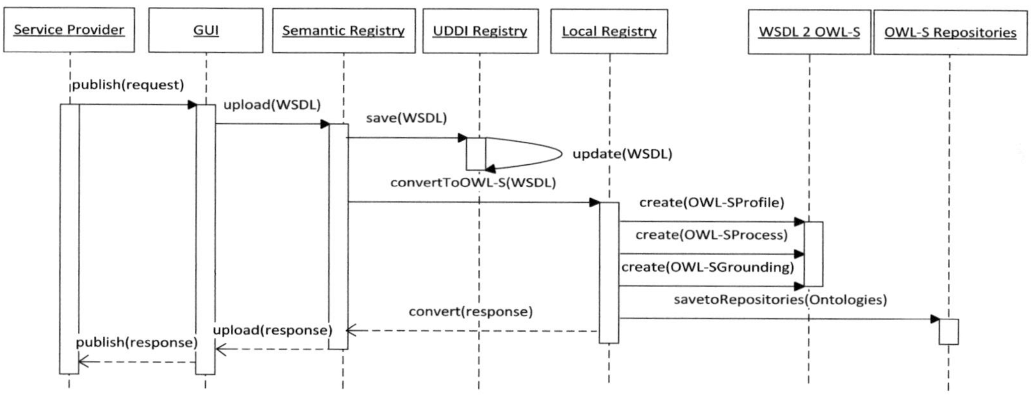

Fig. 8. Healthcare information publication.

The Physician and patients can now query the Semantic Registry by providing service inputs, output, preconditions or effects. As service discovery will use OWL-S service profile and service process model, the service requester have to provide the required service criteria on the basis of service inputs, output, preconditions or effects. Figure 9 explains the working of the demand oriented information provision.

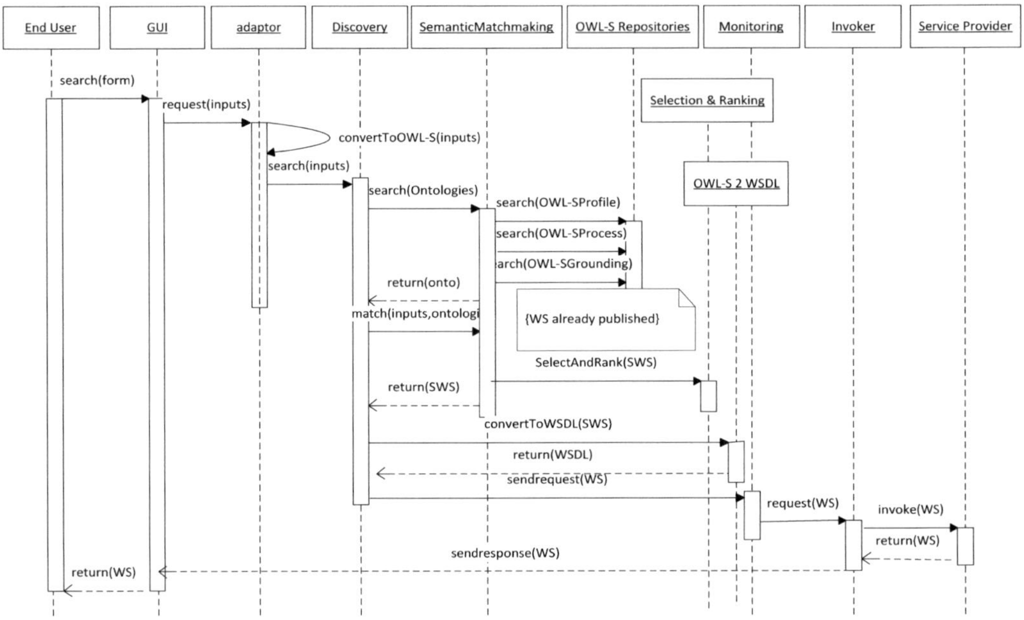

Fig. 9. Healthcare information provision.

2.3.4 Results

A. FindLabReportResult HL7 compliant healthcare web service scenario

We described a "FindLabReportResult" HL7 compliant healthcare web service scenario where our Semantic Registry allows a service provider to give service descriptions of his health service in terms of service inputs, output, preconditions and effects. Service descriptions published with data as well as functional semantics in the Semantic Registry. Our Semantic Registry also allows a service requester to query the HL7 compliant semantic web health service on the bases of service inputs, output, preconditions or effects. We implemented this scenario in our Semantic Registry.

Service publishing

OWL-S based semantic web service is consists of three modules: Service Profile, Process Model, and Service Grounding. Service profile is used for advertisement purpose and provides data semantics. In this paper HL7 compliant health service capabilities are provided for publication to Semantic Registry. In order to provide functional semantics in the service description, process model is also defined for functional description of services. FindLabReportResult scenario is published in the Semantic Registry by defining service profile and service model.

Service profile of FindLabReportResult described below is the capabilities of web services in terms of its inputs, outputs, preconditions and effects. The service profile is described using OWL protégé APIs (protégé API). This service profile is used for publishing health service in the Semantic Registry.

- Service Category: Health_application_services
- ServiceName : FindLabReportResult
- Precondition: The service should be the member of ControlActProcess class of HL7 artifacts.
- Inputs: The service provider enters findResult and labReport as inputs.
- Outputs: The service provider enters resultStatus as output.
- Effects: The service provider mentions that the service should receive an acknowledgement of type ApplicationLevelAck.

Process Model of FindLabReportResult described below is the functional description of the service where the service functionality is termed as a process. One atomic process is defined for the service Inputs, output, preconditions and result, where result contains condition, output constraints and effects to come true for the result outcome.

```
process:AtomicProcess rdf:ID="findResult">
 <process:hasInput rdf:resource="#labRepot"/>
  <process:hasInput rdf:resource="#findResult"/>
  <process:hasOutput rdf:resource="#resultStatus"/>
  <process:hasPrecondition isMember(ControlActProcess)/>
  <process:hasResult>
    <process:Result>
      <process:inCondition>
        <expr:SWRL-Condition>
              correctfindResultInfo(labReport,findResult)
                      </expr:SWRL-Condition>
      </process:inCondition>
      <process:withOutput
rdf:resource="#resultStatus                                                    ">
      <valueType
 rdr:resource="#findResultMsg">
   </process:withOutput>
          <process:hasEffect>
              <expr:SWRL-Condition>
       ApplicationLevelAck(labReport,findResult)
              </expr:SWRL-Condition>
            </process:hasEffect>
    </process:Result>
  </process:hasResult>
</process:AtomicProcess>
```

The service provider publishes service profile and functional service descriptions of health service in OWL-S Profile Repository of Semantic Registry of Figure 2. Service metadata is stored in database for permanent storage purpose. Process model is used in this work to describe the atomic process of service profile. This model will be used further in our future work for service invocation process.

Service discovery

The service requester can now query the Semantic Registry by providing service inputs, output, preconditions or effects. As service discovery will use OWL-S service profile and service process model, the service requester have to provide the required service criteria on the basis of service inputs, output, preconditions or effects. After service publication in OWL-S Profile Repository as described in Figure 2, service requester can query the Semantic Registry. The Capability Matching Module searches the UDDI registry and OWL-S Profile Repository for the requested service parameters. The Capability Matching Module then executes the matchmaking algorithm with OWL-S Service Profile defined through Jena APIs as described below and with healthcare Service Ontology. Healthcare Service ontology is the upper ontology used by our Semantic Registry for implementing service profile publishing and discovery phases. The searched results and matching levels are provided based on scoring and ranking (degree of match: exact match, plugin match, subsume match, no match). The OWL-S Service Profile used for Service Discovery is as follows:

```
<profile:Profile>
<profile:serviceName>FindLabReportResult</profile:serviceName>
<profile:textDescription>
An HL7 compliant semantic web healthcare service
</profile:textDescription>.........
```

How a Physician and a Patient bound on OWL-S Semantic Registry as shown in Figure 6 is better explained through a scenario. We implemented a scenario where a patient registered in a hospital through our semantic registry. The required steps for publishing and discovery phases included as follows:

- **Publishing phase**
  - 2 Web services (WSDL)
  - WSDL 2 OWL-S conversion
  - OWL-S Annotations for these 2 WSDL
  - Service, Profile, Process Model, Grounding
  - Stored in Repositories
- **Discovery phase**
  - User request
  - Convert into OWL-S
  - Map user request, OWL-S Annotations
  - Semantic matchmaking , Selection, Ranking
  - OWL-S 2 WSDL conversion
  - WSDL information from UDDI Registry
  - Service invocation and execution
  - Information provided to End user

B. Publishing phase implemented scenario

The web services description in WSDL for Web service name addPatient is as follows:

```
<message name="addPatient_Request">
<part name="Name" type="xsd:string">
<part name="location" type="xsd:string">
</message>
<message name="addPatient_Response">
<part name="patientId" type="xs:string">
```

```
</message>
 <portType name="addPatientPortType">
<operation name="addPatient">
   <input message="addPatient: addPatient_Request "/>
   <output message="addPatient:addPatient_Response"/>
</operation>
</portType>
<binding  name="addPatientSoapBinding" type="addPatient:addPatientPortType">
<soap:binding style="rpc" transport="http://schemas.xmlsoap.org/soap/http"/>
<operation name="addPatient">
</operation>
</binding>
```

The detailed OWL-S annotations for patient registration web service are as follows:

1. Service

```
<service:Service rdf:ID="regPatient_Service">
<service:presents
rdf:resource="http://www.
regPatient.com/regPatient.wsdl/regPatient_Profile#regPatient_Profile"/>
<service:describedBy                                      rdf:resource="http://www.
regPatient.com/regPatient.wsdl/regPatient_ProcessModel#regPatient_ProcessModel"/>
<service:supports                                         rdf:resource="http://www.
regPatient.com/regPatient.wsdl/regPatient_Grounding#regPatient_Grounding"/>
</service:Service>
```

2. Service Profile

```
<profile:serviceName>patientReg</profile:serviceName>
<profile:textDescription/>
<profile:hasInput rdf:resource=" #regPatientPortType _patientReg_Name_IN"/>
<profile:hasInput rdf:resource="#regPatientPortType _ patientReg_ Location_IN"/>
<profile:hasInput rdf:resource=" #regPatientPortType _ patientReg_isCritical_IN"/>
<profile:hasOutput rdf:resource="#regPatientPortType _ patientReg_patientId_OUT"/>
<profile:hasOutput                    rdf:resource="#regPatientPortType                    _
patientReg_hospitalName_OUT"/>
<profile:hasOutput rdf:resource="#regPatientPortType _ patientReg_contactNo_OUT"/>
 </profile:Profile>
```

3. Process Model

```
<process:AtomicProcess rdf:ID="#regPatientPortType _ patientReg">
<process:hasInput rdf:resource=" #regPatientPortType _ patientReg _Name_IN"/>
<process:hasInput rdf:resource="#regPatientPortType _ patientReg _Location_IN"/>
<process:hasInput rdf:resource="#regPatientPortType _ patientReg_isCritical_ IN"/>
<process:hasResult> <process:Result>
<process:hasOutput rdf:resource="="#regPatientPortType _ patientReg_patientId_OUT"/>
<process:hasOutput          rdf:resource="="#regPatientPortType          _          patientReg
_hospitalName_OUT"/>
```

```
<process:hasOutput rdf:resource="="#regPatientPortType _ patientReg _contactNo_OUT"/>
</process:Result> </process:hasResult>
</process:AtomicProcess>
```

4. Grounding

```
<grounding:WsdlGrounding rdf:ID="regPatient_Grounding">
............
rdf:ID="WSDLGrounding_regPatient_ patientReg ">
<grounding:owlsProcess rdf:resource="http://www. regPatient.com/regPatient.wsdl/regPatient_ProcessModel#regPatientPortType_ patientReg "/>
<xsd:uriReference rdf:value="http://www.regPatient.com/regPatient.wsdl# patientReg"/>
<grounding:wsdlInputMessage> // inputs
<xsd:uriReference rdf:value="http://www. regPatient.com/regPatient.wsdl#patientReg_Request"/>................................
    <xsd:uriReference rdf:value="http://www. regPatient.com/regPatient.wsdl#Name"/> ..................................
<xsd:uriReference rdf:value="http://www. regPatient.com/regPatient.wsdl#Location"/>
 .................. <xsd:uriReference rdf:value="http://www. regPatient.com/regPatient.wsdl#isCritical"/> // Outputs ...............
    <xsd:uriReference rdf:value="http://www. regPatient.com/regPatient.wsdl#hospitalName"/>
..................... <xsd:uriReference rdf:value="http://www. regPatient.com/regPatient.wsdl#contactNo"/> </grounding:wsdlOutputMessageParts>
```

C. Discovery phase implemented scenario

- User request (goal oriented request)
  - Inputs: saman, seecs, true
  - Output: patient id, hospital name, contact no
- Discovered OWL-S Profile

```
<profile:serviceName> </profile:serviceName>
 <profile:textDescription/>  <profile:hasInput rdf:resource=" saman"/>
  <profile:hasInput rdf:resource=seecs"/>
<profile:hasInput rdf:resource=" true"/>
  <profile:hasOutput rdf:resource="patient Id"/>
 <profile:hasOutput rdf:resource="hospital name"/>
 <profile:hasOutput rdf:resource="contact no"/> </profile:Profile>
```

2.3.5 Discussion

We ranked the web services based on service level matching and it varies from 5 as the highest and 0 as the lowest. Ranking helps in displaying the best matching results on top of the list. The default lower bound has the value 3 which filters all the results and displays only those services which have Ranking of 3 or above. We also described concept level matching with these possible degrees of match. (1) Exact Match is applicable when concepts mach exactly. (2) Plug-in Match and Subsume Match are applicable when both request and advertisement have direct parent-child relationship. (3) Enclosure match is applicable when request and advertisement is not direct parent-child but still match in the ontology hierarchy. (4) Unknown matches or Fail when there is no concept in the ontology. Table 2 shows the ranking and degree of matches for the requested service with the advertised services. Similarly the same results achieved for other capabilities of services such as service outputs, preconditions and effects.

Profile Name	Rank	Degree of Match
FindLabReportResult	5	Exact Match
Laboratory Service	4	Subsume Match (Parent Match)
Health-application-service	4	Subsume Match (Parent Match)
....	.....	....

Table 2. Ranking of Found Services

The performance analysis of the system is represented in form of time taken for ontology to be loaded into the memory. Analysis also contains the results of the system in terms of number of relevant results produced by our system comparing with the results of the syntax based systems without ontologies.

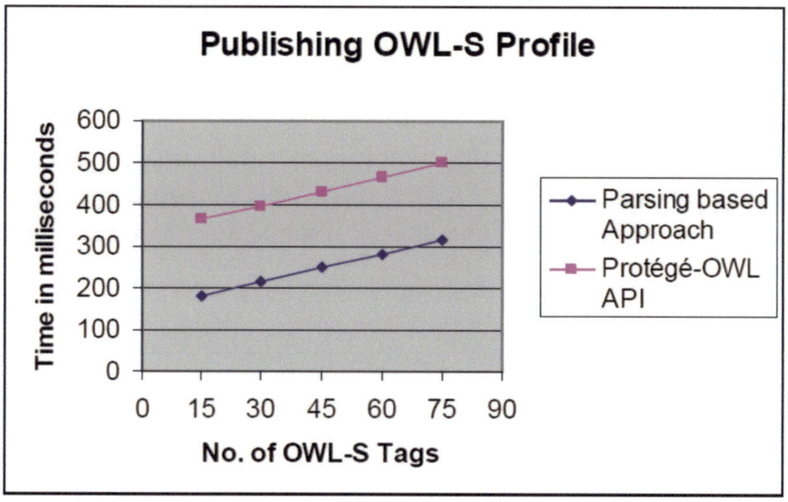

Fig. 10. Performance Analysis of Publishing OWL-S Profile.

The Figure 10 shows the performance of the parsing based approach with the protégé-OWL API. We used protégé-OWL API approach for creation of OWL-S profiles. Though it takes more time as compared to parsing based approach but it captures all required semantics for OWL-S Profiles.

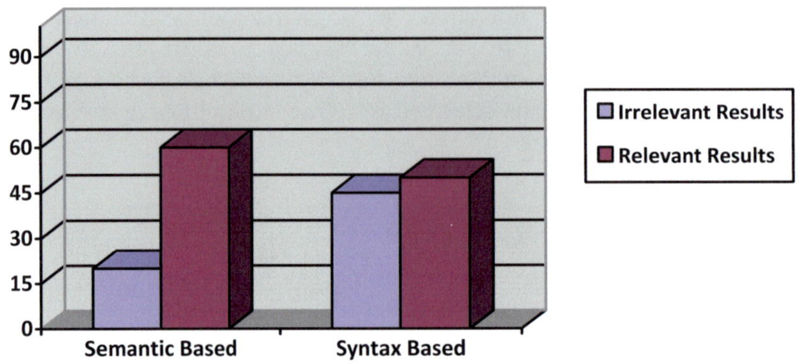

Fig. 11. Performance Analysis of Service Discovery.

For service discovery analysis the system was tested on 100 service profiles. We tested our semantic based approach with the syntax based approach of UDDI. The figure shows the average result of different queries executed on both the systems under same conditions. The relevant result of the syntax based approach is much lower than that of the semantic based approach. With syntax based approach 95 service profiles retrieved out of which 50 were relevant. With our semantic based approach 70 profiles retrieved out of which 62 were relevant. The result is based on the exact matches of IOPE of service capabilities for both systems as shown in Figure 11.

Our semantic based registry or OWL-S framework that provides services and metadata to manage healthcare information and processes in a consistent way that would be compliant with emerging international standards. Our Solution would provide collaboration and give hospitals and clinics the ability to share healthcare semantic information. Semantic web technologies can provide extensible, flexible and efficient information. Semantics can provide interoperable, automated and seamlessly meaningful communication in healthcare domain.

3. Conclusion

This chapter is based on discussion of two major problems of healthcare industry: interoperability and integration. We presented two designing architecture to handle the two common problems and manage large scale medical data, patient records and the technological infrastructure. Healthcare domain is facing challenges of information sharing, interoperability and efficient discovery. These challenges can be handled with the help of semantic web technologies, service oriented architecture and cloud computing by providing automated semantic web health services. This will lead to extensible and flexible data storage, retrieval and sharing among physicians and patients and efficient discovery of information related to diseases and clinical processes.

Cloud computing will change the rules of healthcare service provision globally with adding values to existing platforms as SaaS and will automate processes and knowledge networks through semantic interoperability. The SEMR system will develop a semantic based SaaS service model on top of cloud for healthcare domain to resolve the above mentioned problems. This will result in efficient healthcare provision to patients in a timely manner (Iftikhar et al., 2011).

A framework for semantic registry based on OWL-S - an ontology web language for web services is used for semantic composition. We implemented a scenario where we bound a physician and a patient for registering to a hospital. We also provide service advertisement publication and discovery of service profiles and process model of HL7 compliant healthcare web services. The service description capabilities of Semantic Registry incorporated functional semantics where we also defined preconditions and effects. The service discovery is also more efficient as matchmaking algorithm is also considering service preconditions and effects for fulfilling the user requests. The whole working of the service publication and discovery is described through FindLabReportResult HL7 compliant healthcare semantic web service scenario. The results are evaluated through implementing the UDDI Publish APIs and Inquire APIs as these are without semantics and do not provide discovery on the basis of preconditions and effects (Iftikhar et al., 2011).

4. Acknowledgment

This work is part of Health Life Horizon project initiated at NUST SEECS (http://hl7.niit.edu.pk/index.htm) and is funded by National ICT R&D Funds, Pakistan, http://ictrdf.org.pk.

5. References

Dogac A., Laleci G., Kirbas S., Kabak Y., Sinir S., Yildiz A., and Gurcan, Y.: "Artemis: deploying semantically enriched web services in the healthcare domain". *Proceedings of Information systems journal (Elsevier)*, 2006, 31, (4–5), pp. 321–339

Dogac, Asuman., Gokce, B. Laleci., Kabak, Yildiray., Unal, Seda., Beale, Thomas., Heard, Sam., Elkin, Peter., Najmi, Farrukh., Mattocks, Carl., Webber, David. (2008). Exploiting ebXML Registry Semantic Constructs for Handling Archetype Metadata in Healthcare Informatics. *Proceedings of International Journal of Metadata, Semantics and Ontologies* (IJMSO-08).

Papazoglou, M.P. and W-J. van den Heuvel, "Service-Oriented Architectures: Approaches, Technologies and Research Issues. *Proceedings of VLDB J.*, vol. 16, no. 3, 2007, pp. 389-415.

Beeler, George W., Stan Huff, Wesley Rishel, Abdul-Malik Shakir, Mead Walker, Charlie Mead, Gunther Schadow. (1999) Message Development Framework. Version 3.3, December 1999, Copyright 1999 by Health Level Seven, Inc.

CASCOM: Nadine Fröhlich, Heikki Helin, Heimo Laamanen, Thorsten Möller, Thomas Schabetsberger, Heiko Schuldt, and Christian Stark. (2007). Semantic Service Co-Ordination for Emergency Assistance in Mobile e-Health Environments. *Proceedings of Workshop on Semantic Web in Ubiquitous Healthcare, collocated with the 6th International Semantic Web Conference* (ISWC2007), 2007.

Cesar Cáceresc, Alberto Fernández, Sascha Ossowski, Carlos Matteo Vasirani. (2006). Agent-Based Semantic Service Discovery for Healthcare: An Organizational Approach", IEEE Intelligent Systems, vol. 21, no. 6, 2006, pp. 11-20.

Clement, L. Hately, A. Riegen, C. and Rogers, T. "UDDI Version 3.0.2". OASIS, 2004. UDDI Spec Technical Committee Draft. Available at http://www.uddi.org.

Cocoon: Emanuele Della Valle, and Dario Cerizza. "The mediators centric approach to automatic Web Service discovery of Glue". *CEUR Workshop Proceedings*, vol. 168, 2005, pp. 35–50.

Ginsburg, Mark. Interface Considerations in a Pediatric EMR. *Proceedings of 12th Americans Conference on Information Systems,* Acapulco, Mexico, August 4-6, 2006.

Iftikhar, Saman., Khan, Wajahat Ali., Hussain, Maqbool., Afzal, Muhammad., Ahmad, Farooq. (2011). Design of Semantic Electronic Medical Record (SEMR) system as SaaS service model for Efficient Healthcare. *Proceedings of International Health Interoperability Conference,* March, 2011.

Iftikhar, Saman., Ahmad, Farooq., Fatima, Kiran. (2011). A framework based on OWL-S for health care information provision, *Proceedings of 7th IEEE International Conference on Emerging Technologies,* Islamabad, Pakistan, September, 2011.

Iftikhar, Saman., Nawaz, Falak., Ahmad, Farooq., Fatima, Kiran. (2011). Introducing Semantics in DHTs for Grid Services in a Semantic Registry. *Proceedings of 6th IEEE International Conference on Emerging Technologies,* pp 382 - 387, 18-19 Oct. 2010

Nawaz, F., Pasha, M., Ahmad, F., Suguri, H., (2007). Pushing Semantic Web Service Profiles to Subscribers for Efficient Service Discovery. *Proceedings of the 3rd International Conference on Semantics, Knowledge and Grid* (SKG '07) Xi'an, China, October 2007.

N. Srinivasan, M. Paolucci, K. Sycara. (2004). An Efficient Algorithm for OWL-S based Semantic Search in UDDI. *Proceedings of first International Workshop on Semantic Web Services and Web Process Composition*, SWSWPC 2004 96-110.

Paolucci, M., T. Kawamura, T. Payne, K. Sycara, "Semantic Matching of Web Services Capabilities. *Proceedings of the First International Semantic Web Conference on The Semantic Web*, p.333-347, June 09-12, 2002.

Willmott, S., Willmott, H. Ronsdorf, K. Krempels. (2005)Publish and search versus registries for semantic web service discovery. *Proceedings of Web Intelligence*, 2005.

World Wide Web Sites and Other Electronic Sources

Benefits of SOA, Website 2010, http://www.devshed.com/c/a/Web-Services/Introduction-to-Service-Oriented-Architecture-SOA/2/ [(Last Visited march 2011)]

Benefits of Semantic SOA, http://members.sti2.at/~jacekk/education.sti2.org/slides/1-graham-soa.pdf [(Last Visited march 2011)]

Clear-health-improving practice management. http://www.clear-health.com/ [(Last Visited march 2011)]

CCHIT. http://en.wikipedia.org/wiki/Certification_Commission_for_Healthcare_Information_Technology/. [(Last Visited march 2011)]
CCHIT EMR. http://www.mtbc.com/cchit-emr.aspx/ [(Last Visited march 2011)]
Cocoon. 2011. Available from: http://www.cocoon-health.com
Health Level Seven, http://www.hl7.org/ [(Last Visited March 2011)]
Health Life Horizon (HLH), http://hl7.seecs.nust.edu.pk/ [(Last Visited march 2011)]
HL7 V3 Interoperability Standard, Normative Edition 2009
Health Services Specifications Project (HSSP) http://hssp.wikispaces.com/ [(Last Visited march 2011)]
HIPPA, http://en.wikipedia.org/wiki/Health_Insurance_Portabity_and_Accountability_Act/ [(Last Visited march 2011)]
HL7 V3 Interoperability Standard, Normative Edition 2009.
HIMSS "Selecting the Right EMR Vendor," http://www.himss.org/content/files/selectingemr_flyer2.pdf [(Last Visited March 2011)]
Healthcare Services Specification Project (HSSP) HL7 Services Oriented Architecture SIG; 2011. Available from: http://hssp.wikispaces.com.
LOINC. 2011. Accessed from http://loinc.org/
Neotool "The HL7 Evolution, Comparing HL7 Version 2 to Version 3, Including a History of Version 2"
Object Management Group (OMG), http://www.omg.org/ [(Last Visited march 2011)]
OpenEMR, http://en.wikipedia.org/wiki/OpenEMR/ [(Last Visited march 2011)]
OpenEMR Virtual Appliance, http://en.wikipedia.org/wiki/OpenMRS/ [(Last Visited march 2011)]
OpenMRS, http://en.wikipedia.org/wiki/OpenMRS. [(Last Visited march 2011)]
Protégé API. Jena, 2011. Available from: http://jena.sourceforge.net/.
SequelMed EMR. http://www.sequelmed.com/Products/electronic_medical_records.aspx/. [(Last Visited march 2011)]
SaaS and Healthcare Internet Business Models http://microarray.wordpress.com/2009/01/24/saas-and-healthcare-internet-business-models/ [(Last Visited march 2011)]
Software as a Service (SaaS) http://msdn.microsoft.com/en-us/library/aa905332.aspx#enterprisertw_topic4/ [(Last Visited march 2011)]
SmartCare. http://en.wikipedia.org/wiki/SmartCare/ [(Last Visited march 2011)]
SNOMED Clinical Terms User Guide January 2007 Release
Understanding HIPPA: Health Insurance Portability And Accountability Act. http://www.googobits.com/articles/p0-2899-understanding-hippa-health-insurance-portability-and-accountability-act.html. [(Last Visited march 2011)]
WSMO. http://www.wsmo.org/
Web Services Modeling Ontology. http://www.wsmo.org/
Xchart. http://www.openhealth.org/XChart/ [(Last Visited march 2011)]

ZIMBRA- open source email and collaboration. http://www.zimbra.com/ [(Last Visited march 2011)]

Erl, T., (2005). "Service-Oriented Architecture (SOA). Concepts, Technology, and Design". Prentice Hall PTR.

Kourtesis D. and Paraskakis I. (2008). Combining SAWSDL, OWL-DL and UDDI for Semantically Enhanced Web Service Discovery. In Bechhofer S. et al.(Eds.): ESWC 2008, Lecture Notes in Computer Science 5021, Springer-Verlag Berlin Heidelberg 2008, pp. 614-628.

6

Semantic Based Sport Video Browsing

Xueming Qian
School of Electronic and Information Engineering, Xi'an Jiaotong University, Xi'an, China

1. Introduction

In this chapter, we focus our attention on semantic based sport video highlights detection and semantic based sport video browsing. Users are more interested in sport video highlights than the normal kicks. They site before their TV sets to enjoy the exciting moments that their favorite teams shooting goals. As audiences enjoy the highlight of the video content, usually they have patient to the inserted video Advertisements. For the web based video services, the click rates of sport video highlights are far more than the whole video sequences [56]. Detecting highlights effectively is not only of interest to users/audiences (they are willing to view the highlights) but also of interest to commercial companies. They are interested in inserting their advertisement around the highlights to get more attention from consumers and expand the influences of their products/services. In many online video services websites, the sport video highlights are manually labeled which is very time-consuming and expensive. Thus automatic sport video highlight detection is very urgent [1]-[29]. It is a fundamental step for semantic based video browsing [1,7,8]. However, due to the semantic gaps between computer and human beings, highlights detection is not a trivial.

Two types of approaches have been widely utilized in sport video highlight detection, as shown in Fig.1. The first type of highlights detection approaches are carried out by mapping from low-level features directly or using model-based approaches. In the second type of approaches a mid-level semantic layer is introduced between the low-level features and high-level semantics. Highlights are detected from mid-level semantics rather than from low-level features directly. Thus it is robust against the divergences of low-level features. The second type of sport video highlight detection approaches is more effective than the first type of approaches. Based on the detected high-level semantics, semantics based video browsing can be performed.

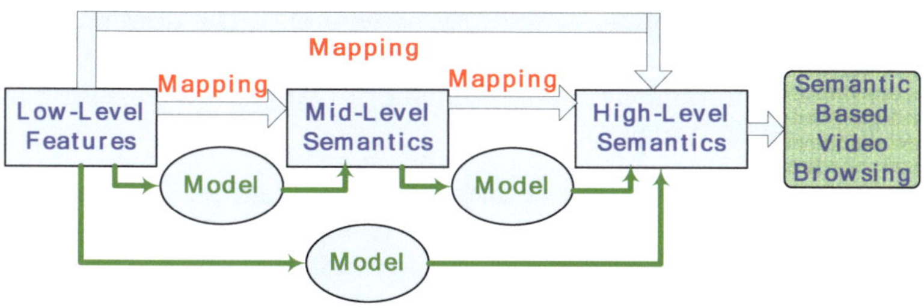

Fig. 1. Block diagram of semantic based sport video browsing.

The conventional video content browsing is based on the summarization of the whole video content. However viewers may be interested to the highlights of sport video. In this chapter, a semantic based sport video browsing approach is introduced. It is a novel book style based approach. Sport video summarization structure is similar to the table of content (ToC) of books. The semantic based video browsing approach has several advantages. Firstly, it is a hierarchical video summarization framework. Secondly, it provides seamless connections with sport video high-level semantics extraction. Thirdly, it is very convenient for users to find their interested content in a large scale database.

In this chapter, firstly learning based soccer video highlight detection approaches are expressed and then semantic based soccer video browsing approach is introduced. The main content of this chapter is organized as follows. Effective low level features representation for sports video is given in Section 2. Middle level semantic classification approaches for soccer video is provided in Section 3. High level semantic detection approaches are introduced in Section 4. Semantic based video browsing is given in Section 5 and conclusions are drawn in Section 6.

2. Low-level feature representation

In this section, several effective low-level visual features for sport video content analysis are introduced. The features are dominant color, motion, texture and overlaid text information. From the low-level visual feature detection results, mid-level semantics classification and high-level events can be determined by using either direct mapping or statistical learning based approaches.

2.1 Dominant color

Dominant color is an effective feature for soccer video analysis. The dominant color is essentially the color of the grass field. The distribution and percentage of grass field region offer significant cues for mid-level semantics categorization and highlights detection.

2.1.1 Related work on dominant color extraction

In [14], Duan et al. classified video shots into eight categories by fusing the global motion pattern, color, texture, shape, and shot length information in a supervised learning framework. Motion and dominant color information of a video shot are fused by multi-layer hidden Markov models (HMM) to determine its categorization [6]. Dominant color ratio and the dominant color projection histogram [12] are utilized for semantic soccer video shot classification. The dominant color extraction approach consists of two stages: dominant color modeling and adaptive dominant color refinement [12]. The dominant color modeling can be viewed as determining a coarse dominant color, which can be utilized for various soccer videos. While the dominant color refinement can be viewed as getting more accurate dominant color for a specific video.

In [56], dominant color detection scheme consists of three steps: 1) Initial dominant color modeling in HSI color space. The accumulative histograms of the HSI components are constructed from training frames of global views randomly selected form wide range of soccer videos and the initial dominant color are determined from the color histogram [36]. 2) Initial dominant color region determination. The initial dominant color and the cylindrical metric [36] are then utilized to classify each pixel of current frame into dominant color or non-dominant color. 3) Adaptive dominant color refinement. For the pixels labeled as initial dominant color, their accumulative histograms of HSI are reconstructed again and the same operations as in initial dominant color modeling step are utilized to obtain the refined dominant color (H_0, S_0, I_0) of the current frame. Let's give a brief overview of this approach.

2.1.2 Coarse to fine dominant color extraction approach

The distance of a pixel located at coordinate (*i*, *j*) with color $(H(i,j), S(i,j), I(i,j))$ to the dominant color (H_0, S_0, I_0) is measured by the cylindrical metric [36] as follows

$$D(i,j) = \sqrt{D_{int}(i,j)^2 + D_{chr}(i,j)^2} \tag{1}$$

where $D_{int}(i,j)$ and $D_{chr}(i,j)$ denote the distance in intensity and chrominance components respectively.

$$D_{int}(i,j) = I(i,j) - I_0 \tag{2}$$

$$D_{chr}(i,j) = \sqrt{S(i,j)^2 + S_0^2 - 2S_0 S(i,j)\cos(\theta(i,j))} \tag{3}$$

$$\theta(i,j) = \begin{cases} |H(i,j) - H_0| & if\ |H(i,j) - H_0| \le 180^\circ \\ 360^\circ - |H(i,j) - H_0| & otherwise \end{cases} \tag{4}$$

Similar to [36], the dominant color region map $DCRM(i,j)$ as follows:

$$DCRM(i,j) = \begin{cases} 0 & D(i,j) > D_{th} \\ 1 & D(i,j) \le D_{th} \end{cases} \tag{5}$$

where D_{th} is learned from several soccer video clips, $DCRM(i,j)$=1 indicates that the pixel (*i*, *j*) belongs to the field region. The dominant color ratio (*DCR*) of a frame is obtained as follows:

$$DCR = \frac{\sum_{i=1}^{H}\sum_{j=1}^{W} DCRM(i,j)}{H \times W} \tag{6}$$

where *H* and *W* are the height and width of a frame. Fig.2 shows the corresponding dominant color region extraction results. The dominant color region of Fig.2(a) is shown in Fig.2 (b) and the field region is extracted as shown in Fig. 2 (c). The dominant color distribution is represented by the dominant color projection vectors of *DCRM*.

Based on *DCRM*, both global or grid based dominant color distributions can be utilized. In [56], the *DCRM* is parsed into 8 equal-sized regions in both vertical and horizontal direction. By calculating the dominant color pixel ratio of each region, a 16-bin dominant color distribution vector is constructed. In addition to the dominant color distribution, a 255 dimensional block wise color moment generated from 5-by-5 grids of the images is also utilized.

(a) Original image (b) dominant color region (c) field and non-field region

Fig. 2. Dominant color region, field region and field lines detection results.

2.2 Texture feature

Texture features are insensitive to lighting, rotation, and other conditions. Two kinds of texture features are utilized for coarse shot classification in [56]. The first is hierarchical wavelet packet texture descriptor (HWVP) [47]. The second is 24 dimensional histogram of oriented gradient (HOG) [46]. HWVP descriptor is a 210 dimensional feature which is extracted under local partitioning pattern Local5 (the image is partitioned into 2x2 grids and a centralized grid), by setting the wavelet packet basis to be db2, with hierarchical wavelet packet transform level 2.

2.3 Title text detection, localization, and tracking

Title texts provide valuable information for event detection in soccer video content analysis. Usually the overlaid text about goal, foul, yellow/red card are followed the corresponding highlight events. In Fig.3, overlaid texts (including bulletin texts and title texts) and replays of a soccer video are plotted. There are 20 replays and 7 overlaid texts. The first text is a bulletin text that shows the players' name of the two teams. The second text shows the initial score of two teams. The 3rd and the 6th texts show the names of the players who got goals. The 4th and 7th texts show the updated scores just after a goal. Moreover, the 5th text shows the score of two teams. From Fig.3, the co-occurrences of the title texts and replays always indicate the appearing of highlights. So, it is reasonable to fuse the title text detection results to improve the highlight detection performance. In [56], the detected title text information is utilized for improving highlight detection performances. Thus from the production knowledge overlaid text information is one of the effective clues for high-level semantics inference.

There are four types of texts in the sport video sequences: 1) long term texts, such as icons of the TV channels, the score-boards which appear at the four corners of video frame, as shown in Fig.4(a) and (b) respectively. This type of texts exists in a fixed location in a frame with long duration. 2) Title texts, e.g. showing the score of two teams after getting a goal, as shown in Fig.4(b). 3) Scene texts, such as the texts appearing in signboard and cloth. 4) Bulletin texts, e.g. showing the name list of a team. This type of text usually appears at the beginning of a soccer video. Except utilizing the text detected in sports video, web-casting text information is incorporated with audio-visual features to improve highlights detection performances [28,29].

In soccer video the title texts usually appeared in the bottom-center of the image. The icon, scoreboard and time tables are appeared in the top-left and top-right parts of an image respectively. This type text always appeared during the whole video sequence, for example, the extracted local text lines of Fig. 4(a), as shown in Fig.4(c) are appeared in the whole video. However, the title text as appeared in Fig.4(b), as shown in Fig. 4(d) usually existed in a limited time range. The title text is usually provides more information on its corresponding highlight event inference than a long term text. They are purposively added during soccer video editing, and they are aimed at providing the audience some indicative information about the video content, such as a card or a goal [56], [62].

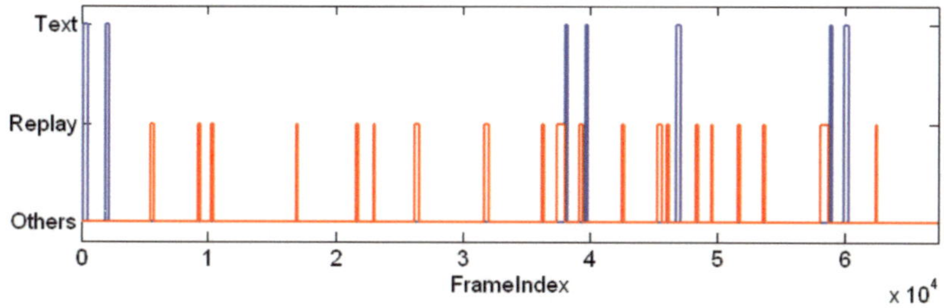

Fig. 3. Overlaid texts (including bulletin texts and title texts) and replays of a soccer video.

Fig. 4. The types of texts appeared in soccer video frames.

2.3.1 Related works on video text detection and tracking

The corresponding text detection approaches can be classified into following 3 types. The first is the connection characteristics of video texts [63], [64]. The text detection methods based on this characteristic assume that text regions have uniform colors and satisfy certain constraints on size, shape, and spatial layout. The second is the texture alike characteristic of the text regions [65, 33, 66, 67]. The text detection methods based on texture information usually assume that the text regions have special texture patterns. And the third is the edge density information [34], [68]. These methods make full use of the fact that the edge densities of background are comparatively sparser than those of the text regions [69], [70]. Usually the corner point number in the text region is larger than that in the background regions.

Video text detection and localization can be carried out both in pixel and compressed domains [71,34,68,65,72]. In order to eliminate false detections, the edge [69], texture [33], and shape information [57] are often utilized in text verifications. In addition, the available redundant temporal information is often used in candidate text region verification and falsely detected text region elimination [71,34,68,65,72,73]. Lyu et al. proposed a multi-resolution based text detection method [34]. Firstly, original edge map is generated for each of target video frames. Multi-resolution text maps of a target frame are generated by down-sampling the original text map. Then text detection, verification and localization are carried out on multi-resolution text maps. Finally, the text detection texts in various resolutions are integrated.

2.3.2 Text detection and tracking

In this chapter, we utilize the corresponding text detection and tracking approaches [56]. The block diagram of the title text detection, localization and tracking is shown in Fig.5. Text line number, spatial location, and temporal duration constraints are utilized during title text detection, localization and tracking. Lyu et al' method [34] is used to detect and localize title texts for a given frame.

It is not necessary to carry out text detection for each of the video frames. In our observations, we find that title texts usually exist for about 5 seconds in soccer video. Detecting text with an interval of one or half second is enough, e.g. detecting text in intra-frames of sport video. Only the texts appeared at the bottom-center of the images and with sufficient duration are determined as candidate title texts. The starting and ending frames of each title text are determined by text line matching and tracking [33].

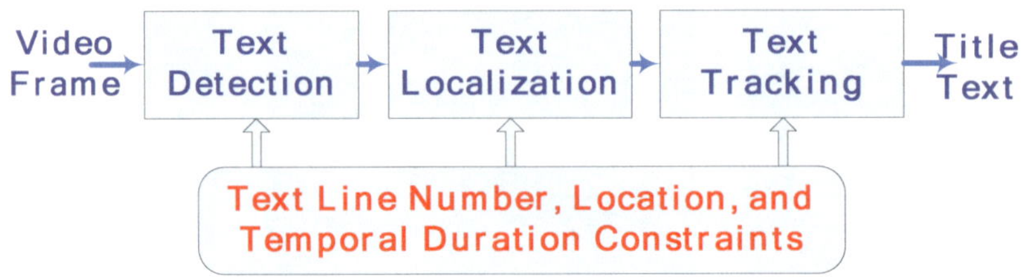

Fig. 5. Title text detection, localization and tracking with text line number, localization and temporal duration constraints.

2.4 Motion feature representation

Motion information is also very important for sport video content analysis [14,15,17]. Typically the camera men operate cameras, by fast track, or zoom in to provide audiences with clearer views of the games. Based on the camera motion (i.e. global motion) patterns and domain related knowledge, high level semantics can be inferred.

In [18], global views of soccer video are further refined into the following three types: stationary, zoom and track in terms of camera motion information using a set of empirical rules with respect to domain and production knowledge. The key-frames of a shot with stationary by means of average motion intensity and average motion intensities of global motion.

Global motions in a video sequence are caused by camera motion, which can be modeled by parametric transforms [30, 32]. The process of estimating the transform parameters is called global motion estimation. The widely used global motion model is perspective model with 8 parameters, which is expressed as follows

$$\begin{cases} x' = \dfrac{m_0 x + m_1 y + m_2}{m_6 x + m_7 y + 1} \\ y' = \dfrac{m_3 x + m_4 y + m_5}{m_6 x + m_7 y + 1} \end{cases} \tag{7}$$

where (x, y) and (x', y') are the coordinates in the current and the reference image respectively, with the set of parameters $\mathbf{m} = [m_0, \cdots, m_7]$ denoting the global motion parameters to be estimated.

Average motion intensities of global motion and local motion are utilized for coarse semantic refinement [56]. The average global motion intensity ($AGMV$) is calculated as follows:

$$AGMV = \frac{1}{M} \sum_{j=1}^{M} \sqrt{GMVx_j^{\,2} + GMVy_j^{\,2}} \tag{8}$$

where $(GMVx_j, GMVy_j)$ is the global motion vector of the block at (x_j, y_j), M is the total block number. The global motion vector $(GMVx_t, GMVy_t)$ at the coordinates (x_t, y_t) is determined as follows

$$\begin{cases} GMVx_t = x'_t - x_t \\ GMVy_t = y'_t - y_t \end{cases} \tag{9}$$

where (x'_t, y'_t) are the warped coordinates in the reference frame by the global motion parameters from the coordinate (x_t, y_t).

The local motion information is represented by average motion intensity (AMV) which is expressed as follows

$$AMV = \frac{1}{M} \sum_{j=1}^{M} \sqrt{MVx_j^{\,2} + MVy_j^{\,2}} \tag{10}$$

where (MVx_j, MVy_j) is the motion vector (MV) of the block with its coordinates (x_j, y_j) and j is the block index.

2.5 Scene change detection and logo detection

Parsing the sequential video sequences into shots is helpful for video content analysis. This is often called scene change detection or shot boundary detection. Thee sport video sequences are different with other video sequences, e.g. the highlights are often replayed. Usually, logos are utilized to connect the live broadcasted clips with the replayed segments. Thus, scene changes and logos are the basis of sport video semantics detection and semantic based sport video content browsing. Scene change detection and logo detection approach consists of the following three steps [3,56]: (1) logo template detection based on the fact that different starting or ending logo transitions, (2) logo transitions detection in the video program using the logo template based on the probability models of pixel-wise intensity-based mean-square difference and color histogram-based mean-square difference, (3) the replay segments identification.

3. Mid-level semantic classification

In this section, the corresponding middle level semantics for sport video are defined and detected. Related work on middle level semantic classification is reviewed.

3.1 Related work on mid-level semantic classification

Xu *et al.* classified each soccer video shot into one of the following 3 views : global, zoom-in and close-up [16]. From the view labels, soccer video sequences are further parsed into play and break. Duan *et al.* classified video shots into predefined mid-level semantics [18]. Based on which, soccer video is coarsely parsed into two type in-play and out-of-play [14]. In [43], global motion and visual features are fused to carry out shot categorization for basketball video. Tan *et al.* also segmented a basketball sequence into wide angle, close-up, fast break and possible shoot at the basket [61]. Motion and dominant color information of a video shot are fused by multi-layer hidden Markov models (HMM) to determine its category [2]. In [37], each shot of a baseball video is classified into predefined semantic scenes by fusing features extracted from visual content of the image, object level feature representations, and camera motion.

(a) Global view (b) Medium view

(c) Close-up (d) Audience

Fig. 6. Four coarse views for soccer video.

3.2 Coarse mid-level semantic classification

Fig.6 shows four coarse mid-level semantics for soccer video. They are global view, medium view, close-up and audience respectively.

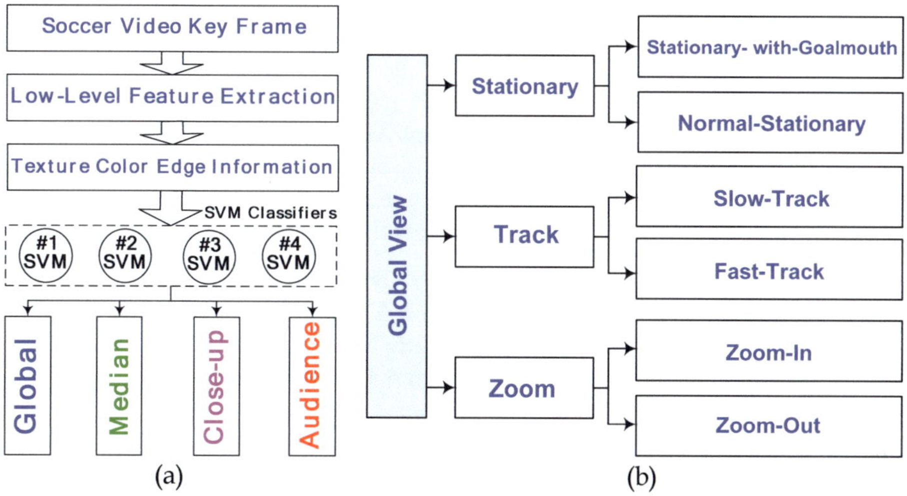

Fig. 7. Coarse to fine soccer video shot categorization. (a) Coarse soccer video shot classification using four one-versus-all SVM classifiers. Replay is refined into replay-global, replay-median and replay-close-up using the first three SVM classifiers. (b) Global view refinement based on camera motion information and field line detection results.

In coarse mid-level semantic categorization, soccer video shots are parsed into four coarse views of global, median, close-up, and audience using four one-versus-all SVM classifiers as shown in Fig.7 (a). The kernels of SVM classifiers are RBF (radius-basis-function). The input of the four SVM classifiers is a 505 dimensional low-level feature, including 255d color moment, 16d dominant color distribution, 24d HOG feature, and 210d HWVP feature.

3.3 Refinement for coarse mid-level semantics

As median, audience, and close-up views are related to the details, which do not need further refinement. Moreover, the audience shots are rarely replayed, the replay into three types: replay-global, replay-median and replay-close-up using the trained SVM classifiers for coarse semantics classification [56]. The block diagram of global view refinement is shown in Fig.7 (b) respectively.

Global view is further refined into one of the following three types: stationary, zoom and track with respect to camera motion information using a set of empirical rules. A shot is determined as with stationary if $AMV<0.5$, otherwise non-stationary. The non-stationary shot is further refined into track if $m_0=m_5=1$, otherwise zoom. A zoom is a zoom-in if $m_0=m_5>1$ and a zoom-out if $m_0=m_5<1$. The track is a slow-track if $AGMV \leq 2$, otherwise a fast-track.

A stationary shot is further refined into stationary-with-goal-post and normal stationary according to the field lines detection results. When the valid field line number is larger than four, then the frame is a stationary with goal-post (SG), otherwise a normal stationary [56].

After mid-level semantic classification and refinement, each segment of a soccer video or event clip is classified into one of 13 mid-level semantics: logo, audience, median, close-up, replay-global, replay-median, replay-close-up, fast-track, slow-track, zoom-in, zoom-out, normal stationary, and stationary-with-goalmouth.

4. High-level semantic detection

In this section, the high level sport video semantics detection approaches are illustrated in details. Statistical learning models such as hidden Markov model (HMM) as shown in Fig.8(a), enhanced hidden Markov model (EHMM), and hidden conditional random field (HCRF) as shown in Fig.8 (b), based soccer video event detection approaches are described. Correspondingly, soccer video highlight detection results are given.

The main content of this section is as follows. Firstly the related works on soccer video highlight detection are briefly overviewed in Section 4.1. Secondly, event clip segmentation in Section 4.2. Thirdly, HMM, EHMM and HCRF based soccer video event detection approaches are provided in Section 4.3 and Section 4.4 respectively. And finally, highlight detection performances are evaluated in Section 4.5.

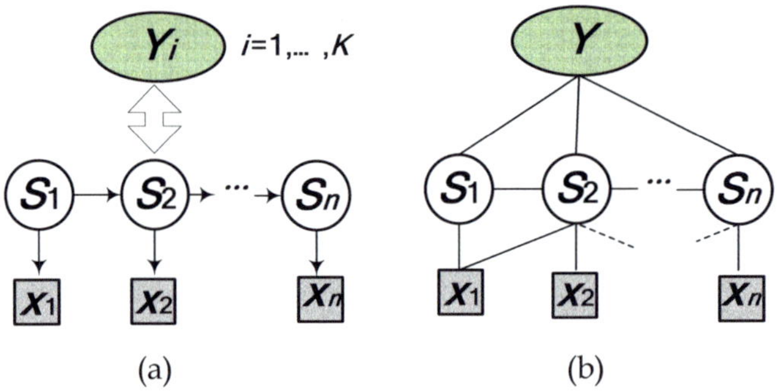

Fig. 8. HMM and HCRF models. (a) HMM and (b) HCRF.

4.1 Related work on soccer video highlight detection

As shown in Fig.1, one type of highlights detection approaches are carried out by mapping from low-level audio-visual features [1], [2], [14], [23], mid-level semantics, coarse events [23], [25], scenes with overlaid text-lines [31] and replays [3]-[5], [31]. Another type of highlight detection approaches are carried out by statistical learning based models. The learning based approaches have been proved to be effective in fusing multi-modal features to improve highlights detection performance [6], [11], [15]-[21], [23]-[27], [35]-[37], [39]-[42], [44], [45].

Xie *et al.* proposed multi-HMMs based method to improve the performance of play-break detection [6]. The HMMs are different structures and with the same input. Dynamic programming is utilized to fuse the outputs of multi-HMMs to determine the shot type (play or break). In [26], soccer video is segmented into sequential event clips: forward pass, shot on goal, placed kick, turnover, counter-attack, and kick-off using a set of domain rules and sport video production knowledge. The placed kicks are further refined into corner kick, free kick and penalty according to the distribution of players' position.

Wang *et al.* proposed conditional random fields (CRF) based soccer video event detection method [11]. Firstly, mid-level semantics are determined by mapping from low-level audio-visual features. Then, highlights are detected by fusing the mid-level semantic using CRF [11]. In [27], dynamic Bayesian networks (DBN) are utilized to model goal, corner kick, penalty, and foul events. Low-level audio-visual features are mapped into mid-level nodes of Bayesian networks directly. Bayesian networks model the dependency of the observations of each shot for event type inference. The shot-based event recognition results are fused by DBN to accumulate evidence in the temporal domain [27].

HCRF is utilized to model highlight events in golf and bowling videos [60]. Different from the existing event detection approaches, the transformed low-level features are utilized to perform event detection. Independent component analysis (ICA) is utilized to determine two main components of the input low-level feature. The HCRF is utilized to fuse the ICA components for event type determination.

In most existing works, events are determined from shot level. It is well known that, a single shot separated from its context does poorly in conveying semantics [22], [56]. That is to say the contextual information among the shots of an event clip is not fully disclosed in event inference [11], [27]. Grouping the sequential shots with the same semantics into unified event clips and then recognizing their event types is an optimal way in event detection [56], [21].

4.2 Event clip segmentation

Let *VS* denote a video sequence. Assuming that it consists of *K* sequential events, the whole video sequence can modeled as follows

$$VS = (E_1, \cdots, E_K) \tag{11}$$

where $E_t (t = 1, \cdots, K)$ belongs to one of the predefined events. Each event clip E_t is composed of several sequential mid-level semantics, which is expressed as

$$E_t = (M_t^1, \cdots, M_t^{N(t)}) \tag{12}$$

where M_t^q ($q = 1, \cdots, N(t)$) corresponds to the predefined mid-level semantics, which can be represented by key-frames of video shots. *N*(*t*) is the total number of mid-level semantics of the *t*-th events. From Eq.(12) and Eq.(11), we have

$$VS = \left(\underbrace{M_1^1, \cdots, M_1^{N(1)}}_{E_1}, \cdots, \underbrace{M_t^1, \cdots, M_t^{N(t)}}_{E_t}, \cdots, \underbrace{M_K^1, \cdots, M_K^{N(K)}}_{E_K} \right) \tag{13}$$

We aimed at segmenting *VS* into event clips by finding event boundaries according to the consistence of semantics. According to domain rules and production knowledge of soccer video, the starting and ending frames of an event clip are the frames at the boundaries where non-global views (including median, close-up, audience, replay and logo) transition to global views [56].

Fig. 9 shows a diagram of event clip (EC) segmentation. The event clips #1 - #4 are composed of global views and several close-up or median views. The event clip #4 is composed of the following mid-level semantics: global, close-up, median, close-up, logo, replays, and logo.

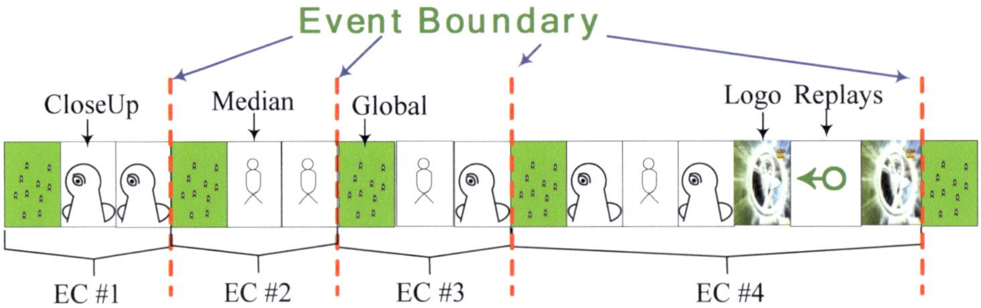

Fig. 9. An example of event boundary determination.

4.2.1 Observations of an event clip

Assuming that an event clip is composed of n mid-level semantics, x_j ($j = 1, \cdots, n$), the temporal transitions of the mid-level semantics of an event clip can be viewed as observations of statistical learning models. Moreover, in [56], the overall feature extracted from each event clip is combined with the temporal observations for event type inference.

The normal observations of an event clip are the temporal transitions of mid-level semantics (i.e. $\mathbf{x} = (x_1, \cdots, x_n)$) as shown in Fig.10. In [56], the enhanced observations $\mathbf{x} = (x_1, \cdots, x_n, \cdots, x_{n+k})$ consist of the normal observations and the overall features are utilized to accumulate the semantics for soccer video highlights detection.

The enhanced observation is composed of k overall features ($k \le 3$). They correspond to the title text (TLT), long time break (LTB), and replay (REP) information respectively. All of them are binary. TLT=0 means that there is no title text in event clip. REP =0 denotes that there is no replay in this event clip. LTB=0 represents that the non-global view segment number is very small.

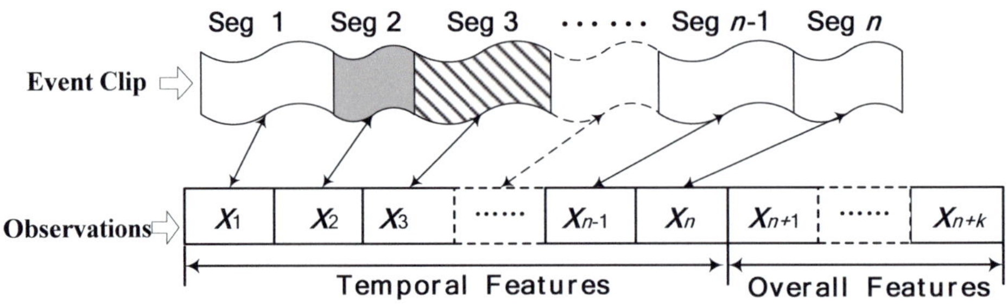

Fig. 10. The temporal and overall features of an event clip. k is the overall feature number.

4.3 HMM based event detection approach

HMM models the state sequence as being Markov, and each observation being independent of all others given the corresponding state [52]. HMM models the joint distribution under two basic independence assumptions: Markov property and independent property.

In this section the hidden Markov and enhanced Markov models based event detection approaches are illustrated in details. The HMM based approach is carried out event inference using the normal observations of an event clip. While, the EHMM based approach carries out event inference using the enhanced observations of an event clip.

4.3.1 Overview of HMM

HMM is a generative model. It defines a joint probability distribution for the observations and their corresponding labels. HMM models a sequence of observations $\mathbf{x} = (x_1, \cdots, x_n)$ with the corresponding label y under the assumption that there is an underlying sequence of state $\mathbf{s} = (s_1, \cdots, s_n)$ drawn from a finite state set. HMM carries out inference under two basic independence assumptions [43]. The first assumption is that each state s_j depends only on its immediate predecessor s_{j-1}, and independent of its previous states (i.e. $s_1, \cdots, s_{j-2}$). The second assumption is that each x_j depends only on the corresponding state s_j. Let $\lambda = (A, B, \pi)$ denote the model parameters. A denotes the state transition probability distribution $A = \{a_{jk}\}$, where a_{jk} is the state transition probability from state j to state k ($a_{jk} \geq 0$). B denotes the observation probability distribution in state j with its observations x_k, $B = \{b_j(k)\}$. $\pi = \{\pi_j\}$ is the initial state distribution. Thus the joint probability of a state sequence **s** and an observation sequence x under a model λ can be modeled as follows

$$P(\mathrm{x} \mid \mathrm{s}, \lambda) = \prod_{j=1}^{n} P(x_j \mid s_j, \lambda) \tag{14}$$

By assuming that observations are statistical independent, then we have

$$P(\mathrm{x} \mid \mathrm{s}, \lambda) = b_{s_1}(x_1) \times b_{s_2}(x_2) \times \cdots \times b_{s_n}(x_n) \tag{15}$$

4.3.2 The training of HMM

Let $D = \{(\mathrm{x}^{(k)}, y^{(k)})\}_{k=1}^{N}$ denote the training data. N is the total number of training event clips. For the k-th training clip, its input is $\mathrm{x}^{(k)} = \{x_1^{(k)}, x_2^{(k)}, \cdots, x_T^{(k)}\}$ and its label is $y^{(k)}$. $x_m^{(k)}$ corresponds to the m-th mid-level semantics in the k-th training clip, and $y^{(k)}$ is its event label.

The flowchart of the training of HMMs is as follows. Firstly, the mid-level semantics of each event clip are determined from the extracted low-level features. Then, the Expectation-maximization (EM) is utilized to estimate the model parameters $\lambda_i = (A_i, B_i, \pi_i)$. The EM algorithm consists of E-steps and M-steps [43]. The E-step computes the forward and backward probability for the given model, and the M-step re-estimates the model parameters. Given an initial model λ, the EM algorithm can find a model λ^t at t-th iteration such that its performance is better than the (t-1)-th iteration. That is to say for the K training samples, the EM algorithm makes the following equation hold.

$$\sum_k P(\mathbf{x}^{(k)}|\lambda^t) \geq \sum_k P(\mathbf{x}^{(k)}|\lambda^{t-1}) \tag{16}$$

4.3.3 The classification of HMM

In event recognition, the type of the event clip with observations **x** is determined as follow

$$y = \arg\max_i P(\mathbf{x}|\lambda_i) = \arg\max_i \sum_{s \in \mathbf{S}} P(\mathbf{x}|\mathbf{S},\lambda_i) \times P(\mathbf{S}|\lambda_i), \tag{17}$$

The probability indicates how well the model λ_i matches the given observations **x**. The probability of the hidden state sequence S can be expressed as

$$P(\mathrm{s}\,|\,\lambda) = \pi_{s_1} a_{s_1 s_2} \times a_{s_2 s_3} \times \cdots \times a_{s_{n-1} s_n} \tag{18}$$

Thus, Eq.(17) can be rewritten as

$$y = \arg\max_i \sum_{s_1,\cdots,s_n} \pi^i_{s_1} b^i_{s_1}(x_1) a^i_{s_1 s_2} \times b^i_{s_2}(x_2) a^i_{s_2 s_3} \times \cdots \times b^i_{s_n}(x_n) a^i_{s_{n-1} s_n}, \tag{19}$$

4.4 HCRF based event detection

Hidden conditional random fields (HCRF) are discriminative models that generalize the hidden Markov models (HMM) and the conditional random fields (CRF) [52]. HCRF models the state sequence as being conditionally Markov given the observations. Unlike HMM, HCRF is also capable of modeling long range dependencies of the observation.

4.4.1 Overview of HCRF

HCRF uses intermediate hidden variables to model the latent structure of the observations as shown in Fig.8 (b). A HCRF models the conditional probability of a label y given the observations $\mathrm{x} = \{x_1,\cdots,x_n\}$ with latent states $\mathrm{s} = \{s_1,\cdots,s_n\}$ as follows:

$$p(y\,|\,\mathrm{x};\lambda) = \frac{1}{Z(\mathrm{x};\lambda)} \sum_{\mathrm{s}} p(y,\mathrm{s}\,|\,\mathrm{x};\lambda) \tag{20}$$

where $p(y,\mathrm{s}\,|\,\mathrm{x};\lambda)$ is a conditional probability, given the labels y, observations x, and hidden states s under the HCRF model parameters λ.

$$p(y,\mathrm{s}\,|\,\mathrm{x};\lambda) = \exp\{\Psi(y,\mathrm{s},\mathrm{x};\lambda)\} \tag{21}$$

where $\Psi(y,\mathrm{s},\mathrm{x};\lambda)$ is a potential function parameterized by the model parameters λ. $Z(\mathrm{x};\lambda)$ is a normalization factor. It ensures that the model be a properly normalized probability over all labels. It is defined as follows

$$Z(\mathrm{x};\lambda) = \sum_{y'}\sum_{\mathrm{s}} \exp\{\Psi(y',\mathrm{s},\mathrm{x};\lambda)\} \tag{22}$$

where y′ is a possible label for the observations x.

4.4.2 The training of HCRF

The parameters of HCRF are trained on the training data $D = \{(\mathrm{x}_i, y_i)\}_{i=1}^{N}$, where each observation $\mathrm{x}_i = \{x_{i,1}, x_{i,2}, \cdots, x_{i,n}\}$ is a sequence of inputs, and each y_i is the label index of the input sequence x_i. The parameters estimations in HCRF is carried out by using the following objective function

$$L(\lambda) = \sum_{t\in\{1,\cdots,N\}} \log p(y_t \mid \mathrm{x}_t;\lambda) - \frac{1}{2\sigma^2}\|\lambda\|^2 \tag{23}$$

The last term $\frac{1}{2\sigma^2}\|\lambda\|^2$ is used for regularization which can reduce the over-fitting of the objective function in optimization. It is the log of a Gaussian prior with variance σ^2 [48, 49]. The limited memory BFGS can be utilized to find the optimal parameters λ^* as follows [50]-[52].

$$\lambda^* = \arg\max_{\lambda} L(\lambda) \tag{24}$$

4.4.3 The classification of HCRF

Given a test event clip with its observations $\mathrm{x} = \{x_1, \cdots, x_n\}$ and trained parameters λ of the HCRFs, the label e^* of this event clip is recognized as follows

$$e^* = \arg\max_{e} P(e \mid \mathrm{x}, \lambda_e) \tag{25}$$

where λ_e is the parameter vector of the event e. In this chapter, we have $e\in$\{Goal, Shoot, Normal Kick, Foul, Placed Kick\}.

4.5 Highlight detection performances evaluation

In this section, high-level semantics detection performances of HMM, EHMM, and HCRF based approaches are evaluated. The training set for the models HMM, EHMM and HCRF is the same which consists of N manually labeled examples $(\mathbf{x}^i, y^i)$ $(i = 1, \cdots, N)$ where each $y^i \in$\{Goal, Shoot, Normal Kick, Foul, Placed Kick\}is the event label, and each observations are $\mathrm{x}^i = \{x_1^i, \cdots, x_n^i\}$. The component x_k^i corresponds to the observation of the k-th segment ($k \in \{1, \cdots, n\}$) of the i-th training event clip. 12 soccer sequences and some highlight event clips which are downloaded from Internet are utilized to train the model parameters of HMM, EHMM and HCRF.

The training steps are as follows: 1) manually label the event clips for the test soccer video sequences. 2) manually label the mid-level semantics. 3) manually label the event boundaries; 4) get the corresponding mid-level semantics for each event clip.

The observations of HMM and HCRF are the temporal transitions of mid-level semantics. The observations of EHMM consist of two parts. The first part is temporal transitions of mid-level semantics which is identical to the observations of HCRF. The second is enhanced observations, including the title texts, long term breaks, and replay information of an event clip [56]. Three overall features are utilized in EHMM. The EHMM and HCRF based event detection approaches are on the basis of event clips and the observation of EHMM and HCRF are mid-level semantics of an event clip.

In order to show the performances of model based event detection approach, in this Section the HMM, EHMM and HCRF based soccer video highlights detection performances are evaluated on seven soccer video sequences. These video sequences are captured from a variety of sources. The total duration of the test video sequences is about 625 minutes. Totally, there are 26 goals, 137 placed kicks, 85 fouls, and 109 shoots. Recall *NR*, precision *NP* and F-measure *F* are used to evaluate objective event detection performances, which are defined as follows:

$$NR = \frac{NC}{NC + NM} \times 100\% \tag{26}$$

$$NP = \frac{NC}{NC + NF} \times 100\% \tag{27}$$

$$F = \frac{2 \times NR \times NP}{NR + NP} \% \tag{28}$$

where *NC*, *NM*, and *NF* denote the correctly, missed, and falsely detected event numbers. Moreover, confusion matrix is utilized to show the discrimination of HCRF based event detection approach for the five events.

The recall, precision and F-measure values of the four highlights of HMM, EHMM and HCRF are shown in TABLE I. The average recall values of the four highlight events are79.55%, 89.08%, and 86.55%. The average precision values of the four highlight events are76.96%, 87.60%, and 88.03%. The average F-measure values of the highlights are 78.24%, 88.33% and 87.29% respectively.

	Placed Kick			Foul			Shoot			Goal		
method	NC	NM	NF	NC	NM	NF	NC	NM	NF	NC	NM	NF
HMM	113	24	18	69	16	25	81	28	28	21	5	14
EHMM	130	7	2	76	9	11	88	21	22	24	2	10
HCRF	120	17	3	73	12	13	90	19	14	26	0	12

Table 1. Comparisons of highlights detection performances of HMM, EHMM and HCRF.

EHMM and HCRF based highlight detection approaches outperform that of HMM based approaches. EHMM is a little better than the HCRF based approach for the events: placed kick and foul. The main reasons are due to the following two aspects: 1) overall features of an event clip are utilized in EHMM. The overall features served as global features which are helpful for highlight event discrimination. 2) The overall features compensate the interior of HMM in modeling the dependence of long term observations and ease the two basic assumptions of HMM. However, HCRF achieves highest performances for detecting shoot and goal events.

5. Semantic based sport video browsing

In this section, a semantic based video browsing framework is proposed. Users can view the video content freely like reading books. The semantic based video content browsing approach is organized as the table-of-content (ToC) of a book. Let's give a brief overlook of the ToC of a book, before illustrating the proposed video browsing method. Fig.11 shows the ToC structure of a book which can be departed into following seven layers: (1) book title (BT); (2) chapter (CH); (3) subchapter (SC); (4) paragraph (PH); (5) page (PG); (6) sentence (ST); and (7) words (WD). With respect to the ToC, readers can know its content very well. They can go straight to the interested content by skipping the irrelevant parts. In order to let readers know the overall content of book, the **preface, introduction** and **summary** of a book give the brief illustrations of the book, a chapter and a subchapter.

If sport video content is organized as the ToC of a book, it will be convenient for us to browsing its content. In this chapter, a novel book style based semantic video browsing approach is expressed. TABLE II gives the correspondences of ToC of book and soccer video. In the first layer the book title corresponds to the video category, such as baseball and soccer video. In the second layer, the chapter of a book is similar to a set of events. In the third layer, the sub-chapter corresponds to the detailed information of an event. In the fourth layer, the paragraph of a book is corresponding to the shot of an event. In the fifth layer, the page of a book is similar to the frame of a video. In the sixth layer, the sentence of a book is corresponding to the object in a video sequence. And in the seventh layer, the word of a book corresponds to the pixel. Fig.12 shows the ToC of soccer videos. Soccer video is parsed into following seven events: normal kick, foul, free kick (FK), penalty, corner kick, shoot and goal. The free kick, penalty and corner kick are refined from placed kick using the distributions of players' positions [7]. The fifth layer of the video provides the original video sequences of event.

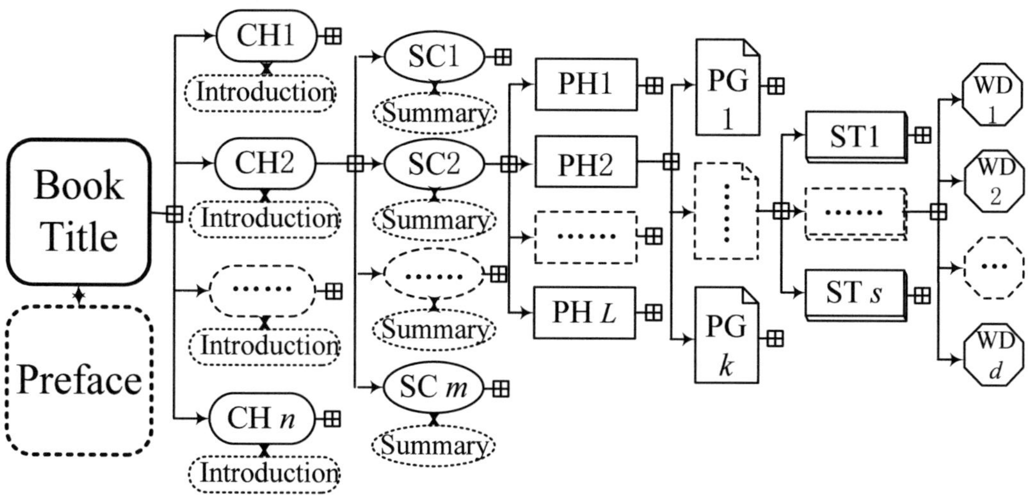

Fig. 11. Table-of-Content of a Book.

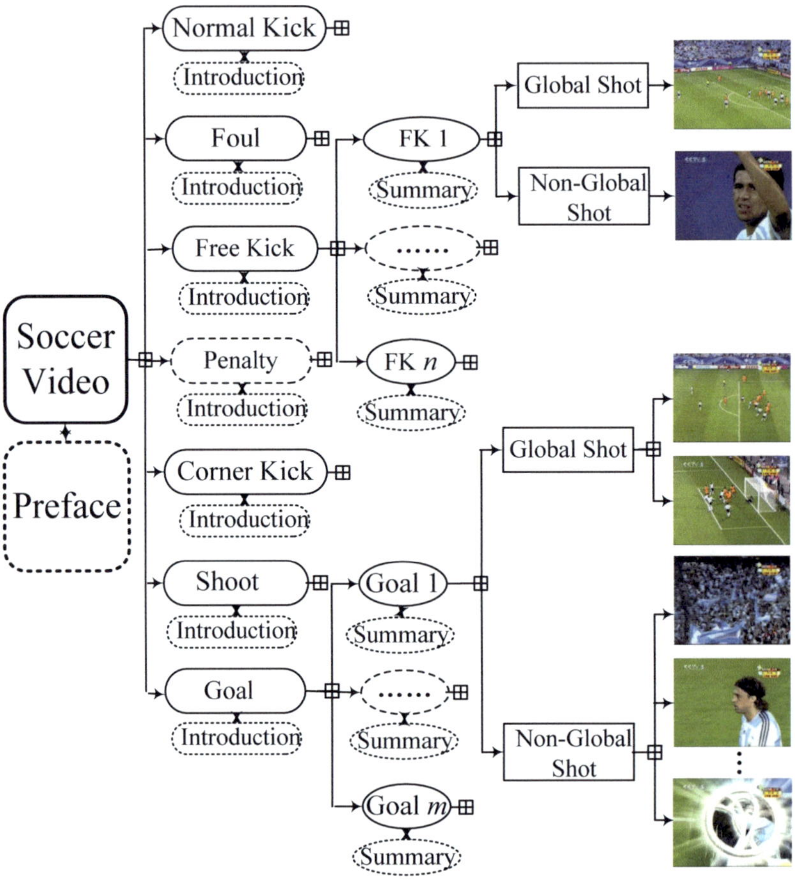

Fig. 12. ToC of soccer video.

The target of us is how to carry out ToC based sport video summarization. According to the correspondence of ToC of Book and sport video, a four layer summarization framework is utilized in this chapter for soccer video summarization. In the fourth layer, the abstraction is carried out for the semantic shots by extracting several key-frames. The third layer abstraction (i.e. **summary**) of a video is the shortened video frames of a specified story unit or event. The summary of the ToC of a video sequences in the third layer is the combination of the summarizations extracted in the fourth layer for the semantic shots. In the sports video, there are also two kinds of semantic shots: global shots and non-global shots. The second layer abstraction (i.e. **introduction**) of a video is the skimmed video frames of story units or events of a certain class. The first layer abstraction (i.e. **preface**) of a video is providing the corresponding abstractions of the video sequences.

Fig.13 shows an example of the proposed sematic based soccer video browsing approach for a goal event. In the fourth layer, it is the continuous video clips of this event. The third layer shows the extracted 11 key-fames of this event clip, which corresponds to the summary of this event. The second layer shows two representative key-frames, which corresponds to the introduction of this event. The first layer is the most representative frames of this event, namely the preface of this event.

Layer	Book	Sports Video
1	Book Title	Soccer video
2	Chapter	A set of Events
3	Sub-Chapter	An Event
4	Paragraph	Mid-level Semantics
5	Page	Frame
6	Sentence	Objects
7	Word	Pixel

Table 2. The Correspondence of ToC structure of different types of video sequences.

(a) The third layer abstraction of an event (summary of ToC)

(b) The second layer abstraction of an event (introduction of ToC)

(c) The first layer abstraction of an event (preface of ToC)

Fig. 13. Video ToC for a soccer event.

6. Conclusion

In this chapter, semantic based sport video browsing is introduced. Soccer video high-level semantics detection approaches using hidden Markov models, enhanced Markov models, and hidden conditional fields are expressed in detail and their performances are evaluated. From the detected highlights, a semantic based soccer video browsing approach is proposed. The proposed semantic based soccer video browsing approach carries out video content browsing using a book-like structure.

7. Acknowledgement

This work is supported in part by National Natural Science Foundations of China (NSFC) No.60903121, No.61173109, and Foundation of Microsoft Research Asia.

8. References

[1] B. Li, J. Errico, H. Pan, and M. Sezan, "Bridging the semantic gap in sports video retrieval and summarization," *J. Vis. Commun. Image R.* vol.17, pp.393-424, 2004.

[2] G. Xu, Y. Ma, H. Zhang, and S. Yang, "An HMM-based framework for video semantic analysis," *IEEE Trans. Circuits and Systems for Video Technology*, vol.15, no.11, Nov. 2005, pp.1422-1433.

[3] H. Pan, B. Li, and M. Sezan, "Automatic detection of replay segments in broadcast sports programs by detecting of logos in scene transitions," in *Proc. Int. Conf. Acoustics, Speech, and Signal Processing*, vol.4, pp. 3385-3388, Orlando, FL, May 2002.

[4] Z. Zhao, S. Jiang, Q. Huang, and G. Zhu, "Highlight summarization in sports video based on replay detection," in *Proc. Int. Conf. Mulmedia and Expo.*, pp. 1613-1616, Toronto, Ontario, Canada, July 2006.

[5] H. Pan, P. Beek, and M. Sezan, "Detection of slow-motion replay segments in sports video for highlights generation," in *Proc. Int. Conf. Acoustics, Speech, and Signal Processing*, vol.3, pp.1649-1652, Salt Lake City, USA, May, 2001.

[6] L. Xie, S. Chang, A. Divakaran, and H. Sun, "Structure analysis of soccer video with hidden Markov models", in *Proc. Int. Conf. Acoustics, Speech, and Signal Processing*,2002, pp. 4096-4099.

[7] A. Ekin, and A. Tekalp, "Generic play-break event detection for summarization and hierarchical sports video analysis," in *Proc. Int. Conf. Mulmedia and Expo*, vol.1, 2003, pp. 169-172.

[8] D. W. Tjondronegoro, Y. Chen, and B. Pham, "Classification of self-consumable highlights for soccer video summaries," in *Proc. Int. Conf. Mulmedia and Expo*, 2004, pp. 579-582.

[9] G. Zhu, C. Xu, Q. Huang, Y. Rui, S. Jiang, W. Gao, and H. Yao, "Event Tactic Analysis Based on Broadcast Sport Video," IEEE Trans. Multimedia, vol.11, no.1, 2009, pp.49-67.

[10] S. Chen, M. Chen, C. Zhang, and M. Shyu, "Exciting event detection using multi-level multimodal descriptors and data classification," in Proc. ISM, 2006.

[11] T. Wang, J. Li, Q. Diao, W. Hu, Y. Zhang, and C. Dulong, "Semantic event detection using conditional random fields," in *Proc. Computer Vision and Pattern Recognition Workshop*, 2006, pp.109-115.

[12] N. Nan, G. Liu, X. Qian, and C. Wang, "An SVM-based soccer video shot classification scheme using projection histograms," PCM 2008.

[13] A. Hanjialic, "Generic approach to highlights extraction from a sports video," in *Proc. Int. Conf. Image Processing*, vol.1, pp. 1-4, 2003.

[14] L. Duan, M. Xu, T. Chua, Q. Tian, and C. Xu, "A mid-level representation framework for semantic sports video analysis," in *Proc. ACM Multimedia*, pp. 29-32,2003.

[15] F. Wang, Y. Ma, H. Zhang, and J. Li, "A generic framework for semantic sports video analysis using dynamic Bayesian networks," in *Proc. Int. Conf. Multimedia Modelling*, pp. 29-32,2005.

[16] P. Xu, L. Xie, and S. Chang, "Algorithms and systems for segmentation and structure analysis in soccer video," in *Proc. Int. Conf. Multimedia & Expo*, 2001, pp. 184-187.

[17] C. Xu, J. Wang, H. Lu, and Y. Zhang, "A Novel Framework for Semantic Annotation and Personalized Retrieval of Sports Video," IEEE Transactions on Multimedia, vol. 10, no. 3, 2008, pp.421-436.

[18] L. Duan, M. Xu, Q. Tian, C. Xu, and J. S. Jin, "A unified framework for semantic shot classification in sports video," *IEEE Trans. Multimedia*, vol.7, No.6, 2005, pp.1066-1083.

[19] X. Qian, H. Wang, G.Liu, Z. Li, and Z. Wang, "Soccer Video Event Detection by Fusing Middle Level Visual Semantics of an Event Clip", in Proc. PCM 2010, pp.439-451.

[20] L. Duan, M. Xu, and Q. Tian, "Semantic shot classification in sports video," in *Proc. SPIE Storage and Retrieval for Media Database*, vol. 5021, 2003, pp. 300-313.

[21] X. Qian, Guizhong Liu, Zhe Wang, Zhi Li, Huan Wang, "Highlight Events Detection in Soccer Video using HCRF," in Proc. ICIMCS, 2010.

[22] X. Zhu, X. Wu, A. Elmagarmid, Z. Feng, and L. Wu, "Video data mining semantic indexing and event detection from the association perspective," IEEE Trans. Knowledge and Data Engineering., vol.17, no.5, pp.665-677, 2005.

[23] Z. Xiong, R. Radhakrishnan, A. Divakaran, and T. Huang, "Highlights extraction from sports video based on an audio-visual marker detection framework, " in Proc. Int. Conf. Multimedia & Expo, pp. 29-32,2005.

[24] C. Xu, Y. Zhang, G. Zhu, Y. Rui, H. Lu, and Q. Huang, "Using Webcast Text for Semantic Event Detection in Broadcast Sports Video," IEEE Trans. Multimedia, vol.10, no.7, 2008, pp.1342-1325.

[25] Y. Wang, Z. Liu, and J. Huang, "Multimedia content analysis using both audio and video clues," IEEE Signal Processing Magazine, 2000.

[26] J. Assfalg, M. Bertini, C. Colombo, A. Bimbo, and W. Nunziati, "Semantic annotation of soccer videos: automatic highlight identification," Computer Vision and Image Understanding, vol.6, No.4, pp.285-305, Aug.2003.

[27] C. Huang, H. Shih, and C. Chao, "Semantic analysis of soccer video using dynamic Bayesian network," IEEE Trans. Multimedia, vol.8, No.4, pp.749-760, Aug. 2006.

[28] M. Dao, and N. Babaguchi, "Mining temporal information and web-casting text for automatic sports event detection," in Proc. MMSP, 2008, pp.616-621.

[29] M. Dao, and N. Babaguchi, "Sports event detection using temporal patterns mining and web-casting text," in Proc. ACM AREA, 2008, pp.33-40.

[30] X. Qian, and G. Liu, "Global motion estimation from randomly selected motion vector groups and GM/LM based applications," Signal, Image and Video Processing, 2007.

[31] D. Zhang, and S. Chang, "Event detection in baseball video using superimposed caption recognition," in Proc. ACM Multimedia, Juan-les- Pins, France, Nov. 1, 2002, pp. 315-318.
[32] Y. Su, M. Sun, and V. Hsu, "Global motion estimation from coarsely sampled motion vector field and the applications", IEEE Trans. Circuits Syst. Video Technol., Vol. 15, No. 2, Feb. 2005, pp. 232-242.
[33] X. Qian, G. Liu, H. Wang, and R. Su, "Text detection, localization and tracking in compressed videos," Signal Processing: Image Communication, vol.22 , 2007, pp.752-768.
[34] M. Lyu, J. Song, and M. Cai, "A comprehensive method for multilingual video text detection, localization, and extraction," IEEE Trans. Circuits and Systems for Video Technology, vol.15, no.2,2005, pp.243-255.
[35] G. Jin, L. Tao, and G. Xu, "Hidden markov model based events detection in soccer video," ICIAR 2004, LNCS 3221, pp.605-612, 2004.
[36] A. Ekin, A. Tekalp, and R. Mehrotra, "Automatic soccer video analysis and summarization," IEEE Trans. Image Processing, vol.12, no.7, 2003, pp. 796-807.
[37] C. Lien, C. Chiang, and C. Lee, "Scene-based event detection for baseball videos," J. Vis. Commun. Image R. 18 (2007) 1–14.
[38] C. Snoek, and M. Worring, "Multimedia event-based video indexing using time intervals," IEEE Trans. Multimedia, vol.7, No.4, pp.638-647, Aug. 2005.
[39] G. Papadopoulos, V. Mezaris, I. Kompatsiaris, and M. Strintzis, "Accumulated motion energy fields estimation and representation for semantic event detection," in Proc. CIVR, 2008, pp.221-230.
[40] F. Wang, Y. Ma, H. Zhang, and J. Li, "Dynamic Bayesian network based event detection for soccer highlight extraction," in Proc. Int. Conf. Image Processing, 2004, pp. 633-636.
[41] D. Sadlier, and N. O'Connor, "Event detection in field sports video using audio-visual features and a support vector Machine," IEEE Trans. Circuits Syst. Video Technol., vol. 15, no. 10, pp. 602-615, Oct. 2005.
[42] K. Wickramaratna, M. Chen, S. Chen, and M. Shyu, "Neural network based framework for goal event detection in soccer videos," in Proc. Int. Symposium on Multimedia. Dec. 2005, pp.21-28.
[43] L. Rabiner, "A tutorial on hidden markov models and selected applications in speech recognition," Proceedings of the IEEE, vol. 77, no. 2, pp. 257-285, 1989.
[44] C. Cheng, and C. Hsu, "Fusion of audio and motion information on HMM-based highlight extraction for baseball games," IEEE Trans. Multimedia, vol.8, No.3, pp.585-599, June. 2006.
[45] A. Mittal, L. Cheong, and T. Leung, "Dynamic bayesian framework for extracting temporal structure in video," in Proc. Int. Conf. Computer Vision and Pattern Recognition, 2001, pp. 110-115.
[46] N. Dalal, and B Triggs, "Histogram of oriented gradients for human detection," in Proc. Int. Conf. Computer Vision and Pattern Recognition, 2005.
[47] X. Qian, G. Liu, D. Guo, Z. Li, Z. Wang, and H. Wang, "Object categorization using hierarchical wavelet packet texture descriptors," in Proc. ISM 2009, pp.44-51.

[48] C. Sutton, and A. McCallum, "An introduction to conditional random fields for relational learning," Introduction to Statistical Relational Learning. MIT Press. 2007.

[49] J. Lafferty, A. McCallum, and F. Pereira, "Conditional random fields: Probabilistic models for segmenting and labeling sequence data," in Proc. Int. Conf. Machine Learning, 2001, pp.282-289.

[50] A. McCallum, "Efficiently inducing features of conditional random fields," in Proc. Uncertainty in Artifical Intelligence, 2003, pp.403-410.

[51] F. Sha, and F. Pereira, "Shallow parsing with conditional random fields," in Proc. Human Language Technology, NAACL, 2003.

[52] M. Mahajan, A. Gunawardana, and A. Acero, "Training algorithms for hidden conditional random fields," ICASSP 2007, vol.1, pp.273-276.

[53] A. Gunawardana, M. Mahajan, A. Acero, and J. Platt, "Hidden conditional random fields for phone classification," in Proc. Int. Conf. Speech Communication and Technology, pp.1117-1120, Sept. 2005.

[54] Y. Sung, C. Boulis, C. Manning, and D. Jurafsky, "Regularization, adaptation, and non-independent features improve hidden conditional random fields for phone classification," in Workshop of Automatic Speech Recognition and Understanding, pp.347-352, 2007.

[55] R. Malouf, "A comparison of algorithms for maximum entropy parameter estimation," in Proc. Int. Conf. National Language Learning, 2002, pp. 49-55.

[56] X. Qian, H. Wang, G. Liu, and X. Hou, "HMM Based Soccer Video Event Detection Using Enhanced Mid-Level Semantic", Multimedia Tools and Applications, 2011. (Accepted)

[57] Z. Liu, and S. Sarkar, "Robust outdoor text detection using text intensity and shape features," in Proc. ICPR 2008

[58] N. Dalal, and B Triggs, "Histogram of oriented gradients for human detection," in Proc. Int. Conf. Computer Vision and Pattern Recognition, 2005.

[59] X. Qian, X. Hua, P. Chen, and L. Ke, "PLBP: An Effective Local Binary Patterns Texture Descriptor with Pyramid Representation", Pattern Recognition, 2011, vol.44, pp. 2502-2515.

[60] X. Wang, and X. Zhang, "ICA mixture hidden conditional random field model for sports event classification," in Proc. ICCV, 2009, pp.562-569.

[61] Y. Tan, D. Saur, S. Kulkarni, and P. Ramadge, "Rapid estimation of camera motion from compressed video with application to video annotation," IEEE Trans. Circuits Syst. Video Technol., vol. 10, no. 1, pp. 133-146, Feb. 2000.

[62] N. Babaguchi, Y. Kawai, and T. Kitashi, "Event based indexing of broadcasted sports video by intermodal collaboration," IEEE Trans. Multimedia, vol.4, no.1, pp.68-75, Mar. 2002.

[63] A. Jain, and B. Yu, "Automatic text location in images and video frames," in Proc. ICPR, 1998, pp. 1497-1499.

[64] V. Mariano, and R. Kasturi, "Locating uniform-colored text in video frames," in Proc. 15th Int. Conf. Pattern Recognit., vol. 4, 2000, pp. 539-542.

[65] X. Qian, and G. Liu, "Text detection, localization and segmentation in compressed videos," in Proc. ICASSP2006., vol. 2, 2006, pp. II385-II388.

[66] T. Sato and T. Kanade, "Video OCR: Indexing digital news libraries by recognition of superimposed caption," ICCV Workshop on Image and Video retrieval. 1998.
[67] Y. Zhong, H. Zhang, and A. Jain, "Automatic Caption Localization in Compressed Video," IEEE Trans. Pattern Analysis and Machine Intelligence, vol.22, no.4, 2000, pp.385-392.
[68] C. Ngo, C. Chan, "Video text detection and segmentation for optical character recognition,". Multimedia Systems, vol.10, no.3, 2005, pp.261-272.
[69] J. Zhang, D. Goldgof, and R. Kasturi, "A New Edge-Based Text Verification Approach for Video," in Proc. ICPR, 2008.
[70] L. Sun, G. Liu, X. Qian, D. Guo, "A Novel Text Detection and Localization Method Based on Corner Response," in Proc. ICME 2009.
[71] U.Gargi, S.Antani, and R. Kasturi, "Indexing text events in digital video databases," in Proc. Int. Conf. Pattern Recognit., vol. 1, 1998, pp.916-918.
[72] X. Tang, B. Gao, J. Liu, and H. Zhang, "A spatial-temporal approach for video caption detection and recognition," IEEE Trans. Neural Networks.,vol. 13, no.4, 2002, pp. 961-971.
[73] H. Jiang, G. Liu, X. Qian, et al., "A Fast and Efficient Text Tracking in Compressed Video," in Proc. ISM 2008.

7

Intelligent Self-Describing Power Grids

Andrea Schröder[1] and Inaki Laresgoiti[2]
[1]*FGH e.V.,*
[2]*TECNALIA*
[1]*Germany*
[2]*Spain*

1. Introduction

The liberalization of the electrical energy market increases the complexity of power grid operation and pushes companies to build cheaper electrical power generation and distribution systems. Automated network management systems based on massively distributed information help to maintain the expected quality performance, manageability and reliability. In this context the European Technology Platform (ETP) Smart Grids was set up in 2005 to create a joint vision for the European networks of 2020 and beyond. Its vision builds both upon an efficient and intelligent integration of distributed resources with other network components and upon two basic concepts upon which the integration of huge amounts of distributed resources is going to be done: "Virtual Power plants" and "Micro Grids" both combined with an extensive use of Information and Communication Technologies (ICT). The Internet and the Web are identified as promising approaches for the integration of large amounts of distributed resources in a dynamic and efficient way.

The EC funded S-TEN (Intelligent Self-describing Technical and Environmental Networks) [1] project running from April 2006 to September 2008 makes a substantial step to let this vision come true by providing decision support in a complex and potentially continuously changing networks based upon the use of semantic web technology [2]. E.g. ontologies are used to represent knowledge associated with the devices, ranging from simple sensors to complex plants such as combined heat and power plants or wind power plants, so that they can register themselves at a registry exposing their capabilities and interfaces to applications searching for a matching service. Besides, semantics describing the equipment design information and measurement data can be used together with the respective data by decision support systems to detect any malfunctioning of the equipment and to trigger corresponding alarms or any other kind of action, such as giving best practice support to the operator.

The following chapters present the work being done to develop and use technologies designed to provide functionalities required by the grid of the future. A clear focus is on the defined ontologies as they form the backbone of intelligent and autonomously acting applications.

2. S-TEN system

In future intelligent grids with lots of distributed resources, such as sensors, photovoltaic plants (PV), wind power plants, combined heat and power plants (CHP) and electrical vehicles, each node has its own intelligence, is able to register in the network autonomously and publishes information about its position, services and data.

This is done by giving devices that may be sensors or plants a semantically interpretable self-description. This self-description is then uploaded into the S-TEN registry. The S-TEN registry is also based on semantically annotated Web Services complemented by a semantically annotated registry schema describing the semantics of data stored in the registry. Authorized control systems can access and query for a particular service (Figure 1).

The registry response contains relevant information to access the Web services offered by the sensor/plant, e.g. monitor current data, browse data for a specific instance in time or a period, control capabilities, subscribe to event notification such as alarms and warnings etc.. In addition, semantic annotation of technical documentation and definition and application of rules support best-practice advice to decision-makers enabling them to react more precisely and faster to unusual situations.

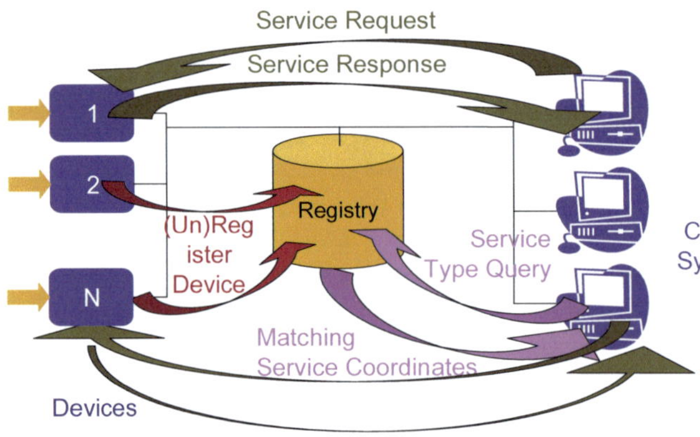

Fig. 1. Overview of the S-TEN system.

3. S-TEN technology

The S-TEN system is based on the S-TEN technology consisting of the following main components:

- **Self-description and registry.** S-TEN systems publish their **self-description** at the S-TEN registry exposing their capabilities and interfaces to applications searching for a matching service. An application first accesses the registry in order to get the endpoints and relevant information of the registered resources.
- **Ontologies. S-TEN top ontologies** and **demonstrator specific ontologies** referencing concepts of the S-TEN top ontologies have been defined.
- **Semantically annotated web services.** The semantics used refer to concepts of the S-TEN ontology for self-describing networks and the S-TEN ontologies for physical quantity space and scale. The web service based implementation of S-TEN services is based on Axis2 [3].

The following section describes the above listed main components of the S-TEN technology in more detail.

3.1 Self-description and registry

For physical devices it is necessary to specify the way in which they announce their presence in a network, so that they can be found when it is necessary to carry out a control or monitoring activity. In the following example, an implementation of the register function is shown: The Register message is used to register an XML-File with the registry. The request to activate this function comprises a HTTP header, a SOAP header with authentication information according to WS-security and an XML-File in the SOAP body which complies with the semantically annotated S-TEN registry schema:

```
POST /STENRegistry/services/Registry HTTP/1.1
Content-Type: text/xml; charset=UTF-8
SOAPAction: "urn:register"
User-Agent: Axis2
....
<?xml version='1.0' encoding='UTF-8'?>
  <soapenv:Envelope>
    <soapenv:Header>
      <wsse:Security>
   <wsse:UsernameToken>
        <wsse:Username>XXX</wsse:Username>
        <wsse:Password    Type="...#PasswordDigest">    1mFoYgXbWQ72/6bvnWNExntatmU=
</wsse:Password>
       </wsse:UsernameToken>
      </wsse:Security>
      ...
    </soapenv:Header>
    <soapenv:Body>
      <ns1:register>
        <xmlfile> the xml file </xmlfile>
      </ns1:register>
    </soapenv:Body>
  </soapenv:Envelope>
```

In reaction to the register request, the registry sends a HTTP response back to the client:

```
HTTP/1.1 200 OK
Content-Type: text/xml;charset=UTF-8
....
<?xml version='1.0' encoding='UTF-8'?>
  <soapenv:Envelope>
    <soapenv:Header> ... </soapenv:Header>
    <soapenv:Body>
      <ns:registerResponse>
        <ns:return>
          <result></result>
        </ns:return>
      </ns:registerResponse>
    </soapenv:Body>
  </soapenv:Envelope>
```

If the registration request was successful, a HTTP response with an empty result is sent back to the client. Otherwise an error message will be returned in the SOAP body of the HTTP response. To enable the invoking client to semantically interpret the register service offered by the registry server, the WSDL [4] specification of the registry service has to be semantically annotated according to SAWSDL [5]. As at this time Axis2 did not fully support WSDL 2.0 it was necessary to base the work on WSDL 1.1, and annotate the respective S-TEN registry WSDL specification accordingly. The data-type associated with the Register Message looks in its semantically annotated form the following way:

```
<xs:element name="register" sawsdl:modelReference="http://www.s-ten.eu/sten-web-services#AddRequestMessage">
    <xs:complexType>
        <xs:sequence>
            <xs:element name="xmlfile" nillable="true"
             sawsdl:modelReference="
             http://www.s-ten.eu/sten-web-services#XMLObject
             http://www.w3.org/2000/01/rdf-schema#isDefinedBy
             http://www.s-ten.eu/sten-web-services#RegistrySchema"/>
        </xs:sequence>
    </xs:complexType>
</xs:element>
```

The referenced registry schema is then again semantically annotated which enables the client using the GetSchema message to arrive at a complete, semantically correct interpretation of the expected registry content.

```
<xsd:schema xmlns:Ontology0="http://www.s-ten.eu/sten#"
xmlns:sawsdl="http://www.w3.org/ns/sawsdl"
 xmlns:xsd="http://www.w3.org/2001/XMLSchema" elementFormDefault="qualified"
attributeFormDefault="unqualified">
 <xsd:complexType name="SystemType" sawsdl:modelReference="http://www.s-ten.eu/sten-web-services#S-TENSystem">
  <xsd:sequence>
   <xsd:element name="SystemID" type="xsd:anyURI"
   sawsdl:modelReference="http://www.s-ten.eu/sten-web-services#ReferenceDesignation"/>
   <xsd:element name="Name" type="xsd:string"
   sawsdl:modelReference="http://www.s-ten.eu/sten-web-services#Designation"/>
   <xsd:element name="S-TENServiceDescriptionEndpoint" type="xsd:anyURI"
   sawsdl:modelReference="http://www.s-ten.eu/sten-web-services#WSDLDescription"/>
   <xsd:element name="TextualDescription" type="xsd:string" minOccurs="0"
   sawsdl:modelReference="http://www.s-ten.eu/sten-web-services#Description"/>
   <xsd:element name="SymbolicLocation" type="xsd:string" minOccurs="0"
   sawsdl:modelReference="http://www.s-ten.eu/sten-web-services#LocationDesignation"/>
   <xsd:element name="S-TENDescriptionEndpoint" type="xsd:anyURI" minOccurs="0"
   sawsdl:modelReference="http://www.s-ten.eu/sten-web-services#OWLDescription"/>
   <xsd:element name="GISLocation" minOccurs="0"
   sawsdl:modelReference="http://www.s-ten.eu/sten-web-services#PointInSpace">
    <xsd:complexType>
     <xsd:sequence>
      <xsd:element name="Longitude" type="xsd:decimal"
      sawsdl:modelReference="http://www.s-ten.eu/sten-web-services#Longitude"/>
      <xsd:element name="Latitude" type="xsd:decimal"
      sawsdl:modelReference="http://www.s-ten.eu/sten-web-services#Latitude"/>
      <xsd:element name="HeightOverSeaLevel" type="xsd:decimal"
      sawsdl:modelReference="http://www.s-ten.eu/sten-web-services#HeightOverSeaLevel"/>
```

```
      </xsd:sequence>
     </xsd:complexType>
    </xsd:element>
    <xsd:element name="ObservedPhysicalQuantitySpace" type="xsd:string" minOccurs="0"
    maxOccurs="unbounded"                    sawsdl:modelReference="http://www.s-ten.eu/sten-web-
services#PhysicalQuantitySpace"/>
    <xsd:element name="MonitoredDevices" type="xsd:string" minOccurs="0" maxOccurs="unbounded"
    sawsdl:modelReference="http://www.labein.es/Microgrid.xml#Device"/>
    <xsd:element name="OfferedServices" type="xsd:string" minOccurs="0" maxOccurs="unbounded"
    sawsdl:modelReference="http://www.labein.es/Microgrid.xml#Service"/>
    <xsd:element name="InventaryNumber" type="xsd:string" minOccurs="0"
    sawsdl:modelReference="http://www.s-ten.eu/sten-web-services#InventaryNumber"/>
    <xsd:element name="Producer" type="xsd:string" minOccurs="0"
    sawsdl:modelReference="http://www.s-ten.eu/sten-web-services#Manufacturer"/>
    <xsd:element name="Owner" type="xsd:string" minOccurs="0"
    sawsdl:modelReference="http://www.s-ten.eu/sten-web-services#Owner"/>
    <xsd:element name="Possessor" type="xsd:string" minOccurs="0"
    sawsdl:modelReference="http://www.s-ten.eu/sten-web-services#Possessor"/>
    <xsd:element name="Operator" type="xsd:string" minOccurs="0"
    sawsdl:modelReference="http://www.s-ten.eu/sten-web-services#Operator"/>
    <xsd:element name="LegacySystemSpecificInformation" minOccurs="0" maxOccurs="unbounded"
    sawsdl:modelReference="http://www.s-ten.eu/sten-web-services#LegacySystemInformation">
     <xsd:complexType>
      <xsd:sequence>
       <xsd:element name="URN" type="xsd:anyURI"/>
       <xsd:element name="Name" type="xsd:string" minOccurs="0"/>
       <xsd:element name="TextualDescription" type="xsd:string" minOccurs="0"/>
       <xsd:element name="Value" type="xsd:string"/>
      </xsd:sequence>
     </xsd:complexType>
    </xsd:element>
   </xsd:sequence>
  </xsd:complexType>
  <xsd:element name="System" type="SystemType"/>
</xsd:schema>
```

3.2 Ontologies

Ontologies are an important part of the Semantic Web and they are thought to be one of the most important advances in software development. They define the terms used to describe and represent an area of knowledge and have the advantage of being a way for a much more formal and less ambiguous definition of the meaning of the concepts.

They are composed of a formal description of concepts (classes) in a domain of discourse, properties of each concept describing various features of the concept, and restrictions on properties. If we add a set of individual instances of classes to the ontology we obtain a knowledge base.

There are different languages that can be used to express ontologies such as XML, RDF(S), SHOE, OWL, etc. In the S-TEN project the Web Ontology Language (OWL) [6] is employed for the definition of the case study because it provides the most expressive language for ontology description.

OWL was the W3C recommended standard for ontologies when the S-TEN project started. It is an extension of RDF(S) [7] that provides additional vocabulary in order to represent more characteristics between concepts. It distinguishes three types of entities: individuals, classes and properties:

- Individuals (or instances) represent objects in the domain of interest (e.g. Transformer_1)
- Classes are groups of individuals (e.g. Equipment, Transformer). Classes can be organised into a superclass-subclass hierarchy, which is also known as taxonomy.
- Properties are binary relations between individuals. There are two main types of properties: object properties that link two individuals and datatype properties that link an individual to an XML Schema Datatype value or an rdf literal (e.g. hasActivePower, name).

There are three different OWL sublanguages:

- OWL-Lite: It is the syntactically simplest sublanguage. It is intended to be used in situations where only a simple class hierarchy and simple constraints are needed.
- OWL-DL: It is much more expressive than OWL-Lite and it is based on Description Logics. It can be used when a maximum expressiveness is required but the computational completeness (all conclusions are guaranteed to be computable) and decidability (all computations will finish in finite time) must be ensured.
- OWL-Full: It provides the maximum expressiveness and the syntactic freedom of RDF with no computational guaranties.

For S-TEN OWL-DL was chosen because the existent reasoners were based on OWL-DL and although they would work also in OWL-Full they could enter into endless loops.

The S-TEN ontology [8] describes all S-TEN system components in a computer understandable way and provides the semantics necessary for exchanging messages between the different components of the S-TEN system including those coming from external users and the ones used internally by the system. Key features of the S-TEN ontology are as follows:

- it specifies an ontology for describing a physical network;
- it can be used by intelligent devices to publish information about their existence and state;
- it encompasses measurements made by sensors within a network and the storage and processing of measurements and
- it enables the use of inferencing to support activities carried out upon a network, including operations and maintenance.

A top level ontology for sensor related information and Web Services has been developed taking into account existing standards such as ISO 15926, IEEE SUMO, IEC 61850 and ISO 10303 (Figure 3). Based on the top S-TEN ontologies, application specific ontologies referencing concepts of the S-TEN top level ontology have been defined for the prototype applications.

The advantage of having an ontology is that automated reasoning can be applied to the data of the network components. Within S-TEN, rules supporting system operations are developed and applied to information available in the Web, e.g. measurements. Rules trigger corresponding alarms and generate Best Practice advice for the system operator based on the currently valid state of the network. Different organisations usually have different views on the same data. Therefore each organisation can have their own rule-bases to generate appropriate Best Practice Advice according to the nature of the system status enabling decision-makers to react more precise and faster to unusual situations and unbalanced systems.

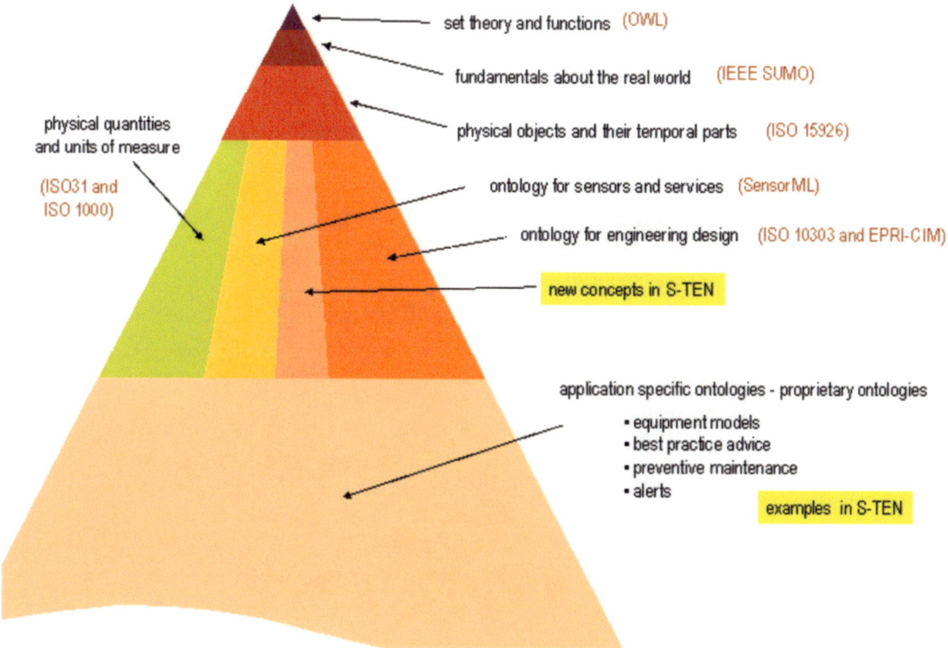

Fig. 2. S-TEN ontology.

The scope of the S-TEN ontology includes:

- **physical objects (physical thing)**

  A network is made up of physical objects. Information about these objects includes:

  - what it is;
  - what it is connected to;
  - where it is (e.g. input from GPS);
  - what it does;
  - what it measures (if it is a measurement device);
  - what the quality of the measurement is (if it is a measurement device).
- **activities**

  An activity can be:

  - a manufacturing or processing activity performed by a physical object within a network as part of its normal operation;

- a measurement activity performed by a measurement device;
- a control, maintenance or measurement activity performed by a person

The information about any activity, can include:

- what it is;
- the performer, which can be a person or device; and
- other physical objects which participate in the activity, particularly the inputs and outputs.

An input or output can be an information object.

- **information**

  It is necessary to record information about both information objects and their information contents.

- **Physical quantities, property and scale**

For physical things the definition of the ontology will be described in detail. The ontologies for the other categories can be found at http://www.s-ten.eu/deliverables/D2.1/.

Physical things

Types of physical thing

The purpose of the structure at the top of the ontology is to specify which relationships are valid for which types of physical thing. These relationships are inherited down the ontology. The principal relationships are discussed in the section Principal relationships. The top of the ontology for S-TEN, is a variant of that in SUMO and ISO 15926-2 as follows:

2. A sten:physical_thing is one of:
   - sten:classical_object which consists of very many interacting particles for a period;
   - sten:classical_object_at_instant which is a sten:classical_object at an instant; or
   - non-classical thing which is everything else, including small numbers of particles isolated from the rest of the universe, and packets of energy.

   For a sten:classical_object, time, position and causality are all valid concepts. Non-classical things are not within the scope of S-TEN.

3. A sten:classical_object can be:
   - sten:persistent_object which is created by a sten:activity and which continues to exist until destroyed by another sten:activity; and
   - sten:ephemeral_object which is a part of a sten:persistent_object which existed before or continued to exist after.

   The different between sten:persistent_object and sten:ephemeral_object is contentious amongst upper ontologists. An sten:ephemeral_object is something which has been defined by a person for a purpose. The beginning and end of an sten:ephemeral_object is not necessarily obvious to another person. Unfortunately, the same can be sometimes be said for a sten:persistent_object.

4. There are many types of sten:persistent_object. These include:
   - sten:facility, which is an object defined by the role it performs, and which is of interest for operations;
   - sten:physical_asset, which is an object defined by its material, and which is of interest for materials management;
   - computer file, which is an information bearing object defined by a computer system.

   EXAMPLE: Consider a pump in a process plant. The switch in the control room which operates this pump is labeled "P_101". On 2007-03-19, the pump with serial number "98-1234" is installed as "P_101". A maintenance activity is carried out overnight, so that on 2007-03-20 the pump with serial number "03-5678" is installed.

   The object "P_101" is a facility, and is defined by the role it performs. The object "98-1234" is an asset and is defined *more or less* by the matter it consists of.

   The qualification *more or less* is important, because a major refurbishment may change many of the parts of asset "98-1234". In this case, whether or not a new asset is created is an administrative choice.

   The justification for regarding a computer file as something physical is discussed in Section Information.

5. There are many types of sten:ephemeral_object. These include:
   - sten:period_of_life, in which a sten:persistent_object operates during a sten:period;
   - sten:activity, which is one or more instances of sten:period_of_life, and which is defined in order to identify a purpose, cause or result.

   NOTE 5: There are particular relationships between an sten:activity and its parts, such as sten:has_input, sten:has_output, sten:creates, sten:destroys, and sten:performed_by.

Top classes in the S-TEN, SUMO and ISO 15926-2 ontologies are shown in Figure 3.

Principal relationships

Relationships which are valid for the different types of physical thing are as follows:

relationship	rdfs:Property	rdfs:domain	rdfs:range
whole-part	sten:part_of	sten:physical_thing	sten:physical_thing
	sten:has_part	sten:physical_thing	sten:physical_thing
temporal whole-part	sten:temporal_part_of	sten:physical_thing	sten:classical_object
	sten:has_temporal_part	sten:classical_object	sten:physical_thing
assembly	sten:component_of	sten:classical_object	sten:classical_object
	sten:has_component	sten:classical_object	sten:classical_object
at time	sten:at_time	sten:classical_object_at_instant	sten:instant
during	sten:during	physical_thing	sten:part_of_time

The difference between the relationships sten:part_of, sten:temporal_part_of and sten:component_of is illustrated by Figure 4.

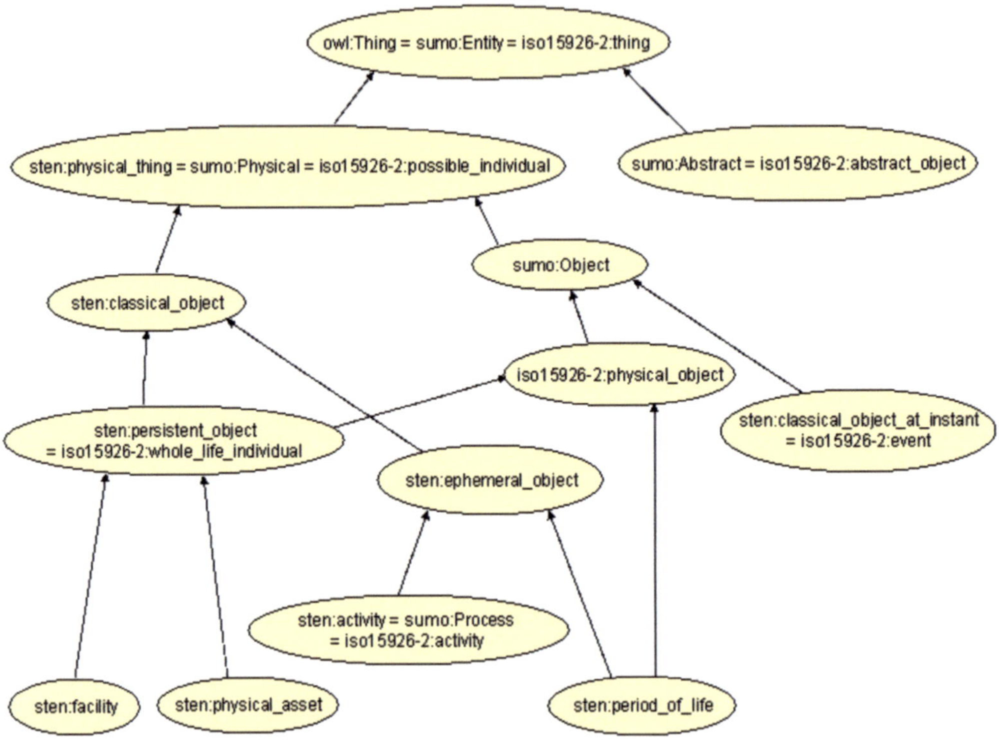

Fig. 3. Top classes in the S-TEN ontology.

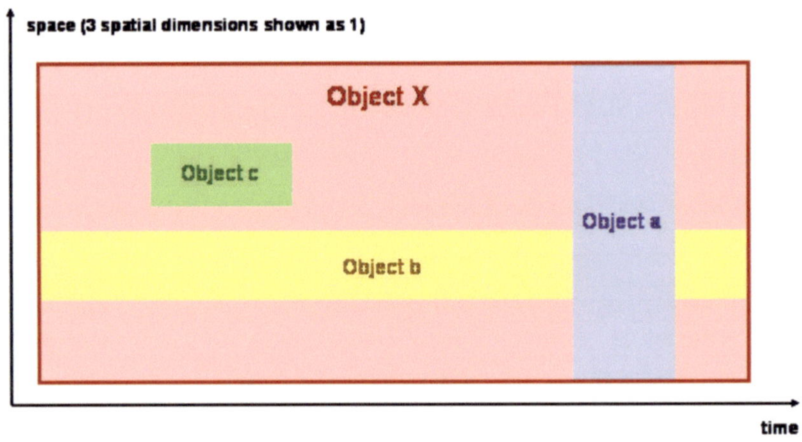

Fig. 4. Temporal part and component.

In this example:

- "object a" has a sten:temporal_part_of relationship with "object X";
- "object b" has a sten:component_of relationship with "object X";
- "object c" has a sten:part_of (but not sten:temporal_part_of or sten:component_of) relationship with "object X";

Activity and role

An sten:activity (= sumo:Process) is defined in order to identify a purpose, cause or result.

S-TEN defines the sten:has_role_player relationship between an sten:activity and a sten:persistent_object. This is not a relationship with a temporal part because an sten:activity is specifically defined to express a relationship between instances of sten:persistent_object.

EXAMPLE 1: Consider the manufacturing sten:activity "F. Bloggs production on 2007-04-23". This sten:activity creates the sten:physical_asset with serial number "07/123456". The sten:activity does not create a temporal part of "07/123456", but instead the sten:persistent_object which continues to exist after the sten:activity has finished.

There are many possible roles in an activity, which are specific to the type of activity.

EXAMPLE 2 A meeting activity has the roles:

- chair person;
- minute taker;
- teller (who counts votes); and
- attender.

For S-TEN, the roles "input" and "output" have been introduced. The part of speech has also been changed so that the relationships are not identified by nouns and cannot be easily mistaken for objects. This gives the following generic roles:

role	**definition**
sten:performed_by	identical to sumo:agent.
sten:has_input	identical to sumo:resource.
sten:has_output	identical to sumo:result.
sten:destroys	a sten:has_input, where the input does not exist after the activity.
sten:creates	a sten:has_output, where the output did not exist before the activity.

A temporal part can be related to an sten:activity by a sten:has_part relationship.

An sten:activity can have a relationship with an object which is neither sten:has_role_player or sten:has_part. Examples of this are:

- sten:causes where one sten:activity causes another to happen;
- sten:has_input_record and sten:has_output_record where a sten:information_carrier is input or output.
- sten:investigates where information is sought about an object which may not play a role in the sten:activity.

Relationships with parts of life

The relationship sten:component_of is a sten:simultaneous_mapping which applies to each temporal part of the part and of the whole.

EXAMPLE 1: The statement *"The gearbox with serial number 98/1234 has a* ***sten:component_of*** *relationship with the car with chassis number 99/4567."* is untrue because the gearbox existed before the car, and may continue to exists after the car if the car is disassembled. If the car has the same gearbox throughout its life, then the correct statement is:

"A temporal part of the gearbox with serial number 98/1234 has a ***sten:component_of*** relationship with the car with chassis number 99/4567." There is no need to be specific about the start and end times of the temporal part of :98/1234, because this can be deduced from the start and end times of :99/4567.

Ontology for physical thing - taxonomy

The following section is an excerpt of the ontology for physical thing and additionally lists some explanations and examples. The ontology is defined in OWL and RDF.

physical_thing

An object is an sten:physical_thing if and only if it exists in space and time.

```
<owl:Class rdf:about="&sten;physical_thing">
 <owl:sameAs rdf:resource="&sumo;Physical"/>
 <owl:sameAs rdf:resource="&iso15926-2;possible_individual"/>
 <meta:defined_by rdf:resource="&D2.1;/physical_things.htm#physical_thing"/>
</owl:Class>
```

classical_object

An object is an sten:classical_object if and only if:

- it is an sten:physical_thing;
- it is a large number of interacting particles which exists for finite periods of time.

A sten:classical_object can have more than one creation and destruction activity because can cease to exist for periods of time.

```
<owl:Class rdf:about="&sten;classical_object">
 <rdfs:subClassOf rdf:resource="&sten;physical_thing"/>
 <meta:defined_by rdf:resource="&D2.1;/physical_things.htm#classical_object"/>
</owl:Class>
```

classical_object_at_instant

An object is an sten:classical_object_at_instant if and only if:

- it is an sten:physical_thing;
- it is a sten:classical_object at an instant.

```
<owl:Class rdf:about="&sten;classical_object_at_instant">
 <rdfs:subClassOf rdf:resource="&sten;physical_thing"/>
 <rdfs:subClassOf rdf:resource="&sumo;Object"/>
 <owl:sameAs rdf:resource="&iso15926-2;event"/>
 <meta:defined_by rdf:resource="&D2.1;/physical_things.htm#classical_object_at_instant"/>
</owl:Class>
```

persistent_object

An object is an sten:persistent_object if and only if:

- it is an sten:classical_object;
- the periods of time during which it exists results from creation and destruction activities.

A single sten:persistent_object can have more than one creation and destruction activity because can cease to exist for periods of time.

```
<owl:Class rdf:about="&sten;persistent_object">
 <rdfs:subClassOf rdf:resource="&sten;classical_object"/>
 <owl:sameAs rdf:resource="&iso15926-2;whole_life_individual"/>
 <rdfs:subClassOf rdf:resource="&iso15926-2;physical_object"/>
 <meta:defined_by rdf:resource="&D2.1;/physical_things.htm#persistent_object"/>
</owl:Class>
```

ephemeral_object

An object is an sten:ephemeral_object if and only if:

- it is an sten:classical_object;
- its spatial and temporal boundaries are a choice to support the recording of information.

A boundary of an sten:ephemeral_object in time or space is not necessarily obvious to an observer.

```
<owl:Class rdf:about="&sten;ephemeral_object">
 <rdfs:subClassOf rdf:resource="&sten;classical_object"/>
 <meta:defined_by rdf:resource="&D2.1;/physical_things.htm#ephemeral_object"/>
</owl:Class>
```

facility

An object is a sten:facility if and only if:

- it is a sten:persistent_object;
- it is created by commissioning activities and is destroyed by decomissioning activities.

A sten:facility is operated. The creation and destruction activities are recognised as such by the operator. A single sten:facility can have more than one creation activity because it can cease to exist for periods of time.

A sten:facility is distinguished from a sten:physical_asset by the nature of the creation and destruction activities. A sten:facility is created when physical assets are combined into a whole that can be operated.

The quantity of matter that is a facility can change during the life of the facility, by the removal of some matter and the addition of other matter. It often changes completely, so that all the matter previously present is removed and replaced by different matter.

EXAMPLE: The feedwater pump for boiler "B_101" is a facility with tag "P_101". Operating the boiler involves operating pump "P_101". The quantity of matter that is pump "P_101" changes a little whenever pump "P_101" is maintained, perhaps by replacing a seal or a bearing.

If the pump with serial number 98-1234 is installed as "P_101" until 2006-10-16, and is then replace by the pump with serial number 06-4567, then the quantity of matter that is pump "P_101" changes completely on 2006-10-16.

```
<owl:Class rdf:about="&sten;facility">
 <rdfs:subClassOf rdf:resource="&sten;persistent_object"/>
 <meta:defined_by rdf:resource="&D2.1;/physical_things.htm#facility"/>
</owl:Class>
```

physical_asset

An object is a sten:physical_asset if and only if:

- it is a sten:persistent_object;
- it is created by an assembly or fabrication activity and is ended by a disassembly or recycling activity.

A sten:physical_asset is owned and maintained. The creation and destruction activities are recognised by the owner or maintainer.

The quantity of matter that is a physical_asset can change during the life of the physical_asset, by the removal of some matter and the addition of other matter. There is only rarely a complete change, in which that all the matter previously present is removed and replaced by different matter.

EXAMPLE: The pump with serial number "98-1234" is a physical_asset. This pump is recorded in the inventory of equipment owned by J. Bloggs and Co..

If the pump with serial number 98-1234 is maintained by replacing the bearings and seals, then the quantity of matter changes, but the physical_asset continues to exist. Replacing the body of the pump would probably be regarded as a manufacturing a new physical_asset, rather than a maintenance activity carried out on a existing physical_asset.

```
<owl:Class rdf:about="&sten;physical_asset">
 <rdfs:subClassOf rdf:resource="&sten;persistent_object"/>
 <meta:defined_by rdf:resource="&D2.1;/physical_things.htm#physical_asset"/>
</owl:Class>
```

period_of_life

An object is a sten:period_of_life if and only if:

- it is an sten:ephemeral_object;
- the sten:period during which it exists is a choice to support the recording of information.

```
<owl:Class rdf:about="&sten;period_of_life">
 <rdfs:subClassOf rdf:resource="&sten;ephemeral_object"/>
 <rdfs:subClassOf rdf:resource="&iso15926-2;physical_object"/>
 <meta:defined_by rdf:resource="&D2.1;/physical_things.htm#period_of_life"/>
</owl:Class>
```

activity

An object is an sten:activity if and only if:

- it is an sten:ephemeral_object;
- it is defined in order to identify a purpose, cause or result.

The ISO 15926 term "activity" is prefered to the SUMO term "process", because it is more general and does not imply that there is an intention or that there is a well defined outcome.

```
<owl:Class rdf:about="&sten;activity">
 <rdfs:subClassOf rdf:resource="&sten;ephemeral_object"/>
 <owl:sameAs rdf:resource="&sumo;Process"/>
 <owl:sameAs rdf:resource="&iso15926-2;activity"/>
 <meta:defined_by rdf:resource="&D2.1;/physical_things.htm#activity"/>
</owl:Class>
```

3.3 Semantically annotated web services

S-TEN data access is based on semantically annotated Web Services or on agent based systems using as a system component semantically annotated Web Services, too. This approach was chosen, as standard Web Services take into account only the functional or syntactical aspects of a service. This means semantic information is either not available or offered only in an informal and human-interpretable way. It's therefore not possible to derive the intended semantics of input, output, and function or the meaning of parameters of a Web service from its WSDL description only. In that way, two Web services may have the same syntactical definition and, yet, implement different functionality. In this situation, Semantic Web services constitute a promising path to automate the tasks of Web service discovery, composition and invocation and to improve the integration of applications within and across enterprise boundaries. At present, there are three main approaches to enable Semantic Web services: SAWSDL [5], OWL-S [9] and WSMO [10], ranging from pragmatic to more comprehending extensions of standard Web services. Within S-TEN, SAWSDL, as the most pragmatic approach was selected as the only one suitable for implementation at this time, because SAWSDL was supported by the many of the widely used tools of WSDL while the other two had a lack of tools. The basic idea behind SAWSDL is to enhance the WSDL specification with the aim to go beyond a mere syntactical description of a Web service by adding semantics to the functions and the data delivered by a service. As it can be seen in the code excerpt below, featuring a BrowseRequest service, SAWSDL model references provide the link to the semantics defined in the S-TEN top-level ontology.

```
<xs:element name="BrowseRequest">
 <xs:complexType>
  <xs:sequence>
   <xs:element name="SessionID" type="xs:string"
    sawsdl:modelReference="http://www.s-ten.eu/sten-web-services#SessionID"/>
   <xs:element name="ObservedBy" type="xs:string" sawsdl:modelReference="http://www.s-ten.eu/sten-
core#observedBy"/>
   <xs:element name="Observes" type="xs:string" minOccurs="0"
    maxOccurs="unbounded" sawsdl:modelReference="http://www.s-ten.eu/sten-core#observes"/>
   <xs:element name="PhysicalProperty" type="xs:string" minOccurs="0" maxOccurs="unbounded"
       sawsdl:modelReference="http://www.s-ten.eu/sten-core#PhysicalProperty"/>
   <xs:choice>
    <xs:element name="TimeSpan" type="ns0:TimeSlice"/>
     <xs:element name="At" type="xs:long" nillable="true"
       sawsdl:modelReference="http://www.s-ten.eu/sten-core#ClassicalObjectAtInstant
                              http://www.s-ten.eu/sten-core#atTime
                              http://www.s-ten.eu/sten-core#Time
                              http://www.s-ten.eu/sten-core#milliSecondsSince1970-01-01
                              http://www.s-ten.eu/sten-core#Integer"/>
     <xs:element name="Quantity" type="xs:int" nillable="true"
       sawsdl:modelReference="http://www.s-ten.eu/sten-web-services#NumberOfMembers"/>
    </xs:choice>
   </xs:sequence>
  </xs:complexType>
</xs:element>
```

Fig. 5. Browse Request Service.

4. S-TEN applications

Prototype applications have been developed within the S-TEN project validating the S-TEN technology and showing the advantages of the use of web-services, agents and ontologies. Among these prototype applications the following two applications demonstrate the monitoring and control functionality of future power systems:

- Control of Distributed Resources in Electrical Power Networks.
- Secondary control of microgrids

For these prototypes application-specific ontologies have been defined referencing concepts of the S-TEN top ontology and taking into account existing standards such as IEC 61850 and ISO 15926. The development of these applications has been supported by a user-group set up within the S-TEN project. This user-group, consisting of supply companies, manufacturers and research organizations, assisted in defining the requirements of the various applications thereby ensuring its practical relevance. The following section describes the two applications mentioned above in more detail.

4.1 Control of distributed resources in electrical power networks

The integration of distributed energy resources will influence the structure of future power systems considerably. Power generation will not take place only in a few central power stations but also in a constantly increasing number of distributed energy generators such as wind power plants, photovoltaic plants and combined heat and power plants located in the medium and low voltage system. The prototype application "Control of Distributed Resources in Electrical Power Networks" will enable the monitoring of distributed generators with the aim to improve the management of the distribution network in terms of remote control capabilities and automated network control. The monitoring includes both the observation of measuring values and events (alarms and warnings) and provides event handling. The application has a public presence on the web where its client software can be downloaded at www.s-ten.eu.

Ontology

Based on the S-TEN top-level ontology an application specific ontology has been defined featuring combined heat and power plants (CHP), photovoltaic (PV), wind power devices and additional network devices such as circuit-breakers, inverters, batteries, etc.. An excerpt of the CHP ontology is given in Figure 6.

The Web Services the network resources offer are semantically annotated that is they link to the application ontology and the S-TEN top-level ontology. The XML document (Fig. 7.) shows an example of a browse request and the browse response written according to the S-TEN ontology.

Also, rules definition uses concepts from the S-TEN top-level ontology and the application specific ontology.

Architecture and functionality

A hierarchical architecture has been chosen for the demonstrator (Figure 6). For each DER an S-TEN server has been established. The hierarchical architecture allows adding S-TEN

```
<?xml version="1.0"?>

<rdf:RDF xml:base="[redacted]" xmlns="[redacted]"
xmlns:chp="[redacted]" xmlns:der="[redacted]"
xmlns:owl="http://www.w3.org/2002/07/owl#" xmlns:rdf="http://www.w3.org/1999/02/22-rdf-syntax-ns#"
xmlns:rdfs="http://www.w3.org/2000/01/rdf-schema#" xmlns:sten-PhysicalQuantitySpace="http://www.s-ten.eu/sten-
PhysicalQuantitySpace#" xmlns:sten-core="http://www.s-ten.eu/sten-core#"
xmlns:xsd="http://www.w3.org/2001/XMLSchema#">
        <owl:Ontology rdf:about="">
                <owl:versionInfo xml:lang="en">version 0.1</owl:versionInfo>
                <rdfs:comment xml:lang="en">Ontology describing CHP systems</rdfs:comment>
                <owl:imports rdf:resource="http://www.s-ten.eu/sten-core"/>
                <owl:imports rdf:resource="[redacted]"/>
                <owl:imports rdf:resource="http://www.s-ten.eu/sten-PhysicalQuantitySpace"/>
        </owl:Ontology>
        <owl:Class rdf:ID="CHPSystem">
                <rdfs:subClassOf rdf:resource="#DER"/>
                <rdfs:comment xml:lang="en">A Combined heat and power (CHP) system uses the exhaust heat of an
                engine to simultaneously generate both electricity and useful heat.</rdfs:comment>
        </owl:Class>
        <owl:Class rdf:ID="CHPModule">
                <sten-core:partOf rdf:resource="#CHPSystem"/>
                <rdfs:comment xml:lang="en">A CHP module forms part of a CHP system. The CHP system may consist of
                various CHP Modules.</rdfs:comment>
        </owl:Class>
        <!--        CHP specific data     -->
        <owl:ObjectProperty rdf:about="#nominalMaximumActivePower">
                <rdf:type rdf:resource="http://www.w3.org/2002/07/owl#FunctionalProperty"/>
                <rdfs:label xml:lang="en">nominal maximum active power</rdfs:label>
                <rdfs:domain rdf:resource="#CHPModule"/>
                <rdfs:range rdf:resource="http://www.s-ten.eu/sten-PhysicalQuantitySpace#ActivePower"/>
                <rdfs:comment xml:lang="en">nominal maximum active power (W)</rdfs:comment>
        </owl:ObjectProperty>

        <owl:ObjectProperty rdf:about="#nominalMaximumThermalPower">
                <rdf:type rdf:resource="http://www.w3.org/2002/07/owl#FunctionalProperty"/>
                <rdfs:label xml:lang="en">nominal maximum heating power</rdfs:label>
                <rdfs:domain rdf:resource="#CHPModule"/>
                <rdfs:range rdf:resource="http://www.s-ten.eu/sten-PhysicalQuantitySpace#Power"/>
                <rdfs:comment xml:lang="en">nominal maximum thermal power (kW)) </rdfs:comment>
        </owl:ObjectProperty>
        <owl:ObjectProperty rdf:about="#nominalHeatToPowerEfficiency">
                <rdf:type rdf:resource="http://www.w3.org/2002/07/owl#FunctionalProperty"/>
                <rdfs:label xml:lang="en">nominal heat to power efficiency</rdfs:label>
                <rdfs:domain rdf:resource="#CHPModule"/>
                <rdfs:range rdf:resource="http://www.s-ten.eu/sten-core#Real"/>
        </owl:ObjectProperty>
        <owl:ObjectProperty rdf:about="#typeOfHeatingMedium">
                <rdf:type rdf:resource="http://www.w3.org/2002/07/owl#FunctionalProperty"/>
                <rdfs:label xml:lang="en">type of heating medium</rdfs:label>
                <rdfs:domain rdf:resource="#CHPModule"/>
                <rdfs:range rdf:resource="http://www.s-ten.eu/sten-core#Integer"/>
                <rdfs:comment xml:lang="en">0: not applicable; 1: water; 2: steam; 3: air; 99: other</rdfs:comment>
        </owl:ObjectProperty>

        <!--
        Measured values and time dependent values, respectively     -->
        <owl:Class rdf:about="#CHPModuleAtInstant">
                <rdfs:subClassOf rdf:resource="http://www.s-ten.eu/sten-core#ClassicalObjectAtInstant"/>
                <rdfs:comment xml:lang="en">A CHP at an instant in time</rdfs:comment>
        </owl:Class>
        <!-- Measured active power (W) -->
        <owl:ObjectProperty rdf:about="#measuredActivePower">
                <rdf:type rdf:resource="http://www.w3.org/2002/07/owl#FunctionalProperty"/>
                <rdfs:label xml:lang="en">measured active power</rdfs:label>
                <rdfs:domain rdf:resource="#CHPModuleAtInstant"/>
                <rdfs:range rdf:resource="http://www.s-ten.eu/sten-PhysicalQuantitySpace#ActivePower"/>
        </owl:ObjectProperty>
        <!-- Measured thermal power (W) -->
        <owl:ObjectProperty rdf:about="#measuredThermalPower">
                <rdf:type rdf:resource="http://www.w3.org/2002/07/owl#FunctionalProperty"/>
```

Fig. 6. Excerpt of ontology for Combined Heat and Power plants.

```
<?xml version="1.0" encoding="UTF-8"?>
<BrowseRequest>
  <SessionID>012154782</SessionID>
  <ObservedBy>http://www.fgh.de/sten/DER.xml#MDevice_CHP_1</ObservedBy>
  <Observes>http://www.fgh.de/sten/DER.xml#CHP_1</Observes>
  <PhysicalProperty>http://www.fgh.de/sten/CHP.xml#ActivePower</PhysicalProperty>
  <After>1201508970325</ After>
  <Before>1201512570325</Before>
</BrowseRequest>
```


Fig. 7. Browse request example.


```
<?xml version="1.0" encoding="UTF-8"?>
<BrowseResponse>
 <ObservedBy>http://www.fgh.de/sten/DER.xml#MDevice_CHP_1</ObservedBy>
 <Observes>http://www.fgh.de/sten/DER.xml#CHP_1</Observes>
 <PhysicalProperty>http://www.labein.es/sten/CHP.xml#Active_Power</PhysicalProperty>
  <Scale>http://www.fgh.de/sten/SIUnits.xml#Watts</Scale>
  <DataTimeValue>
    <TimeSpec>1201508970325</TimeSpec>
    <DecimalValue>25400</DecimalValue>
  </DataTimeValue>
  <DataTimeValue>
    <TimeSpec>1201508932630325</TimeSpec>
    <DecimalValue>30000</DecimalValue>
  </DataTimeValue>
  <DataTimeValue>
    <TimeSpec>1201508932690325</TimeSpec>
    <DecimalValue>31200</DecimalValue>
  </DataTimeValue>
  <BrowseResponseMessage>
    < SuccessIndicator>Browse succeeded</SuccessIndicator>
  </BrowseResponseMessage>
</BrowseResponse>
```


Fig. 8. Browse response example.

systems (servers) that aggregate other S-TEN systems, where the high level S-TEN system provides low level systems' aggregated information and functionalities.

Currently, an operator can access "level 1" S-TEN systems in order to browse data and events and monitor data of a DER. This implies that he only sees the contribution of one DER upstream the feeder per started client application. A future control system embedded in an upper level could aggregate data of all available S-TEN systems within the control area and be in charge of sending the corresponding operation commands to "level 1" S-TEN systems in order to balance the system.

Three servers have been implemented in the application: one for a wind turbine, a second for a PV plant and a third for a CHP unit (Figure 10).

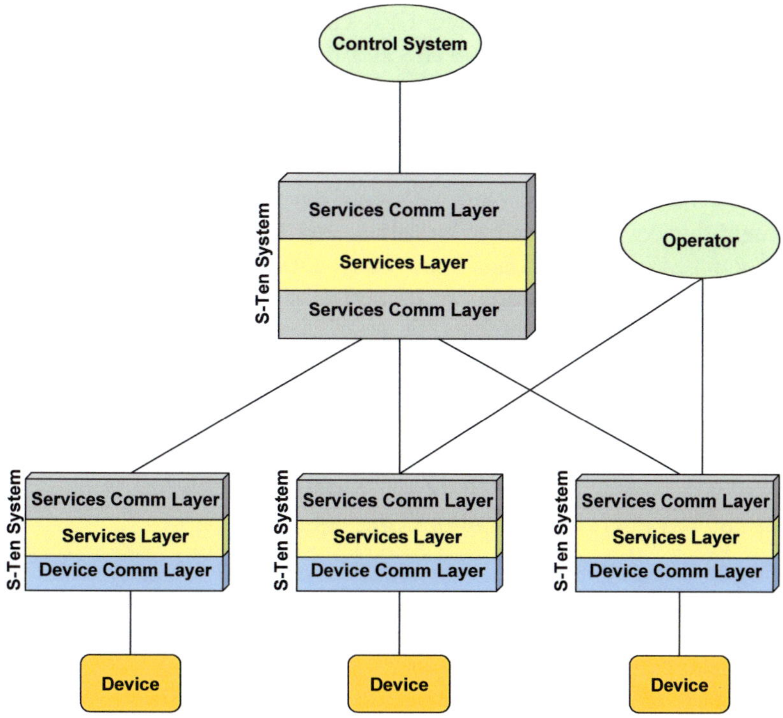

Fig. 9. Hierarchical S-TEN system.

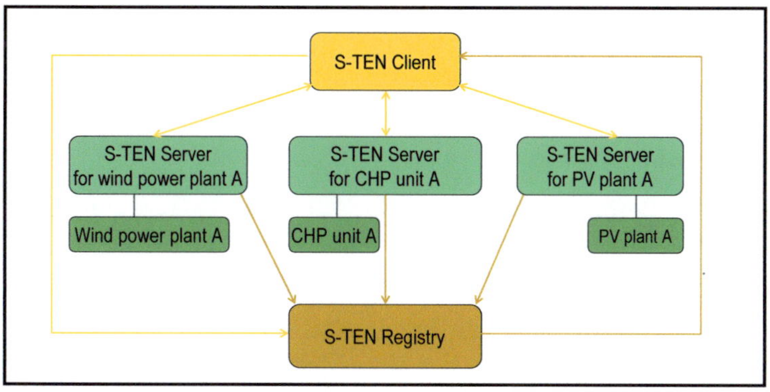

Fig. 10. Design of the prototype application.

The S-TEN server registers its monitored resource in the S-TEN Registry as soon as it is in operation. The registration file contains both the URL of the resource and the services it offers. Each resource sends its data via a communication interface to the S-TEN server where the data is stored in a database.

The registry can be queried for its registered DERs with the option to ask for all DERs, a special DER type or a DER belonging to a certain system area. As result of this query a list of all registered DERs matching the searching criteria is sent back. The user can now select a DER and access it via its URL known from the self-description file held in the S-TEN registry.

Besides, the web services of the selected DER can be viewed and with the help of the semantic web service validator it can be checked if the offered services match the ones the client understands. If the client and server services match, the user can login the DER of interest.

After successful connection with the DER that is after authorisation and authentication the DER tree is displayed revealing the components of the DER, its measured values along with the measurement devices that measure the values and the warnings and alarms available for the measured value. Within the client application data of the DER can then be monitored and browsed and event subscriptions can be performed leading to a notification when the event occurs. When a web service such as "Browse" is selected, a SOAP query is launched in which the data of interest, e.g. the actual power of wind turbine C belonging to wind power plant A, is held. The SOAP query is sent to the S-TEN server of the requested DER which retrieves the data of interest and sends it back to the client. If a control operation is performed (e.g. drive up a CHP), the way of interaction is the same as described for the monitoring data service only that the client gets a status information of the executed service. The responses and requests can be monitored on request.

Event handling is implemented modeling notifications that are sent when warnings and alarms coming from legacy systems occur. E.g. if a wind turbine is equipped with IEC 61850 IEDs (Intelligent Electronic Device) providing alarms, these events will be made available in the prototype application.

Based on semantically interpretable information rules can be defined enabling automatically derivations and subsequent actions, e.g. switching on or off a disconnector within a ring where a short-circuit occured. Besides, observations and data derived from network resources can be linked together and activated with formal rules in order to provide best practise support for the user.

4.2 Secondary control of microgrids

A microgrid can be defined as an integrated Power Delivery system consisting of interconnected loads and distributed energy resources which as an integrated system can operate in parallel with the grid or in an intentional island mode.

It is important for microgrids that the integration of their resources into the LV (Low Voltage) grids, and their relation with the MV (Medium Voltage) network upstream, will contribute to optimize the general operation of the system. For that purpose a hierarchical system control architecture has been designed, that comprises three critical control levels:

- Local Microsource Controller (MC) and Load Controllers (LC): It responds in milliseconds and uses local information and the requests from the microgrid system Central Controller (MGCC).
- Microgrid system Central Controller: It is the interface with the distribution network and responds to the requests of the Distribution System Operator and optimizes the operation of the equipment that it controls.
- Distribution Management system (DMS): The Distribution Management System is the replica of the Energy Management System (EMS), but for managing distribution networks instead of transmission networks.

In this application a secondary power-frequency control problem is addressed, such that any variation in the power exchange between the Microgrid and the distribution network is detected and the plan to recover from that situation is generated. Once the plan has been generated, the assigned resources are monitored and any deviation from its scheduled behaviour raised and corrected.

Use of the ontology

In order to monitor an industrial process it is necessary to have an operating plan for the physical resources participating in the process, and data from sensors within the system. These are used together to check that everything is taking place according to the plan. Deviations from the plan are detected, and these may require a quick reaction to ensure the safe or economic continuation of the process. The S-TEN project has defined an ontology which covers:

- an observation and measurement activity;
- a time history of a physical property;
- definition of features of a time history.

This ontology is being used to monitor changes of the output active power of generators within a MicroGrid. The monitoring process has two stages, firstly the measurement of values and their recording using RDF, and secondly the monitoring of these values to make higher level statements about the state of the process which are used by the supervisory control to modify the operating plan.

A simple example of monitoring is the detection of changes. The monitoring activity MonitoringActivity_2_OfGenerator_01 is tasked with looking for changes in the output active power of Diesel_01. The following statements are input to the activity and specify what it does.

```
:MonitoringActivity_2_OfGenerator_01
 a                            sten::MonitoringActivity;
 sten:monitors                :activePowerOfDiesel_01;
 sten:hasMonitoringCriterion  :ChangeCriterion1.
```

The time history activePowerOfDiesel_01 is defined as:

```
:activePowerOfDiesel_01
 a                            sten:TimeVariationOfPhysicalProperty;
 rdfs:subPropertyOf           sten:outputActivePower;
 rdfs:domain                  :Diesel_01.
```

A change event is reported (sent as a message or added to the journal formula) if the generator output gets bigger than the 36 kW threshold. Hence the monitoring criterion is defined as follows:

```
:ChangeCriterion1
 a                            sten:ChangeCriterion;
 sten:setlevel                  [scale:kilowatt 36].
```

If the measurement crosses this level between 13:10and 13:20 on 2008-07-22, then the monitoring activity reports the event as follows:

```
[sten:partOfTimeVariation  : activePowerOfDiesel_01;
 rdfs:domain
  [sten:during [t:hasBeginning [t:inXSDDateTime 2008-07-22T13:10]];
               [t:hasEnd       [t:inXSDDateTime 2008-07-22T13:20]]]]
  a  :ChangeCriterion1.
```

Description of the control scenario

The technology has been applied for the secondary regulation control of the MicroGrid shown in figure 1. A typical scenario is as follows:

1. A sudden unbalance between generation and load is dealt within the short term by the modification of the exchange of energy between the MicroGrid and the Distribution Network.
2. The controller of the MicroGrid then reacts to the situation and dispatches (instructs) DieselEgine_01 to increase power to 36 kW in order to return the system to the normal balance between generation and load.
3. As soon as the generator is scheduled a "Scheduling Monitoring activity" is started. The main objective of this application is to monitor the ability of DieselEgine_01 to fulfil its assignment. It may not be able to do so, because of a break down of the generator, a loss of efficiency caused by the need to support CHP, or some other reason.
4. If the scheduling application detects that the plan cannot be fulfilled it reports the problem.
5. The plan Plan_Generator_01_1074528964 is defined as the class of time history that:
6. is the outputActivePower of DieselEgine_01;
7. begins at the current time - millisecond count 1074528964;
8. ends when a final output of 36 kW has been reached or when the expected time to achieve it has been exceeded.

The "Scheduling Monitoring activity" assigned to this task is concerned with the time history of active power of DieselEgine_01 beginning at the current time and ending when the new required output level has been reached. The application reports when the requirement has been fulfilled, i.e. when a member of the required class has been found, or when it is clear that the requirement cannot be fulfilled.

The specification of the monitoring activity is as follows:

```
:MonitoringActivity_Generator_01_1074528964
 a                             sten:MonitoringActivity;
 sten:monitors                 :activePowerOfDieselEgine_01;
 sten:hasMonitoringCriterion :Plan_Generator_01_1074528964.
```

The knowledge stored in the ontology greatly facilitates the development of decision support systems and in this case only one simple rule has to be programmed to detect that DieselEgine_01 has achieved its objective. At time T, the time history from the start of the plan to T is assessed as follows:

```
If
activePowerOfDieselEgine01_1074528964 is P1 and
```

```
Current output of DieselEgine_01 is P2 and
Ramping capacity of DieselEgine_01 is R and
Current Time is T and
P2 >= 36 kW and
T < 1074528964 + (36 - P1)/R
Then
DieselEgine_01 has successfully fulfilled his planned schedule.
```

This can be reported by the statement:

```
activePowerOfDieselEgine01_1074528964_T
 a                                   :Plan_Generator_01_1074528964.
```

Another rule is used to detect that the DieselEgine_01 can not arrive at its scheduled value and that another generator has to be re-scheduled to cover the difference. In this case, as in the previous rule, design knowledge such as the "ramping" capacity1 of the generator is used to detect the situation. The rule used by the application is as follows:

```
IF
activePowerOfDieselEgine01_1074528964 is P1 and
Current output of DieselEgine_01 is P2 and
Ramping capacity of DieselEgine_01 is R and
Current time is T and
P2 < 36 kW and
T - 1074528964 > (36 kW -P1)/R
Then
Set DieselEgine_01 as unavailable for further scheduling and
schedule anotherGenerator to generate 36 minus P2 kW.
```

5. Outlook

The integration of innovative technologies used by the Semantics Web Community has been proved to be effective for the control of industrial applications and in particular for the control of a MicroGrid. Ontologies derived from standards have been demonstrated to pave the way towards building complex applications by integrating powerful representation mechanisms together with complex decision support systems. The prototype applications have demonstrated that building decision support tools using rule based techniques on top of standard ontologies is a promising way to facilitate the coding of industrial applications and to customize them to the user needs.

Currently the integration of electrical vehicles into the electrical power system is a challenging task that is worked on worldwide. Controllable electrical vehicles could contribute to a reliable and secure power system operation by charging their batteries when the energy demand is low and feeding back energy when the energy demand is high. Applying Web technologies and agent technologies in combination with ontologies and rules to Vehicle To Grid (V2G) applications is a promising approach for realizing the smart grids of the future.

---

[1] The ramping capacity represents the amount of Power per Time unit that a generator can raise its power.

6. Acknowledgment

The research described in the paper has been carried out within the S-TEN project ('Intelligent Self-describing Technical and Environmental Networks', www.s-ten.eu, FP6-IST-2005-027683) co-funded by the European Community in the Information Society Technologies program.

7. References

[1] S-TEN Project: Intelligent Self-describing Technical and Environmental Networks, Available from: www.s-ten.eu

[2] Berners-Lee, T. Handler, J., Lassila, O. (2001). The Semantic Web, In: *Scientific American Magazine,* Available from: http://www.dblab.ntua.gr/~bikakis/SW.pdf

[3] The Apache Software Foundation: AXIS 2, Available from: http://axis.apache.org/axis2/java/core/

[4] W3C: Web Services Description Language (WSDL) 1.1, Available from: http://www.w3.org/TR/wsdl

[5] W3C: Semantic Annotations for WSDL, Available from: http://www.w3.org/2002/ws/sawsdl/

[6] W3C: OWL Web Ontology Language - W3C Recommendation 10 February 2004, Available from: http://www.w3.org/TR/owl-features/

[7] W3C: RDF Vocabulary Description Language 1.0: RDF Schema W3C Recommendation 10 February 2004, Available from: http://www.w3.org/TR/rdf-schema/

[8] S-TEN consortium(2007): Ontology for self-describing networks (D2.1), Available from: http://www.s-ten.eu/deliverables/D2.1/.

[9} W3C: OWL-S: Semantic Markup for Web Services - W3C Member Submission 22 November 2004, Available from: http://www.w3.org/Submission/OWL-S/

[10] W3C: Web Service Modeling Ontology (WSMO) - W3C Member Submission 3 June 2005, Available from: http://www.w3.org/Submission/WSMO/

Section 3

Visualization

8

Facet Decomposition and Discouse Analysis: Visualization of Conflict Structure

Hayeong Jeong[1], Kiyoshi Kobayashi[1],
Tsuyoshi Hatori[2] and Shiramatsu Shun[3]
[1]*Kyoto University*
[2]*Ehime University*
[3]*Nagoya Institute of Technology*
Japan

1. Introduction

Public debate has become an important process in the planning of public projects where stakeholders including citizens, experts, enterprises, and administrators meet face-to-face to discuss the desirability of a public project in its early planning stages. The roles of public debate are: to clarify the pros and cons of a project, that is, evaluate available information and proposed approaches; to promote mutual understanding of the stakeholders' different perspectives; and to find resolutions that are mutually beneficial for all stakeholders.

The stakeholders or debate participants have varying values, concerns, and expectations on the benefits and costs of a project and as such, their interests do not necessarily coincide with or complement each other. To promote their interests, debate participants strategically reiterate and legitimize their opinions. The debate facilitator must identify appropriate methods for recognizing and managing uncooperative communication in order for a debate to arrive at a fair consensus. To facilitate effective group communication such as debates, it is important to develop scientific management tools for managing debate content and conflict situations.

Advances in information technology has led to the development of various debate support systems based on corpus linguistics (Shiramatsu *et al.*, 2007; Jeong *et al.* 2007) designed to assist facilitators and participants in achieving clear communication and arriving at a consensus by analyzing information from actual dialogue data. Unfortunately, these systems are yet to be fully applied to studies in public discourse. There have been few studies that examined the effectiveness of debate support systems in alleviating stakeholder interest conflict. In addition, systematic and objective means for summarizing and analyzing debate content have not been sufficiently developed. In order to effectively and efficiently manage public debate, techniques that enable deeper understanding of participant opinions and management of conflict are essential.

This study proposes a method for visualizing conflict structures in public debates by analyzing debate minutes using a corpus-based discourse analysis. In this method, the opinion of participants recorded in the debate minutes (hereafter called "primary corpus") are decomposed into four facets based on the following defined conceptual categories—debate purpose, means, evidences, and attitudes toward the subject project. Using this facets-tagged corpus (hereafter called "secondary corpus"), this study quantitatively measures the content similarity among the recorded opinions and the level of interest dissonance among the participants. The rest of this paper is organized as follows. Section 2 describes the basic idea of the study. Section 3 explains the definition and decomposition of the facets using a support vector machine (SVM). Section 4 presents the discourse analysis using the secondary corpus and visualizes the conflict structure and debate pattern changes. The applicability of the proposed methodology is then discussed by applying it to a real case of public debate. Section 5 presents the conclusions and limitations of the study.

2. The basic idea

2.1 Related studies

Previous studies on debate support systems have focused on summarizing debate contents by extracting important topics and exploring semantic meanings using statistical indicators of term frequency and co-occurency (Horita and Kanno, 2001; Hiromi *et al*, 2006). While these techniques clarify the main topic of debate and participants' interests from a debate minute using natural language processing and text mining, they do not identify conflict structures and underlying dynamic interaction in a multiple debate process.

Nasukawa and Yi (2003) proposed a sentiment analysis approach for extracting polar opposite sentiments of subjects from a document by identifying the semantic relationship between the subject term and semantic expressions such as "good" and "bad," instead of classifying the entire document as positive or negative. By defining the terms of sentiment expression, it is possible to calculate an individual's attitude toward the subject term and determine whether participants in a discussion have different attitudes toward to subject term While this method certainly has its merits, it is unable to determine the reason for the differences in attitude and the underlying relationships in the debate. In order to enhance mutual understanding and consensus building in debates, it is necessary to clarify the conflict structure and its change throughout multiple debates, evaluate the significance of debate context on participants' sentiments, and develop facilitation techniques for managing conflict structures.

Opinion mining is a relatively new research field that includes review analysis, opinion extraction, and answering opinion questions. Opinion mining utilizes natural language processing techniques and facilitates deep semantic classification of opinions. Sophisticated techniques for deep semantic classification have not yet been developed for and applied to public debates as they require substantial linguistic knowledge and the ability to process additional non-literal information such as heuristic rules. The rules-based approaches to opinion mining also have some limitations. Somasundaran and Wiebe (2010) examined opinions in ideological online debates by developing an argument lexicon using the Multi-Perspective Question Answering (MPQA) annotations. Meanwhile, the Statement Map (Murakami *et al.*, 2010) and WISDOM (Akamine *et al.*, 2009) methods focus on analyzing information credibility through opinion mining techniques. These methods classify semantic relationships between subjective statements such as agreement and conflict relationships using rules-based approaches that work well with experimental data but generally are more difficult to implement than machine learning approaches. Recognizing Textual Entailment (RTE) Challenges (Dagan, 2006; PASCAL, 2005) is a method that focuses on the semantic relationships between texts to determine whether the meaning of one text is derived from another text. Although the RTE datasets included semantic relations such as agreement and conflict, Marnefe (2008) found that opinions in real world debates were much more difficult to classify and as such, more sophisticated classification methods are required for RTE to work in the real world. Cross-document Structure Theory (CST) is another approach for identifying semantic relationships between sentences (Radev, 2000). The CSTBank Corpus built by Radev (2000) is annotated with 18 kinds of semantic relationships including agreement and conflict. As with the RTE, the CST approach does not effectively classify opinions in debates.

The rules-based approaches discussed above clarify linguistic characteristics using detailed categorizations and rules to ensure accuracy in analysis. However, they are limited in that they are difficult to implement and their classifications are too simplified to accurately classify more complicated opinions in real-world debates. This study proposes a simpler, more effective approach based on machine learning techniques for visualizing conflict structures in terms of rapid prototyping. Machine learning approaches are more effective and perform better than rules-based approaches. We then apply this approach to a series of real public debates where participants with different backgrounds argue their opinions.

2.2 Content Analysis

Debate participants' different cognitive frames and subjective interests lead to differing opinions. In order to effectively summarize the debate contents, we need to maintain the relevance between textual and contextual information using qualitative and descriptive analyses (Hashiuchi, 2003). In this study, we used the method of content analysis proposed by Stone *et al.* (1966). Content analysis refers to ". . . any research technique for making inferences by systematically and objectively identifying specified characteristics within text" (Stone *et al.*, 1966). The purpose of content analysis is to examine the corpus data of dialogue (e.g., debate minutes), taking into consideration the relevance between the words and the context embedded in the dialogue. Krippendorff (1980) identified the three most important features of content analysis: it is an *unobtrusive* technique; it can assess *unstructured* material; and is *context-sensitive*. These features allow researchers to examine relatively unstructured data for meanings, symbolism, expressed information, and the role this information plays in the lives of the data sources, while at the same time acknowledging the textuality of the data, that is, recognizing that the data are read and understood by others and interpreting this data based their own contexts (Koreniusa *et al.*, 2007).

Discourse analysis is a type of content analysis that clarifies debate content and structure by targeting language use in the real world (Schiffrin *et al.*, 2003). Discourse analysis reveals the structural and functional mechanism of language in relation to the utterances in their context. Discourse has traditionally been defined as "anything beyond the sentence." Schiffrin (1994) referred to "utterances" rather then "sentences" because utterances are *contextualized* sentences, that is, they are context- and text-bound. In discourse analysis, context refers to the information that surrounds a sentence and determines its meaning, and includes a broad range of information such as the speaker's knowledge, beliefs, facial expressions, gestures, and social circumstance, and culture.

Hatori *et al.* (2006) suggested a discourse analysis based on facet theory. In this method, utterances in a debate are decomposed into three conceptual units (hereafter called "facets")—"what" should be solved, "how" it should be solved, and "why" it should be solved, in order to effectively examine interest conflict and cognitive dissonance among debate participants. This facet decomposition task depends on how researchers analyze and interpret the utterances in a debate. However, to be able to analyze multiple debates with huge amounts of language data, improved reproducibility and computational approaches are required (Francis, 1982).

This study develops a computational method of facet decomposition and discourse analysis based on corpus linguistics. Corpus is generally defined as a collection of text or written and spoken material that highlights how a language is used. Corpus linguistics is a linguistic method that explains the meanings of words and phrases using a corpus. It is a reconstructive method for analysis of language data using a computer (Sinclair, 1991; Stubbs, 2002; Wang, 2005; McCarthy, 1998). In this study we use SVM learning to decompose debate utterances into facets. Then, using this facets-tagged corpus, we propose an approach for calculating the differences among the utterances of the debate participants and visualize their dynamic change.

2.3 Management of public debate

A public debate is essentially a third-party committee where stakeholders, including experts, public enterprises, and citizens, share their perspectives on public projects in their early planning stage. The purpose of this third-party committee is to promote mutual understanding among the debate participants and ensure transparency of the debate system by opening the discussion process to the various stakeholders and making available information on related projects. The third-party committee is not involved in the decision-making, but rather in the collection of information related to public project and the building of public trust in the decision makers (Hatori *et al.*, 2008).

The third-party committee is directly entrusted by the government and the citizens and as such, must suggest solutions that are socially desirable and beneficial to the government and its citizens. As representatives of the government and its citizens, committee members must assess solutions based on their social perspective (i.e., check for adequacy) and technical and professional perspectives (i.e., check for rigor). In short, the third-party committee is expected to assess project-related information for adequacy and rigor to facilitate decision making.

Previous studies have used questionnaires and interviews to understand the perspectives of stakeholders on public projects. According to Giddens (1990), these methods are based on the segmented, asynchronous communication between the stakeholders and thus suffer from the problem of faceless commitments. These methods are limited in that questionnaire may contain the subjective perspectives of the researchers and as such both the researcher and participants readily trust the questions and answers on the questionnaire, respectively. In addition, the questionnaire may contain the assumptions and perspectives of the researchers on the projects which the respondents or citizens do not necessarily recognize. In contrast, a debate within a third-party committee realizes the richness of social communication facilitated by the direct meeting among stakeholders. Such debates ensure the effective collection of information and transparency in the decision-making process.

Debate participants are interested only in certain aspects of an issue, and as such, are motivated to steer the discussion toward their desired goals. Debate participants such as experts and engineers usually evaluate the benefits of the projects based on scientific and professional evidences highlighting rigor, while general citizens evaluate them based on their common sense and their interests, checking for adequacy. If debate participants consider only one aspect of the issue, that is, either rigor or adequacy only, the debate would not reach a consensus. The most important role of public debate involving the third-party committee is to achieve a common perspective on the project under discussion by recognizing each stakeholder's interest and point of view. To evaluate the progress of the debate toward mutual understanding and consensus, it is necessary to accumulate the debate minutes and summarize the discussions. This study proposes a method of discourse analysis that manages public debate by summarizing the debate contents and tracking the progress of the debate process toward its goal.

3. Creating the facet-tagged corpus

3.1 Facet decomposition and the Support Vector Machine (SVM)

In this study, we define utterance as the language used to establish one's position on an issue by addressing the position's pros and cons. During a debate, participants legitimize their positions with technical and scientific evidences or their common sense and self-interests. They strengthen their positions by expressing positive or negative attitudes toward another participant's utterances depending on whether those utterances coincide or contrast their positions. Based on these assumptions, we identified the four facets to be used in this study: facet A refers the positions of participants or their pros and cons on the issue; facet B refers their efforts to strengthen their positions using evidence; facet C refers the characteristics of evidences, that is, whether they pertain to either adequacy or rigor; and facet D refers to the participants' interpretation of each other's utterances, that is, their expression of positive or negative attitudes toward each other's utterances. We coded the utterances using a combination of four facets (i.e., stractable). In this study, the utterances in the debate minutes comprise the primary corpus and the utterances encoded with facet stractables comprise the secondary corpus. Utterances that do not explicitly pertain to a position are considered neutral and as such, classified under a third category for each facet. Section 3.2 presents the facet stractables in more detail.

In order to create the secondary corpus, we encoded the utterances with the facet stractables. Owing to the enormous amount of data in the primary corpus, decomposing the utterances based on facets is not easy. As such, we created the secondary corpus using a statistical facet learning model that reduces the efforts required of researcher while at the same time maintaining the logical consistency of the primary corpus. This statistical facet learning model is based on a pattern recognition technique that classifies the huge amount of primary corpus into the secondary corpus through the SVM, a type of statistical learning machine. Pattern recognition is generally defined as a method for extracting data features such as those in letters, video, and audio and determining the data categories based on the standard pattern of the features. This study decomposed the facets using the SVM model originally developed by Vapnik (see Kudo, 2002). The SVM is a binary sorter where there is only one border identifying a sample's location. Because there are three categories for each facet, that is, $X \in \{A,B,C,D\}$, this study uses two bounding hyperplanes $y_h{}^X(U_i),(h=1,2)$. These bounding hyperplanes are defined by a high-dimensional discrimination function that determines the amount of terms included in the primary corpus and maximizes the distance between the border and each utterance. Although the discrimination function is usually represented by a nonlinear kernel function, we used a d-dimensional polynomial function that flexibly approximates the function. The SVM model used in this study is able to process large amounts of data and produces good estimation results. In this model, the utterances in the primary corpus, $U_i(i=1,\cdots,m)$, are each classified into one of the three categories of facets, $F^X(U_i) \in \{X(-1),X(0),X(1)\}$. $F^X(U_i)$ determines the corresponding relationship and is defined as:

$$F^X : U_i \mapsto \{X(-1),X(0),X(1)\} \tag{1}$$

$$(X \in \{A,B,C,D\})$$

The two types of kernel functions, $y_1{}^X(U_i)$, $y_2{}^X(U_i)$ for the facets $X \in \{A,B,C,D\}$ with m units of utterances $U_i(i=1,\cdots,m)$ which are located in the n dimensional space$'$(n is the total number of terms in the primary corpus) are defined as follows:

i. $F^X(U_i) = X(1)$ if $y_1{}^X(U_i) > 0$;

ii. $F^X(U_i) = X(0)$ if $y_1{}^X(U_i) \le 0$ and $y_2{}^X(U_j) > 0$; and

iii. $F^X(U_i) = X(-1)$ if $y_2{}^X(U_i) \le 0$.

In addition, we define the facet vector $\mathbf{G}_i$ for an utterance U_i using 0–1 variables $(\delta_i^y \in \{0,1\})$ in order to represent the four facets $X \in \{A,B,C,D\}$ corresponding to each of the categories $y \in \{X(-1),X(0),X(1)\}$:

$$\begin{aligned}\mathbf{G}_i = \{&\delta_i^{A(-1)},\delta_i^{A(0)},\delta_i^{A(1)},\delta_i^{B(-1)},\delta_i^{B(0)},\delta_i^{B(1)},\\ &\delta_i^{C(-1)},\delta_i^{C(0)},\delta_i^{C(1)},\delta_i^{D(-1)},\delta_i^{D(0)},\delta_i^{D(1)}\}\end{aligned} \tag{2}$$

The set of facet vector $\mathbf{G}_i$ for the all utterances $U_i(i=1,\cdots,m)$ is the secondary corpus.

3.2 Case study

This paper's case study examines the debates of the Yodo-River committee which was established in 2001 in order to obtain advice for the planning and policy handling of a river improvement project related to the building of a dam and gather the opinions of the representatives of affected citizens and public organizations. The Yodo-river committee meetings consists of a general meeting, four regional meetings, five theme meetings, five working group meetings, and three meetings of the sub-working group. A total of 400 meetings have been held since 2001. The debate minutes are available from the committee website and are downloadable as PDF files. The minutes record the names of speakers and their utterances chronologically.

From these meetings, we selected 14 debates between citizens and experts or between administrators (i.e., river managers) and experts. Participants were classified into five groups according to their roles: facilitator; expert; citizen with a "con" opinion; citizen with a "pro" opinion; and administrator. The minutes from the 14 debates consisted of 8,831 utterances. A unit of utterance is a single sentence ended by punctuation mark.

3.3 Outline of the facet decomposition

Four researchers from construction consulting companies with experience in mobilizing public involvement made a training set of facet decomposition. To maintain the objectivity of the training set, two researchers conducted facet decomposition on the same utterances. We completed the training set the corresponding facet decomposition. Table 1 shows the framework of the four facets with the facet elements and the typical language use.

An utterance is coded as facet A(1) if it describes the pros of the project. Statements about the advantages of the project are examples of A(1). Meanwhile, disapproving opinions are classified as facet A(-1) and include statements that mention the disadvantages of the project and suggest new alternatives. Utterances that include evidences are coded as facet B(1) and those without evidences as B(-1). Utterances with rigorous or adequate evidences are coded as C(1) or C(-1), respectively. Facet C(1) includes statements that cite evidences from studies or experiments while facet C(-1) includes statements with evidences based on individual experiences or feelings. Finally, facet D(1) represents positive attitudes toward the project, signaling affirmation or belief in the project. Facet D(-1) represents negative attitudes toward the project. Conflicts can be identified by comparing the difference between the responses in facet A and those in facet D. Facet B determines the plausibility of arguments while facet C sheds light on the participants' reasoning systems. If an utterance cannot be easily coded using the above facets, it is classified under the neutral category, $X(0)$, $X \in \{A,B,C,D\}$.

Below are two examples of how utterances are encoded using the facets framework:

Example 1: The dam construction is the only way to ensure the safety of the town's residents given the limited public finances. → A (1) B (1) C (-1) D (-1)
Example 2: There have been many regional development projects that constructed dams but only a few of them succeeded. → A (-1) B (1) C (1) D (-1)

The first utterance example is decomposed into facet A(1)B(1)C(-1)D(-1). The expression "is the only way" indicates that the speaker agrees to the dam construction, hence, A (1), but does not have a positive attitude toward it, hence, D(-1). The expression "given the limited public finances" is an evidence and is therefore classified as B(1); however, this evidence is also based on the speaker's anxiety and concern, and as such, is classified as C(-1). Meanwhile, the second utterance example expresses pessimism regarding the dam construction, hence, A(-1). The phrase "only a few of them have succeeded" expresses the speaker's reason for his negative view and thus is denoted as B(1), C(1), and D(-1).

As mentioned earlier, researchers created and completed the training utterance set of facet decomposition. Of the total 8,831 utterances, 34% were decomposed as facet A, 65% as facet B, 59% as facet C, and 52% as facet D. Over half of the utterances are selected as training utterence excepting facet A. The training utterance set determines the statistical facet

	Definition	Elements		
		$X(1)$	$X(-1)$	$X(0)$
Facet A	Refers to the position of the participants (i.e., whether they have taken a "pro" or "con" position on the project.	Pros	Cons	Neutral utterances including greetings, questions, and other utterances during the progress of the debate. These utterances are categorized as X(0) and not X(1) or X(-1).
Facet B	Refers to whether participants provided evidences to strengthen their position and help others understand their perspectives	With evidence, including scientific, mathematical, and psychological evidence	Without Evidence	
Facet C	Refers to the characteristics of the evidences (i.e., whether they are rigorous or adequate)	Rigor of evidence focusing on statistical facets, scientific facts, existing facts, and engagement	Adequacy of evidence focusing on psychological facts (e.g., anxiety, trust, impression), sensitizing concepts (values, norms, belief), community spirit, ethical facts, fairness, rightfulness, etc.	
Facet D	Refers to the participants' bargaining attitudes to the project	Positive attitudes such as agreement, esteem, encouragement, compromise, etc.	Negative attitudes such as avoidance, constraint, doubt, distrust, disregard, ignorance, disruption, etc.	

Table 1. Framework of Facet Decomposition.

decomposition using the SVM. We then investigate the accuracy of the SVM decomposition by calculating the matching rate between the results done by the researchers and that by the SVM.

The accuracy of the SVM decomposition was estimated by using kernel-fold cross validation wherein we divide the 8,831 utterances into K subgroups and use K-1 subgroups as the training set (i.e., the utterances facet-encoded by researcher) while the remaining subgroup is decomposed into facets using the SVM. In this study, $K = 10$. By changing the subgroup of the training set to the other subgroup, the statistical facet decomposition for all the utterances using the SVM can be implemented a total of K times. The dummy variable δ_i^y indicates the categorized elements $y \in \{X(-1), X(0), X(1)\}$ of each facet $X \in \{A, B, C, D\}$ of utterances $U_i (i = 1, \cdots, m)$. α refers to the matching frequency of the results of the facet decomposition from both the researchers and the SVM where $\delta_i^y = 1$. β refers to the frequency that training set was $\delta_i^y = 1$ but was categorized by the SVM as $\delta_i^y = 0$. γ refers to the frequency that training set was $\delta_i^y = 0$ but was identified by the SVM as $\delta_i^y = 1$. Finally, λ refers to the frequency that both the researchers and the SVM decomposed the utterance as $\delta_i^y = 0$. The accuracy of the SVM model was determined by the F-value calculated as follows:

$$A = \frac{\alpha + \lambda}{\alpha + \beta + \gamma + \lambda} \tag{3a}$$

$$F = \frac{2P \times R}{P + R} \tag{3b}$$

where $P = \frac{\beta}{\alpha + \beta}$, and $R = \frac{\alpha}{\alpha + \gamma}$.

3.4 Results

Table 2 presents the results of the facet decomposition. The total number of facet decomposition performed by the researchers exceeded that of the utterances as each utterance can be classified into multiple facet elements. 35% of the utterances expressed the pros of the dam project; 33% mentioned the cons percent of the project; 31% of the utterances had evidences while 24% did not; 21% had rigorous evidence while 41% had adequate evidence; 12% expressed a positive attitude toward the project and 55% expressed a negative attitude. Over 50% of the utterances were negative responses to the project that had rigorous evidence. This result does not mean, however, that over half of the debate participants had a negative opinion of the project because the utterances were only the opinions of those who spoke. Meanwhile, in the facet decomposition resulting from the SVM, 4% expressed the pros of the project and 1% expressed the cons; 26% had evidences and 20% did not; 10% presented rigorous evidence and 24% presented adequate evidence; 5% expresses positive attitudes toward the project and 34% negative attitudes. The accuracy of the SVM decomposition was calculated using Equation 3b which resulted in an F-measure between 0.48 and 0.66. In general, the accuracy level should be between 0.6 and 0.7. There are at least two possible reasons for this low level of accuracy. First, many of the utterances were decomposed into the third category, neutral (X(0)). Second, the accuracy of the decomposition for facet A was particularly low because most participants imply rather than express the pros and cons of the project and as such, their utterances cannot be easily decomposed into the appropriate facets. The final facet classification lies on the researcher. To ensure the objectivity of the researchers' decomposition, a feedback system is used to review and revise the facet decomposition based on the discourse patterns. Subsection 4.2 presents the analysis of the discourse patterns.

The less than ideal accuracy level of the SVM decomposition is not uncommon, as only few classification techniques utilizing natural language processing for discourse data have achieved sufficient accuracy. As such, the results of the SVM decomposition in this study are still useful for determining facet decomposition. The final facet decomposition was improved by adjusting the two classifications by the SVM which supported and facilitated the researchers' tasks.

The SVM decomposition provides useful information that helps researchers in their final analysis and significantly reduces their efforts for confirming the secondary corpus. In addition, the SVM helps monitor and improve the performance of rule-based approaches for opinion mining (e.g., Dagan, 2006; Radev, 2000). The SVM method is facilitates the comparison of the results of two approaches using disagreements to track changes in the discourse rules. Future studies should test the applicability of the SVM method to rules-based approaches.

Total 8,831 utterances		Facet A		Facet B		Facet C		Facet D	
		Cons/Pros		With/Without Evidences		Rigor/adequacy		Positive/Negative	
		#	%	#	%	#	%	#	%
Researchers	○	6130	35	5447	31	3715	21	2088	12
	●	5839	33	4214	24	7252	41	9716	55
	×	5693	32	8045	45	6739	38	5902	33
SVM	○	313	4	2292	26	904	10	452	5
	●	49	1	1793	20	2142	24	2959	34
	×	8469	95	4746	54	5785	66	5420	61
Final Decomposition	○	3532	40	2914	33	2031	23	1236	14
	●	3267	37	2296	26	3533	40	4946	56
	×	2782	23	3621	41	3267	37	2649	30
Accuracy		48		66		55		50	
F-value		35		54		44		34	

Note: The symbols ○, ●, and × indicate categories X(1), X(-1), and neutral, respectively.

Table 2. Facet Decomposition Results.

4. Discourse analysis of the public debate

4.1 Similarity of utterance meaning

Using the secondary corpus (i.e., the facet-encoded utterance developed in the previous section), we conducted the discourse analysis in order to examine the interest conflict among the participants and visualize the discourse patterns during the debate process. Using non-metric multi-dimensional scaling (MDS), we distributed the participants on a two-dimensional space based on the similarity of their utterance meanings (Kruskal, 1964a and 1964b; Qian, 2004). Among the Z participants $p_i \in (p_1,...,p_z)$, the dissimilarity of interest $dsim(p_i,p_j)$ between two participants p_i and p_j is represented as the distance $dis(p_i,p_j)$ in a two-dimensional space. If the interest dissimilarity between the participants is $dsim(p_i,p_j) < dsim(p_i,p_k)$, then the distance is $dis(p_i,p_j) < dis(p_i,p_k)$.

For a participant p_k, the relative frequency of dummy variables $\delta_j^y(y = A(-1), A(0), A(1),\cdots, D(-1), D(0), D(1))$ is defined, making up the facet vector from the secondary corpus as illustrated below:

$$W_y^{pk} = \frac{\sum_{j \in \Omega pk} \delta_j^y}{\sum_{j \in \Omega pk} \sum_{y=A(-1)}^{D(1)} \delta_j^y} \tag{4}$$

Here, Ωp_k indicates a set of facet vector. Facet matrix S is defined as:

$$\mathbf{S} = \begin{bmatrix} \mathbf{F}_{p1} \\ \vdots \\ \mathbf{F}_{pz} \end{bmatrix} = \begin{bmatrix} W_{A(-1)}^{p_1} & \cdots & W_{D(1)}^{p_1} \\ \vdots & \ddots & \vdots \\ W_{A(-1)}^{p_z} & \cdots & W_{D(1)}^{p_z} \end{bmatrix} \tag{5}$$

The similarity between the facet vectors of two participants is calculated based on the cosine angle distance:

$$sim(p_i, p_j) = \cos(\mathbf{F}_{pi}\mathbf{F}_{pj}) = \frac{\mathbf{F}_{pi}\mathbf{F}_{pj}}{|\mathbf{F}_{pi}| \cdot |\mathbf{F}_{pj}|} = \frac{\sum_{y=A(-1)}^{D(1)} W_y^{p_i} W_y^{p_j}}{\sqrt{\sum_{y=A(-1)}^{D(1)} (W_y^{p_i})^2} \sqrt{\sum_{y=A(-1)}^{D(1)} (W_y^{p_j})^2}} \tag{6}$$

We can determine the dissimilarity of the facet vectors through the inverse of the cosine function:

$$dsim(p_i, p_j) = \cos^{-1}\{sim_i(p_i, p_j)\} \tag{7}$$

All distances $dis(p_i, p_j)$ are arranged in a correlation matrix D:

$$\mathbf{D} = \begin{pmatrix} dis(p_1, p_1) & \cdots & dis(p_1, p_z) \\ \vdots & \ddots & \vdots \\ dis(p_z, p_1) & \cdots & dis(p_z, p_z) \end{pmatrix} \tag{8}$$

MDS reproduces the distance $dis(p_i, p_j)$ on a two-dimensional space by minimizing the sum of the squares of the distance between $dis(p_i, p_j)$ and the dissimilarities $dsim(p_i, p_j)$. Using stress, which represents the degree of incompatibility between the dissimilarity and the distance, an accurate coordinate value is produced:

$$Stress = \sqrt{\frac{\sum_{i=1}^{z-1} \sum_{j>i}^{z} \{dis(p_i, p_j) - dsim(p_i, p_j)\}^2}{\sum_{i=1}^{z-1} \sum_{j>i}^{z} \{dis(p_i, p_j) - \overline{dis}\}^2}} \tag{9}$$

$\overline{dis}$ denotes the average of the distance between two participants:

$$\overline{dis} = \sqrt{\frac{\sum_{i=1}^{z-1} \sum_{j>i}^{z} \{dis(p_i, p_j)\}^2}{{}_zC_2}} \tag{10}$$

By changing the dimension value to a lower value, the optimal arrangement for the coordinate value in a two-dimensional space can be defined. Consequently, the semantic similarity of all individuals is illustrated as the distances in a two-dimensional space.

Figure 1 shows the distribution of the participants in this study (49 professionals, 27 administrators [i.e., river managers], and 5 citizens) on a two-dimensional space based on the similarity of the facet vectors derived from 14 debates minutes (i.e., the primary corpus). The symbols ◆, ✳, and □ denote citizens, experts, and administrators, respectively. As shown in Figure 1, the participant groups usually have similar interests. For instance, citizens are located on the leftmost part of the graph. Meanwhile the administrators are distributed on the top portion of the space, while, the experts are positioned on the bottom of the space, indicating that these two groups have interest conflict.

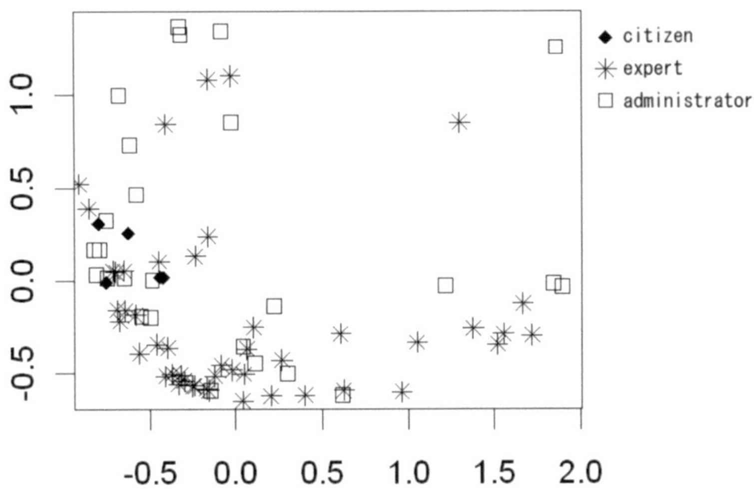

Fig. 1. Similarity of Interest Structures of Debate Participants.

Figure 2 illustrates the five types of participants who expressed their utterances: the facilitators (⊗); experts (✳); citizens with a "pro" opinion (◆); citizens with a "con" opinion (◇), and administrators (□). As shown in the figure, the distance between facilitator and expert is wider than that between facilitator and citizen or administrator, which means that the interest structure of facilitators is similar to that of experts, but substantially differs from that of citizens and administrators. In this case, it is important to examine the change in the interest structure during the debate rather than the different interest structures themselves. It is also important to remember that different interest structures are not necessarily a negative thing. On the contrary, it will help groups obtain and understand the diverse perspectives of the various stakeholders on a project. In the following subsection, we will analyze the change in interest structure during the debate process using Figure 2 once again.

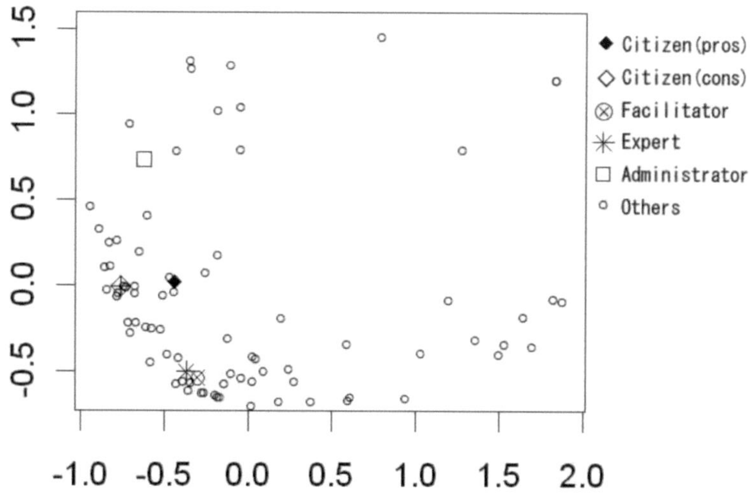

Fig. 2. The Five Types of Participants.

4.2 The change of discourse pattern

We created a time-sequence of the primary corpus and calculated the cumulative frequency of the facet in order to analyze the change in the discourse patterns of the five types of participants. Figures 3 to 7 illustrate the discourse change for the different types of participants. The horizontal axis on the graphs represents the number of time-sequence of utterances while the vertical axis represents the cumulative frequency of the elements of each facet. The line will go up if the frequency of category $X(1)$ of facet X increases. The line will go down if the frequency of category $X(-1)$ of facet X increases. The line will remain constant if the frequency of $X(1)$ matches that of $X(-1)$.

Figure 3 illustrates the temporal variation of the cumulative frequency of the facets of the facilitator. The facilitator expresses a total of 849 utterances in 8 out of the 14 debates. The results of the facet decomposition for facilitators show that the facilitators do not take a "pro" or "con" position on the project; expressed utterances without evidence; when they do provide evidence, they presented rigorous evidence during the debate in general and used adequate evidence on certain issues; and expressed more negative attitudes rather than positive attitudes throughout the debates.

In contrast, the cumulative frequency of the facets of the other types of participants exhibits a stable pattern (Figures 4 to 7). Experts had a total of 444 utterances in 6 out of the 14 debates; administrators expressed 151 utterances in one debate; citizens (pros) expressed 143 utterances in one debate; and citizens (cons) had 228 utterances in one debate. Except for the facilitators and experts, the participants were involved in only one debate; as such, their opportunities for expressing their perspectives on the project was limited, only managing to gain mutual understanding and knowledge during the debate. The results also show that administrators and experts have a tendency to take a neutral position on many facets while citizens have a tendency to repeat same categories of facets, that is, the pros or cons.

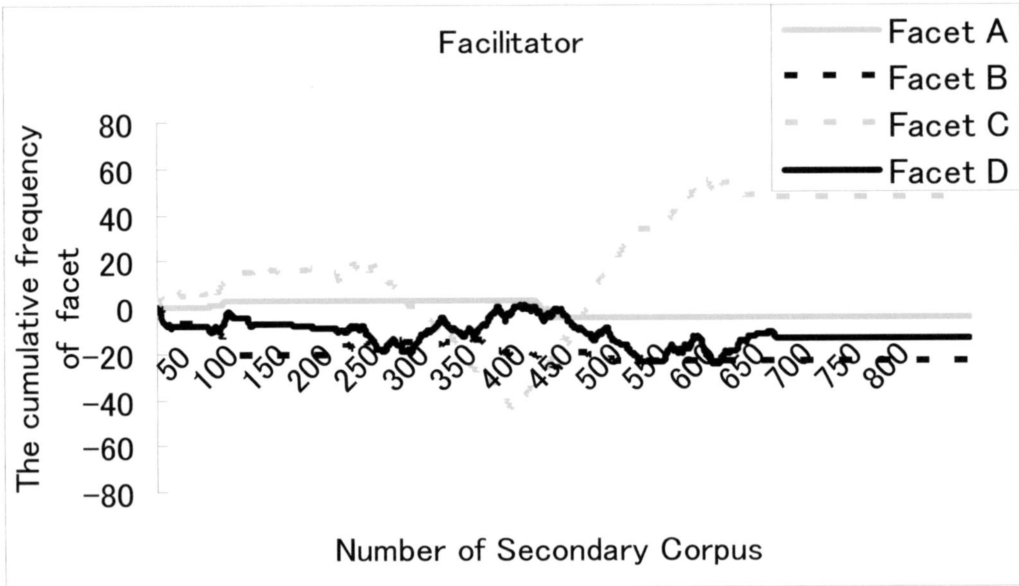

Fig. 3. The Discourse Pattern Change of the Facilitator.

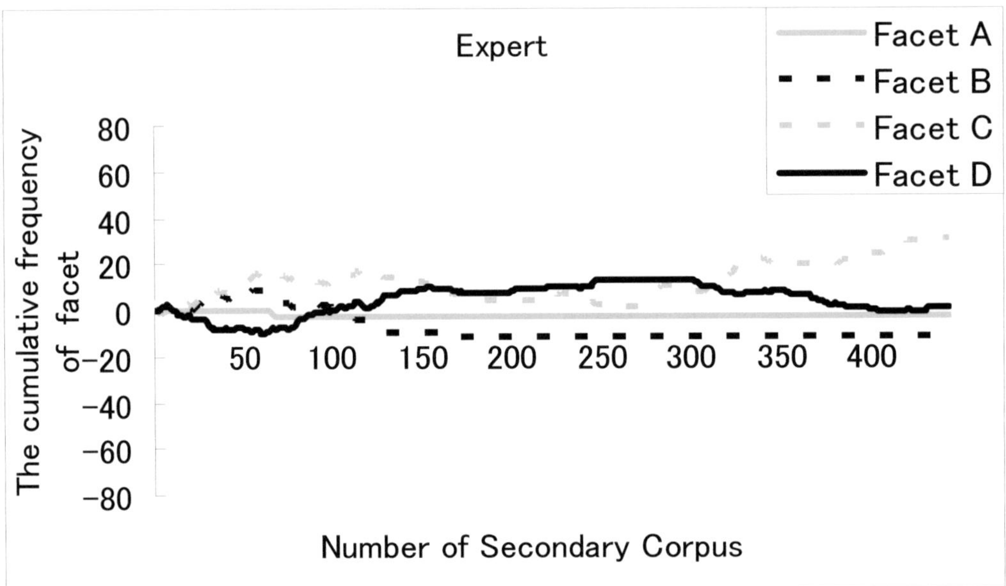

Fig. 4. The Discourse of Pattern Change of the Experts.

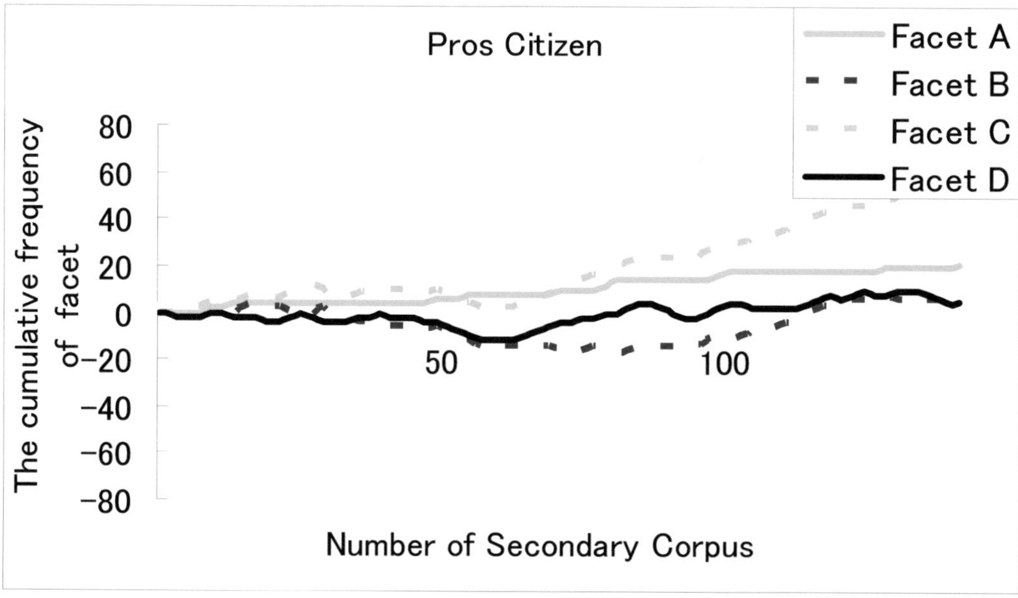

Fig. 5. The Discourse Pattern Change of Citizens (Pros).

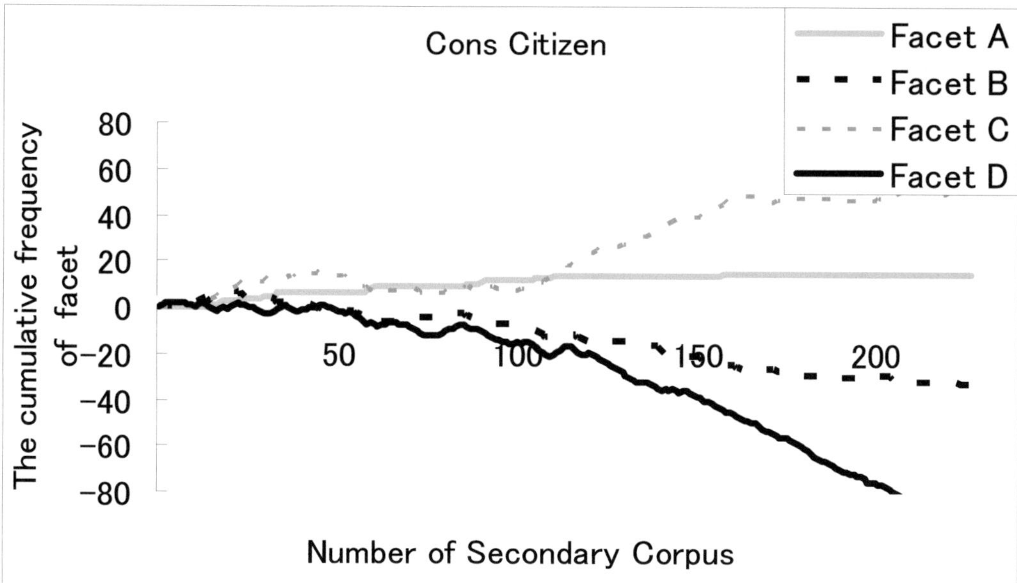

Fig. 6. The Discourse Pattern Change of Citizens (Cons).

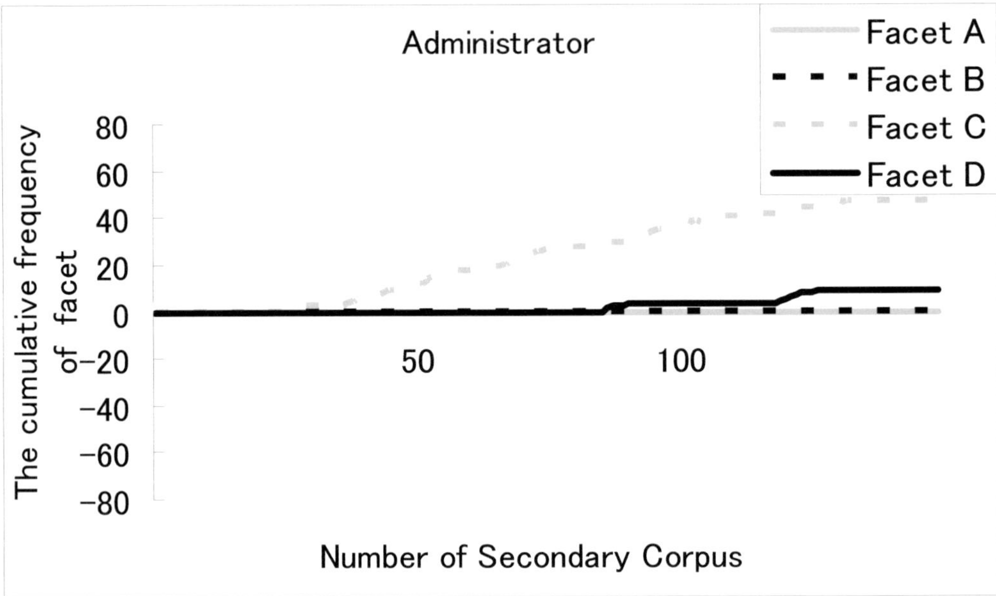

Fig. 7. The Discourse Pattern Change of the Administrators.

The cumulative frequency of facet is a simple and useful indicator for understanding the change in discourse and consequently the change in the interest structures. By examining the changes in the discourse patterns, we can uncover the possible causes of the interest conflicts.

In sum, this study's proposed method of discourse analysis enables us to identify debate content and structure and consequently the conflict structure and dynamic change throughout the debate process. This new approach overcomes the limitations previous existing approaches.

5. Conclusions

This study proposed a new method for examining the interest conflict of participants and discourse pattern changes in the process of debate using discourse analysis. We applied this method to a series of debates on a real public project during which we uncovered interest conflict among certain types of participants.

Results of our analysis suggest that during public debates, it is important to identify and adopt facilitation techniques that help identify discourse patterns, which in turn uncovers the cause of interest conflicts. This will help the debate participants examine the different perspectives of stakeholders and arrive at a consensus.

While the proposed discourse analysis method in this study helps manage and support the debate progress, it is not without its limitations. First, the validity of the proposed method relies mainly on the facet decomposition framework. Further empirical analysis is needed to confirm this validity. Second, the accuracy of the facet decomposition needs to be improved. Facet decomposition resulting from the use of the SVM has low accuracy levels for highly context-dependent utterances. Further studies may address this problem using a feedback system that reviews the results of discourse pattern changes. Third, utterances are dependent on the debate context and the characteristics of the participants. As such, it is necessary to improve the method by taking into account latent variables such as social context and unobservable individual characteristics. Fourth, it is easy to lose diverse contextual information in the process of facet decomposition. It is therefore necessary to build a database that includes other contextual information such as the right to speak (e.g., utterance turn or length of utterance) or the social relationship between participants. Finally, further normative research of public debate is needed. This involves developing normative rules of public debate and evaluating models of desirability of public debate. By overcoming these limitations, facilitation techniques can be vastly improved.

6. References

Akamine, S., Kawahara, D., Kato, Y., Nakagawa, T., Inui, K., Kurohashi, S., and Kidawara, Y. (2009). WISDOM: A web information credibility analysis system, *Proceedings of the ACL-IJCNLP 2009 Software Demonstrations*, pp. 1-4.

Dagan, I., Glickman, O., and Magnini, B. (2006). The PASCAL recognising textual entailment challenge, *Machine learning challenges. Lecture notes in computer science*, Vol. 3944, Springer, pp. 177-190.

Ericsson, K.A. and Simon, H.A. (1993). *Protocol analysis: verbal reports as data*, MIT Press.Francis, N. (1982). Problems of assembling and computerizing large corpora, In: Johansson, S. (ed.): *Computer corpora in English language research*, Norwegian Computing Centre for the Humanities, Bergen, pp. 7-24.

Giddens, A. (1990). *The consequences of modernity*. Cambridge: Polity Press.

Horita, M. and Kanno, Y. (2001). Development an information based CRANES for Public involvement Management, *Journal of Japan Society of Civil Engineers, VI*, Vol. 686, No. 52, pp. 109-120 (in Japanese).

Hashiuchi, T. (2003). *Disukōsu: Danwa no orinasu sekai*, Tokyo: Kuroshio Publishers (in Japanese).

Hatori, T., Kawayoke, T., Kobayashi, K., Natsume, T., and Fujisaki, E. (2006). Protocol analysis of a public debate using facet theory, *Journal of Japan Society of Civil Engineers*, Vol. 23, No.1, pp. 91-102 (in Japanese).

Hatori, T., Jeong, H., and Kobayashi, K. (2008). The open public debate and the impacts upon trust formation, *Journal of Japan Society of Civil Engineers D*, Vol. 64, pp. 148-169.

Hiromi, W., Tomonari, M., Atsuhiro, T., and Jun, A. (2006). Topic-oriented term extraction and term clustering for query focusing, *Transactions of Information Processing Society of Japan database*, Vol. 47, No. SIG19 (TOD32), pp. 72-85.

Jeong, H., Hatori, T., and Kobayashi, K.(2007). Discourse analysis of public debates: a corpus-based approach, *IEEE, SMC*.

Koizumi, T. (2001). *Nyumon goyoron kenkyu: riron to ouyou*, Kenkyusya (in Japanese).

Koreniusa, T., Laurikkalaa, J., and Juhola, M. (2007). On principal component analysis, cosine and Euclidean measures in information retrieval, *Information Sciences*, Vol. 177 pp. 4893-4905.

Krippendorff, K. (1980). *Content analysis: an introduction to its methodology*, Sage Publication, Inc.

Kruskal, J.B. (1964a). Multidimensional scaling by optimizing goodness of fit to a nonmetric hypothesis, *Psychometrica*, Vol. 29, pp. 1-29.

Kruskal, J.B. (1964b). Nonmetric multidimensional scaling: a numerical method, *Psychometrica*, Vol. 29, pp. 115-129.

Kudo, T. and Matsumoto,Y. (2002). Chunking with Support Vector Machines, *Journal of Natural Language Processing*, Vol. 9, pp. 3-22.

Lupia, A. and McCubbins, M.D. (1998). The democratic dilemma; can citizens learn what they need to know?, Cambridge University Press.

McCarthy, M.(1998). *Spoken language and applied linguistics*, Cambridge University Press.

Murakami, K., Nichols, E., Mizuno, J., Watanabe, Y., Masuda, S., Goto, H., Ohki, M., Sao, C., Matsuyoshi, S., Inui, K., and Matsumoto, Y. (2010). Statement map: reducing web information credibility noise through opinion classification. *Proceedings of the 4th Workshop on Analytics for Noisy Unstructured Text Data*, pp. 59-66.

Nasukawa, T. and Yi, J. (2003). Sentiment analysis: capturing favorability using natural language processing, Second International Conference on Knowledge Capture.

PASCAL (2005). Recognising textual entailment challenge, http://www.pascal-network.org/Challenges/RTE/.

Ong, B. S. (2005). *Towards automatic music structural analysis: identifying characteristic within –song excerpts in popular music*, Universitat Pompeu Fabra Barcelona.

Qian, G., Sural, S., Gu, Y., and Pramanik, S. (2004). Similarity between Euclidean and cosine angle distance for nearest neighbor queries, *Proceedings of The 19th Annual ACM Symposium on Applied Computing*.

Radev, D.R. (2000). Common theory of information fusion from multiple text sources step one: Cross-document structure. *Proceedings of The 1st SIGdial workshop on Discourse and dialogue*, pp. 74-83.

Schiffrin, D. (1994). *Approaches to discourse*, Blackwell Publishers.

Schiffrin, D., Tannen, D., and Hamilton, H. *(Eds.)* (2003). *The handbook of discourse analysis*, Blackwell Publishers.

Shiramatsu, S., Komatani, K., Hasida, K., Ogata, T., and Okuno, H.G. (2007). A game-theoretic model of referential coherence and its statistical verification based on large Japanese and English corpora, *Journal of Natural Language Processing*, Vol. 14(5), pp. 199-239 (in Japanese).

Sinclair, J. (1991). *Corpus, concordance, collocation*, Oxford University Press.

Sinclair, J. (1996). The search for units of meaning, *Textus*, Vol. 9, pp. 75-106.

Somasundaran, S and Wiebe, J. (2010). Recognizing stances in ideological on-line debate, *Proceedings of the NAACL HLT 2010 Workshop on Computational Approaches to Analysis and Generation of Emotion in Text*, pp. 116-124.

Stone, P.J., Dunphy, D. C., Smith, M. S., and Ogilvie, D. G. (1966). *The general inquirer: a computer approach to content analysis*, MIT Press.

Stubbs, M. (2002). *Words and phrases: corpus studies of lexical semantics*, Blackwell Publishers.

Takubo, Y., Nishiyama, Y., Mitoh, H., Kameyama, M., and Katagiri, Y. (1999). *Danwa to bunmyaku*, Tokyo, Japan: Iwanami Publishers (in Japanese).

Wang, S.-P. (2005). Corpus-based approaches and discourse analysis in relation to reduplication and repetition, *Journal of Pragmatics*, Vol. 37, pp. 505-540.

9

Visualizing Program Semantics

Guofu Zhou and Zhuomin Du
Wuhan University
China

1. Introduction

Generally, any program is designed for computing one problem based on one special architecture computing machine. It is unavoidable that some machine constraint will be transferred to the program code. When the program is formalized for being verified or validated the machine constraints will be treated as properties of program .

Turing model,the theory model of program(mainstream), has two special features: Only one storage tape that determines the changing status is sequent; Only one write-read head that determines the sequence of action operating is serialization; Accordingly, research on program semantics is focus on two areas: the first viewpoint thinks that a program is a set of status. the operating is a procedure of status changing. So, for that the formalization tools describe status. The other one viewpoint thinks that a program is a set of processes. A status is abstracted for understanding the process. So, for that the formalization tools describe the processes, and a status only is the composition of processes by timeline.

One target of formalizing a program is,not for a special machine, to get one general and one abstract specification Bjorner et al. (1987); Spivey (1998). So, one program specification must describe the following basic properties:

- variables and theeir changing;
- the consumptive or the nonconsumptive resources;
- the semantics of operation;
- the control flow in program, not one in computing machine.

For the problems, Petri nets is an ideal theory tool. By both extending and applying Petri nets theory, the semantics of program can be formalized visually Breuer & Lano (1999); Girault & Valk (2002); Jensen et al. (2007).

2. Model

Informally, a program is composed of data structure and algorithm Harel (1987); Khedker et al. (2009); Woodcock & Davies (1996). We know data structure is a discrete description of entity attributes based on one special computing machine. For example, the data structure of tree can be described as in figure 1(if the tree only has such attributes)

From figure 1, we can conclude the tree is composed of attributes *right*,*left* and *data*. But we can't make out any relation among *right*,*left* and *data*. In fact, the relations are the key to

```
Tree: structure
    Right:tree;
    Left:tree;
    Data:integer;
End Tree.
```

Fig. 1. Tree structure

```
x := 1    o1
y := 1    o2
```

Fig. 2. Segment of algorithm

```
y := 1    o1
x := 1    o2
```

Fig. 3. Another segment of algorithm

understand that is a tree but not any others. So, the discrete description of attributes does not help to understand an entity .

And there is another characteristics in coding a program. For example, there is a segment of algorithm in figure 2, o_1 and o_2 are labeled as a statement on x and a statement on y respectively(ignore other unconcern processes).

Also, we can design another algorithm(figure 3) to fulfill the same function as in figure 2.

The reason to explain the case is in design phase designer only concerns the result produced by the algorithm, and thinks the algorithm is right if and only if the algorithm can produce an expected result. However, the same result the two algorithms can produce but not the same semantics the two algorithms have.

In a word, when designing an algorithm, the designer transforms some constraints into the algorithm unconsciously, for example, serialization(discussed above). Once the algorithm finished, the additional relations are fixed into the code. So, two aftereffects are forged:

1. Two independent operations will be serialized, a new relation is added; or
2. The two concurrent operations will be serialized and the relation of concurrence is lost.

For convenience, the relation between variables, variable and operation, or operations is called control.

Asynchronous control, A-control for short, is a kind of relation between operation and variable that has no directive or indirected causality. A-control has two types: concurrent control and noncorrelation control.

A concurrent control denotes there are one or more common direct or indirect causality sets among operations (variables), e.g., o in figure 4 is a common result of b_1, b_2 and b_3. Dashed line shows there are more than one node, the straight line show there is a directive relation.

A noncorrelation control denotes there is no any common direct or indirect causality among operations (variables) . A noncorrelation control is no necessary in program. However, in a large-scale software system, noncorrelation controls are usual. The noncorrelative variables or operations in a system may be associated for building a new system. For example, in figure 5(1), $\{a_1, a_2, \cdots, a_i\}$ is non correlative with $\{b_1, b_2, \cdots, b_i\}$ in a system, however, in figure

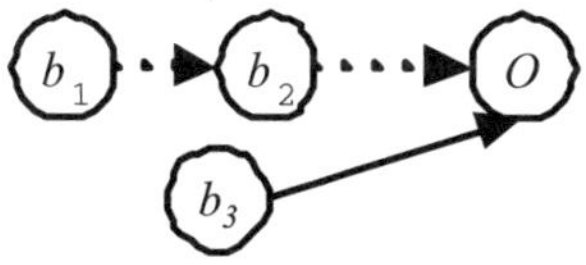

Fig. 4. Concurrent control

5(2), $\{a_1, a_2, \cdots, a_i\}$ is associated with $\{b_1, b_2, \cdots, b_i\}$ because of c_i in a new system. c_i is a common result among $\{a_1, a_2, \cdots, a_i\}$ and $\{b_1, b_2, \cdots, b_i\}$. Obviously, the noncorrelation control between $\{a_1, a_2, \cdots, a_i\}$ and $\{b_1, b_2, \cdots, b_i\}$ disappears.

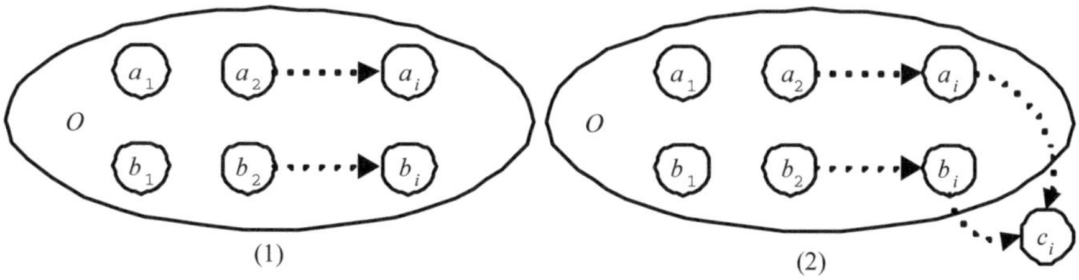

Fig. 5. Asynchronous Control

Linear control, L-control for short, describes causality among variables and operations. L-control has two kinds of types: direct associated and indirect associated.

one variable is a direct composition of another one, e.g., X is composed of b as in figure 6(1); or one variable is a indirect sub-composition of another one, e.g., in figure 6(2), Y is directly composed of both a and b. Specially, c is an indirect sub-composition of Y.

Fig. 6. Linear Variables

For operations, L-control denotes one operation is a run condition of another one , e.g., in figure 7(1), c_i run only after a_i finished (direct associated); or one operation is one of run conditions of another one (indirect associated), e.g., in figure 7(2), c_i can not run immediately after a_i finish if b_i do not finish.

Fig. 7. Linear Operations

Loop control is a special L-control(figure 8). because of the recursive attributes not being permitted, A loop control can only describe relations among operations.

Parallel control , P-control for short, denotes variables or operations are parallel. On one hand, parallel operations have direct common pre-operations or post-operations as in figure 9(1). A is parallel to B because C is a direct common post-operation of A and B.

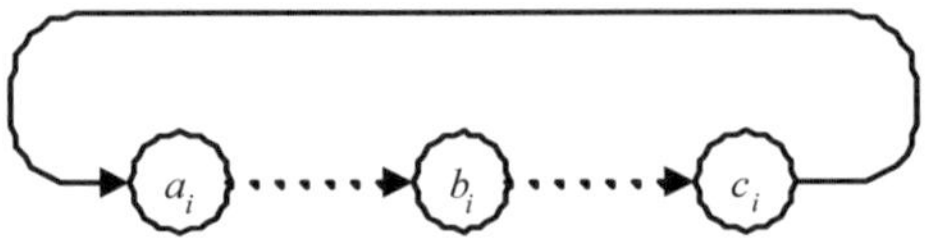

Fig. 8. Linear LOOP

On the other hand, parallel variables have direct common target variables. In figure 9(2), both *right* and *left* construct a tree, a parallel control exists between *left* and *right*.

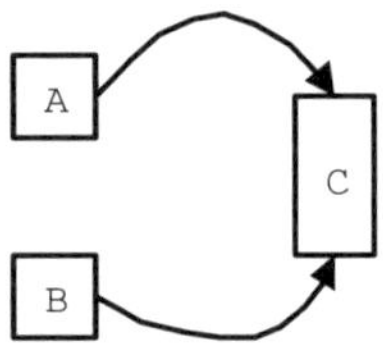

(1)

tree:

left: tree;

right:tree;

P-control(left, right)

(2)

Fig. 9. Parallel Control

P-control is relative. In figure 10(1), a is parallel to b. But, if another P-control is inserted between a and b (figure 10(2)), then the new a is the direct run condition of b. Obviously, the new a is not parallel to b and the P-control between a and b losts.

(1) (2)

Fig. 10. Relative Parallel Control

Trigger Action Control is the logic relation that regulates how to run, delay and terminate operations. Any operation can only run after it gets (satisfied) a control handle of computing machine. In other words, computing machine determines how to run a program.

In figure 11, a control handle arrives at the statement *doingsomething*. Here, $controlofprogram = true$ and controls of other statements can not be satisfied ($controlofo_i = false$), the statement *doingsomething* is running. and the other statements do not run. So, Control mechanism can help to describe the dynamic properties.

Regulate Order Single control handle determines a program is sequent. If a program has more than one control handles, how about a program should be? For example, a program in figure 11 has one control handle, statements only run in turn. When the program has two control handles, the program can run by many ways, such as in figure 12.

Resource is physical and depend on a computing machine. Running a program needs resources, such as RAM, CPU, communication channel, and so on. Generally, resources are managed by an operation system.

o_1:	*control* of o_1 = *false*;
	...
doing something :	*control* of program = *true*;
	...
o_2:	*control* of o_3 = *false*;
	...

Fig. 11. Trigger Action

o_1:	contro of o_1 = *true*;	o_1:	contro of o_1 = *true*;	o_1:	contro of o_1 = false;
o_2:	contro of o_2 = *true*;	o_2:	contro of o_2 = *false*;	o_2:	contro of o_2 = *true*;
o_3:	contro of o_3 = *false*;	o_3:	contro of o_3 = *true*;	o_3:	contro of o_3 = *true*;
	(1)		(2)		(3)

Fig. 12. Regulate Order

Resource can be either consumable or inconsumable . Consumable resource will be consumed out during a program run. Consumable resources are exclusive, such as RAM ,CPU. Inconsumable resource can be shared, such as system clock and any program can read the system clock any time.

We know, the mathematics model of program is Turing machine. Accordingly, a program is a set of variables and read-writes.

- Operation is to process variables, such as to update the current value of variable;
- Variable records the result produced by operation(s). An operation can be described by the track of changing value of variable.

Any operation of program can be broken down a set of more fine grained read-write. Generally, read-write operation appears in assignment statement.

Assignment is composed of read and write(not concerns arithmetic). Read refers the current value of variable. Write updates the current value of variable. In an assignment statement, read variable(s) is located in the right side and write variable(s) is located in the left side , such as

$$X := \underline{a + b + c}$$

Where,a,b,c are read variables. The current values of a,b and c are not modified. In the following

$$\underline{X} := a + b + c$$

X is a write variable. The current value of X will be updated.

Read-write not only refers the current value of variable, but also updates the current value. The read-write variable will appear both sides of assignment statement, such as X in the following,

$$\underline{X := X} + c$$

Accordingly, the model of program should be composed of :

1. resources, including consumable resource and nonconsumable resource;
2. variables, recording status;
3. operations, including read and write;

4. relations, including read, write and control.

3. Extending definitions

Compare to general Petri net theory Jensen et al. (2007); Reisig (1985), Here concepts are extended.

Place

two kinds of places: control place (Figure 13.a) and variable place (Figure 13.b). The definition of control place is same as the definition of place in Petri net. Resources described by variable place are inconsumable. Generally, variable place can describe all data types, such as real type, boolean type, structure type and so on. The graphic representation of variable place is same as that of control place. However, the type of arc connecting with control place is different to that with variable place. Control place can only connect with control arc (flow); Variable place can connect with read arc, write arc or the combinatorial arc of read arc and write arc, but not with control arc. The arc types are discussed in the later this section.

Fig. 13. Extending Place

Token

As same as Petri net, token is expressed by symbol "•". Here, token has two functions: firstly, the flowing track of token denotes control flow; secondly, token in a variable place is expressed by the value instead of symbol "•", and the number of tokens in variable place is the current value of variable place, such as in figure 14.b. To hold consistency, the number of token in control place is mapped to a value of integer type. In figure 14.a, the data type denoted by the place is integer and the current value is 1. So, the number of token in place is 1.

Fig. 14. Extending Token

Arc

four kinds of arcs: control arc, read arc, write arc and read-write arc. The graphic representations of arcs are drawn as in figure 15.

(a) represents the relation of control flow which denotes the firing of transition t_1 will consume resource s_1;

(b) represents the read relation which denotes the firing of transition t_2 will read the current value of s_2 but not modify the current value of s_2;

(c) represents the write relation which denotes the firing of transition t_3 will modify the current value of s_3;

(d) represents the read-write relation which is the combination of a read relation and a write relation, i.e. the firing of transition t_4 not only read the current of s_4, but also modifies the current value of s_4.

The four kinds of relations are classified into two categories: flow relationship(a) and read-write relationship(b, c, d). Flow relationship is a kind of consumable relationship. Control place can only hold flow relationship(control arc)and tokens in a control place must flow. Read-write relationship is a kind of inconsumable relationship;Read-write do not consume any token and tokens in a variable place can not flow around. Variable place can only hold read-write relationship(read arc, write arc or both).

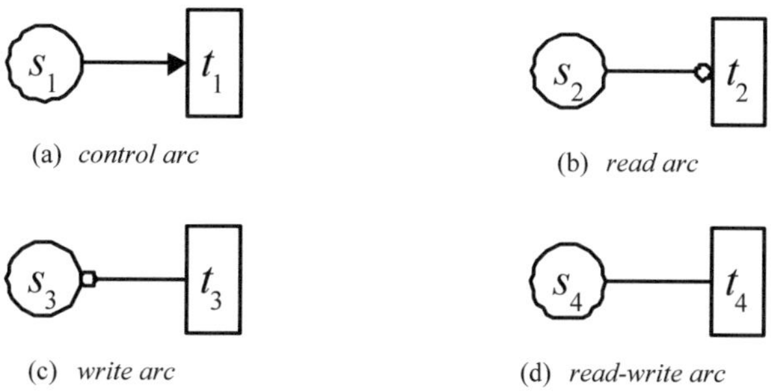

Fig. 15. Extending Arc

Transition

Extension of transition defines a new kind of transition called variable transition. Variable transition can not only connect with control place but also variable place. In other words, the firing of transition may either consume resources(e.g. need some tokens) or not. Contrast to variable transition, transition defined in Petri net is called control transition . The structure of control transition is represented as in figure 16.a. Guard is a mechanism to control the firing of control transition. Control guard holds false only if the firing condition is not satisfied, i.e., the transition can not fire; When the firing condition is satisfied, the control guard hold true and the transition fire. The structure of variable transition is composed of three parts (figure 16.b):

E denotes a control guard which is same as control guard of control transition;

B is called variable guard which denotes the condition satisfied by variables(places).

I operations script .

Because Petri nets is a self-explain system, places need not be declared explicitly. Variables are described by variable places. In figure 17, places are variable places. Assignment $X := a + b + c$ can be described as a variable transition(figure 18), where a,b and c connect with the variable transition. Read operation is described by read arc between a variable transition and a variable place. Write operation is described by write arc between a variable transition and a variable place. Figure 20 describes assignment $X := a + b + c$, where Figure 19(1) is read operation. Figure 19 (2) is write operation.

When a variable is both read and write, readwrite relation can be applied. Figure 20 is a readwrite relation. Consumable resource is described by control place. The number of tokens

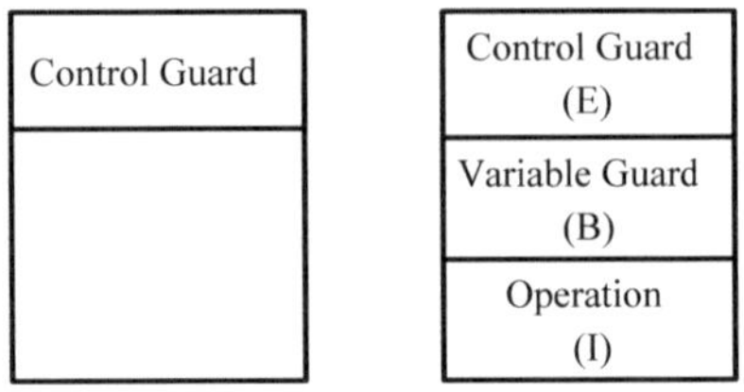

(a) *control transition* (b) *variable transition*

Fig. 16. Extending Transition

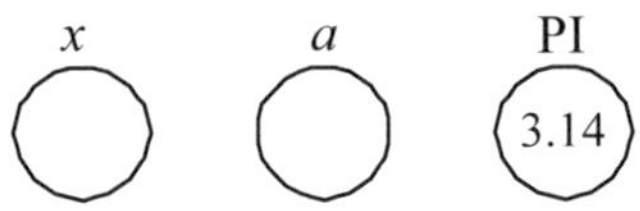

Fig. 17. Variable Place

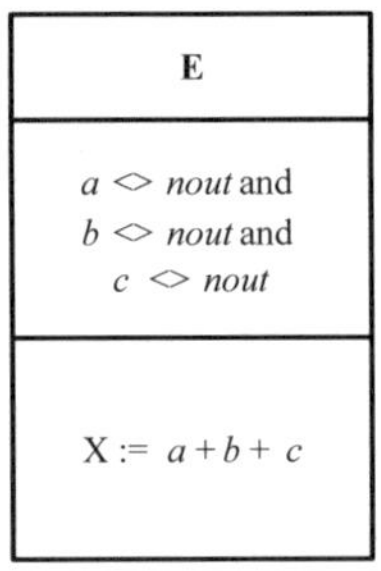

Fig. 18. Inside Transition

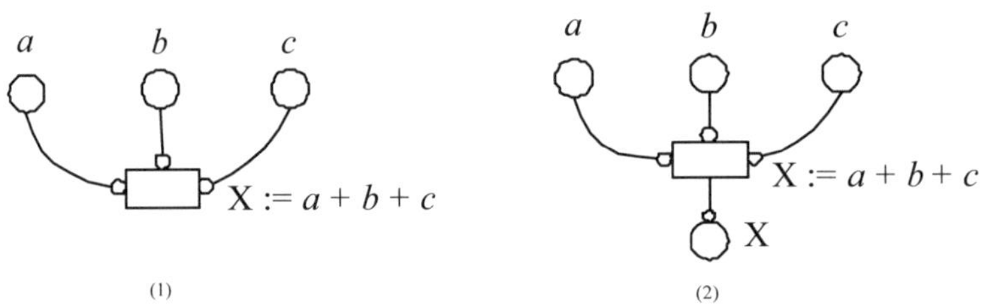

Fig. 19. Read and Write

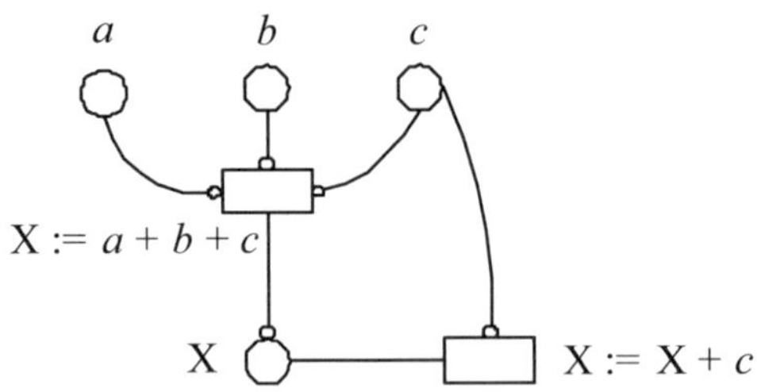

Fig. 20. ReadWrite

in a control place denotes the number of available resource described by the control place. The weight of arc denotes the number of resource consumed by a transition. For example, RAM consumption can be described as in figure **??**. Place denotes the resource RAM; the number of tokens in place denotes the available number of RAM; o_1 denotes an operation; the weight of arc denotes that operation o_1 will consume two units of RAM during firing.

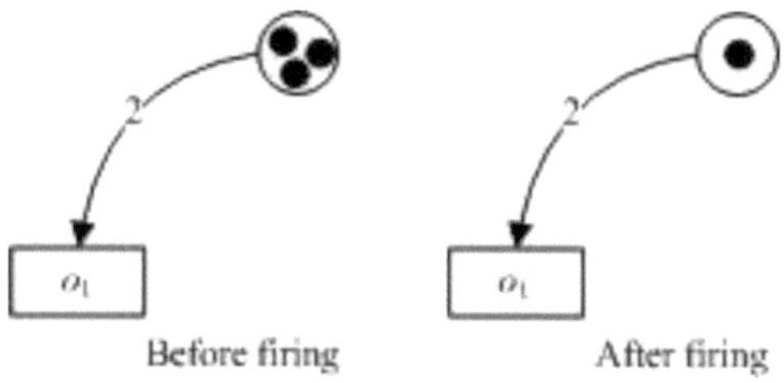

Fig. 21. Resource consumption

4. Formal definitions

For a convenience, the extension is called *rwPN* (*r*eadable and *w*ritable Petri Net). The following discussion will refer some concepts of Petri Net or Coloured Petri Net.

Definition 4.1 (*rwPN*). *6-tuple* $N = (S_c, S_v, T; R, W, F)$, *where*

1. $S_c \cap S_v = \emptyset$;
   $(S_c \cup S_v) \cap T = \emptyset$;
   $S_c \cup S_v \cup T \neq \emptyset$;
2. $R \subseteq S_v \times T$;
   $W \subseteq T \times S_v$;
   $F \subseteq S_c \times T \cup T \times S_c$;
3. $S_v = dom(R) \cup cod(W)$;
   $S_c \subseteq dom(F) \cup cod(F)$;
   $T \subseteq dom(F) \cup dom(W) \cup cod(F) \cup cod(R)$.

where S_c, S_v, T are finite sets and R, W, F are relations respectively.

Let $\mathscr{S}$ be a function from a set of *place*s to a set of colors, such as

$$\mathscr{S} : S \to \mathbb{C}$$

$$S = S_v \cup S_c$$

where S is a set of *places* , S_v is a set of *Variable places* , S_c is a set of *control places* , $\mathbb{C}$ is a set of colors. Here and afterward, sets are finite .

Because $dom(F) \cup cod(F)$ can contain *places* , *transitions* , or both. For a convinence and in a discussion context, $dom(F) \cup cod(F)$ can be viewed as a set of *place*s , a set of *transition*s or both on need.

F only connects between S_c and T or T and S_c, and is defined as

$$F \subseteq S_c \times T \cup T \times S_c$$

where T is a set of *transitions* . F describes a situation in which *token*s are flowable, i.e. *tokens* can flow out of this *place* and into another one along *Control Flow F*.

R only connects between S_v and T, and is defined as

$$R \subseteq S_v \times T$$

R is represented graphically by a line with circle $\multimap$ which points to a *transition* .

W also only connects between T and S_v, and is defined as

$$W \subseteq T \times S_v$$

W is represented graphically by a line with circle $\multimap$ but which points to a *variable place* .

Semantically similar to Coloured Petri Net, a *transition* is also controlled by a *GUARD* that is a boolean value. Let $\mathscr{G}_c$ denote this kind of *GUARD* , called *control guard* .

$$\mathscr{G}_c : T \rightarrow BOOL$$

T is a set of *transitions* , and $\mathscr{G}_c$ changes from *TRUE* to *FALSE* alternatively. When the *preset* of a *transition* has enough *tokens* , the *control guard* of *transition* is *TRUE*. Otherwise, the *control guard* of *transition* is *FALSE*.

Additionally, there has another *GUARD* to monitor the *Variable place*s in the *preset* of *transition* . Such a *GUARD* called *variable guard* . Let $\mathscr{G}_v$ be a *variable guard* and

$$\mathscr{G}_v : T \rightarrow BooleanExpression$$

where the boolean expression specifies a variable-related condition to fire a *transition* . Any operand in *BooleanExpression* either holds a constant or just is a *variable place* .

Accordingly, the two *GUARDS* codetermine whether a *transition* can be fired.

The third part of a *transition* is statements which describes the expected action of a *transition* . Statements can be written by a program language, such as C, Java, etc. Let function $\mathscr{L}$ be the action script of a *transition* , then

$$\mathscr{L} : T \rightarrow statement$$

Summarily, a *transition* has three components: $\mathscr{G}_c$, $\mathscr{G}_v$ and $\mathscr{L}$. Let function $\mathscr{H}$ be

$$\mathscr{H} : T \rightarrow \mathscr{G}_c \cup \mathscr{G}_v \cup \mathscr{L}$$

Obviously, $\forall t \in T$,

when $R(t) = \emptyset$ and $W(t) = \emptyset$ then $\mathscr{L}(t) = \emptyset$ and $\mathscr{G}_v(t) = \emptyset$.

when $\mathscr{G}_v(t) = \emptyset$ and $\mathscr{L}(t) = \emptyset$, the *transition* is the same as that of Coloured Petri Net.

when $\mathscr{G}_c(t) = \emptyset$, the *transition* can fire without any *Control Flow* .

when $\mathscr{G}_v(t) = \emptyset$, the *transition* can fire when the *preset* of *transition* has enough *tokens* .

As a default, if $\mathscr{G}_v(t) = \emptyset$, let $\mathscr{G}_v(t) = TRUE$, and if $\mathscr{G}_c(t) = \emptyset$, let $\mathscr{G}_c(t) = TRUE$.

Definition 4.2 (*cvNet*). *given a* rwPN $N = (S_c, S_v, T; R, W, F)$, N_{cv} *is called* cvNet *(control view net) of N, and*

$$N_{cv} = (S_c, T|_{S_c}; F)$$

where $T|_{S_c}$ *is a set of* transitions *connecting with* control places .

Definition 4.3 (*dvNet*). *given a* rwPN $N = (S_c, S_v, T; R, W, F)$, N_{dv} *is called* dvNet *(data view net) of N, and*

$$N_{dv} = (S_v, T|_{S_v}, R, W)$$

where $T|_{S_v}$ *is a set of* transitions *connecting with* Variable places .

Theory 4.1. *If* N_{cv} *is* cvNet *and* N_{dv} *is* dvNet *of* rwPN *N respectively, then*

$$N = N_{cv} \cup N_{dv}$$

Proof: where $\cup$ is the operator of graph union, based on definitions *rwPN N*, *cvNet* N_{cv} and *dvNet* N_{dv}, the conclusion holds obviously.

So, if a system is modeled by *rwPN* , the system features can be captured from two views. One view is from *Control View Net* which describes the control flow relationship of system. The other one is from *Data View Net* which describes the entity relationship of system.

Definition 4.4 (*rwPNs*). 4-*tuple* $\Sigma = (N, \mathscr{S}, \mathscr{H}, M_0)$, *where*

1. $N = (S_c, S_v, T; R, W, F)$ *is a* rwPN .
2. $\mathscr{S} : S \rightarrow \mathbb{C}$,
   $S = S_c \cup S_v$;
   $\mathbb{C} = Integer \cup DATATYPE$ *is a set of colors;*
   $\forall s_c \in S_c, \mathscr{S}(s_c) = Integer$;
   $\forall s_v \in S_v, \mathscr{S}(s_v) = DATATYPE$;
3. $\mathscr{H} : T \rightarrow \mathscr{G}_c \cup \mathscr{G}_v \cup \mathscr{L}$
   $\mathscr{G}_c : T \rightarrow BOOL$
   $\mathscr{G}_v : T \rightarrow BooleanExpression$
   $\mathscr{L} : T \rightarrow statement$
4. *M is the marking of N,* $M = M_c \cup M_v$; *and*
   $M_c : S_c \rightarrow \mathbb{N}$
   $M_v : S_v \rightarrow \{1\}$
   M_0 *is the initial marking;* M_{C_0} *is the initial marking of* S_c; M_{v_0} *is the initial marking of* S_v;

Specially, if let color set $C = \mathbb{C} \cup Integer \cup DATATYPE \cup BOOL \cup BooleanExpression \cup statement$ and $cd = \mathscr{S} \cup \mathscr{H}$, *rwPNs* can be mapped to Coloured Petri Net $\mathscr{N} =< P, T, Pre, Post, C, cd >$. The mapping from *rwPNs* to Coloured Petri Netwill further be discussed in the next section.

Definition 4.5 (*cvNets*). *Given* rwPNs $\Sigma = (N, \mathscr{S}, \mathscr{H}, M_0)$, *call* N^{cs} cvNets *and*

$$N^{cs} = (N_{cv}, \mathscr{S}|_{S_c}, \mathscr{H}|_{S_c}, M_0|_{S_c})$$

where
$M_0|_{S_c} = M_{c_0}$; *the initial marking of* control places ;

$\mathscr{S}|_{S_c} : S_c \rightarrow$ *integer; the colors of* control places *;*
$\mathscr{H}|_{S_c} = \mathscr{G}_c$*; only the* Control Guards *of* transitions *are concerned.*

Definition 4.6 (*dvNets*). *Given* rwPNs $\Sigma = (N, \mathscr{S}, \mathscr{H}, M_0)$*, call* N^{ds} dvNets *and*

$$N^{ds} = (N_{dv}, \mathscr{S}|_{S_v}, \mathscr{H}|_{S_v}, M_0|_{S_v})$$

where
$M_0|_{S_v} = M_{v0}$*; the initial marking of* Variable places *;*
$\mathscr{S}|_{S_v} : S_v \rightarrow DATATYPE$ *; the colors of* Variable places *;*
$\mathscr{H}|_{S_v} = \mathscr{G}_v \cup \mathscr{L}$*;the* Variable Guards *of* transitions *and the action script are concerned.*

Theory 4.2. *If* N^{cs} *is* cvNets *and* N^{ds} *is* dvNets *of* rwPNs *N respectively, then*

$$N = N^{cs} \cup N^{ds}$$

Proof: where $\cup$ is the operator of graph union, based on definitions *rwPNs* N, *cvNets* N^{cs} and *dvNets* N^{ds}, the conclusion also holds.

When the dynamic features of system are concerned, there are also two views to study the system, *cvNets* and *dvNets* . Specially, Because *GUARD* $\mathscr{G}_c$ and *GUARD* $\mathscr{G}_v$ in $\mathscr{H}$ will determine whether transitions can be fired, some properties of program, e.g.,the code coverage and key path in the program testing, can be computed automatically based on $\mathscr{H}$.

5. Dynamic semantics

Definition 5.1. $x \in S \cup T$,
$r_s(x) = \{a|(a,x) \in R \wedge x \in T\}$*, the set of* Variable places *read by* transition *x;*
$w_s(x) = \{a|(x,a) \in W \wedge x \in T\}$*, the set of* Variable places *written by* transition *x;*
$r_t(x) = \{a|(x,a) \in R \wedge x \in S\}$*, the set of* transition *read* variable place *x;*
$w_t(x) = \{a|(a,x) \in W \wedge x \in S\}$*, the set of* transition *write* variable place *x;*
$r(x) = r_s(x) \cup r_t(x)$*, read on x;*
$w(x) = w_s(x) \cup w_t(x)$*, write on x;*
$^\bullet t = \{p|(p,t) \in F\}$*, the* preset *of* transition *t;*
$t^\bullet = \{p|(t,p) \in F\}$*, the* postset *of* transition *t;*

Definition 5.2. *In marking* $M = M_c \cup M_v$*, t is C_enabled, iff*

$$C\_enabled(M,t) \equiv enabled(M_c,t)$$

where, $enabled(M_c,t)$ *denotes* $^\bullet t$ *has enough number of* tokens *and leads to* control guard $\mathscr{G}_c =$ TRUE. *If* $^\bullet t = \emptyset$*, let* $\mathscr{G}_c =$ TRUE.

t is V_enabled, iff

$$V\_enabled(M,t) \equiv enabled(M_v,t)$$

where, $enabled(M_v,t)$ *denotes* variable guard $\mathscr{G}_v$ *holds. If* $r(t) \cup w(t) = \emptyset$*, let* $\mathscr{G}_v =$ TRUE.

Definition 5.3. *t is firable in marking M, called* $M[t>$*, iff in marking M, t is both C_enabled and V_enabled ,*

$$M[t> \equiv C\_enabled(M,t) \wedge V\_enabled(M,t))$$

Accordingly, *transition t* is controlled by both $\mathscr{G}_v$ and $\mathscr{G}_c$. t can fire iff all required resource have been provided and all the related variables hold legal values.

Definition 5.4. *if $M[t>$, let M' be the succession marking of M, then $M[t> M'$, and M' is, if $s \in S_c$:*

$$M'(s) = \begin{cases} M(s) - 1 & \text{if } s \in^{\bullet} t - t^{\bullet} \\ M(s) + 1 & \text{if } s \in t^{\bullet} -^{\bullet} t \\ M(s) & \text{if } s \notin {}^{\bullet}t^{\bullet} \text{ or } s \in^{\bullet} t \cap t^{\bullet} \end{cases}$$

if $s \in S_v$:

$$M'(s) = \begin{cases} Val(\mathscr{H}(t)) & \text{if } s \in w(t), \\ M(s) & \text{if } s \in r(t) \end{cases}$$

where $Val(\mathscr{H}(t))$ denotes the current value of s updated by t.

From above definition, a transition will be affected by three factors: tokens in control place, *variable guard*(B) and *control guard*(E).

Definition 5.5. *$t_1, t_2 \in T$ and $t_1 \neq t_2$. In marking M , $M[t_1 > \wedge M[t_2 >$,*

1. *if $s \in {}^{\bullet}t_1 \cap {}^{\bullet}t_2, M(s) < 2$, Then, between t_1 and t_2, there exists* P_confilict, *call $P\_conflict(t_1, t_2)$.*
2. *if $t_1, t_2 \in T_v$, $w(t_1) \cap w(t_2) \neq \emptyset$, then between t_1 and t_2, there exists* W_conflict, *call $W\_conflict(t_1, t_2)$.*
3. *if $t_1, t_2 \in T_v$, $(w(t_1) \cap r(t_2)) \cup (r(t_1) \cap w(t_2)) \neq \emptyset$, then between t_1 and t_2, there exists* RW_conflict, *call $RW\_conflict(t_1, t_2)$.*

t_1 is conflict with t_2, call $conflict(t_1, t_2)$, iff

$$conflict(t_1, t_2) \equiv P\_conflict(t_1, t_2) \vee W\_conflict(t_1, t_2) \vee RW\_conflict(t_1, t_2)$$

Definition 5.6. *$t_1, t_2 \in T$ and $t_1 \neq t_2$, in marking M, t_1 is concurrent with t_2 , iff*

$$M[t_1 > \wedge M[t_2 > \wedge \neg conflict(t_1, t_2)$$

Definition 5.7. *A directed net $N = (B, E; F)$ is a general occurrence net, if N satisfies the condition:*

$$F^+ \cap (F^{-1})^+ = \emptyset$$

where,

$F^+ = F \cup F \circ F \cup F \circ F \circ F \cup \cdots;$
$F^{-1} = \{(x, y) | (y, x) \in F\};$
$(F^{-1})^+ = F^{-1} \cup F^{-1} \circ F^{-1} \cup F^{-1} \circ F^{-1} \circ F^{-1} \cup \cdots.$

"$\circ$" is a symbol of relation composition.

A general occurrence net $N = (B, E; F)$, if $x, y \in E$ or $x, y \in B(x \neq y)$, and $(x, y) \in F^+$, then there is a partial order relation between x and y, denoted as $x \prec y$, or more strictly $x \prec_N y$.

Definition 5.8. *A general occurrence net $N' = (B, E; F')$, if there is a mapping between N' and Net system $\Sigma = (N, C, I, M_0)$, i.e. : $\rho : N' \to \Sigma$ satisfies conditions:*

1. $B = B' \cup \{\varepsilon\}$;
   $\rho(B') \subseteq S_p \cup S_v, \rho(\varepsilon) = \emptyset$;
   $\rho(E) \subseteq T$;
   $\rho(F') \subseteq F \cup R \cup W$;
   $\exists(x,y) \in F' \wedge (x = \varepsilon \vee y = \varepsilon) \Rightarrow \rho(x,y) = \emptyset$;
2. $\forall(x,y) \in F' : \rho(x) \in S_p \vee \rho(y) \in S_p$
   $\Rightarrow \rho(x,y) = (\rho(x), \rho(y)) \in F$;
   let $\widetilde{N} = (B, E, F' - \{(x,y)\})$,
   $\rho(x) \in S_v \wedge (\rho(x), \rho(y)) \notin R$
   $\Rightarrow (\rho(x), \rho(y)) \in W - R \wedge^{\bullet} x \neq \emptyset \wedge \neg(x \prec_{\widetilde{N}} y)$;
   $\rho(y) \in S_v \wedge (\rho(x), \rho(y)) \notin W$
   $\Rightarrow (\rho(x), \rho(y)) \in R - W \wedge |y^{\bullet}| = 1 \wedge (\rho(y), \rho(y^{\bullet})) \in W$;
3. $\forall e \in E :$
   $\rho(^{\bullet}e) \cap S_p =^{\bullet} \rho(e)$;
   $\rho(e^{\bullet}) \cap S_p = \rho(e)^{\bullet}$;
   $r(\rho(e)) \subseteq \rho(^{\bullet}e) \cap S_v$;
   $w(\rho(e)) \subseteq \rho(e^{\bullet}) \cap S_v$;
   $\forall b \in B :$
   $|b^{\bullet}| > 1 \Rightarrow \rho(b) \in S_v \wedge \forall e \in b^{\bullet} : (\rho(b), \rho(e)) \in R - W$;
   $|^{\bullet}b| > 1 \Rightarrow \rho(b) \in S_v \wedge^{\bullet} b \subseteq r(\rho(b)) - w(\rho(b))$
   $\wedge \exists b' \in B : \rho(b) = \rho(b') \wedge^{\bullet} b \subseteq b'^{\bullet}$;
4. $\forall b_1, b_2 \in B : \rho(b_1), \rho(b_2) \in S_v \wedge \rho(b_1) = \rho(b_2)$
   $\Rightarrow b_1 \prec b_2 \vee b_2 \prec b_1 \vee b_2 = b_1$,
   $\forall e_1, e_2 \in E, \forall x \in S_v : x \in v(\rho(e_1)) \cap v(\rho(e_2))$
   $\Rightarrow \exists b(\rho(b) = x \wedge \{e_1, e_2\} \subseteq b^{\bullet}) \vee e_1 \prec e_2 \vee e_2 \prec e_1$;
5. $\forall b_1, b_2 \in B : b_1 \neq b_2 \wedge \rho(b_1) = \rho(b_2)$
   $\Rightarrow^{\bullet} b_1 \cap^{\bullet} b_2 = b_1^{\bullet} \cap b_2^{\bullet} = \emptyset$;
6. $\forall s \in S_p : |\{b | \rho(b) = s \wedge^{\bullet} b = \emptyset\}| \leq M_0(x) \neq nout.$

Then (N', ρ) is a process of system Σ . Where,

1. Process may have a special place ε which is not appeared in *rwPNs* . ε denotes the partial order of transitions. Transition labels in process are transition names in *rwPNs* . Place labels in process are place names in *rwPNs* or label ε . Accordingly, the process may have special arc(s) (complementary arc) ,associated with ε, which are also not appeared in *rwPNs* .
2. N will guarantee the less complexity through removing the redundant arcs.
3. Elements of S_p mapped from $^{\bullet}e^{\bullet}$ are similar to places of Petri nets. Elements of S_v mapped from $^{\bullet}e^{\bullet}$ can be :
   (a) variables read by $\rho(e)$ are mapped from the set $^{\bullet}e$, maybe including variable(s) associated with complementary arc(s) and written by $\rho(e)$;
   (b) variables written by $\rho(e)$ are mapped from the set $e^{\bullet}$, maybe including variable associated with complementary arc(s) and read by $\rho(e)$.
4. If a variable accessed by two different transitions in occurrence net, the mapped elements of the two transitions in *rwPNs* either have a partial order relation or concurrently read the variable.

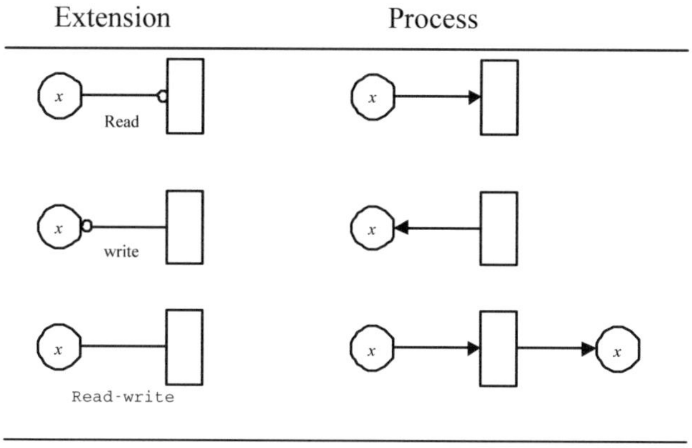

Fig. 22. Basic Place-Arc-Transition

5. The preset and the postset of transitions in N must be labeled by different elements in Σ. This condition is similar to general petri net theory except that the tail part of condition is $^\bullet b_1 \neq ^\bullet b_2 \wedge b_1^\bullet \neq b_2^\bullet$.
6. Not all processes need all initial resources described by the initial marking M_0. This condition requires $|\{b\}| \leq M_0(s)$ instead of $|\{b\}| = M_0(s)$. If the first operation upon an element of S_v is read action, the element must have an initial value.

The process of Petri nets is an observational record of system . Based on the above definition of process, the mapping rules to process can be summarized by the graphic representation. In Figure 22, one variable place is only operated by one transition.

- *Read* relation is mapped to *input arc*(a out-arc with arrowhead);
- *write* relation is mapped to *output arc*(a in-arc with arrowhead);
- *read-write* relation is mapped to *input-output arc*(one read and one writečľ.

Figure 23 lists the process mapping rules on read-write concurrent or conflict relations between two transitions. When one transition writes after the other transition has read, place ε is introduced to denote a sequential relation between the two transitions. When two transitions write the same place at the same time, place ε is introduced to denote the sequential order relation.

Based on above rules, more complex mapping specification can be work out.

6. Analysis

To verify the formal specification, all petri net theory can be applied. In this section, we will discuss some special features.

Theory 6.1. *A program has only one place* $s, ^\bullet s = \emptyset$.

Proof: The computing target is initialized by only one computing unit. The unit must provide all initial condition for the computing target. Meanwhile the unit will also ask for cooperation with other units because the unit can not fulfill the special computing. If the number of $^\bullet s \neq \emptyset$ and greater than 1, the computing target will be more than 1 and are initialized by different

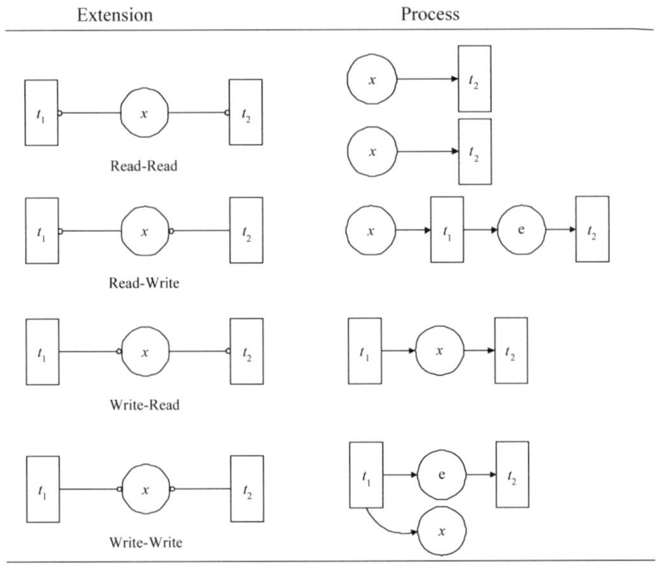

Fig. 23. One Place and Two Transition

computing units. In this case, we can make a more abstract computing unite S covers these initialized computing units. Obviously, the new abstract computing unit S is one and only.

Theory 6.2. *if* $s^\bullet = \emptyset$, *then s is a finished status.*

Proof: When a computing task reach a status in which all other status are no changed anymore, i.e. the program reach a fixed point.

The above two theorems show there exists the boundary in a program specification.

Let S is a step in marking M of system, then S's successive marking is $M, \forall p \in P$, P is a set of all status.

$$M'(p) = M(p) + \sum_{t \in T} I_+(p,t)X(t) - \sum_{t \in T} I_-(p,t)X(t)$$

where, $X(t)$ denotes the number of transition t appearing in step X. M' is the succession of M, written as $M[X > M'$, i.e. , after X firing, reaches from marking M to M'. I_- denotes the number of consumed tokens or the value for one variable. I_+ denotes the number of produced tokens or the updated value for one variable.

So, system will step into a new status, and

1. In the same step, more than one action can be fired.
2. Based on the preset of transition, I_- , I_+ and M , the marking M' can be determined.

Resources or control flow are described by tokens, the number of tokens in system must be conserved. The property of conservation of token number is called invariant. Invariable(including T invariant and S invariant) is limited within boundary, i.e. local invariant and system invariant. The invariant can be computed through reference matrix.

From initializing computing to result returning, the task must be fulfilled in n steps. occurrence sequence:

$$M_0[S_1 > M_1[S_2 > \cdots M_n[S_n > M$$

we can get two sequences:

1. sequence of status changing:$M_0M_1M_2 \cdots M_nM$;
2. sequence of transition changing:$S_1S_2 \cdots S_n$.

Theory 6.3. *Any marking M_i can reach at from the initial marking M_0, i.e. there exists one sequence:*

$$M_0[S_1 > M_1[S_2 > \cdots M_j[S_j > M_i$$

Proof:

If such a sequence is not exists, then there are two cases:

- Net is not connective. So, there are at least two no connective subnet and the two subnet have no any intercourse. Because any subnet has its special computing target, the two computing targets are not interactive.

  That is inconsistency with the one and only of computing target. Therefore, the two computing targets are unsure.
- If net is connective, but there exists a marking M_k can not reach. In M_k, place p_k has no token. p_k is not isolated and has pre-transition t_k. So, there is a function I_+. Because p_k has no token, therefore t_k is not enable, i.e., t_k can not fire. In other words, the program has an operation and the operation will never be executed. So, such a computing procedure is not optimization and even wrong.

From above, any marking M_i is reachable from the initial marking M_0.

Theory 6.4. *elements in net are partial order and there exists least upper bound and greatest lower bound*

Proof: In any system , every operation or status serves for the computing target. Therefore, all operations and status are correlation, i.e. all are useful for the computing target. So, there does not exist any independent subnet, and all elements are in the same partial order set. The initial set $^{\bullet}s = \emptyset$ is greatest lower bound. $s^{\bullet} = \emptyset$ is least upper bound.

In the following discussion, let $\mathscr{C}$ is a Coloured Petri Nets , $\mathscr{R}$ is a *rwPNs* . $\mathscr{C}$ is the Coloured Petri Netmapping of $\mathscr{R}$. For any element $x \in \mathscr{R}$, x' is the mapping element in $\mathscr{C}$, and vice versa.

Theory 6.1. *if $t' \in \mathscr{C}$ is firable, then t is also firable.*

Proof: If $t' \in \mathscr{C}$ is firable , then three condition must be satisfied.

1. the *preset* of t' has enough tokens;
2. the *postset* of t' has enough capacity;
3. the arc expression $^{\bullet}t' \times \{t'\}$ can be evaluated correctly.

In $\mathscr{R}$, whether t fires or not depends on *preset* of t. Let p be the *preset* of t. p may contain *control place* p_p,*variable place* p_v or both. For a convenient, suppose p_p and p_v respectively contains only one single *place*. for *control place* , p_p is same as the *preset* of t'. For *variable place* , If $(p_v, t) \in R$, then there are two corresponding arcs,

$(p'_v, t') \in F;$

$(t', p'_v) \in F;$

Because $t' \in \mathscr{C}$ is firable, p_v has enough token and capacity.

If $(t, p_v) \in W$, then there are two corresponding arcs,

$(p'_v, t') \in F;$

$(t', p'_v) \in F;$

Because $t' \in \mathscr{C}$ is firable, p_v has enough token and capacity.

The arc expression ${}^{\bullet}t' \times \{t'\}$ can be evaluated correctly, and the number of tokens in *variable place* remain unchanged. Meanwhile, the logical condition in arc expression ${}^{\bullet}t' \times \{t'\}$ are removed and put into the *variable guard* of t, consequently, the three condition of t's firing

1. *control guard* holds;
2. *variable guard* holds;
3. the value of *variable place* can be evaluated correctly.

can be satisfied. Therefore, t also is firable.

Theory 6.2. *If $b' \in \mathscr{C}$ is reachable, then $b \in \mathscr{R}$ is reachable.*

Proof:

Because b' is reachable, therefore *transitions* in the *preset* of b' can fire. Let the *preset* of b' is T' and the *preset* of T' is P'. To prove b is reachable, the *preset* of b must be firable. Let the *preset* of b is T and the *preset* of T is P.

for $\forall p \in P$, if p is a *control place* , obviously t is firable. If p is a *variable place* , the expression of arc (p', t') in $\mathscr{C}$ contains *variable guard* of t as the logical conditions of arc expression. And the arc expression (p', t') can be evaluated correctly , therefore p's *variable guard* can hold *TRUE*, i.e., in *rwPNs* t can fire, because b is the *postset* of t, accordingly b is reachable.

Theory 6.3. *Let M'_1 is a marking of $\mathscr{C}$ and M_1 is a marking of $\mathscr{R}$. if M'_1 is reachable, then M_1 is also reachable, and there is a occurrence sequence $M_0[t_1 > \cdots t_i > M_i[t_{t+1} \cdots t_n > M_1$.*

Proof: According to theorem 6.2, the theorem holds.

Theory 6.4. *if $\mathscr{C}$ is live, then $\mathscr{R}$ is also live.*

Proof: because $\mathscr{C}$ is live, therefore for any transition in $\mathscr{C}$ can fire and any marking of $\mathscr{C}$ can be reachable. Accordingly to 6.2 and 6.3, the theorem can be proved.

Theory 6.5. *Let M' is the marking of $\mathscr{C}$. $\mathscr{R}$ is bounded iff there exists a natural number bound n so that for every reachable marking $M' \leq n$.*

Proof: 1. If $M' \leq n$. $\forall p' \in M'$, if $p \in \mathscr{R}$ is a *control place* , obviously the number of tokens in p is same as the number of tokens in p'. if p is a *variable place* , then based on the definition of *variable place* in *rwPNs* , the number of tokens in a *variable place* always is 1. $\forall p \leq n$ holds. Therefore $\mathscr{R}$ is bounded.
2. If $\mathscr{R}$ is bounded. $\forall p \in \mathscr{R}$, if p is a *variable place* , then the number in p is 1. If p is a *control place* , because $\mathscr{R}$ is bounded, therefore there exists a natural number bound n and $p \leq n$ holds. Because the mapping rules don't change the number of tokens in a *place*, therefore $\forall p' \in \mathscr{C}$, the number in p' is same as the number in p. Accordingly, there exists a natural number bound n and $p' \leq n$. Therefore $M' \leq n$ holds.

7. Example

In this section, we formalize several programs to illustrate *rwPNs* usage.

7.1 Min

A function, foo, computes the value of $5 * min(x, y)$ with parameters, x and y. Suppose the code is such as

```
int foo(int x,int y)
 {
     int z;
     if x<y
          z := x;
     else
          z:=y;
     z:=5*z;
     return z;
 }
```

Obviously *foo* contains three variables, x,y and z. Let

$$S_v = \{x, y, z\}$$

Generally, one statement can be modeled as one transition. Omitting the function head , the variables declaration and statement *return*, three main statements are left,

1. if $x < y \;\; z := x$
2. else $z := y$
3. $z := 5 * z$

Let *transition* t_{if},*transition* t_{else} and *transition* t_{min} describe the three statements respectively, then $\mathscr{L}$ can respectively be

$$\mathscr{L}(t_{if}) : z := x$$

$$\mathscr{L}(t_{else}) : z := y$$

$$\mathscr{L}(t_{min}) : z := 5 * z$$

In the three main statements, statement 1 and statement 2 are enclosed by *if-else*. The boolean expressions in statement *if-else* can be *GUARDS* .

Let us focus on *transition* t_{if}. In t_{if}, two variables z and x are concerned. t_{if} has two *GUARDS* . One, *control guard* , is to test whether $^{\bullet}t_{if}$ has enough *tokens* . When $^{\bullet}t_{if}$ have one *token* , *control guard* is *TRUE*, otherwise *FALSE*. The *control guard* determines whether statement 1 can be continued or not. The other one, *variable guard* , is to test whether $x < y$ holds. The *variable guard* also determines whether statement $z := x$ can be continued or not. Therefore, the two guards are

$$\mathcal{G}_c(t_{if}) = \{TRUE, FALSE\}$$
$$\mathcal{G}_v(t_{if}) = \{x < y\}$$

In $\mathcal{G}_v(t_{if})$, variable x and variable y are read. Therefore, in $\mathcal{L}(t_{if})$, variables z is written,and variable y is read. Consequently, *transition* t_{if} concerns three variables , x(read),y(read) and z(written). The specification can be represented as that in Figure 24. Similarly, *Transition* t_{else} can be described in figure 25.

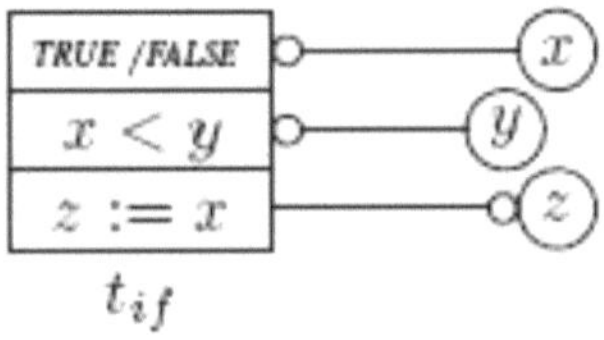

Fig. 24. Transition t_{if}

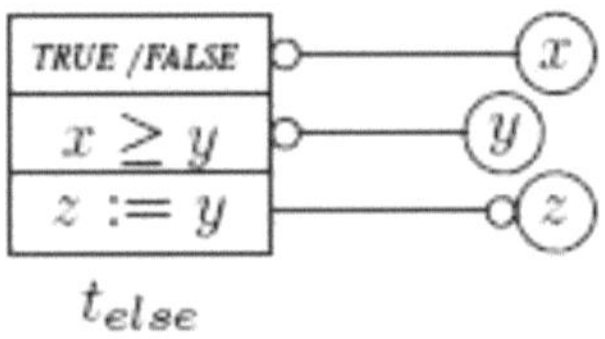

Fig. 25. Transition t_{else}

Statements in *if-else* are mutual exclusive, i.e. statement 1 and statement 2 are mutual exclusive. To guarantee the mutual exclusion, one *control place* is applied. Let C_{ifelse} is the *control place* (Figure 26). When C_{ifelse} has one *token* , there is only one is *TRUE*between $\mathcal{G}_c(t_{if})$ and $\mathcal{G}_c(t_{else})$. Suppose $\mathcal{G}_c(t_{if})$ is *TRUE*. After t_{if} fires and the *token* is consumed, then C_{ifelse} loses the *token* . And then $\mathcal{G}_c(t_{if})$ changes to *FALSE*. Generally, $\mathcal{G}_c(t_{if})$ will be *TRUE*or *FALSE*alternatively on whether C_{ifelse} has enough *tokens* .

In statement $z := 5 * z$, z appears in both sides of the assignment that means z will be both read and written. Moreover, statement $z = 5 * z$ only executes after statement *if-else* finishes, i.e. t_{min} follows both t_{if} and t_{else}. Let *control place C* determine the consecutive order. Then the program specification can be represented as that in figure 27.

t_{min} will execute when C has one *token* , therefore the *variable guard* of t_{min} is not necessary. Of course, any *GUARD* can be added if need.

In *rwPNs* , if all *Variable places* , *Read Arcs* and *Write Arcs* are omitted, the *cvNets* of program can abstracted as figure 28. In fact, that in figure 28 is a P/T nets and the analysis techniques of Petri nets can be applied . Obviously *cvNets* describes the *Control Flow* framework of program.

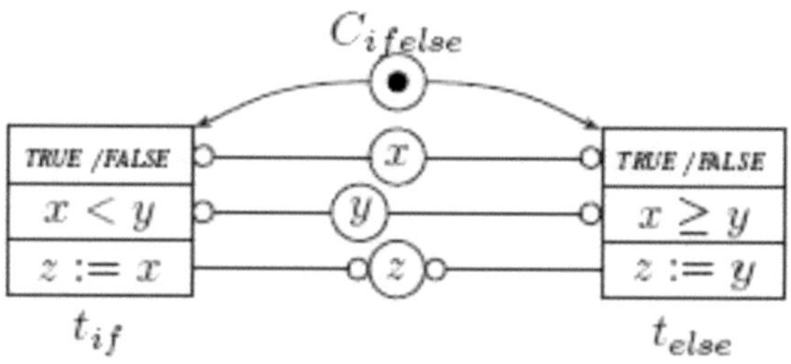

Fig. 26. Exclusive transitions

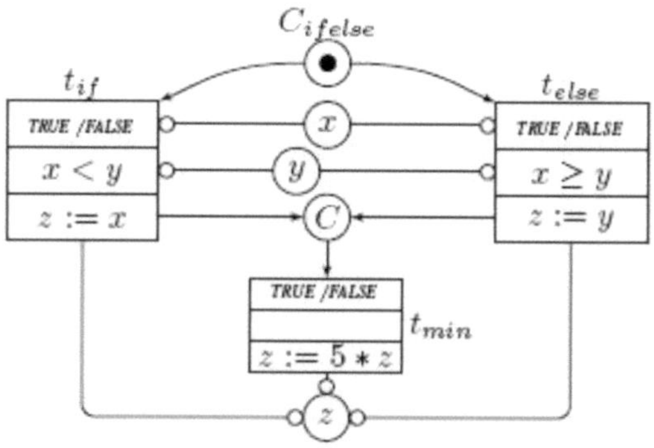

Fig. 27. *rwPN* Specification of $5 * min(x, y)$

Similarly, if all *control places* , *Control Arcs* and *transitions* without write/read arcs are omitted, then the *dvNets* of program can be abstracted as that in figure 29. Because *dvNets* has not *Control Flow* , all transitions are concurrent theoretically. *dvNets* describes the dataflow relationship among entities of program.

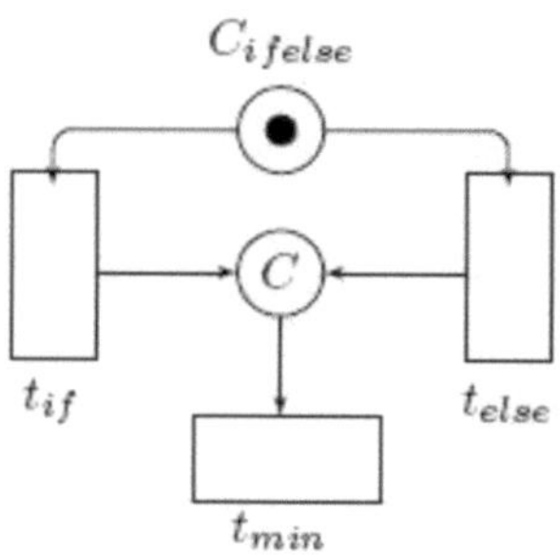

Fig. 28. *cvNets* of $5 * min(x, y)$

Informally, when an engineer starts to design a program, he can push *Control Flow* (*cvNets*) aside first, and only focus on data flow(*dvNets*), i.e., entity relations. When a computing machine has be chosen to implement the program, the *Control Flow* (*cvNets*) can be integrated at later. Accordingly, the final model of program just is composed of *cvNets* and *dvNets* .

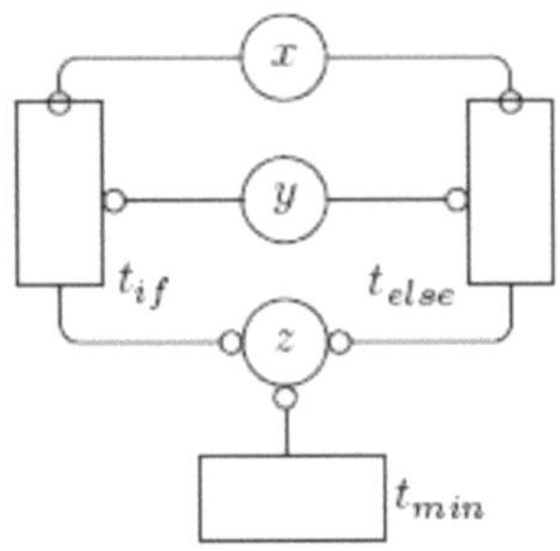

Fig. 29. *dvNets* of $5 * min(x, y)$

7.2 SORT

$n(n \geq 2)$ numbers should be sorted ascendingly. Let these n numbers be $x_1, x_2, \cdots, x_n$. *rwPN* specification is described as in figure 30, where, $\Sigma = (N, C, I, M0)$, and $N = (S_p, S_v, T; R, W, F)$.

Control place set: $S_p = \phi$;

Variable control set: $S_v = \{v_i | 1 \leq i \leq n\}$;

(Variable) Transition set: $T = \{t_i | 1 \leq i < n\}$;

Control flow set: $F = \phi$;

Read relation (R) and write relation (W): $R = W = \{< v_i, t_i >, < v_{i+1}, t_i > | 1 \leq i < n\}$;

C is the type set of x_i;

Initial markings M_0: $\{E_0(t_i) = false, M_{0v}(v_i) = x_i | 1 \leq i \leq n\}$;

I, the specification of transition t_i: for $\forall t_i T$: $B(t_i) \equiv v_i > v_{i+1}$;
$A(t_i) \equiv v_i, v_{i+1} = v_{i+1}, v_i$; This statement denotes that v_i exchanges the value with v_{i+1};

The semantics of marking varying is: If $\forall t_i\ T : M[t_i > M' \leftrightarrow M(v_i) > M(v_{i+1}) \wedge M(v_i) = M(v_{i+1}) \wedge M'(v_{i+1}) = M(v_i)$, then $E(t_i) = true$; If not, then $E(t_i) = false$.

In figure 30, transitions firing may reduce the number of descending arrays of $M(v_i)(1 \leq i \leq n)$. When marking satisfies $\forall v_i\ S_v \wedge i \neq n : M(v_i) \leq M(v_{i+1})$, then $\forall t_i\ T : B(t_i) = false \wedge E(t_i) = true$, and the sort arrives at the fixpoint, the sort accomplishes the purpose.

Fig. 30. SORT Specification

In figure 30, there is no sequential relation among $t_1, t_2, \cdots, t_{n-1}$, that is to say, transitions can fire concurrently. The semantics of sort in figure 30 is: Transition t_i is to compare the current value of $v_i(M(v_i) = x_k)$ and that of $v_{i+1}(M(v_{i1}) = x_j)$. If the current value of v_i is bigger than that of v_{i+1}, then v_i exchanges the current value with v_{i+1}; and then the guard of transition t_i

$(E(t_i)$ and $B(t_i))$ holds false. When every transition guard holds false, the sort arrives at the fixpoint and terminates.

The specification in figure 30 has not any resources restriction and n transitions can fire concurrently. If resources are restricted, e.g., only one control handle, the new specification is described as in figure 31. Where, additional sets,

Control place set: $S_p = \{s_i|1 \leq i < n\}$;

Control transition set: $T = \{g_i|1 \leq i < n\}$;

Control flow set: $F = \{< s_i, t_i >, < s_i, g_i > |1 \leq i < n\} \cup \{< t_i, s_{i+1} >, < g_i, s_{i+1} > |1 \leq i < n-1\} \cup \{< t_{n-1}, s_1 >, < g_{n-1}, s_1 >\}$;

M_{0p}, initial marking of control place s_i : $\{M_0(s_1) = 1\} \cup \{M_0(s_i) = 0|1 < i < n\}$;

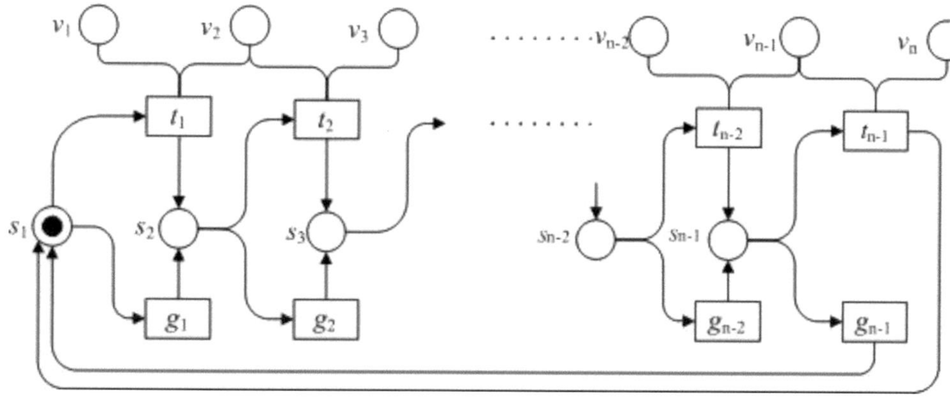

Fig. 31. Constraint SORT Specification

In figure 31, t_i can fire only if s_i, which is the preset of t_i, has at least one token. After t_i fires, the token in s_i is consumed and a new token flows into s_{i+1}, which is the postset of t_i. Because of the nondeterminacy, the firing possibility of g_i is the same as that of t_i. If there are not g_i, when $v_i v_{i+1}$, t_i cant fire and the sort terminates though $t_j > t_{j+1} (j > i)$. While transitions is fired continually, the token flows along place $s_1, s_2, \cdots, s_{n-1}$, and s_1. In fact, the specification in figure 31 is bubble sort . Similarly, if other resources are restrained, many different sorts can be designed based on the specification in figure 30.

In system Σ, let $n = 4$, $S_v = \{v_1, v_2, v_3, v_4\}$, $T_v = \{t_1, t_2, t_3\}$, $C(v_i) = Integer$ and initial markings of v_i and t_i are: $M_0(v_1) = 4$, $M_0(v_2) = 2$, $M_0(v_3) = 3$, $M_0(v_4) = 1$, $M_0(t_i) = false$. We can get a process of system Σ (Fig.9). This process describes the sort procedure from 4, 2, 3, 1 to 1, 2, 3, 4.

7.3 Dining philosophy

In this section, DPP(Dining philosophy problem) is treated as a program . Five philosophers, No.1 to No.5, sit around a table orderly and the No.1 is next to the No.5. Each philosopher is in one of three states: *thinking*, *hungry* and *eating*. Thinking independently for a while, each philosopher stops thinking to eat for hungriness. Each philosopher has one fork at his left hand, but he can eat only when he holds two forks, i.e. the left fork is owned by himself and the right fork is borrowed from his right neighbor. If borrows the right fork successfully, the philosopher can eat, otherwise he must wait for the right fork. After his

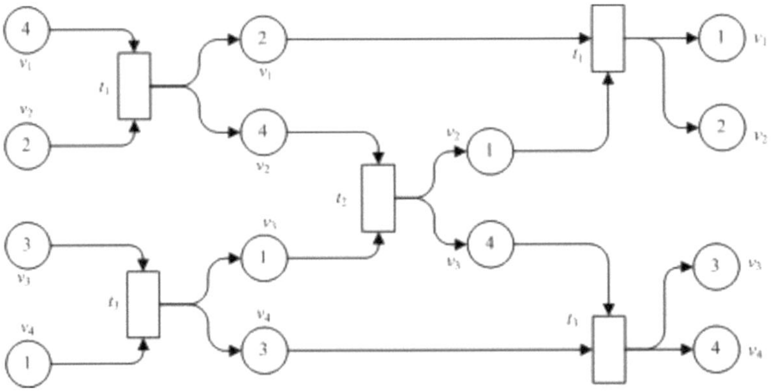

Fig. 32. SORT Process

eating, the philosopher returns the borrowed fork and frees his own fork for being lent, and then he starts to think. We suppose it is fair to use forks and there isn't any priority. In addition, a premise is that a philosopher doesn't free his holding fork(s) until he finishes his eating. Obviously, forks are the shared resources. To guarantee each philosopher can eat, each dining philosopher must finish his eating in a while and free his holding forks. Therefore, no philosopher can eat or be hungry forever.

Let $PHIL$ be the type philosophers belong to, $P_i \in PHIL$ denotes the ith philosopher. Variable place $P_i.state$ records the current state of philosopher, i.e. $thinking, hungry$ or $eating$. Concisely, $P_i.state = thinking, P_i.state = hungry$ and $P_i.state = eating$ are abbreviated as $P_i.thinking, P_i.hungry$ and $P_i.eating$ respectively, here the data type of $thinking, hungry$ and $eating$ are $Boolean$. Let $FORK$ be the type forks belong to, $f_i \in FORK$ denotes the fork owned by the ith philosopher. Variable transitions T_i, H_i and E_i denote operations that make philosopher P_i to think, be hungry and eat respectively (see Fig.33). T_i, H_i and E_i all can modify the current value of $P_i.state$. In figure 33, *Control guard* locates at top level and its initial value is $false$. *Control guard* is $false$ denotes that the fire condition of transition can't be satisfied, so the transition can't fire. When the fire condition of transition is satisfied, *control guard* is *true* and the transition is *enabled*. *Control guard* is just the first control of transition's firing. *Variable guard* locates at the middle level and it represents the condition that the associated variables must satisfy. Similar to *Control guard*, when *variable guard* is *true*, the transition is *enabled*. *Variable guard* is the second control of transition's firing. The transition fires only when both *control guard* and *variable guard* are *true*. *Variable guard* is fixed once it is assigned, but *control guard* can alternate between *true* and $false$. Action description locates at bottom level and it is a collection of assignments. For example, the semantics of T_i is: when *control flow* arrives at T_i (*control guard* is *true*) and P_i is *eating* (*variable guard* is *true*), P_i changes its state (*eating*) and starts thinking. Meanwhile P_i sets the current state to *thinking*. The semantics of E_i and H_i are similar to T_i's.

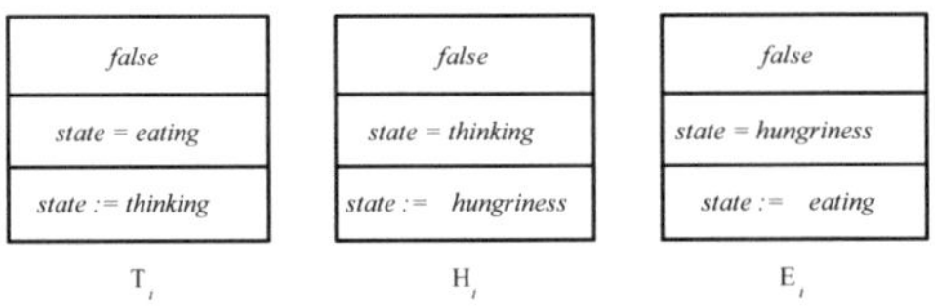

Fig. 33. Transition specification of *thinking*, *hungriness* and *eating*

In figure 34, the initial marking of P_i is: $M_0(f_i) = 1, M_0(St_i) = 1$ and $P_i.state = thinking$, i.e. the initial state of P_i is *thinking* and the next *enable* transition is H_i. When H_i fires, P_i is in the state of *hungriness* and requests two forks to eat, i.e. the *weight* of arc (H_i, Sa_i) is 2. When $M(f_i) = 1$ and $M(Sa_i) \geq 1$, Lf_i fires. Consequently, fork f_i is held by P_i. Similarly, When $M(f_{i-1}) = 1$ and $M(Sa_i) \geq 1$, Rf_i fires. Consequently, fork f_{i-1} is held by P_i. If Ff_i has two tokens, i.e. $M(Ff_i) = 2$, E_i fires and P_i starts to eat with two forks. Marking $M(Sf_i) = 1$ denotes P_i is eating. T_i's firing denotes P_i finishes eating and start to think, at the same time, P_i frees forks f_i and f_{i-1} (P_1 uses f_1 and f_5), i.e. $M(f_i) = 1$ and $M(f_{i-1}) = 1$. In Fig.34 and other figures, *arc with arrow* denotes *control flow* and *arc without arrow* denotes *read/write* relationship.

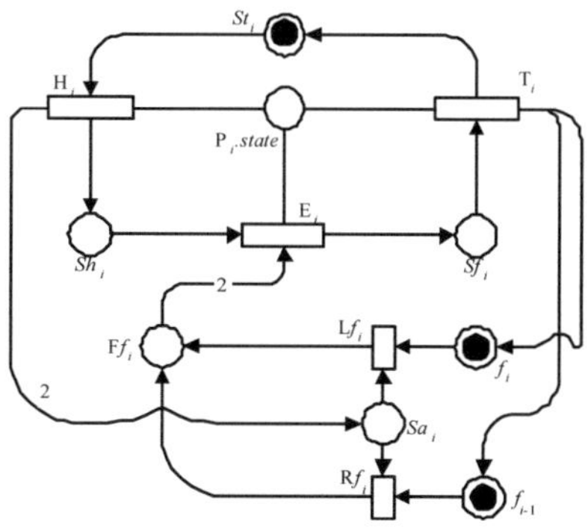

Fig. 34. Specification of P_i

In figure 34, *token* denotes the *control* inside P_i and flows among *control places*. Although *control place* can't be read or written, we can observe the *control flow* through the change of *state*. For example, in figure 33, *variable guards* of T_i, H_i and E_i imply the change order of states. The current state of philosopher can be checked through *state*.

The specifications of five philosophers are similar to that in figure.34. With shared forks, the specification of DPP (figure.35) can be got from interaction among five individual philosopher specifications (figure.34).

Control place set: $S_p = \{St_i, Sh_i, Sf_i, f_i, Sa_i, Ff_i | i = 1,2,3,4,5\}$.

Variable place set: $S_v = \{P_i.state | i = 1,2,3,4,5\}$.

Transition set: $T_v = \{T_i, H_i, E_i | i = 1,2,3,4,5\}, T_p = \{Lf_i, Rf_i | i = 1,2,3,4,5\}$.

Read/Write relationship: $R = W = (P_i.state, T_i), (P_i.state, H_i), (P_i.state, E_i)$.

Control flow relationship: $F = \{(T_i, St_i), (St_i, H_i), (H_i, Sh_i), (Sh_i, E_i), (E_i, Sf_i), (Sf_i, T_i), (T_i, f_i), (T_i, f_{i-1}), (H_i, Sa_i), (Sa_i, Lf_i), (f_i, Lf_i), (f_{i-1}, Rf_i), (Sa_i, Rf_i), (Lf_i, Ff_i), (Rf_i, Ff_i), (Ff_i, E_i) | i = 1,2,3,4,5\}$, where $f_0 = f_5$.

The individual weight of other arcs is 1 respectively, but $\{W(Ff_i, E_i) = 2, W(H_i, Sa_i) = 2 | i = 1,2,3,4,5\}$.

Description of *(variables) transition I* is in figure.33.

Initial marking $M_0 : \{M_0(f_i) = 1, M_0(St_i) = 1, M_0(P_i.state) = thinking | i = 1,2,3,4,5\}$.

In figure.35, non-neighboring philosophers hasn't the shared resource (fork), so they can be concurrent, such as P_1 and $P_3(P_4)$, P_2 and $P_4(P_5)$, P_3 and $P_5(P_1)$. These properties can be

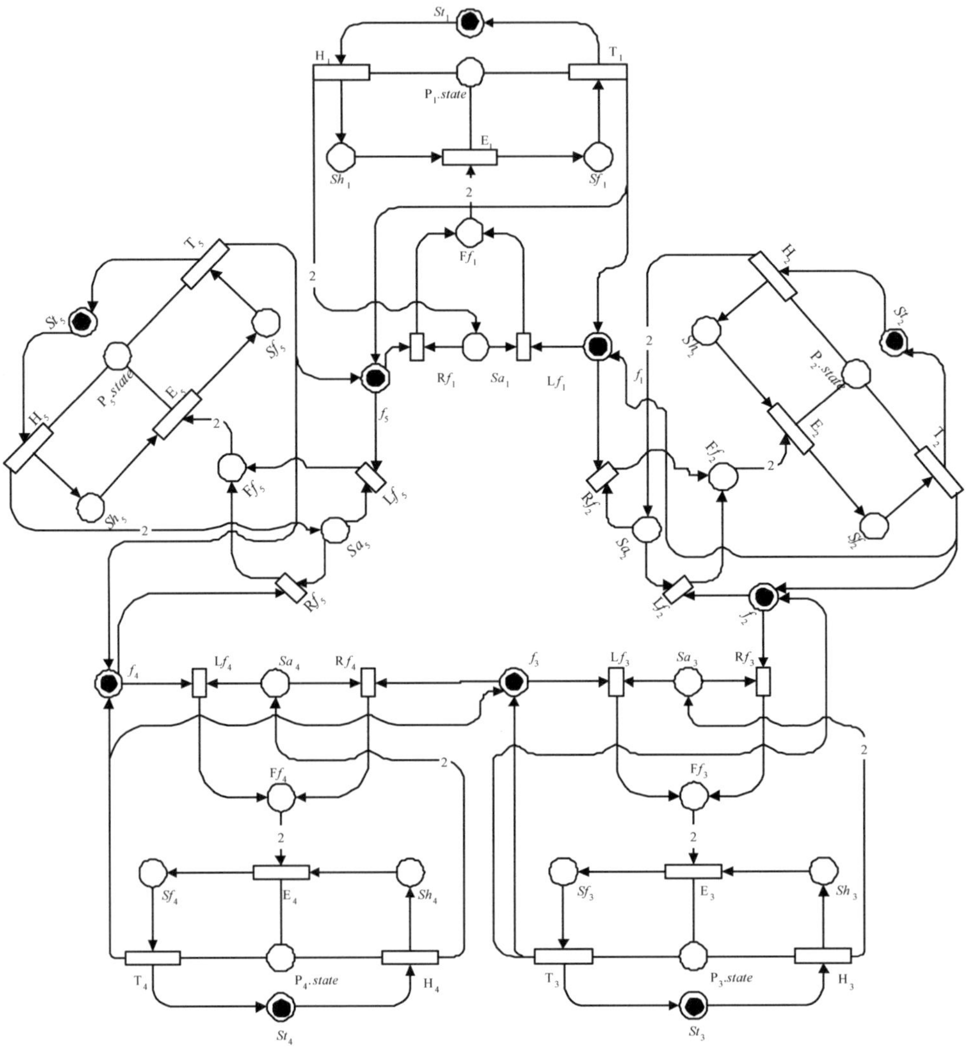

Fig. 35. *rwPN* Specification of Dining Philosopher Problem

observed from figure.35. For convenience, predicate $R_p(P_i, P_j)$ denotes that P_i is next to P_j; predicate $T_f(f_i, f_j)$ denotes f_i is next to f_j and they are used by P_i,. Under no confusion circumstances, $M(St_i) = 1$ is abbreviated to St_i; and $\neg St_i$ to $M(St_i) = 0$; f_i means fork f_i is free and marking $M(f_i)$ is 1; $\neg f_i$ means fork f_i is being used and marking $M(f_i)$ is 0.

Control places Sf_i, St_i and Sh_i are unreadable and to some extent are encapsulated. However, variable place *state* is readable and writable, so the state of philosopher can be observed through variable place *state*. We call *state* the *observe window* of the inner state of philosopher. Therefore, *control flow* inside a philosopher can be checked indirectly through *variable place*, and *variable place* also can be called as *interface*. On the other hand, properties on *state* can be proved through *control flow*. The following properties are expressed by UNITY logic but the proofs are Petri nets style.

P_i.*thinking* ensures P_i.*hungriness*.	P_i will stop thinking because of hungriness.
P_i.*hungriness* ensures P_i.*eating*.	The hungry philosopher has opportunity to eat.
P_i.*eating* ensures P_i.*thinking*.	The dining philosopher must finish his eating in a while and start to think.

These properties ensure each philosopher is in one of three states by turn, i.e. any philosopher can't be in one of states forever. Therefore, the individual philosopher could be live.

Proof: Because St_i is a *control place*, $M(St_i) = 1$ implies that P_i is in the state of *thinking*, i.e. $St_i \rightarrow P_i.thinking$. Similarly, $Sh_i \rightarrow P_i.hungriness$ and $Sf_i \rightarrow P_i.eating$. Therefore, property 1 can be rewritten as

$$St_i \text{ ensures } Sh_i$$
$$Sh_i \text{ ensures } Sf_i$$
$$Sf_i \text{ ensures } St_i$$

From figure.34, we can get a segment of process (figure.36). For conciseness, some detail parts are neglected in figure.36, e.g. P_i must have an opportunity to hold two forks.

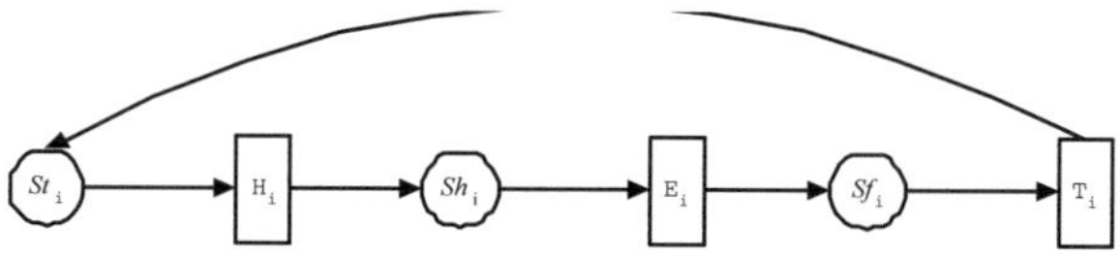

Fig. 36. A process segment of P_i

As showed in figure.36, *control*(token) flows from St_i through H_i, and then into Sh_i. Accordingly, there is an *occurrence sequence* $St_i[H_i > Sh_i$. Obviously, H_i is the operation which guarantees St_i ensures Sh_i. Consequently, based on the premise $St_i \rightarrow P_i.thinking$ and $Sh_i \rightarrow P_i.hungriness$, H_i also guarantees P_i.*thinking* ensures P_i.*hungriness*.

Similarly, P_i.*hungriness* ensures P_i.*eating* and P_i.*eating* ensures P_i.*thinking* hold *true*.

Property 1. invariant $R_p(P_i, P_j) \rightarrow \neg(P_i.eating \wedge P_j.eating)$.

The neighboring philosophers can't eat at the same time.

Proof: Similar to property 1, property 2 can be rewritten as

$$invariantR_p(P_i, P_j) \rightarrow \neg(Sf_i \wedge Sf_j)$$

Suppose P_i is in the state of *eating*, the firing condition of E_i is

$$M(Ff_i) = 2$$

At that time, tokens in Sf_i and Sf_j must respectively be consumed, i.e.

$$M(Sf_i) = 0 \quad M(Sf_j) = 0$$

Similarly, P_j is in state of *eating*, the firing condition of E_j is

$$M(Ff_j) = 2$$

Because P_i and P_j are neighboring, and $M(Ff_i) = 2$ has caused $M(Sf_j) = 0$. Therefore, Lf_j can't fire. Accordingly, $M(Ff_j) = 2$ can't be satisfied. So, P_j can't be in the state of *eating*, i.e.

$$R_p(P_i, P_j) \rightarrow P_i.eating \wedge \neg P_j.eating \tag{1}$$

Similarly, when P_j is in the state of *eating*, the firing condition of E_i can't be satisfied. Accordingly, P_i can't be in the state of *eating*, i.e.

$$R_p(P_i, P_j) \rightarrow \neg P_i.eating \wedge P_j.eating \tag{2}$$

When the neighboring philosopher P_i and P_j both are not in the sate of *eating*, obviously,

$$R_p(P_i, P_j) \rightarrow \neg P_i.eating \wedge \neg P_j.eating \tag{3}$$

From (1)(2)(3), we can find that

$$R_p(P_i, P_j) \rightarrow \neg (P_i.eating \wedge P_j.eating) \tag{4}$$

Because (4) has no other restrictive condition besides a premise that P_i and P_j are neighboring. Therefore, (4) holds *true* when the program is initializing. Therefore, (4) always holds *true*. Accordingly, property 2 holds *true*.

Property 2. $P_i.eating \longmapsto \neg P_i.eating \wedge f_i \wedge f_j \wedge T_f(f_i, f_j)$.

the dining philosopher will finish eating and free the holding forks.

Proof: Similar to property 1, property 3 can be rewritten as:

$$Sf_i \longmapsto \neg Sf_i \wedge f_i \wedge f_j \wedge T_f(f_i, f_j)$$

From property 1, Sf_i ensures St_i holds *true*. A philosopher is thinking implies that the philosopher is not in the state of *eating*, i.e. $St_i \rightarrow \neg Sf_i$. Accordingly, Sf_i *ensures*$\neg Sf_i$ hold *true*. From figure 35, we can get an *occurrence sequence* $Sf_i[T_i > \{St_i, f_i, f_j\}$, so T_i's firing causes $M(f_i) = M(f_j) = 1$. Accordingly, the two forks used by $P_i(T_f(f_i, f_j))$ are free, i.e.

$$Sf_i \text{ ensures } \neg Sf_i \wedge f_i \wedge f_j$$

Consequently, property $P_i.eating \longmapsto \neg P_i.eating \wedge f_i \wedge f_j \wedge T_f(f_i, f_j)$ holds *true*.

Property 3. $P_i.hungriness \longmapsto P_i.eating \wedge (\neg f_i \wedge \neg f_j) \wedge T_f(f_i, f_j)$.

The hungry philosopher has opportunity to eat with two forks.

Proof: Similar to property 1, property 4 can be rewritten as

$$Sh_i \longmapsto Sf_i \wedge (\neg f_i \wedge \neg f_j) \wedge T_f(f_i, f_j)$$

From figure 34, we can get a process segment as figure.37 ($f_0 = f_5$).

In figure.37, $^\bullet E_i = \{Sh_i, Ff_i\}$ and $E_i^\bullet = \{Sf_i\}$, accordingly, there is *occurrence sequence*:

$$\{Sh_i, M(Ff_i) = 2\}[E_i > \{Sf_i\} \tag{5}$$

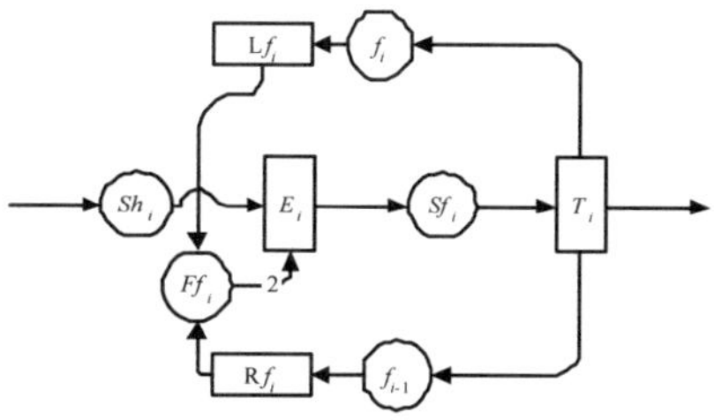

Fig. 37. The process segment of P_i's eating

Moreover, there also is *occurrence sequence*:

$$\{f_i, f_j\}[\{Lf_i, Rf_i\} > \{M(Ff_i) = 2\} \tag{6}$$

therefore, $M(Ff_i) = 2$ cause $M(f_i) = 0$ and $M(f_j) = 0$.

According to property 1 and (5), Sh_i ensures Sf_i and E_i's firing needs $M(Ff_i) = 2$. According to (6), $M(Ff_i) = 2$ causes $M(f_i) = 0$ and $M(f_j) = 0$, i.e. E_i's firing causes $M(f_i) = 0$ and $M(f_j) = 0$. f_i and f_j are neighboring is the premise, so

$$Sh_i \text{ ensures } Sf_i \wedge (\neg f_i \wedge \neg f_j) \wedge T_f(f_i, f_j)$$

i.e. $Sh_i \longmapsto Sf_i \wedge (\neg f_i \wedge \neg f_j) \wedge T_f(f_i, f_j)$ holds *true*.
Therefore, property 4 holds *true*.

Proof of liveness

T is a set of transitions, M is a set of system markings. Let $r = \{(m, m')|m, m' \in M \wedge t \in T : m[t > m'\}$, then

$$r^* = r^0 \cup r^1 \cup r^2 \cup \cdots = \bigcup_{i=0}^{\infty} r^i$$

is called as reachable relation, expression $m\ r^*\ m'$ denotes that marking m can be changed to marking m' after finite transitions fire.

If $m \in M, t \in T, m' \in M : mr^*m' \wedge m'[t >$, then the system is live.

If the system is live, and $m, m' \in M : mr^*m'$, then the system is circular.

From the above definition, we can prove the liveness of the dining problem.

Proof: The state of each philosopher changes in turn:

$$thinking \rightarrow hungry \rightarrow eating \rightarrow thinking \cdots$$

The state change of philosopher P_i is controlled by a flow (directed circle): $\delta_i = \cdots T_i H_i E_i T_i \cdots$, The two neighbor philosophers must share one fork. P_i requests the fork is controlled by (directed circle)

The right fork: $\varepsilon_{r_i} = f_i E_i S f_i T_i f_i$

The left fork: $\varepsilon_{l_i} = f_{i+1} E_i S f_i T_i f_{i+1}$

If $value(Pi) \neq nout$, the fire condition of the element in $T = \{T_i, H_i, E_i | i = 1 \cdots 5\}$ are $\{\cdots, Sf_i\}, \{\cdots, St_i\}$ and $\{\cdots, f_i, f_{i+1}, Sh_i\}$ respectively.

Given $m \in M$, the next firable transition t must be an element of T, arbitrarily let $t = H_i$, obviously, if let $m' = \{\cdots, St_i\}$, the fire condition of H_i can be satisfied and H_i can fire.

Similarly, if let $t = T_i$ or $t = E_i$, there are $m' = \{\cdots, Sf_i\}$ or $m' = \{\cdots, f_i, f_{i+1}, Sh_i\}$ can satisfy the fire condition of T_i or E_i respectively. Thus,

$$t \in T, m' \in M : m'[t > \quad (1)$$

If $m' \subseteq m$, then $mr^* m'$ holds true obviously.

If $m' \nsubseteq m$, since there are directed circles δ_i, ε_{l_i} and ε_{r_i}, arbitrarily set a_i be a place of the directed circles δ_i, ε_{l_i} or ε_{r_i} in marking m', and $m'(a_i) > 0$.

If $a_i \in \delta_i$. Because δ_i is a directed circle, therefore δ_i has a place b_i in marking m, and there must be a path from b_i to a_i (the token in b_i will arrive at a_i at some time). Otherwise, the philosopher P_i can't be in one state of three states in m. So, $b_i r^* a_i$.

Similarly, if $a_i \in \varepsilon_{l_i}, b_j \in \varepsilon_{l_i}, b_j r^* a_i$; if $a_i \in \varepsilon_{r_i}, \exists b_k \in \varepsilon_{r_i}, b_k r^* a_i$;

Hence, if $m' \nsubseteq m$, m can reach m'. i.e.

$$mr^* m' \quad (2)$$

From (3.1) and (3.2), we conclude that the system is live.

Because there exists directed circles δ_i, ε_{l_i} and ε_{r_i}, the tokens must flow along the circles, so the markings of system change circularly. We can conclude that any marking m can reach any other marking m', i.e., $m, m' \in M : mr^* m'$. Hence, the system is circular.

8. References

Bjorner, D., Jones, C. B., Airchinnigh, M. M. a. & Neuhold, E. J. (1987). *VDM '87 VDM – A Formal Method at Work*, Vol. 252, Springer-Verlag, Germany. ø.

Breuer, P. T. & Lano, K. C. (1999). Creating specifications from code: Reverse-engineering techniques, *Journal of Software Maintenance: Research and Practice* 3: 145–162.

Girault, C. & Valk, R. (2002). *Petri Nets for Systems Engineering:a guide to modeling,verification,and applications*, Springer-Verlag.

Harel, D. (1987). *Statecharts: A Visual Formalism for Complex Systems.* Sci. Comput. Programming 8.

Jensen, K., Kristensen, L. M. & Wells, L. (2007). Coloured petri nets and cpn tools for modelling and validation of concurrent systems, *Int. J. Softw. Tools Technol. Transf.* 9(3): 213–254.

Khedker, U., Sanyal, A. & Karkare, B. (2009). *Data Flow Analysis: Theory and Practice*, CRC Press (Taylor and Francis Group).

Reisig, W. (1985). *Petri Nets, an Introduction*, EATCS Monographs in Theroetical Computer Science, Springer. EATCS Monographs in Theroetical Computer Science.

Spivey, J. M. (1998). The z notation: A reference manual.

Woodcock, J. C. P. & Davies, J. (1996). *Using Z-Specification,Refinement,and Proof*, Prentice-Hall.

Section 4

Natural Language Disambiguation

10

Resolving Topic-Focus Ambiguities in Natural Language

Marie Duží
VŠB-Technical University Ostrava
Czech Republic

1. Introduction

Natural language has features that are not found in logically perfect artificial languages. One such feature is *redundancy*, where two or more terms/expressions share exactly the same semantic and logical (but perhaps not pragmatic or rhetoric) properties. Another feature is its converse, namely *ambiguity*, where one term/expression has more than one meaning. A logical analysis of such a piece of natural language will typically translate each of its unambiguous meanings into logically perfect notation. Frege's Begriffsschrift was the first major attempt in modern logic to create such a notation (though he primarily intended it for mathematical language).[1] There are various origins and various manifestations of ambiguity, not least cases bearing on quantifier scopes, like "Every boy dances with one girl". Another sort of example is "John loves his wife, and so does Peter", which is ambiguous between Peter loving John's wife and Peter loving his own wife, because it is ambiguous which property 'so' picks up.[2] A third, and perhaps less-noticed, sort of ambiguity is pivoted on whether the *topic* or the *focus* of a sentence is highlighted. For instance, "John only introduced Bill to Sue", to use Hajičová's example,[3] lends itself to two different kinds of construal: "John did not introduce other people to Sue except for Bill" and "The only person Bill was introduced to by John was Sue". There are two sentences whose semantics, logical properties and consequences only partially overlap. A similar phenomenon also crops up in the case of propositional attitudes and their less-attended 'cousins' of notional attitudes like seeking and finding, calculating and proving.

In this chapter I will deal in particular with ambiguities in natural language exemplifying the difference between *topic* and *focus articulation* within a sentence. This difference is closely related to the disambiguation stemming from supposition *de dicto* and *de re* with which a particular expression is used. I will show that whereas articulating the topic of a sentence activates a presupposition, articulating the focus frequently yields merely entailment. Based on an analysis of topic-focus articulation, I propose a solution to the almost hundred-year old dispute over Strawsonian vs. Russellian definite descriptions.[4] The point of departure is

---

[1] See (Frege, 1884).
[2] See (Neale, 2004), and also (Duží & Jespersen, submitted).
[3] See (Hajičová, 2008).
[4] See, for instance, (Donellan, 1966); (Fintel, 2004); (Neale 1990); (Russell, 1905, 1957); (Strawson 1950, 1964).

that sentences of the form "The *F* is a *G*" are ambiguous. Their ambiguity is, in my view, not rooted in a shift of meaning of the definite description 'the *F*'. Rather, the ambiguity stems from different topic-focus articulations of such sentences. Russell and Strawson took themselves to be at loggerheads; whereas, in fact, they spoke at cross purposes. The received view still tends to be that there is room for at most one of the two positions, since they are deemed incompatible. And they are, of course, incompatible - *if* they must explain the same set of data. But they should not, in my view. One theory is excellent at explaining one set of data, but poor at explaining the data that the other theory is excellent at explaining; and *vice versa*. My novel contribution advances the research into definite descriptions by pointing out how progress has been hampered by a false dilemma and *how to move beyond that dilemma*. The point is this. If 'the *F*' is the topic phrase then this description occurs with *de re* supposition and Strawson's analysis appears to be what is wanted. On this reading the sentence *presupposes* the existence of the descriptum of 'the *F*'. The other option is '*G*' occurring as topic and 'the *F*' as focus. This reading corresponds to Donnellan's *attributive* use of 'the *F*' and the description occurs with *de dicto* supposition. On this reading the Russellian analysis gets the truth-conditions of the sentence right. The existence of a unique *F* is merely entailed.

Ancillary to my analysis is a *general analytic schema* of sentences coming with a presupposition. This analysis makes use of a definition of the '*if-then-else*' connective known from programming languages. A broadly accepted view of the semantic nature of this connective is that it is a so-called non-strict function that does not comply with the principle of compositionality. However, the semantic nature of the connective is contested among computer scientists. I will show — and this is also a novel contribution of mine — that there is no cogent reason for embracing a non-strict definition and context-dependent meaning, *provided* a higher-order logic making it possible to operate on hyperintensions is applied. The framework of Tichý's Transparent Intensional Logic (TIL) possesses sufficient expressive power, and will figure as background theory throughout my exposition.[5]

Tichý's TIL was developed simultaneously with Montague's Intensional Logic, IL.[6] The technical tools of disambiguation will be familiar from IL, with two exceptions. One is that we λ-bind separate variables $w, w_1, \ldots, w_n$ ranging over possible worlds and $t, t_1, \ldots, t_n$ ranging over times. This dual binding is tantamount to *explicit intensionalization and temporalization*. The other exception is that *functional application* is the logic both of extensionalization of intensions (functions from possible worlds) and of predication.[7] Application is symbolized by square brackets, '[...]'. Intensions are extensionalized by applying them to worlds and times, as in $[[Intension\ w]\ t]$, abbreviated by subscripted terms for world and time variables: $Intension_{wt}$ is the extension of the generic intension *Intension* at $\langle w, t\rangle$. Thus, for instance, the extensionalization of a property yields a set (possibly an empty one), and the extensionalization of a proposition yields a truth-value (or no value at all). A general objection to Montague's IL is that it fails to accommodate *hyperintensionality*, as indeed any formal logic interpreted set-theoretically is bound to unless a domain of primitive hyperintensions is added to the frame. Any theory of natural-language analysis needs a hyperintensional (preferably procedural) semantics in order to crack the hard nuts

5 For details on TIL see, in particular, (Duží et al., 2010a); (Tichý, 1988, 2004).

6 For a detailed critical comparison of TIL and Montague's IL, see (Duží et al., 2010a, § 2.4.3);

7 For details, see (Jespersen, 2008).

of natural language semantics. In global terms, without procedural semantics TIL is an anti-contextualist (i.e., transparent), explicitly intensional modification of IL. With procedural semantics, TIL rises above the model-theoretic paradigm and joins instead the paradigm of hyperintensional logic and structured meanings.

The structure of this chapter is as follows. In Section 2 I briefly summarise the history of the dispute between Russell and Strawson (as well as their proponents and opponents) on the semantic character of sentences containing definite descriptions. Section 3 is an introduction to TIL. In paragraph 3.1 I introduce the semantic foundations of TIL and in 3.2 its logical foundations. Sections 4 and 5 contain the main results of this study. In Section 4 I propose a solution to the dispute over Strawsonian vs. Russellian definite descriptions. Paragraph 4.1 is an introduction to the problem of ambiguities stemming from different topic-focus articulation and a solution based on this distinction is proposed in paragraph 4.2. Section 5 generalizes the method of topic-focus disambiguation to sentences containing not only definite descriptions but also general terms occurring with different suppositions. To this end I make use of the strict analysis of the *if-then-else* function that is defined in paragraph 5.1. The method is then illustrated by analysing some more examples in paragraph 5.2. Finally, Section 6 summarizes the results.

2. Russell vs. Strawson on definite descriptions

There is a substantial difference between proper names and definite descriptions. This distinction is of crucial importance due to their vastly different logical behaviour. Independently of any particular theory of proper names, it should be granted that a *proper* proper name (as opposed to a definite description grammatically masquerading as a proper name) is a rigid designator of a numerically particular individual. On the other hand, a definite *description* like, for instance, 'the Mayor of Dunedin', 'the King of France', 'the highest mountain on Earth', etc., offers an *empirical criterion* that enables us to establish which individual, if any, satisfies the criterion in a particular state of affairs.

The contemporary discussion of the distinction between names and descriptions was triggered by Russell (1905). Russell's key idea is the proposal that a sentence like

(1) "The F is a G", containing a definite description 'the F' is understood to have, in the final analysis, the logical form

(1') $\exists x\,(Fx \wedge \forall y\,(Fy \supset x{=}y) \wedge Gx)$, rather than the logical form $G(\iota x\, Fx)$.

Though Russell's quantificational theory remains to this day a strong rival of referential theories, it has received its fair share of *criticism*. *First*, Russell's translation of simple sentences like "The F is a G" into the molecular form "There is at least one F and at most one thing is an F and that thing is a G" is rather enigmatic, because Russell disregards the standard constraint that there must be a fair amount of structural similarity between analysandum and analysans. *Second*, Russell proposed the elimination of Peano's descriptive operator 'ι' understood as 'the only', and deprived definite descriptions of their self-contained meaning. *Third*, Russell simply got the truth-conditions wrong in important cases of using descriptions when there is no such thing as the unique F. This criticism was launched by Strawson who in (1950) objected that Russell's theory predicts the wrong truth-conditions for sentences like 'The present King of France is bald'. According to Russell's analysis, this sentence is false, but according to Strawson, this outcome does not conform to our intuitions about its truth or falsity. In Strawson's view, the sentence can be neither true nor false whenever there is no King of France. Obviously, in such a state of affairs the sentence is not true. However, if it were false then its negation, "The King of France is not bald", would be true, which entails that there is a unique King of France, contrary to the assumption that there is none. Strawson held that sentences like these *not only entail* the existence of the present King of France, but also *presuppose* his existence. If 'the present King of France' fails to refer, then the presupposition is false and the sentence fails to have a determinate truth value.[8]

Russell (1957) in response to Strawson's criticism argued that, despite Strawson's protests, the sentence was in fact false:

> Suppose, for example, that in some country there was a law that no person could hold public office if he considered it false that the Ruler of the Universe is wise. I think an avowed atheist who took advantage of Mr. Strawson's doctrine to say that he did not hold this proposition false would be regarded as a somewhat shifty character. (Russell, 1957)

Donnellan (1966) observed that there is a sense in which Strawson and Russell are both right (and both wrong) about the proper analysis of definite descriptions, because definite descriptions can be used in two different ways. On a so-called *attributive use*, a sentence of the form 'The *F* is a *G*' is used to express a proposition equivalent to 'Whatever is uniquely *F* is a *G*'. Alternatively, on a *referential use*, a sentence of the form 'The *F* is a *G*' is used to pick out a specific individual, *a*, and to say of *a* that *a* is a *G*. Donnellan suggested that Russell's quantificational account of definite descriptions might capture attributive uses, but that it does not work for referential uses. Ludlow in (2007) interprets Donnellan as arguing that in some cases descriptions are Russellian and in other cases they are Strawsonian.

Kripke (1977) responded to Donnellan by arguing that the Russellian account of definite descriptions could, by itself, account for both referential and attributive uses, and that the difference between the two cases could be entirely a matter of pragmatics, because there is an important distinction between what one literally says by an utterance and what one intends to communicate by that utterance. Neale (1990) supported Russell's view by collecting a number of previously observed cases in which intuitions about truth conditions clearly do not support Strawson's view. On the other hand, a number of linguists have recently come to Strawson's defence on this matter. For a detailed survey of the arguments supporting Strawson's view and also arguments supporting Russell's, see (Ludlow, 2007). Here it might suffice to say that Strawson's concerns have not delivered a knock-out blow to Russell's theory of descriptions, and so this topic remains very much alive. Recently, von Fintel in (2004) argues that every sentence containing a definite description 'the *F*' comes with the existential presupposition that there be a unique *F*. For instance, he argues against the standpoint that the sentence "Last week, my friend went for a drive with the king of France" is false. He claims that this sentence presupposes that there be a king of France and that in the technical sense the sentence has no truth-value.

---

[8] Nevertheless, for Strawson, *sentences* are meaningful in and of themselves, independently of the empirical facts like contingent non-existence of the King of France.

In this chapter I am not going to take into account Kripke's pragmatic factors like the intentions of a speaker. In other words, I am not going to take into account what a speaker might have meant by his/her utterance, for this is irrelevant to a *logical* semantic theory. So I am disregarding Donnellan's troublesome notion of having somebody in mind. Instead, I will propose a *literal semantic analysis* of sentences of the form "The *F* is a G". What I want to show is this. First, definite descriptions are not deprived of a self-contained meaning and they denote one and the same entity in any context. Thus they are never Russellian. Second, Russell's insight that a definite description 'the *F*' does not denote a definite individual is spot-on. Rather, according to TIL, 'the *F*' denotes a *condition* to be contingently satisfied by the individual (if any) that happens to be the *F*. I will explicate such conditions in terms of possible-world intensions, *viz.* as individual roles or offices to be occupied by at most one individual per world/time pair. Third, I am going to show that Donnellan was right that sentences of the form "The *F* is a *G*" are ambiguous. However, their ambiguity does not concern a shift of meaning of the definite description 'the *F*'. Rather, the ambiguity concerns different *topic-focus* articulations of these sentences. There are two options. The description 'the *F*' may occur in the topic of a sentence and property *G* (the focus) is predicated of the topic. This case corresponds to Donnellan's *referential* use; using medieval terminology I will say that 'the *F*' occurs with *de re* supposition. The other option is '*G*' occurring as topic and 'the *F*' as focus. This reading corresponds to Donnellan's *attributive* use of 'the *F*' and the description occurs with *de dicto* supposition. Consequently, such sentences are ambiguous between their *de dicto* and *de re* readings. On their *de re* reading they *presuppose* the existence of a unique *F*. Thus Strawson's analysis appears to be adequate for *de re* cases. On their *de dicto* reading they have the truth-conditions as specified by the Russellian analysis. They do not presuppose, but only entail, the existence of a unique *F*. However, the Russellian analysis, though being equivalent to the one I am going to propose, is not an adequate literal analysis of *de dicto* readings.

I am going to bring out the *semantic* nature of the topic-focus difference by means of a logical analysis. As a result, I will furnish sentences differing only in their topic-focus articulation with different structured meanings producing different possible-world propositions.[9] Moreover, the proposed solution of the problem of definite descriptions generalizes to any sentences differing in their topic-focus articulation. Thus I am going to introduce a *general analytic schema* of sentences that come with a presupposition. Since our logic is a hyperintensional logic of *partial functions*, I am able to analyse sentences with presuppositions in a natural way. It means that I furnish them with hyperpropositions, *viz.* procedures that produce partial possible-world propositions, which occasionally yield truth-value gaps.[10]

3. Foundations of TIL

TIL is an overarching semantic theory for all sorts of discourse, whether colloquial, scientific, mathematical or logical. The theory is a *procedural* (as opposed to denotational) one, according to which sense is an abstract, extra-linguistic procedure detailing what operations to apply to what procedural constituents to arrive at the product (if any) of the

[9] For details on structured meanings, see (Duží, et al., 2010b).

[10] For an introduction to the notion of hyperproposition, see (Jespersen, 2010).

procedure. Such procedures are rigorously defined as TIL *constructions*. The semantics is tailored to the hardest case, as constituted by hyperintensional contexts, and generalized from there to simpler intensional and extensional contexts. This entirely anti-contextual and compositional semantics is, to the best of my knowledge, the only one that deals with all kinds of context in a uniform way. Thus we can characterize TIL as an extensional logic of hyperintensions.[11] The sense of an empirical sentence is an algorithmically structured *construction* of the proposition denoted by the sentence. The denoted proposition is a flat, or unstructured, mapping with domain in a logical space of possible worlds. Our motive for working 'top-down' has to do with anti-contextualism: any given unambiguous term or expression (even one involving indexicals or anaphoric pronouns) expresses the same construction as its sense whatever sort of context the term or expression is embedded within. And the meaning of an expression determines the respective denoted entity (if any), but not vice versa. The denoted entities are (possibly 0-ary) functions understood as set-theoretical mappings. Thus we strictly distinguish between a procedure (construction) and its product (here, a constructed function), and between a function and its value. What makes TIL suitable for the job of disambiguation is the fact that the theory construes the semantic properties of the sense and denotation relations as remaining invariant across different sorts of linguistic contexts.[12] Thus logical analysis disambiguates ambiguous expressions in such a way that an ambiguous expression is furnished with more than one context-invariant meaning that is TIL construction. However, *logical* analysis cannot dictate *which* disambiguation is the intended one. It falls to *pragmatics* to select the intended one.

3.1 Semantic foundations of TIL

The context-invariant semantics of TIL is obtained by universalizing Frege's reference-shifting semantics custom-made for 'indirect' contexts.[13] The upshot is that it becomes trivially true that all contexts are transparent, in the sense that pairs of terms that are co-denoting outside an indirect context remain co-denoting inside an indirect context and vice versa. In particular, definite descriptions that only contingently describe the same individual never qualify as co-denoting.[14] Our term for the extra-semantic, factual relation of contingently describing the same entity is '*reference*', whereas '*denotation*' stands for the intra-semantic, pre-factual relation between two words that pick out the same entity at the same world/time-pairs.

The syntax of TIL is Church's (higher-order) typed λ-calculus, but with the all-important difference that the syntax has been assigned a *procedural* (as opposed to denotational) semantics. Thus, abstraction transforms into the molecular procedure of forming a function, application into the molecular procedure of applying a function to an argument, and variables into atomic procedures for arriving at their values. Furthermore, TIL constructions represent our interpretation of Frege's notion of *Sinn* (with the exception that constructions are not truth-bearers; instead some present either truth-values or truth-conditions) and are kindred to Church's notion of *concept*. Constructions are linguistic

---

[11] For the most recent application, see (Duží & Jespersen, fothcoming).

[12] *Indexicals* being the only exception: while the sense of an indexical remains constant, its denotation varies in keeping with its contextual embedding. See (Duží et al., 2010a, § 3.4).

[13] See (Frege, 1892).

[14] See Definition 7.

senses as well as modes of presentation of objects and are our hyperintensions. While the Frege-Church connection makes it obvious that constructions are not formulae, it is crucial to emphasize that constructions are not functions(-in-extension), either. They might be explicated as Church's 'functions-in-intension', but we do not use the term 'function-in-intension', because Church did no define it (he only characterized functions-in-intension as rules for presenting functions-in-extension). Rather, technically speaking, some constructions are modes of presentation of functions, including 0-place functions such as individuals and truth-values, and the rest are modes of presentation of other constructions. Thus, with constructions of constructions, constructions of functions, functions, and functional values in our stratified ontology, we need to keep track of the traffic between multiple logical strata. The ramified type hierarchy does just that. What is important about this traffic is, first of all, that constructions may themselves figure as functional arguments or values. Thus we consequently need constructions of one order higher in order to present those being arguments or values of functions. With both hyperintensions and possible-world intensions in its ontology, TIL has no trouble assigning either hyperintensions or intensions to variables as their values. However, the technical challenge of operating on constructions requires two (occasionally three) interrelated, non-standard devices. The first is *Trivialization*, which is an atomic construction, whose only constituent part is itself. The second is the function *Sub* (for 'substitution'). (The third is the function *Tr* (for 'Trivialization'), which takes an object to its Trivialization.) We say that Trivialization is *used* to *mention* other constructions.[15] The point of mentioning a construction is to make it, rather than what it presents, a functional argument. Hence for a construction to be mentioned is for it to be Trivialized; in this way the context is raised up to a hyperintensional level.

Our neo-Fregean semantic schema, which applies to all contexts, is this triangulation:

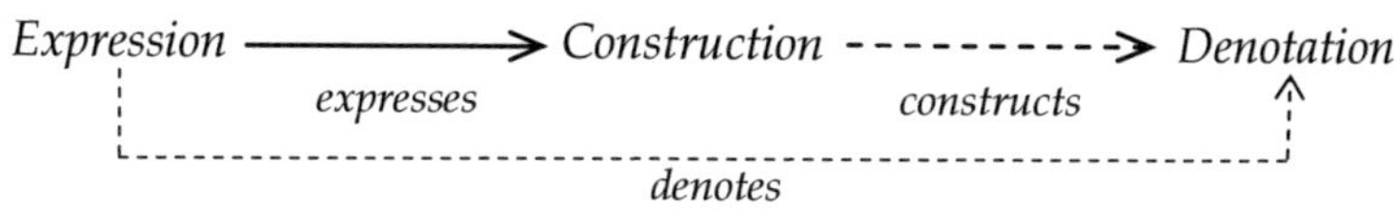

Fig. 1. TIL semantic schema.

The most important relation in this schema is between an expression and its meaning, i.e., a construction. Once *constructions* have been defined, we can logically examine them; we can investigate *a priori* what (if anything) a construction constructs and what is entailed by it. Thus meanings/constructions are semantically primary, denotations secondary, because an expression denotes an object (if any) *via* its meaning that is a construction *expressed* by the expression. Once a construction is explicitly given as a result of logical analysis, the entity (if any) it constructs is already implicitly given. As a limiting case, the logical analysis may reveal that the construction fails to construct anything by being *improper*.

[15] The use/mention distinction normally applies only to *words*; in TIL it applies to the *meanings* of words (i.e., constructions). See (Duží, et al., 2010a, §2.6). In theory, a construction may be mentioned by another construction than Trivialization; but in this chapter we limit ourselves to Trivialization.

3.2 Logical foundations of TIL

In this section we set out the definitions of *first-order types* (regimented by a simple type theory), *constructions*, and *higher-order types* (regimented by a ramified type hierarchy), which taken together form the nucleus of TIL, accompanied by some auxiliary definitions.

The type of first-order object includes all objects that are not constructions. Therefore, it includes not only the standard objects of individuals, truth-values, sets, etc., but also functions defined on possible worlds (i.e., the intensions germane to possible-world semantics). Sets, for their part, are always characteristic functions and insofar extensional entities. But the domain of a set may be typed over higher-order objects, in which case the relevant set is itself a higher-order object. Similarly for other functions, including relations, with domain or range in constructions. That is, whenever constructions are involved, we find ourselves in the ramified type hierarchy.[16] The definition of the ramified hierarchy of types decomposes into three parts: firstly, simple types of order 1; secondly, constructions of order n; thirdly, types of order $n + 1$.

Definition 1 (*types of order 1*). Let B be a *base*, where a base is a collection of pair-wise disjoint, non-empty sets. Then:

i. Every member of B is an elementary *type of order 1 over B*.
ii. Let α, β_1, ..., β_m ($m > 0$) be types of order 1 over B. Then the collection $(\alpha\ \beta_1 \ldots \beta_m)$ of all m-ary partial mappings from $\beta_1 \times \ldots \times \beta_m$ into α is a functional *type of order 1 over B*.

Nothing is a *type of order 1 over B* unless it so follows from (i) and (ii).

Definition 2 (*construction*)

i. The *Variable* x is a *construction* that constructs an object X of the respective type dependently on a valuation v; x v-constructs X.
ii. *Trivialization*: Where X is an object whatsoever (an extension, an intension or a *construction*), ${}^0X$ is the *construction Trivialization*. It constructs X without any change.
iii. The *Composition* $[X\ Y_1 \ldots Y_m]$ is the following *construction*. If X *v-constructs* a function f of a type $(\alpha\beta_1 \ldots \beta_m)$, and Y_1, ..., Y_m *v-construct* entities B_1, ..., B_m of types β_1, ..., β_m, respectively, then the *Composition* $[X\ Y_1 \ldots Y_m]$ *v-constructs* the value (an entity, if any, of type α) of f on the tuple-argument $\langle B_1, \ldots, B_m \rangle$. Otherwise the *Composition* $[X\ Y_1 \ldots Y_m]$ does not *v-construct* anything and so is *v-improper*.
iv. The *Closure* $[\lambda x_1 \ldots x_m\ Y]$ is the following *construction*. Let x_1, x_2, ..., x_m be pair-wise distinct variables v-constructing entities of types β_1, ..., β_m and Y a construction v-constructing an α-entity. Then $[\lambda x_1 \ldots x_m\ Y]$ is the *construction* λ-*Closure* (or *Closure*). It *v-constructs* the following function f of the type $(\alpha\beta_1 \ldots \beta_m)$. Let $v(B_1/x_1, \ldots, B_m/x_m)$ be a valuation identical with v at least up to assigning objects B_1/β_1, ..., B_m/β_m to variables x_1, ..., x_m. If Y is $v(B_1/x_1, \ldots, B_m/x_m)$-improper (see iii), then f is undefined on the argument $\langle B_1, \ldots, B_m \rangle$. Otherwise the value of f on $\langle B_1, \ldots, B_m \rangle$ is the α-entity $v(B_1/x_1, \ldots, B_m/x_m)$-constructed by Y.

[16] Attempting to type constructions within the simple type theory (as though constructions were first-order objects) is the source of some misconceptions of TIL found in (Daley 2010).

v. The *Single Execution* ^1X is the *construction* that either v-constructs the entity v-constructed by X or, if X v-constructs nothing, is *v-improper* (yielding nothing relative to v).
vi. The *Double Execution* ^2X is the following *construction*. Where X is any entity, the *Double Execution* ^2X is *v-improper* (yielding nothing relative to v) if X is not itself a construction, or if X does not v-construct a construction, or if X v-constructs a v-improper construction. Otherwise, let X v-construct a construction Y and Y v-construct an entity Z: then ^2X v-constructs Z.

Nothing is a *construction*, unless it so follows from (i) through (vi).

Definition 3 (ramified hierarchy of types)

$\mathbf{T_1}$ (*types of order 1*). See Definition 1.

$\mathbf{C_n}$ (*constructions of order n*)

i. Let x be a variable ranging over a type of order n. Then x is a *construction of order n over B*.
ii. Let X be a member of a type of order n. Then ^0X, ^1X, ^2X are *constructions of order n over B*.
iii. Let X, $X_1,\ldots, X_m$ $(m > 0)$ be constructions of order n over B. Then $[X\ X_1\ldots\ X_m]$ is a *construction of order n over B*.
iv. Let $x_1,\ldots x_m$, X $(m > 0)$ be constructions of order n over B. Then $[\lambda x_1\ldots x_m\ X]$ is a *construction of order n over B*.
v. Nothing is a *construction of order n over B* unless it so follows from $\mathbf{C}_n$ (i)-(iv).

$\mathbf{T}_{n+1}$ (*types of order n + 1*). Let $*_n$ be the collection of all constructions of order n over B. Then

i. $*_n$ and every type of order n are *types of order n + 1*.
ii. If $0 < m$ and α, $\beta_1,\ldots,\beta_m$ are types of order $n + 1$ over B, then $(\alpha\ \beta_1\ \ldots\ \beta_m)$ (see T_1 ii)) is a *type of order n + 1 over B*.

Nothing is a *type of order n + 1 over B* unless it so follows from $\mathbf{T}_{n+1}$ (i) and (ii).

Remark. For the purposes of natural-language analysis, we are currently assuming the following base of ground types, which is part of the ontological commitments of TIL:

- o: the set of truth-values {**T**, **F**};
- ι: the set of individuals (the universe of discourse);
- τ: the set of real numbers (doubling as discrete times);
- ω: the set of logically possible worlds (the logical space).

Empirical languages incorporate an element of *contingency*, because they denote *empirical conditions* that may or may not be satisfied at some world/time pair of evaluation. Non-empirical languages (in particular the language of mathematics) have no need for an additional category of expressions for empirical conditions. We model these empirical conditions as *possible-world intensions.* They are entities of type $(\beta\omega)$: mappings from possible worlds to an arbitrary type β. The type β is frequently the type of the *chronology* of α-objects, i.e., a mapping of type $(\alpha\tau)$. Thus α-intensions are frequently functions of type $((\alpha\tau)\omega)$, abbreviated as '$\alpha_{\tau\omega}$'. *Extensional entities* are entities of a type α where $\alpha \neq (\beta\omega)$ for any type β. *Examples* of frequently used intensions are: *propositions* of type $o_{\tau\omega}$, *properties of individuals* of type $(o\iota)_{\tau\omega}$, binary *relations-in-intension* between individuals of type $(o\iota\iota)_{\tau\omega}$, *individual offices/roles* of type $\iota_{\tau\omega}$. Our *explicit intensionalization and temporalization* enables us to encode constructions of possible-world intensions, by means of terms for possible-world variables and times, directly in the logical syntax. Where variable w ranges over possible worlds (type ω) and t over times (type τ), the following logical form essentially characterizes the logical syntax of any empirical language: $\lambda w \lambda t\ [\ldots w \ldots . t \ldots]$. Where α is the type of the object v-constructed by $[\ldots w \ldots . t \ldots]$, by abstracting over the values of variables w and t we construct a function from worlds to a partial function from times to α, that is a function of type $((\alpha\tau)\omega)$, or '$\alpha_{\tau\omega}$' for short.

Logical objects like *truth-functions* and *quantifiers* are extensional: $\wedge$ (conjunction), $\vee$ (disjunction) and $\supset$ (implication) of type (ooo), and $\neg$ (negation) of type (oo). The *quantifiers* $\forall^{\alpha}$, $\exists^{\alpha}$ are type-theoretically polymorphous functions of type $(o(o\alpha))$, for an arbitrary type α, defined as follows. The *universal quantifier* $\forall^{\alpha}$ is a function that associates a class A of α-elements with **T** if A contains all elements of the type α, otherwise with **F**. The *existential quantifier* $\exists^{\alpha}$ is a function that associates a class A of α-elements with **T** if A is a non-empty class, otherwise with **F**. Another kind of partial polymorphic function we need is the *Singularizer* I^{α} of type $(\alpha(o\alpha))$. A singularizer is a function that associates a singleton S with the only member of S, and is otherwise (i.e. if S is an empty set or a multi-element set) undefined.

Below all type indications will be provided outside the formulae in order not to clutter the notation. Furthermore, 'X/α' means that an object X is (a member) of type α. '$X \rightarrow_v \alpha$' means that the type of the object v-constructed by X is α. We write '$X \rightarrow \alpha$' if what is v-constructed does not depend on a valuation v. This holds throughout: $w \rightarrow_v \omega$ and $t \rightarrow_v \tau$. If $C \rightarrow_v \alpha_{\tau\omega}$ then the frequently used Composition $[[C\ w]\ t]$, which is the intensional descent (a.k.a. extensionalization) of the α-intension v-constructed by C, will be encoded as 'C_{wt}'. When using constructions of truth-functions, we often omit Trivialisation and use infix notation to conform to standard notation in the interest of better readability. Also when using constructions of identities of α-entities, $=_{\alpha}/(o\alpha\alpha)$, we omit Trivialization, the type subscript, and use infix notion when no confusion can arise. For instance, instead of

$$`[{}^0\!\supset [{}^0\!=_{\iota}\ a\ b]\ [{}^0\!=_{((o\tau)\omega)}\ \lambda w \lambda t\ [P_{wt}\ a]\ \lambda w \lambda t\ [P_{wt}\ b]]]'$$

where $=_{\iota}/(o\iota\iota)$ is the identity of individuals and $=_{((o\tau)\omega)}/(oo_{\tau\omega}o_{\tau\omega})$ the identity of propositions; a, b constructing objects of type ι, P objects of type $(o\iota)_{\tau\omega}$, we write

$$`[[a = b] \supset [\lambda w \lambda t\ [P_{wt}\ a] = \lambda w \lambda t\ [P_{wt}\ b]]]'.$$

We invariably furnish expressions with procedural structured meanings, which are explicated as TIL constructions. The analysis of an unambiguous sentence thus consists in discovering the logical construction encoded by a given sentence. The *TIL method of analysis* consists of three steps:

1. *Type-theoretical analysis*, i.e., assigning types to the objects that receive mention in the analysed sentence.
2. *Type-theoretical synthesis*, i.e., combining the constructions of the objects *ad* (1) in order to construct the proposition of type $o_{\tau\omega}$ denoted by the whole sentence.
3. *Type-theoretical checking*, i.e. checking whether the proposed analysans is type-theoretically coherent.

To illustrate the method, we analyse the notorious sentence "The King of France is bald" in the Strawsonian way. The sentence talks about the office of the King of France (topic) ascribing to the individual (if any) that occupies this office the property of being bald (focus). Thus it is presupposed that the King of France exist, i.e., that the office be occupied. If it is not, then the proposition denoted by the sentence has no truth-value.[17] This fact has to be revealed by our analysis. Here is how.

Ad (1) $King\_of/(\iota\iota)_{\tau\omega}$: an empirical function that dependently on $\langle w, t\rangle$-pairs assigns to one individual (a country) another individual (its king); $France/\iota$; $King\_of\_France/\iota_{\tau\omega}$; $Bald/(o\iota)_{\tau\omega}$.

Ad (2) and (3). For the sake of simplicity, I will demonstrate the steps (2) and (3) simultaneously. In the second step we combine the *constructions* of the objects *ad (1)* in order to construct the proposition (of type $o_{\tau\omega}$) denoted by the whole sentence. Since we intend to arrive at the *literal* analysis of the sentence, the objects denoted by the semantically simple expressions are constructed by their Trivialisations: $^0King\_of$, ^0France, ^0Bald. In order to construct the office *King_of_France*, we have to combine $^0King\_of$ and ^0France. The function *King_of* must be extensionalised first *via* the Composition $^0King\_of_{wt} \rightarrow_v (\iota\iota)$, and the result is then applied to *France*; we get $[^0King\_of_{wt}\ ^0France] \rightarrow_v \iota$. Abstracting over the values of w and t we obtain the Closure that constructs the office: $\lambda w\lambda t\ [^0King\_of_{wt}\ ^0France] \rightarrow \iota_{\tau\omega}$. But the property of being bald cannot be ascribed to an individual office. Rather, it is ascribed to the individual (if any) occupying the office. Thus the office has to be subjected to intensional descent first: $\lambda w\lambda t\ [^0King\_of_{wt}\ ^0France]_{wt} \rightarrow_v \iota$. The property itself has to be extensionalised as well: $^0Bald_{wt}$. By Composing these two constructions, we obtain either a truth-value (**T** or **F**) or nothing, according as the King of France is, or is not, bald, or does not exist, respectively. Finally, by abstracting over the values of the variables w and t, we construct the proposition:

$$\lambda w\lambda t\ [^0Bald_{wt}\ \lambda w\lambda t\ [^0King\_of_{wt}\ ^0France]_{wt}]$$

Gloss. In *any* world (λw) at *any* time (λt) do this. First, find out who is the King of France: $[^0King\_of_{wt}\ ^0France]$. If there is none, then terminate with a truth-value gap because the Composition $[^0King\_of_{wt}\ ^0France]$ is v-improper. Otherwise, check whether the so obtained individual has the property of being bald: $[^0Bald_{wt}\ [^0King\_of_{wt}\ ^0France]]$. If he is, then **T**, otherwise **F**. So much for the method of analysis and the semantic schema of the logic of TIL.

4. Definite descriptions: Strawsonian or Russellian?

Now I am going to propose a solution to the Strawson-Russell standoff. In other words, I am going to analyse the phenomena of presupposition and entailment connected with using definite descriptions with supposition *de dicto* or *de re*, and I will show how the topic-focus distinction determines which of the two cases applies.

[17] On our approach this does not mean that the sentence is meaningless. The sentence has a sense, namely an instruction of how to evaluate in any possible world w at any time t its truth-conditions. (Such instructions are encoded in our language of constructions.) Only if we evaluate these conditions in such a state-of-affairs where there is no King of France does the process of evaluation yield a truth-value gap.

4.1 Topic-focus ambiguity

When used in a communicative act, a sentence communicates something (the focus F) about something (the topic T). Thus the schematic structure of a sentence is $F(T)$. The topic T of a sentence S is often associated with a presupposition P of S such that P is entailed both by S and *non-S*. On the other hand, the clause in the focus usually occasions a mere entailment of some P by S. To give an example, consider the sentence "Our defeat was caused by John".[18] There are two possible readings of this sentence. Taken one way, the sentence is about our defeat, conveying the snippet of information that it was caused by John. In such a situation the sentence is associated with the presupposition that we were defeated. Indeed, the negated form of the sentence, "Our defeat was not caused by John", also implies that we were defeated. Thus 'our defeat' is the topic and 'was caused by John' the focus clause. Taken the other way, the sentence is about the topic John, ascribing to him the property that he caused our defeat (focus). Now the scenario of truly asserting the negated sentence can be, for instance, the following. Though it is true that John has a reputation for being rather a bad player, Paul was in excellent shape and so we won. Or, another scenario is thinkable. We were defeated, only not because of John but because the whole team performed badly. Hence, our being defeated is not presupposed by this reading, it is only entailed.

Schematically, if $\models$ is the relation of entailment, then the logical difference between a mere entailment and a presupposition is this:

P is a *presupposition* of S: $(S \models P)$ and $(non\text{-}S \models P)$

Corollary: If P is not true, then *neither S nor non-S* is true. Hence, S has no truth-value.

P is only *entailed* by S: $(S \models P)$ and neither $(non\text{-}S \models P)$ nor $(non\text{-}S \models non\text{-}P)$

Corollary: If S is not true, then we cannot deduce anything about the truth-value of P.

More precisely, the entailment relation obtains between hyperpropositions P, S; i.e., the *meaning* of P is analytically entailed or presupposed by the *meaning* of S. Thus $\models/((o*_n*_n)$ is defined as follows. Let C^S, C^P be constructions assigned to sentences S, P, respectively, as their meanings. Then *S entails P* ($C^S \models C^P$) iff the following holds:[19]

$$\forall w \forall t\ [[{}^0True_{wt}\ C^S] \supset [{}^0True_{wt}\ C^P]]$$

Since we work with properly *partial* functions, we need to apply the propositional property $True/(o o_{\tau\omega})_{\tau\omega}$, which returns **T** for those $\langle w, t\rangle$-pairs at which the argument proposition is true, and **F** in all the remaining cases. There are two other propositional properties: *False* and *Undef*, both of type $(o o_{\tau\omega})_{\tau\omega}$. The three properties are defined as follows. Let P be a propositional construction ($P/*_n \rightarrow o_{\tau\omega}$). Then

$[{}^0True_{wt}\ P]$ v-constructs the truth-value **T** iff P_{wt} v-constructs **T**, otherwise **F**.
$[{}^0False_{wt}\ P]$ v-constructs the truth-value **T** iff $[\neg P_{wt}]$ v-constructs **T**, otherwise **F**.
$[{}^0Undef_{wt}\ P]$ v-constructs the truth-value **T** iff

$$[\neg[{}^0True_{wt}\ P] \wedge \neg[{}^0False_{wt}\ P]]\ v\text{-constructs } \mathbf{T}, \text{ otherwise } \mathbf{F}.$$

[18] This and some other examples were taken from Hajičová (2008).
[19] For the general definition of entailment and the difference between analytical and logical entailment, see (Duží 2010).

Thus we have:

$$\neg[{}^0Undef_{wt}\ P] = [[{}^0True_{wt}\ P] \vee [{}^0False_{wt}\ P]]$$

$$\neg[{}^0True_{wt}\ P] = [[{}^0False_{wt}\ P] \vee [{}^0Undef_{wt}\ P]]$$

$$\neg[{}^0False_{wt}\ P] = [[{}^0True_{wt}\ P] \vee [{}^0Undef_{wt}\ P]]$$

Hence, though we work with truth-value gaps, we do not work with a third truth-value, and our logic is in this weak sense bivalent.

4.2 The King of France revisited

Above we analysed the sentence "The King of France is bald" on its perhaps most natural reading as predicating the property of being bald (the focus) of the individual (if any) that is the present King of France (the topic). Yet there is another, albeit less natural reading of the sentence. Imagine that the sentence is uttered in a situation when we are talking about baldness, and somebody asks "Who is bald?" The answer might be "Well, among those who are bald there is the present King of France". If you got such an answer, you would most probably protest, "This cannot be true, for there is no King of France now". On such a reading the sentence is about baldness (topic) claiming that this property is instantiated, among others, by the King of France *(focus)*. Since there are no rigorous grammatical rules in English to distinguish between the two variants, the input of our *logical* analysis is the result of a *linguistic* analysis, where the topic and focus of a sentence are made explicit.[20] In this chapter I will mark the topic clause in italics. The two readings of the above sentence are:

(S) "*The King of France* is bald" (Strawsonian) and
(R) "The King of France is *bald*" (Russellian).

The analysis of (S) is as above:

$$\lambda w\lambda t\ [{}^0Bald_{wt}\ \lambda w\lambda t\ [{}^0King\_of_{wt}\ {}^0France]_{wt}]$$

The meaning of 'the King of France', *viz.* $\lambda w\lambda t\ [{}^0King\_of_{wt}\ {}^0France]$, occurs in (S) with *de re* supposition, because the object of predication is the unique *value* in a $\langle w, t\rangle$-pair of evaluation of the office rather than the office itself.[21] The following *two de re principles* are satisfied: the principle of *existential presupposition* and the principle of *substitution of co-referential* expressions. Thus the following arguments are valid (though not sound):

<u>*The King of France* is/is not bald</u>
The King of France exists

[20] For instance, the Prague linguistic school created The Prague Dependency Treebank for the Czech language, which contains a large amount of Czech texts with complex and interlink annotation on different levels. The tectogrammatical representation contains the semantic structure of sentences with topic-focus annotators. For details, see *http://ufal.mff.cuni.cz/pdt2.0/*.

[21] For details on *de dicto* vs. *de re* supposition, see (Duží *et al.*, 2010a), esp. §§ 1.5.2 and 2.6.2, and also (Duží 2004).

The King of France is bald
The King of France is Louis XVI
Louis XVI is bald

Here are the proofs.

(a) *existential presupposition*:

First, existence is here a property of an individual *office* rather than of some non-existing individual (whatever it might mean for an individual not to exist). Thus we have $Exist/(o\iota_{\tau\omega})_{\tau\omega}$. To prove the validity of the first argument, we define $Exist/(o\iota_{\tau\omega})_{\tau\omega}$ as the property of an office's being occupied at a given world/time pair:

$$^{0}Exist =_{of} \lambda w \lambda t\ \lambda c\ [^{0}\exists \lambda x\ [x =_{i} c_{wt}]],$$
$$\text{i.e. } [^{0}Exist_{wt}\ c] =_{o} [^{0}\exists \lambda x\ [x =_{i} c_{wt}]]$$

Types: $\exists/(o(o\iota))$: the class of non-empty classes of individuals; $c \rightarrow_{v} \iota_{\tau\omega}$; $x \rightarrow_{v} \iota$; $=_{o}/(ooo)$: the identity of truth-values; $=_{of}/(o(o\iota_{\tau\omega})_{\tau\omega}(o\iota_{\tau\omega})_{\tau\omega})$: the identity of properties of individual offices; $=_{i}/(o\iota\iota)$: the identity of individuals, $x \rightarrow_{v} \iota$. Now let $Louis/\iota$, $Empty/(o(o\iota))$ the singleton containing the empty set of individuals, and $Improper/(o*_{1})_{\tau\omega}$ the property of constructions of being v-improper at a given $\langle w, t\rangle$-pair, the other types as above. Then at any $\langle w, t\rangle$-pair the following proof steps are truth-preserving:

1)	$(\neg)[^{0}Bald_{wt}\ \lambda w\lambda t\ [^{0}King\_of_{wt}\ ^{0}France]_{wt}]$	Ø
2)	$\neg[^{0}Improper_{wt}\ ^{0}[\lambda w\lambda t\ [^{0}King\_of_{wt}\ ^{0}France]_{wt}]]$	by Def. 2, iii)
3)	$\neg[^{0}Empty\ \lambda x\ [x =_{i} [\lambda w\lambda t\ [^{0}King\_of_{wt}\ ^{0}France]]_{wt}]]$	from (2) by Def. 2, iv)
4)	$[^{0}\exists \lambda x\ [x =_{i} [\lambda w\lambda t\ [^{0}King\_of_{wt}\ ^{0}France]]_{wt}]]$	EG
7)	$[^{0}Exist_{wt}\ [\lambda w\lambda t\ [^{0}King\_of_{wt}\ ^{0}France]]]$	by def. of *Exist.*

(b) *substitution*:

1)	$[^{0}Bald_{wt}\ \lambda w\lambda t\ [^{0}King\_of_{wt}\ ^{0}France]_{wt}]$	Ø
2)	$[^{0}Louis =_{i} \lambda w\lambda t\ [^{0}King\_of_{wt}\ ^{0}France]_{wt}]$	Ø
3)	$[^{0}Bald_{wt}\ ^{0}Louis]$	substitution of identicals

As explained above, the sentence (R) is not associated with the presupposition that the present King of France exist, because 'the King of France' occurs now in the focus clause. The truth-conditions of the Russellian "The King of France is *bald*" are these:

- True, if among those who are bald there is the King of France
- False, if among those who are bald there is no King of France (either because the present King of France does not exist or because the King of France is not bald).

Thus the two readings (S) and (R) have different truth-conditions, and they are not equivalent, albeit they are co-entailing. The reason is this. Trivially, a valid argument is *truth-preserving from premises to conclusion*. However, due to partiality, the entailment relation may fail to be *falsity-preserving from conclusion to premises*. As a consequence, if A, B are constructions of propositions such that $A \models B$ and $B \models A$, then A, B are not necessarily equivalent in the sense of constructing the same proposition. The propositions they construct may not be identical, though the propositions take the truth-value **T** at exactly the same world/times, because they may differ in such a way that at some $\langle w, t\rangle$-pair(s) one takes the value **F** while the other is undefined. The pair of meanings of (S) and (R) is an example of such co-entailing, yet non-equivalent hyperpropositions. If the value of the proposition constructed by the meaning of (S) is **T** then so is the value of the proposition constructed by the meaning of (R), and *vice versa*. But, for instance, in the actual world now the proposition constructed by (S) has *no truth-value* whereas the proposition constructed by (R) takes value **F**.

Now I am going to analyse (R). Russell argued for his theory in (1905, p. 3):

> The evidence for the above theory is derived from the difficulties which seem unavoidable if we regard denoting phrases as standing for genuine constituents of the propositions in whose verbal expressions they occur. Of the possible theories which admit such constituents the simplest is that of Meinong. This theory regards any grammatically correct denoting phrase as standing for an object. Thus 'the present King of France', 'the round square', etc., are supposed to be genuine objects. It is admitted that such objects do not subsist, but nevertheless they are supposed to be objects. This is in itself a difficult view; but the chief objection is that such objects, admittedly, are apt to infringe the law of contradiction. It is contended, for example, that the existent present King of France exists, and also does not exist; that the round square is round, and also not round, etc. But this is intolerable; and if any theory can be found to avoid this result, it is surely to be preferred.

We have such a theory at hand, *viz.* TIL. Moreover, TIL makes it possible to avoid the other objections against Russell's analysis as well. Russellian rephrasing of the sentence "The King of France is *bald*" is this: "There is a unique individual such that he is the King of France and he is bald". This sentence expresses the construction

(R^*) $\lambda w \lambda t\, [{}^0\exists \lambda x\, [x =_i [\lambda w \lambda t\, [{}^0King\_of_{wt}\, {}^0France]_{wt}] \wedge [{}^0Bald_{wt}\, x]]]$.[22]

TIL analysis of the 'Russellian rephrasing' does not deprive 'the King of France' of its meaning. The meaning is invariably, in all contexts, the Closure $\lambda w \lambda t\, [{}^0King\_of_{wt}\, {}^0France]$. Thus the second objection to the Russellian analysis is not pertinent here. Moreover, even the third objection is irrelevant, because in (R^*) $\lambda w \lambda t\, [{}^0King\_of_{wt}\, {}^0France]$ occurs intensionally unlike in the analysis of (S) where it occurs extensionally.[23] The existential quantifier $\exists$ applies to *sets* of individuals rather than a particular individual. The proposition constructed by (R^*) is true if the *set* of individuals who are bald contains the individual who occupies the office of King of France, otherwise it is simply false. The truth conditions specified by (R^*) are Russellian. Thus we might be content with (R^*) as an adequate analysis of the Russellian reading (R). Yet we should not be. The reason is this. Russell's analysis has another defect; it does not comply with *Carnap's principle of subject-matter*, which states, roughly, that only those entities that receive mention in a sentence can become constituents of its meaning.[24] In

---

[22] Note that in TIL we do not need the construction corresponding to $\forall y\, (Fy \supset x{=}y)$ specifying the uniqueness of the King of France, because it is inherent in the meaning of 'the King of France'. This holds also in a language like Czech, which lacks grammatical articles. The meaning of descriptions 'the King of France', 'král Francie' is a construction of an individual office of type $\iota_{\tau\omega}$ occupied in each $\langle w, t\rangle$-pair by at most one individual.

[23] For the definition of extensional, intensional and hyperintensional occurrence of a construction, see (Duží et al., 2010a, § 2.6).

[24] See (Carnap 1947, §24.2, §26).

other words, (R^*) is not the literal analysis of the sentence "The King of France is *bald*"., because existence and conjunction do not receive mention in the sentence. Russell did avoid the intolerable result that the King of France both does and does not exist, but the price he paid is too high, because his rephrasing of the sentence is too loose a reformulation of it. TIL, as a hyperintensional, typed *partial* λ-calculus, is in a much better position to solve the problem.

From the logical point of view, the two readings differ in the way their respective *negated* form is obtained. Whereas the Stawsonian negated form is "The *King of France* is *not* bald", which obviously lacks a truth-value if the King of France does not exist, the Russellian negated form is "It is not true that the King of France is bald", which is true at those $\langle w, t\rangle$-pairs where the office is not occupied. Thus in the Strawsonian case the property of not being bald is ascribed to the individual, if any, that occupies the royal office. The meaning of 'the King of France' occurs with *de re* supposition, as we have seen above. On the other hand, in the Russellian case the property of not being true is ascribed to the whole proposition that the King is bald, and thus (the same meaning of) the description 'the King of France' occurs with *de dicto* supposition. Hence we simply ascribe the property of being or not being true to the whole proposition. To this end we apply the propositional property $True/(o o_{\tau\omega})_{\tau\omega}$ defined above. Now the analysis of the sentence (R) is this construction:

(R') $\lambda w \lambda t\ [{}^0True_{wt}\ \lambda w \lambda t\ [{}^0Bald_{wt}\ \lambda w \lambda t\ [{}^0King\_of_{wt}\ {}^0France]_{wt}]]$

Neither (R') nor its negation

(R'_neg) $\lambda w \lambda t\ \neg[{}^0True_{wt}\ \lambda w \lambda t\ [{}^0Bald_{wt}\ \lambda w \lambda t\ [{}^0King\_of_{wt}\ {}^0France]_{wt}]]$

entail that the King of France exists, which is just as it should be. (R'_neg) constructs the proposition *non-P* that takes the truth-value **T** if the proposition that the King of France is bald takes the value **F** (because the King of France is not bald) or is undefined (because the King of France does not exist).

Consider now another group of sample sentences:

(1) "*The King of France* visited London yesterday."
(1′) "*The King of France* did not visit London yesterday."

The sentences (1) and (1′) talk about the (actual and current) King of France (the topic), ascribing to him the property of (not) having visited London yesterday (the focus). Thus both sentences share the presupposition that the King of France actually exist *now*. If this presupposition fails to be satisfied, then neither of the propositions expressed by (1) and (1′) has a truth-value. The situation is different in the case of sentences (2) and (2′):

(2) "*London* was visited by the King of France yesterday."
(2′) "*London* was not visited by the King of France yesterday."

Now the property (the focus) of having been visited by the King of France yesterday is predicated of London (the topic). The existence of the King of France (now) is presupposed neither by (2) nor by (2′). The sentences can be read as "Among the visitors of London yesterday was (not) the King of France". The existence of the King of France *yesterday* is only *entailed* by (2) and *not presupposed*.[25] Our analyses respect these conditions. Let *Yesterday*/$((o\tau)\tau)$ be the function that associates a given time *t* with the time interval that is yesterday with respect to *t*; *Visit*/$(o\iota\iota)_{\tau\omega}$; *King_of*/$(\iota\iota)_{\tau\omega}$; *France*/$\iota$; $\exists^{\tau}/(o(o\tau))$: the existential quantifier that assigns to a given set of times the truth-value **T** if the set is non-empty, otherwise **F**. In what follows I will use an abbreviated notation without Trivialisation, writing '$\exists x\ A$' instead of '$[{}^{0}\exists^{\tau}\lambda x\ A]$', when no confusion can arise. The analyses of sentences (1), (1′) come down to

(1*) $\lambda w\lambda t\ [\lambda x\ \exists t'[[[{}^{0}Yesterday\ t]\ t'] \wedge [{}^{0}Visit_{wt'}\ x\ {}^{0}London]]\ \lambda w\lambda t\ [{}^{0}King\_of_{wt}\ {}^{0}France]_{wt}]$

(1′*) $\lambda w\lambda t\ [\lambda x\ [\exists t'[[[{}^{0}Yesterday\ t]\ t'] \wedge \neg[{}^{0}Visit_{wt'}\ x\ {}^{0}London]]\ \lambda w\lambda t\ [{}^{0}King\_of_{wt}\ {}^{0}France]_{wt}]$

At such a $\langle w, t\rangle$-pair at which the King of France does not exist neither of the propositions constructed by (1*) and (1′*) has a truth-value, because the extensionalization of the office yields no individual, the Composition $\lambda w\lambda t\ [{}^{0}King\_of_{wt}\ {}^{0}France]_{wt}$ being v-improper. We have the Strawsonian case, the meaning of 'King of France' occurring with *de re* supposition, and the King's existence being presupposed. On the other hand, the sentences (2), (2′) express

(2*) $\lambda w\lambda t\ \exists t'[[[{}^{0}Yesterday\ t]\ t'] \wedge [{}^{0}Visit_{wt'}\ \lambda w\lambda t\ [{}^{0}King\_of_{wt}\ {}^{0}France]_{wt'}\ {}^{0}London]]$

(2′*) $\lambda w\lambda t\ \exists t'[[[{}^{0}Yesterday\ t]\ t'] \wedge \neg[{}^{0}Visit_{wt'}\ \lambda w\lambda t\ [{}^{0}King\_of_{wt}\ {}^{0}France]_{wt'}\ {}^{0}London]]$

At such a $\langle w, t\rangle$-pair at which the proposition constructed by (2*) is true, the Composition $\exists t'[[[{}^{0}Yesterday\ t]\ t'] \wedge \lambda w\lambda t\ [{}^{0}King\_of_{wt}\ {}^{0}France]_{wt'}\ {}^{0}London]]$ v-constructs **T**. This means that the second conjunct v-constructs **T** as well and the Composition $\lambda w\lambda t\ [{}^{0}King\_of_{wt}\ {}^{0}France]_{wt'}$ is not v-improper. Thus the King of France *existed at some time t′* belonging to *yesterday*. On the other hand, if the King of France did not exist at any time yesterday, then the Composition $\lambda w\lambda t\ [{}^{0}King\_of_{wt}\ {}^{0}France]_{wt'}$ is v-improper for any t' belonging to yesterday and the time interval v-constructed by $\lambda t'[[[{}^{0}Yesterday\ t]\ t'] \wedge [{}^{0}Visit_{wt'}\ \lambda w\lambda t\ [{}^{0}King\_of_{wt}\ {}^{0}France]_{wt'}\ {}^{0}London]]$, as well as by $\lambda t'[[[{}^{0}Yesterday\ t]\ t'] \wedge \neg[{}^{0}Visit_{wt'}\ \lambda w\lambda t\ [{}^{0}King\_of_{wt}\ {}^{0}France]_{wt'}\ {}^{0}London]]$, is empty. The existential quantifier takes this interval to **F**. This is as it should be, because (2*) *only implies the existence* of the King of France *yesterday* but *does not presuppose* it. We have the Russellian case. The meaning of the definite description 'the King of France' occurs with *de dicto* supposition in (2) and (2′).[26]

5. Topic-focus ambivalence in general

Up until now we have utilised the singularity of definite descriptions like 'the King of France' that denote functions of type $\iota_{\tau\omega}$. If the King of France does not exist in some particular world *W* at some particular time *T*, the office is not occupied and the function does not have a value at $\langle W, T\rangle$. Due to the partiality of the office constructed by $\lambda w\lambda t\ [{}^{0}King\_of_{wt}\ {}^{0}France]$ and the principle of compositionality, the respective analyses construct purely partial propositions associated with some presupposition, as desired. Now I am going to generalize the topic-focus phenomenon to sentences containing general terms.

---

[25] Von Fintel (2004) does not take into account this reading and says that any sentence containing 'the King of France' comes with the presupposition that the King of France exist *now*. In my opinion, this is because he considers only the *neutral* reading, thus rejecting topic-focus ambiguities.

[26] More precisely, the meaning of 'the King of France' occurs with *de dicto* supposition with respect to the temporal parameter *t*.

To get started, let us analyse Strawson's example

(3) "All *John's children* are asleep."
(3') "All *John's children* are not asleep."

According to Strawson both (1) and (1') entail[27]

(4) John has children.

In other words, (4) is a presupposition of (3) and (3'). If each of John's children is asleep, then (3) is true and (3') false. If each of John's children is not asleep, then (3) is false and (3') is true. However, if John has no children, then (3) and (3') are neither true nor false. Note that applying a classical regimentation of (3) in the language of the first-order predicate logic (FOL), we get

$$``\forall x\, [JC(x) \supset S(x)]"$$

This formula is true under every interpretation assigning an empty set of individuals to the predicate *JC* ('is a child of John's'). In other words, FOL does not make it possible to render the truth-conditions of a sentence equipped with a presupposition, because FOL is a logic of *total* functions. We need to apply a richer logical system in order to express the instruction how to evaluate the truth-conditions of (3) in the way described above. By reformulating the above specification of the truth-conditions of (3) in a rather technical jargon of English, we get

"*If* John has children *then* check whether all his children are asleep,
else fail to produce a truth-value."

We now analyse the particular constituents of this instruction. As always, we start with assigning types to the objects that receive mention in the sentence: $Child\_of/((o\iota)\iota)_{\tau\omega}$: an empirical function that dependently on states-of-affairs assigns to an individual a set of individuals, its children; $John/\iota$; $Sleep/(o\iota)_{\tau\omega}$; $\exists/(o(o\iota))$; $All/((o(o\iota))(o\iota))$: a restricted general quantifier that assigns to a given set the set of all its supersets.

The presupposition that John have children receives the analysis

$$\lambda w \lambda t\, [^0\exists \lambda x\, [[^0Child\_of_{wt}\, ^0John]\, x]].$$

Now the literal analysis of the sentence "All John's children are asleep" on its *neutral* reading (that is, without existential presupposition), is best obtained by using the restricted quantifier *All*, because using a general quantifier $\forall$ would involve implication that does not receive mention in the sentence. Composing the quantifier with the set of John's children at the world/time pair of evaluation, $[^0All\, [^0Child\_of_{wt}\, ^0John]]$, we obtain the set of all supersets of John's children in w at t. The sentence claims that the population of those who are asleep, $^0Sleep_{wt}$, is one such superset:

$$\lambda w \lambda t\, [[^0All\, [^0Child\_of_{wt}\, ^0John]]\, ^0Sleep_{wt}].$$

The schematic analysis of sentence (3) on its topic-like reading that comes with the presupposition that John have children translates into this procedure:

[27] See (Strawson, 1952, in particular pp. 173ff.)

(3[s]) $\lambda w \lambda t$ [If [$^0\exists\lambda x$ [[$^0Child\_of_{wt}$ ^0John] x]] then [[^0All [$^0Child\_of_{wt}$ ^0John]] $^0Sleep_{wt}$] else Fail.

To finish the analysis, we must define the *if-then-else* function. This I am going to do in the next paragraph.

5.1 The *if-then-else* function

In a programming language the *if-then-else* conditional forces a program to perform different actions depending on whether the specified *condition* evaluates true or else false. This is always achieved by *selectively* altering the control flow based on the specified condition. For this reason, an analysis in terms of material implication, ⊃, or even 'exclusive *or*' as known from propositional logic, is not adequate. The reason is this. Since propositional logic is strictly compositional, *both* the 'then clause' *and* the 'else clause' are always evaluated. For instance, it might seem that the instruction expressed by "The only number n such that if 5 = 5 then n equals 1, else n equals the result of 1 divided by 0" would receive the analysis

$$[^0\mathrm{I}^\tau\ \lambda n\ [[[^05{=}^05] \supset [n{=}^01]] \wedge [\neg[^05{=}^05] \supset [n{=}[^0Div\ ^01\ ^00]]]]]$$

Types: $\mathrm{I}^\tau/(\tau(o\tau))$; $n \rightarrow_v \tau$; 0, 1, 5/τ; $Div/(\tau\tau\tau)$: the division function.

But the output of the above procedure should be the number 1 because the *else* clause is never executed. However, due to the strict principle of compositionality that TIL observes, the above analysis fails to produce anything, the construction being improper. For, the Composition [^0Div ^{01} ^{00}] does not produce anything: it is improper because the division function takes no value at the argument ⟨1, 0⟩. Thus [n = [^0Div ^{01} ^{00}]] is v-improper for any valuation v, because the identity relation = does not receive a second argument, and so any other Composition containing the improper Composition [^0Div ^{01} ^{00}] as a constituent also comes out v-improper. The underlying principle is that partiality is being strictly propagated up. This is the reason why the *if-then-else* connective is often said to denote a *non-strict* function not complying with the principle of compositionality. However, as I wish to argue, there is no cogent reason to settle for non-compositionality. I suggest applying a mechanism known in computer science as *lazy evaluation*. As we have seen, the *procedural* semantics of TIL operates smoothly even at the hyperintensional level of constructions. Thus it enables us to specify a definition of *if-then-else* that meets the compositionality constraint. The analysis of

"If P then C, else D"

reveals a procedure that decomposes into two phases. First, on the basis of the condition P, select one of C, D as the procedure to be executed. Second, execute the selected procedure. The first phase, *viz.* selection, is realized by the Composition

$$[^0\mathrm{I}^*\ \lambda c\ [[P \supset [c = {}^0C]] \wedge [\neg P \supset [c = {}^0D]]]]$$

Types: $P \rightarrow_v o$ (the condition of the choice between the execution of C or of D); C, $D/*_n$; variable $c \rightarrow_v *_n$; $\mathrm{I}^*/(*_n(o*_n))$: the singularizer.

The Composition $[[P \supset [c{=}^0C]] \wedge [\neg P \supset [c{=}^0D]]]$ v-constructs **T** in two cases. If P v-constructs **T** then the variable c receives as its value the *construction* C, and if P v-constructs **F** then the variable c receives the *construction* D as its value. In either case the set v-constructed by

$\lambda c\ [[P \supset [c={}^0C]] \wedge [\neg P \supset [c={}^0D]]]$ is a singleton whose element is a construction. Applying I* to this set returns as its value the only member of the set, i.e. either C or D.[28]

Second, the chosen construction c is executed. To execute it we apply Double Execution; see Def. 2, vi). As a result, the schematic analysis of "If P then C, else D" turns out to be

(*) $\quad {}^2[{}^0\mathrm{I}^*\ \lambda c\ [[P \supset [c={}^0C]] \wedge [\neg P \supset [c={}^0D]]]]$

Note that the evaluation of the first phase does not involve the execution of either of C or D. In this phase these constructions figure only as arguments of other functions. In other words, we operate at hyperintensional level. The second phase of execution turns the level down to intensional or extensional one. Thus we define:

Definition 4 (*If-then-else, if-then-else-fail*). Let $p/*_n \rightarrow_v o$; $c, d_1, d_2/*_{n+1} \rightarrow *_n$; ${}^2c, {}^2d_1, {}^2d_2 \rightarrow_v \alpha$. Then the polymorphic functions *if-then-else* and *if-then-else-fail* of types $(\alpha o *_n *_n)$, $(\alpha o *_n)$, respectively, are defined as follows:

$${}^0\mathit{If\text{-}then\text{-}else} = \lambda p\ d_1\ d_2\ {}^2[{}^0\mathrm{I}^*\ \lambda c\ [[p \supset [c = d_1]] \wedge [\neg p \supset [c = d_2]]]]$$

$${}^0\mathit{If\text{-}then\text{-}else\text{-}fail} = \lambda p\ d_1\ {}^2[{}^0\mathrm{I}^*\ \lambda c\ [[p \supset [c = d_1]] \wedge [\neg p \supset {}^0\mathbf{F}]]]$$

Now we are ready to specify a **general analytic schema of an (empirical) sentence S associated with a presupposition *P*.** In a technical jargon of English the evaluation instruction can be formulated as follows:

At any $\langle w, t\rangle$-pair do this:
if P_{wt} is true then evaluate S_{wt}, else *Fail* (to produce a truth-value).
Let $P/*_n \rightarrow o_{\tau\omega}$ be a construction of a presupposition, $S/*_n \rightarrow o_{\tau\omega}$ the meaning of the sentence S and $c/*_{n+1} \rightarrow_v *_n$ a variable. Then the corresponding TIL construction is this:

$$\lambda w \lambda t\ [{}^0\mathit{If\text{-}then\text{-}else\text{-}fail}\ P_{wt}\ {}^0S_{wt}] =$$

$$\lambda w \lambda t\ {}^2[{}^0\mathrm{I}^* \lambda c\ [[P_{wt} \supset [c = {}^0S_{wt}]] \wedge [\neg P_{wt} \supset {}^0\mathbf{F}]]]$$

The evaluation of S for any $\langle w, t\rangle$-pair depends on whether the presupposition P is true at $\langle w, t\rangle$. If true, the singleton v-constructed by λc […] contains as the only construction to be executed ${}^0S_{wt}$ that is afterwards double executed. The first execution produces S_{wt} and the second execution produces a truth-value. If $\neg P_{wt}$ v-constructs **T**, then the second conjunct becomes the Composition $[{}^0\mathbf{T} \supset {}^0\mathbf{F}]$ and thus we get $\lambda c\ {}^0\mathbf{F}$. The v-constructed set is *empty*. Hence, $[\mathrm{I}^*\lambda c\ {}^0\mathbf{F}]$ is v-improper, and the Double Execution *fails* to produce a truth-value.

Now we can finish the analysis of Strason's example (3). *First*, make a choice between executing the Composition $[[{}^0\mathit{All}\ [{}^0\mathit{Child\_of}_{wt}\ {}^0\mathit{John}]]\ {}^0\mathit{Sleep}_{wt}]$ and a v-improper construction that fails to produce a truth-value. If the Composition $[{}^0\exists\lambda x\ [[{}^0\mathit{Child\_of}_{wt}\ {}^0\mathit{John}]\ x]]$ v-constructs **T** then the former, else the latter. The choice itself is realized by this Composition:

$$[{}^0\mathrm{I}^*\lambda c\ [[\exists x\ [[{}^0\mathit{Child\_of}_{wt}\ {}^0\mathit{John}]\ x] \supset [c={}^0[[{}^0\mathit{All}\ [{}^0\mathit{Child\_of}_{wt}\ {}^0\mathit{John}]]\ {}^0\mathit{Sleep}_{wt}]]]$$
$$\wedge\ [\neg\exists x\ [[{}^0\mathit{Child\_of}_{wt}\ {}^0\mathit{John}]\ x] \supset {}^0\mathbf{F}]]]$$

---

28 In case P is v-improper the singleton is empty and *no* construction is selected to be executed so the execution aborts.

Second, execute the chosen construction. To this end we apply *Double Execution*:

$$^2[^0\mathrm{I}^*\lambda c\ [[\exists x\ [[^0Child\_of_{wt}\ ^0John]\ x] \supset [c{=}^0[[^0All\ [^0Child\_of_{wt}\ ^0John]]\ ^0Sleep_{wt}]]] \wedge [\neg\exists x\ [[^0Child\_of_{wt}\ ^0John]\ x] \supset {}^0\mathbf{F}]]]$$

The evaluation of this construction for any $\langle w, t\rangle$ depends on whether the presupposition condition $\exists x\ [[^0Child\_of_{wt}\ ^0John]\ x]$ is true at $\langle w, t\rangle$:

a. $\exists x\ [[^0Child\_of_{wt}\ ^0John]\ x] \rightarrow_v \mathbf{T}$.
Then $\lambda c\ [^0\mathbf{T} \supset [c{=}^0[[^0All\ [^0Child\_of_{wt}\ ^0John]]\ ^0Sleep_{wt}] \wedge [^0\mathbf{F} \supset {}^0\mathbf{F}]]$ v-constructs this singleton: $\{^0[[^0All\ [^0Child\_of_{wt}\ ^0John]]\ ^0Sleep_{wt}]\}$. Hence the value of I* is its only member and we have:
$^2[^0\mathrm{I}^*\ \lambda c\ [^0\mathbf{T} \supset [c{=}^0[[^0All\ [^0Child\_of_{wt}\ ^0John]]\ ^0Sleep_{wt}] \wedge [^0\mathbf{F} \supset {}^0\mathbf{F}]] =$
$^{20}[[^0All\ [^0Child\_of_{wt}\ ^0John]]\ ^0Sleep_{wt}] = [[^0All\ [^0Child\_of_{wt}\ ^0John]]\ ^0Sleep_{wt}]$.

b. $\exists x\ [[^0Child\_of_{wt}\ ^0John]\ x] \rightarrow_v \mathbf{F}$.
Then $\lambda c\ [^0\mathbf{F} \supset [c{=}^0[[^0All\ [^0Child\_of_{wt}\ ^0John]]\ ^0Sleep_{wt}] \wedge [^0\mathbf{T} \supset {}^0\mathbf{F}]] = \lambda c\ {}^0\mathbf{F}$. The v-constructed set is *empty*, function I* being undefined at such set. Hence, $^2[^0\mathrm{I}^*\lambda c\ {}^0\mathbf{F}]$ is v-improper, *fails*.

Finally, we must abstract over the values of w and t in order to construct a proposition of type $o_{\tau\omega}$ denoted by the sentence. The resulting analysis of (3) is this:

(3*) $$\lambda w\lambda t\ ^2[^0\mathrm{I}^*\lambda c\ [\exists x\ [[^0Child\_of_{wt}\ ^0John]\ x] \supset [c{=}^0[[^0All\ [^0Child\_of_{wt}\ ^0John]]\ ^0Sleep_{wt}] \wedge [\neg\exists x\ [[^0Child\_of_{wt}\ ^0John]\ x] \supset {}^0\mathbf{F}]]]$$

In the interest of better readability I will in the remainder use a more standard notation. Hence instead of either "$\lambda w\lambda t\ [^0\textit{If-then-else-fail}\ P_{wt}\ ^0S_{wt}]$" or "$\lambda w\lambda t\ ^2[^0\mathrm{I}^*\lambda c\ [[P_{wt} \supset [c = {}^0S_{wt}]] \wedge [\neg P_{wt} \supset {}^0\mathbf{F}]]]$" I will simply write "$\lambda w\lambda t$ [If P_{wt} then S_{wt} else Fail]".

5.2 Additional examples

Consider now another pair of sentences differing only in terms of topic-focus articulation:

(4) "The *global financial and economic crisis* was caused by the Bank of America."
(5) "The *Bank of America* caused the global financial and economic crisis."

While (4) not only entails but also presupposes that there be a global financial and economic crisis, the truth-conditions of (5) are different, as our analysis clarifies. First, (4) as well as

(4′) "The *global financial and economic crisis* was not caused by Bank of America"

are about the global crisis, and that there is such a crisis is not only entailed but also presupposed by both sentences. The instruction encoded by (4) formulated in logician's English is this:

"*If* there is a global crisis *then* return **T** or **F** according as the crisis was caused by the Bank of America, *else fail* (to produce a truth-value)"

Since every TIL analysis is fully compositional, we first need to analyse the particular constituents of this instruction, and then combine these constituents into the construction expressed by the sentence. As always, we start with assigning types to the objects that receive mention in the sentence. Simplifying a bit, let the objects be: *Crisis*/$o_{\tau\omega}$: the proposition that there is a global financial and economic crisis; $Cause/(o\iota o_{\tau\omega})_{\tau\omega}$: the relation-in-intension between an individual and a proposition which has been caused to be true by the individual; $Bank\_of\_America/\iota_{\tau\omega}$: the individual office occupiable by a corporation belonging to the American financial institutions.

A schematic analysis of (4) comes down to this procedure:

$$\lambda w\lambda t\ [\text{If } {}^0Crisis_{wt} \text{ then } [{}^0True_{wt}\ \lambda w\lambda t\ [{}^0Cause_{wt}\ {}^0Bank\_of\_America_{wt}\ {}^0Crisis]] \text{ else Fail}]$$

Here we are again using the propositional property *True* in the then-clause, because this clause occurs in the focus of the sentence, and thus with *de dicto* supposition. The existence of the Bank of America is not presupposed.

The truth-conditions of the other reading with 'Bank of America' as topic are different. Now the sentence (5) is about the Bank of America (topic), ascribing to this corporation the property that it caused the crisis (focus). Thus the scenario of truly asserting that (5) is *not true* can be, for instance, this. Though it is true that the Bank of America played a major role in risky investments in China, the President of USA played a positive role in enhancing financial-market transparency and passed new laws that prevented a global crisis from arising. Or, a less optimistic scenario is thinkable. The global financial and economic crisis is not due to the Bank of America's bad investments but because in the era of globalisation the market economy is unpredictable, hence uncontrollable. Hence, that there is a crisis is not presupposed by (5), and its analysis is this Closure:

$$\lambda w\lambda t\ [\text{If } [{}^0Exist_{wt}\ {}^0Bank\_of\_America] \text{ then } [{}^0True_{wt}\ \lambda w\lambda t\ [{}^0Cause_{wt}\ {}^0Bank\_of\_America_{wt}\ {}^0Crisis]] \text{ else Fail}]$$

Note that (5) presupposes the existence of the Bank of America, while the existence of the crisis is not presupposed. Yet, if (5) is true, then the existence of the crisis can be validly inferred. To capture such truth-conditions, we need to refine the analysis. A plausible explication of this phenomenon is this: x is a cause of a proposition p iff p is true and if it is so then x affected p so as to become true. Schematically,

$$\lambda w\lambda t\ [{}^0Cause_{wt}\ x\ p] = \lambda w\lambda t\ [p_{wt} \wedge [p_{wt} \supset [{}^0Affect_{wt}\ x\ p]]]$$

Types: $Cause, Affect/(o\alpha o_{\tau\omega})_{\tau\omega}$; $x \rightarrow \alpha$, α: any type; $p \rightarrow o_{\tau\omega}$.

If x is not a cause of p, then either p is not true or p is true but x did not affect p so as to become true: $\lambda w\lambda t\ \neg[{}^0Cause_{wt}\ x\ p] = \lambda w\lambda t\ [\neg p_{wt} \vee [p_{wt} \wedge \neg[{}^0Affect_{wt}\ x\ p]]]$.[29] By applying such an explication to our sentence, the construction corresponding to the 'then clause', *viz.* $\lambda w\lambda t\ [{}^0Cause_{wt}\ {}^0Bank\_of\_America_{wt}\ {}^0Crisis]$, is refined to:

$$\lambda w\lambda t\ [{}^0Crisis_{wt} \wedge [{}^0Crisis_{wt} \supset [{}^0Affect_{wt}\ {}^0Bank\_of\_America_{wt}\ {}^0Crisis]]]$$

This Closure entails that there is a crisis, which is the desired (logical, though not economic) outcome.

The topic-focus ambiguity also crops up in the case of propositional and notional attitudes, as noted in the Introduction.[30] Imagine one is referring to the tragedy in Dallas, November

[29] For the sake of simplicity, I ignore here the past tense 'affected'; a more precise analysis is this: $\lambda w\lambda t\ [p_{wt} \wedge [p_{wt} \supset \exists t'\ [[t' < t] \wedge [{}^0Affect_{wt'}\ x\ p]]]]$.

[30] For an analysis of propositional attidues *de dicto* and *de re*, see (Duží *et al.*, 2010a, § 5.1.2).

22, 1963, by "The police were seeking the murderer of JFK, but never found him". The sentence is again ambiguous due to a difference in topic-focus articulation, as evidenced by (6) and (7):

(6) The *police* were seeking the murderer of JFK, but never found him.
(7) The police were seeking *the murderer of JFK*, but never found him.

The existence of the murderer of JFK is not presupposed by (6), unlike (7). The sentence (6) can be true in such states-of-affairs where JFK was not murdered, unlike (7). The latter can be reformulated in a less ambiguous way as "*The murderer of JFK* was looked for by the police, but was never found". This sentence expresses the construction

$$\lambda w \lambda t\ [\text{If } [{}^0Exist_{wt}\ \lambda w \lambda t\ [{}^0Murderer\_of_{wt}\ {}^0JFK] \text{ then}$$
$$[[{}^0Seek_{wt}\ {}^0Police\ \lambda w \lambda t\ [{}^0Murderer\_of_{wt}\ {}^0JFK]] \wedge \neg[{}^0Find_{wt}\ {}^0Police\ \lambda w \lambda t\ [{}^0Murderer\_of_{wt}\ {}^0JFK]]]$$
$$\text{else } Fail.$$

Types: *Seek, Find*/$(o\iota\iota_{\tau\omega})_{\tau\omega}$: the relation-in-intension between an individual and an individual office (the seeker wants to find out who is the holder of the office); *Police*/ι; *Murderer_of*/$(\iota\iota)_{\tau\omega}$; *JFK*/$\iota$.[31]

On the other hand, the analysis of (6) comes down to this construction:

$$\lambda w \lambda t\ [[{}^0Seek_{wt}\ {}^0Police\ [\lambda w \lambda t\ [{}^0Murderer\_of_{wt}\ {}^0JFK]]] \wedge$$
$$\neg[{}^0Find_{wt}\ {}^0Police\ [\lambda w \lambda t\ [{}^0Murderer\_of_{wt}\ {}^0JFK]]]].$$

If the police did not find the murderer then either the murderer did not exist or the murderer did exist; only the search was not successful. However, if the foregoing search was successful, then it is true that police found the murderer and the murderer exists. Hence, a successful search, i.e. *finding* after a foregoing search, merely entails that the murderer exists and the following argument is valid:

$$\frac{\lambda w \lambda t\ [{}^0Find_{wt}\ {}^0Police\ [\lambda w \lambda t\ [{}^0Murderer\_of_{wt}\ {}^0JFK]]]}{\lambda w \lambda t\ [{}^0Exist_{wt}\ [\lambda w \lambda t\ [{}^0Murderer\_of_{wt}\ {}^0JFK]]]}$$

In order to logically reproduce this entailment, we explicate *finding after a foregoing search* in a manner similar to *causing* ($x \rightarrow_v \iota$; $c \rightarrow_v \iota_{\tau\omega}$; *Success_Search*/$(o\iota\iota_{\tau\omega})_{\tau\omega}$):

$$\lambda w \lambda t\ [{}^0Find_{wt}\ x\ c] = \lambda w \lambda t\ [[{}^0Exist_{wt}\ c] \wedge [[{}^0Exist_{wt}\ c] \supset [{}^0Success\_Search_{wt}\ x\ c]]];$$
$$\lambda w \lambda t\ \neg[{}^0Find_{wt}\ x\ c] = \lambda w \lambda t\ [\neg[{}^0Exist_{wt}\ c] \vee [[{}^0Exist_{wt}\ c] \wedge \neg[{}^0Success\_Search_{wt}\ x\ c]]].$$

Thus the analysis of such an explication of the sentence "The *police* found the murderer of JFK" is this Closure:

$$\lambda w \lambda t\ [[{}^0Exist_{wt}\ \lambda w \lambda t\ [{}^0Murderer\_of_{wt}\ {}^0JFK]] \wedge [[{}^0Exist_{wt}\ \lambda w \lambda t\ [{}^0Murderer\_of_{wt}\ {}^0JFK]] \supset$$
$$[{}^0Success\_Search_{wt}\ {}^0Police\ \lambda w \lambda t\ [{}^0Murderer\_of_{wt}\ {}^0JFK]]]]$$

From this analysis one can validly infer that the murderer exists and that the search was successful, just as we ought to be able to. And if the so constructed proposition is not true,

[31] For the sake of simplicity, past tense and anaphoric reference are ignored. For a more detailed analysis of this kind of seeking and finding, see, for instance, (Duží 2003) or (Duží *et al.*, 2010a, § 5.2.2).

then the murderer does not exist or the murder does exist, only the search did not meet with success.

The next example I am going to analyse is again due to (Hajičová, 2008):

(8) "John only introduced *Bill* to Sue."
(9) "John only introduced Bill to *Sue*."

Leaving aside the possible disambiguation "John introduced only *Bill* to Sue" vs. "John introduced Bill only to *Sue*", (8) can be truly affirmed only in a situation where John did not introduce other people to Sue than Bill. This is not the case of (9). This sentence can be true in a situation where John introduced other people to Sue, but the only person Bill was introduced to by John was Sue. Hence the presuppositions of (8) and (9) are constructed by these Closures:

Presupposition of (8): $\lambda w \lambda t\ [\forall x\ [[{}^0Int\_to_{wt}\ {}^0John\ x\ {}^0Sue] \supset [x = {}^0Bill]]]$
Presupposition of (9): $\lambda w \lambda t\ [\forall y\ [[{}^0Int\_to_{wt}\ {}^0John\ {}^0Bill\ y] \supset [y = {}^0Sue]]]$

The construction C that is to be executed in case a relevant presupposition is true is here the Closure $\lambda w \lambda t\ [{}^0Int\_to_{wt}\ {}^0John\ {}^0Bill\ {}^0Sue]$. *Types*: $Int\_to/(o\iota\iota\iota)_{\tau\omega}$: a relation-in-intension between the individual *who* does the introducing, another individual *who* is introduced, and yet another individual to *whom* the second individual was introduced; *John, Sue, Bill*/ι.

The resulting analyses are

(8*) $\lambda w \lambda t\ [\text{If } \forall x\ [[{}^0Int\_to_{wt}\ {}^0John\ x\ {}^0Sue] \supset [x = {}^0Bill]] \text{ then } [{}^0Int\_to_{wt}\ {}^0John\ {}^0Bill\ {}^0Sue]$ else fail];
(9*) $\lambda w \lambda t\ [\text{If } \forall y\ [[{}^0Int\_to_{wt}\ {}^0John\ {}^0Bill\ y] \supset [y = {}^0Sue]] \text{ then } [{}^0Int\_to_{wt}\ {}^0John\ {}^0Bill\ {}^0Sue]$ else fail].

Using technical jargon, the truth-conditions constructed by the construction (8*) are, "If the only person that was introduced by John to Sue is Bill, then it is true that John introduced only *Bill* to Sue, otherwise there is no truth-value". Similarly for (9*).

For the last example, consider the sentence

"All students of VSB-TU Ostrava who signed up for the Logic course in the winter term of 2011 passed the final exam."

There are again two readings matching two possible scenarios.

Scenario 1: We are talking about the students of VSB-Technical University Ostrava, and somebody then asks, "What about the students of VSB-TU Ostrava who signed up for the Logic course in the winter term of 2011 – how did they do?". The answer is, "They did well, they all passed the final exam".

In this case the topic of the sentence is the students enrolled in the Logic course. Thus the sentence comes with the presupposition that there should be students of VSB-TU Ostrava having signed up for Logic in the winter term of 2011. If this presupposition is not satisfied (for instance, because the course runs only in the summer term) then the sentence is neither true nor false, leaving a truth-value gap. For the negated sentence cannot be true, either: "Some students of VSB-TU Ostrava who signed up for Logic in the winter term of 2011 did not pass the final exam". Moreover, the positive sentence merely entails (and so does not presuppose) that the final exam has taken place. This is so because the sentence can be false for either of two reasons: Either some of the students did not succeed, or none of the students succeeded because the exam has yet to take place.

Scenario 2: The topic is the final exam. Somebody asks, "What about the final exam in Logic, what are the results?" One possible answer is, "All students passed". Now the sentence presupposes that the final exam have already taken place. If it has not then the sentence is neither true nor false, because the negated sentence ("The final exam has not been passed by all students ...") cannot be true, either. In this situation the (positive) sentence does not presuppose, but only entails, that some students signed up for the course.

The logical machinery of TIL, thanks not least to the application of Definition 4, makes it easy to properly distinguish between those two non-equivalent readings. In the situation corresponding to the first scenario the meaning of the sentence is this Closure:

$$\lambda w \lambda t\ [\text{If } [{}^0\exists\ [{}^0\mathit{Students\_enrolled\_in}_{wt}\ {}^0\mathit{Logic}]$$
$$\text{then } [[{}^0\mathit{All}\ [{}^0\mathit{Students\_enrolled\_in}_{wt}\ {}^0\mathit{Logic}]]\ [{}^0\mathit{Passed}_{wt}\ {}^0\mathit{Exam}]$$
$$\text{else } \mathit{Fail}]$$

The second scenario receives this Closure as analysis:

$$\lambda w \lambda t\ [\text{If } \mathit{Exam}_{wt} \text{ than } [[{}^0\mathit{All}\ [{}^0\mathit{Students\_enrolled\_in}_{wt}\ {}^0\mathit{Logic}]]\ [{}^0\mathit{Passed}_{wt}\ {}^0\mathit{Exam}]$$
$$\text{else } \mathit{Fail}]$$

Types: $\exists/(o(o\iota))$: the existential quantifier; $\mathit{Students\_enrolled\_in}/((o\iota)\iota)_{\tau\omega}$: an attribute (i.e. empirical function) that dependently on a given state-of-affairs assigns to an individual a set of individuals; Logic/ι (for the sake of simplicity); $\mathit{All}/((o(o\iota))(o\iota))$: a restricted quantifier, which is a function assigning to a set S of individuals the set of all supersets of S; $\mathit{Passed}/((o\iota)o_{\tau\omega})_{\tau\omega}$: a function that dependently on a given state-of-affairs associates a proposition (in this case an event) with the set of individuals (who are the successful actors of the event); $\mathit{Exam}/o_{\tau\omega}$: the proposition that the final exam takes place.[32]

6. Conclusion

In this chapter I brought out the *semantic*, as opposed to pragmatic, character of the ambivalence stemming from topic-focus articulation. The procedural semantics of TIL provided rigorous analyses such that sentences differing only in their topic-focus articulation were assigned different constructions producing different propositions (truth-conditions) and having different consequences. I showed that a definite description occurring in the topic of a sentence with *de re* supposition corresponds to the Strawsonian analysis of definite descriptions, while a definite description occurring in the focus with *de dicto* supposition corresponds to the Russellian analysis. While the clause standing in topic

[32] For the sake of simplicity we are ignoring the past tense of the sentence. For the TIL analysis of tenses, see (Duží et al., 2010a, § 2.5.2). Similarly as above, see the sentence (3), we again apply the restricted quantifier *All* in the analysis of the clause "All students who signed up for Logic passed the exam'.

position triggers a presupposition, a focus clause usually entails rather than presupposes another proposition. Thus both opponents and proponents of Russell's quantificational analysis of definite descriptions are partly right and partly wrong.

Moreover, the proposed analysis of the Russellian reading does not deprive definite descriptions of their meaning. Just the opposite; 'the *F*' receives a context-invariant meaning. What is dependent on context is the way this (one and the same) meaning is used. Thus I also demonstrated that Donnellan-style referential and attributive uses of an occurrence of 'the *F*' do not bring about a shift of meaning of 'the *F*'. Instead, one and the same context-invariant meaning is a constituent of different procedures that behave in different ways.

The proposed analysis of topic-focus ambivalence was then generalized to sentences containing not only singular clauses like 'the *F*' but also general clauses like 'John's children', 'all students' in the topic or focus of a sentence. As a result, I proposed a general analytic schema for sentences equipped with a presupposition. This analysis makes use of the definition of the *if-then-else* function that complies with the desirable principle of compositionality. This is also my novel contribution to the old problem of the semantic character of the specification of the *if-then-else* function. I demonstrated the method by analysing several examples including notional attitudes like seeking and finding.

The moral to be drawn from my contribution is this. Logical analysis disambiguates ambiguous expressions, but cannot dictate *which* disambiguation is the intended one (leaving room for pragmatics here). Yet, our fine-grained method of analysis contributes to language disambiguation by making its hidden features *explicit* and *logically tractable*. In case there are more senses of a sentence we furnish the sentence with different TIL logical forms. Having a formal, fine-grained encoding of linguistic senses at our disposal, we are in a position to automatically infer the relevant consequences.

7. Acknowledgments

This research was funded by Grant Agency of the Czech Republic Project 401/10/0792 *Temporal Aspects of Knowledge and Information*. Versions of this study were read by the author as an invited talk at the University of Western Australia, Perth, Australia, March 4th, 2011. Portions of this chapter elaborate substantially on points made in (Duží, 2009a, 2009b). I am indebted to Bjørn Jespersen for valuable comments that improved the quality of this study.

8. References

Carnap, R. (1947). *Meaning and Necessity*, Chicago: Chicago University Press.

Donnellan, K. S., (1966). Reference and definite descriptions, *Philosophical Review*, vol. 77, 281-304.

Duží, M. (2003). Notional Attitudes (On wishing, seeking and finding). *Organon F*, vol. X, No. 3, pp. 237-260, ISSN 1335-0668

Duží, M. (2004). Intensional Logic and the Irreducible Contrast between *de dicto* and *de re*. *ProFil*, vol. 5, No. 1, pp. 1-34, ISSN 1212-9097

Duží, M. (2009a). Strawsonian vs. Russellian definite descriptions. *Organon F*, vol. XVI, No. 4, pp. 587-614, ISSN 1335-0668

Duží, M. (2009b). Topic-focus articulation from the semantic point of view. In: *Computational Linguistics and Intelligent Text Processing*, A. Gelbukh (Ed.), Berlin, Heidelberg: Springer-Verlag LNCS, vol. 5449, 220-232.

Duží, M. (2010). The paradox of inference and the non-triviality of analytic information. *Journal of Philosophical Logic*, vol. 39, No. 5, pp. 473-510. ISSN 0022-3611

Duží, M & Jespersen, B. (forthcoming). 'Transparent quantification into hyperpropositional contexts *de re*', *Logique et Analyse*.

Duží, M. & Jespersen, B. (submitted). An argument against unrestricted beta-reduction.

Duží, M., Jespersen, B. & Materna, P. (2010a): *Procedural Semantics for Hyperintensional Logic; Foundations and Applications of Transparent Intensional Logic.* Berlin: Springer, series Logic, Epistemology, and the Unity of Science, vol. 17, 2010, ISBN 978-90-481-8811-6, 550 pp.

Duží, M., Jespersen, B. & Materna, P. (2010b). The *logos* of semantic structure. In: *Philosophy of Language and Linguistics*, vol. 1: The Formal Turn. P. Stalmaszczyk (ed.) Frankfurt: Ontos Verlag, ISBN 978-3-86838-070-5, pp. 85-102.

Fintel, Kai von (2004). Would you believe it? The King of France is Back! (Presuppositions and Truth-Value Intuitions). In: *Descriptions and Beyond*, Reimer, M., Bezuidenhout, A. (eds.), Oxford: Clarendon Press, ISBN 0-19-927051-1, pp. 315 - 341.

Frege, G. (1884). *Die Grundlagen der Arithmetik*, Breslau: W. Koebner.

Frege, G. (1892). Über Sinn und Bedeutung. *Zeitschrift für Philosophie und philosophische Kritik*, vol. 100, pp. 25-50.

Hajičová, E. (2008). What we are talking about and what we are saying about it. In: *Computational Linguistics and Intelligent Text Processing*, A. Gelbukh (Ed.), Berlin, Heidelberg: Springer-Verlag LNCS, vol. 4919, 241-262.

Jespersen, B. (2008). Predication and extensionalization. *Journal of Philosophical Logic*, vol. 37, pp. 479 - 499.

Kripke, S., (1977). Speaker reference and semantic reference. In: *Contemporary Perspectives in the Philosophy of Language*, French, Uehling and Wettstein (eds.), Minneapolis: University of Minnestoa Press, p. 6-27.

Ludlow, P. (2007). Descriptions. Available from
http://plato.stanford.edu/entries/descriptions/#2.

Neale, S., (1990). *Descriptions*. Cambridge: MIT Press Books.

Neale, S., (2004). This, that, and the other. In: *Descriptions and Beyond*, A. Bezuidenhout and M. Reimer (eds.), Oxford: Oxford University Press, pp. 68-182.

Russell, B. (1905). On denoting. *Mind* vol. 14, pp. 479-493.

Russell, B., (1957). Mr. Strawson on referring, *Mind* vol. 66, pp. 385-389.

Strawson, P. F. (1950). On referring, *Mind* vol. 59, pp. 320-334.

Strawson, P. F. (1952). *Introduction to Logical Theory*. London: Methuen.

Strawson, P.F., (1964). Identifying reference and truth-values, *Theoria* vol. 3, pp. 96-118.

Tichý, P. (1988). *The Foundations of Frege's Logic*, Berlin, New York: De Gruyter.

Tichý, P. (2004). *Collected Papers in Logic and Philosophy*, V. Svoboda, B. Jespersen, C. Cheyne (eds.), Prague: Filosofia, Czech Academy of Sciences, and Dunedin: University of Otago Press.